صلى الله عليه وسلم

THE HOLY PROPHET OF ISLĀM

ḤAḌRAT MUḤAMMAD MUṢṬAFĀ

(Peace and Blessings of Allāh be Upon Him)

محمد رسول الله

صلی اللہ علیہ وسلم

THE HOLY PROPHET OF ISLĀM

ḤAḌRAT MUḤAMMAD MUṢṬAFĀ

(Peace and Blessings of Allāh be Upon Him)

وہ پیشوا ھمارا ‘ جس سے ھے نور سارا

نام اس کا ھے محمد ‘ دلبر مرا یھی ھے

That leader of ours, from whom radiates all light;

His name is Muḥammad, he is the one who has captivated my heart

The Promised Messiah and Mahdī[as]

Dr. Karimullah Zirvi

First Edition Published in September 2009

By

KZ Publications
14-21 Saddle River Road
Fair Lawn, NJ 07410
USA

ISBN 978 1 882494 26 2

بِسْمِ اللّٰهِ الرَّحْمٰنِ الرَّحِيْمِ

In the name of Allāh, the Gracious, the Merciful

THE HOLY PROPHET OF ISLĀM

ḤAḌRAT MUḤAMMAD MUṢṬAFĀ

(Peace and Blessings of Allāh be upon him)

TABLE OF CONTENTS

Foreword: Ḥaḍrat Mirzā Masroor Aḥmad, Khalīfatul Masīḥ V[aba] 11

Comments: Maulānā Daud A. Ḥanif, Nā'ib Amīr and Missionary In-charge, USA 13

Publisher's Note 14

System of Transliteration 16

Introduction: Karimullah Zirvi 19

1. The World Before Islām **25**

Arabian Peninsula Before Islām 30

Mecca, the Birthplace of the Holy Prophet[sa] 31
Prophethood in Ḥaḍrat Nūḥ's[as] (Noah) Progeny 34
Ḥaḍrat Ibrāhīm[as] and Ḥaḍrat Ismāī'l[as] 34

2. The Holy Prophet[sa] of Islām 42

Birth and Childhood 42
Joined *Ḥilful Fuḍūl* Association During
His Youth 50
As a Shepherd 51
Marriage with Ḥaḍrat Khadījah[ra] 51
Rebuilding of the Sacred House of Allāh (*Ka'bah*) 52

3. The Beginning of Islām 53

Worship of Allāh in Solitude 53
Receiving the First Revelation 53
The Pause in Revelation 55

4. Conveying the Message of Islām 57

Invitation to Abū Jahl to Accept Islām 62
Rejection of the Message by the Meccans 63
Hostility Towards the Holy Prophet[sa] and
His Companions[ra] 63
Migration of Muslims to Abyssinia (*Ḥabshah*) 65
Ḥaḍrat Ḥamzah[ra] Accepts Islām 68
Ḥaḍrat 'Umar[ra] Accepts Islām 68
Confinement in Shi'bi Abī Ṭālib 70
The Year of Sorrow and Grief: Death of Abū Ṭālib
and Ḥaḍrat Khadījah[ra] 72

Conveying the Message to the People of Ṭā'if 72

5. **The Night Journey 77**

Journey From Mecca to Jerusalem (*Isrā'*) 77
Ascension to Heaven (*Mi'rāj*) 81

6. **Migration to Medina 91**

Migration of Early Muslims to Medina 91
The First Covenant of 'Aqabah 94
The Second Covenant of 'Aqabah 94
Conditions of the Last Pledge of 'Aqabah .. 95
Migration of the Holy Prophet[sa] to Medina 96
A Plan to Assassinate the Holy Prophet[sa] 96
Stay in the Cave Thaur 100
Stop at the Camp of Umm Ma'bad 103
Arrival of the Holy Prophet[sa] in Medina 104
Construction of *Masjid Nabawī* 105
Early Days of the Holy Prophet[sa] in Medina.............. 107
Establishment of Fraternity Among *Anṣār* and *Muhājirīn* 108
The Covenant of Medina 110
The Hypocrites of Medina 113
Pact Among the Various Tribes of Medina.............. 114
The First Written Constitution 116
Facing the *Ka'bah* in Prayer 118
Divine Protection for the Holy Prophet[sa] 119

7. **Battles of Badr and Uḥud 123**

Battle of Badr 123

Charter of Freedom 134
Murder of Ka'b bin Ashraf 135
Ghazwah Ghaṭafān (Ghazwah Qarqarat Al-Kudr) .. 135
Ghazwah Al-Sawīq 136
Battle of Uḥud 137
Reconnaissance Mission Sent by the Holy Prophet[sa] 142
Martyrdom of Muslims at Bi'r Ma'ūnah 145

8. Encounter with Banū Muṣṭaliq and Battle of Aḥzāb (Battle of the Ditch) 147

Encounter with Banū Muṣṭaliq 147
Battle of Aḥzāb (Battle of the Ditch) 149
The *Banū Quraiẓah* Punished for Their Treachery 153

9. Ḥudaibiyyah Pact *(Ṣulḥ Ḥudaibiyyah)* 162

The Oath of Riḍwān *(Bai'at-e-Riḍwān)* 163
Ghazwah Dhī Qarad (Ghazwah Gābah) 167

10. Invitations Sent to Various Rulers to Accept Islām 170

Heraclius, the Emperor of Rome 170
Chosroes, the King of Persia 174
The Negus, the King of Abyssinia 178
Muqawqis, the King of Egypt 179
Various Tribal Chiefs 181

11. The Jews of Medina 184

Fall of Khaibar 186
Peace Agreement With the Inhabitants of Fadak 188
Ghazwah Wādī al-Qurā 189
Ghazwah Taymā' 191
Ghazwah Dhātur Riqā' 191

12. Battle of Mu'tah 193

13. The Conquest of Mecca 197

The House of Allāh *(Ka'bah)* Cleared of the Idols 200
The Holy Prophet's[sa] Dream Regarding Migration and Future Successes 202

14. Battles of Ḥunain and Auṭās 203

Battle of Ḥunain 203
Divine Help 207
Battle of Auṭās 208
Distribution of the Spoils of the Battles of Ḥunain and Auṭās 209

15. The Expedition of Tabūk 212

The Case of the Three Companions[ra] Who Remained Behind in the Expedition of Tabūk 215
Establishment of Mosques 224

16. Demolition of the Conspiracy Centers 225

Demolition of the Mosque Built by Hypocrites (*Ḍirār* Mosque) 225
Demolition of the House Used by the Hypocrites . 228
Death of 'Abdullāh bin Ubayy bin Salūl 229

17. Basic Teachings of Islām 232

The Five Fundamentals of Islām 232
Shahada (Declaration of Faith) 234
Ṣalāt (Daily Prayers) 235
Ṣaum (Fasting of Ramaḍān) 236
Zakāt 237
Ḥajj (Pilgrimage) 240
Compilation of the Holy Qur'ān 242

18. The Exalted Status of the Holy Prophet[sa] 246

As Stated in the Holy Qur'ān 246
The Holy Prophet[sa] States About His High Status ... 274
Two Phases of the Life of the Holy Prophet[sa] 277
The Exalted Status of the Holy Prophet[sa] in the Sight of the Promised Messiah[sa] 280

19. Physical Description and Habits of the Holy Prophet[sa] 285

The Holy Prophet[sa] Describes About Himself 285
Physical Description and Personality of the Holy Prophet[sa] 287
The Daily Routine 292

Patience in Adversity 293
Simple Lifestyle 294
Humility 297
Pleasing Sense of Humor 300

20. A Synopsis of the High Moral Excellences of the Holy Prophet[sa] 302

His Character 302
Trust and Faith in God 305
Rejected Help from an Infidel 307
Love of God and Submission to Him 307
Miraculous Divine Help 309
Revelations, Visions and Prophecies 312
Marriage with Ḥaḍrat 'Ā'ishah[ra] 313
False Claimants: Musailimah ibn Ḥabīb (al-Kadhdhāb) and Aswad 'Ansī 313
Death of Aswad 'Ansī 314
Death of Quraish Leaders of Mecca in the Battle of Badr 314
Prophecy Regarding the Death of Chosroes Pervaiz 315
Chosroes' Bracelets and Surāqah bin Mālik. 316
The Prophecy Regarding Sea Conquests 316
Prophecy Regarding the Glory of Islām 317
Acceptance of His Prayers 318
Love of the Holy Qur'ān 325
His Worship and Love for Prayers 326
Thankfulness for Divine Bounties 328
Truthfulness 329
Excellences in Dealing with Others 331
Devotion Towards Moral Training of the Muslims 331
Justice and Fair Dealings 333
Fulfillment of the Covenants 336

Trustworthiness 336
Generosity 337
Bravery 338
Kindheartedness 340
Self-Control and Tolerance 342
Love for Humanity 346
Love for the Companions[ra] 347
Treatment of the Non-Muslims 348
Respect for the Non-Muslim Delegates 348
Charter of Privileges 349
Respect for the Dead 351
Appreciation of the Service to Mankind 352
Treatment of the Uncultured 353
Serving a Disbeliever 353
Helping the Oppressed and Orphans 353
Love for the Poor 356
Love for Children 357
Treatment of Women 359
Treatment of Neighbors 361
Treatment of Slaves 362
Treatment of Servants and Laborers 363
Treatment of Animals 364
Visiting the Sick 366
Extraordinary Patience 367
As a Judge 369
Loving Father and Grandfather 370

21. Wives of the Holy Prophet[sa] 374

Ḥaḍrat Khadījah[ra] 374
Ḥaḍrat Saudah[ra] 376
Ḥaḍrat 'Ā'ishah[ra] 378
Age at the Time of Her Marriage 381
Slander Against Her 382
An Interesting Episode 384

The Battle of *Jamal* (Camel) 386
Ḥaḍrat Ḥafṣah[ra] 387
Ḥaḍrat Zainab bint Khuzaimah[ra] 388
Ḥaḍrat Ummi Salamah[ra] 388
Ḥaḍrat Zainab bint Jaḥsh[ra] 390
Ḥaḍrat Juwairiyyah[ra] 394
Ḥaḍrat Ṣafiyyah[ra] 396
An Interesting Episode 399
Ḥaḍrat Ummi Ḥabībah[ra] 399
Ḥaḍrat Mariah al-Qibṭiyyah[ra] 402
Ḥaḍrat Maimūnah[ra] 404

22. Life of the Wives of the Holy Prophet[sa] 405

Separation of the Holy Prophet[sa] from His Wives for One Month 406
Some Other Events in the Life of the Wives of the Holy Prophet[sa] 408
The Incident of Honey 412

23. Children of the Holy Prophet[sa] 414

Sons of the Holy Prophet[sa] 414
Daughters of the Holy Prophet[sa] 415
Ḥaḍrat Zainab[ra] 415
Ḥaḍrat Ruqayyah[ra] and Ḥaḍrat Ummi Kulthūm[ra] 415
Ḥaḍrat Fāṭimah[ra] 416

It is ironic that it is only Aḥmadi Muslims who have accepted the responsibility of suggesting solutions to the kind of problems in which the world is immersed today by reflecting on the life of the Prophet and respond to the many objections raised against his character by the opponents of Islām. In a way that was also the primary purpose of the advent of Ḥaḍrat Mirzā Ghulām Aḥmad of Qadian (1835-1908) who claimed that he was the Promised Messiah and Reformer expected by the world. This is why it is our obligation to make manifest in the English language the life and excellent example of the Holy Prophet of Islām, may peace and blessings of Allāh be upon him, so that the maximum number of people in the English speaking world should become aware of his life and his character.

For instance: Decisions in respect of Jewish persons in Madinah were made according to the teaching of Moses, on whom be peace. Once, a very near Companion of the Holy Prophet, peace and blessings of Allāh be upon him, said, "The Holy Prophet is superior to Prophet Moses, on whom be peace." He was severely reprimanded for this action by the Holy Prophet, peace and blessings of Allāh be upon him, who declared:

"Do not express my superiority over Moses, peace be on him, because it has broken the heart of a Jewish person." Despite the superior position of the Holy Prophet, peace and blessings of Allāh be upon him, in the heart of the Muslims and regardless of the greatest position bestowed to the Holy Prophet in the Holy Qur'ān, the proclamation made by the Holy Prophet, peace and blessings of Allāh be upon him, not to call him superior to Moses on whom be peace, was meant to prevent disturbance in the peace of the society.

Such was the life of the Holy Prophet a life worth emulating.

MIRZA MASROOR AHMAD
Khalifatul Masih V
Head of the worldwide Aḥmadiyya Muslim Community
11 June 2009

بِسْمِ اللّٰهِ الرَّحْمٰنِ الرَّحِيْمِ

In the name of Allāh, the Gracious, the Merciful

Comments About the Book by Maulānā Daud A. Hanif, Nā'ib Amīr and Missionary In-charge, USA

Many biographies of the Holy Prophet Muḥammad[sa] have been written by different authors. These books cover many aspects of his life. Each book has a different hue and color. The book, "The Holy Prophet of Islām, Ḥaḍrat Muḥammad Muṣṭafā (May Peace and Blessings of Allāh be upon Him)" by Dr. Karimullah Zirvi has a very special charm. I have read its final manuscript thoroughly and have found that this 450 page text has been prepared by the author by delving deep into the original sources of Islāmic history on the life of the Holy Prophet[sa]. He has provided authentic references for the quotes from the earlier records. He has thus produced a novel history of the Holy Prophet[sa], which covers most of the aspects of his life. Its reading creates a yearning for a deep study into the life of the Holy Prophet[sa] and has a great attraction, especially for the young readership and researchers. Anyone who reads it would love to have it in their personal library so that future generations may also benefit from this authentic source. It is a very praiseworthy effort. May Allāh reward him for this difficult and arduous task which he has carried out incessantly for a long period of time to accomplish this valuable work!

Daud A. Hanif
Nā'ib Amīr and Missionary In-charge, USA

July 29, 2009

PUBLISHER'S NOTE

Please note that in referencing the Holy Qur'ān we have counted the verse:

بِسْمِ اللّٰهِ الرَّحْمٰنِ الرَّحِيْمِ

In the Name of Allāh, the Gracious, the Merciful

as the first verse of the Chapter in which it appears. Some publishers of the Holy Qur'ān, however, begin counting the verses after the verse

بِسْمِ اللّٰهِ الرَّحْمٰنِ الرَّحِيْمِ

Should the reader not find the relevant verse under the number given in the book, it would be found in the adjacent lower number. For instance, the reader would find the referred verse under 3 instead of 4.

The translation of the verses of the Holy Qur'ān mentioned in the book is taken from Ḥaḍrat Maulawī Sher 'Alī Ṣāḥib's[ra] translation. In addition, the translation done by Ḥaḍrat Khalīfatul Masīḥ IV[rh] in the appendix of the Holy Qur'ān with Ḥaḍrat Maulawī Sher 'Alī Ṣāḥib's[ra] translation has been given. Many translators add explanatory words in their translation, which are not found in the Qur'ānic text. But they see to it that the reader is not misled to consider them as words of the Qur'ān. Ḥaḍrat Maulawī Sher 'Alī Ṣāḥib[ra] has italicized such words.

The name of Muḥammad[sa], the Holy Prophet of Islām, has been followed by the symbol [sa], which is an abbreviation for the salutation *Ṣallallāhu 'Alaihi Wasallam* (may peace and blessings of Allāh be upon him). The names of other Prophets and Messengers are followed by the symbol [as], an abbreviation for *'Alaihissalām* (on whom be peace). The symbol [ra] is used with the name of the Companions of the Holy Prophet[sa] and those of the Promised Messiah[as]. It stands for *Raḍī Allāhu 'anhu/'anhā/'anhum* (May Allāh be pleased with him/with her/with them). The symbol [rh] stands for *Raḥimahullāhu Ta'ālā* (may Allāh grant him peace). The symbol [aba] stands for *Ayyadahullāhu Ta'ālā bi naṣrihil 'azīz* (May Allāh the Almighty help him with His powerful support). The actual salutations have not been set out in full for the sake of brevity and ease for the reader. Muslim readers should treat the full salutation as implicit.

SYSTEM OF TRANSLITERATION

TRANSLITERATION

In transliterating Arabic words we adhere to the following system adopted by the Royal Asiatic Society:

ا at the beginning of a word, pronounced as *a*, *i*, *u* preceded by a very slight aspiration, like *h* in the English word 'honour'.

ث *th*, pronounced like th in the English word 'thing'.

ح *ḥ*, a guttural aspirate, stronger than h.

خ *kh*, pronounced like the Scotch *ch* in 'loch'.

ذ *dh*, pronounced like the English *th* in 'that'.

ص *ṣ*, strongly articulated s.

ض *ḍ*, similar to the English th in 'this'.

ط *ṭ*, strongly articulated palatal t.

ظ *ẓ*, strongly articulated z.

ع ‘, a strong guttural, the pronunciation of which must be learned by the ear.

غ *gh*, a sound approached very nearly in the *r 'grasseye'* in French, and in the German *r*. It requires the muscles of the throat to be in the gargling position whilst pronouncing it.

ق *q*, a deep guttural k sound.

ء ’, a sort of catch in the voice.

Short vowels are represented by *a* for ـَـ (like *u* in 'bud'); *i* for ـِـ (like *i* in 'bid'); u for ـُـ (like *oo* in 'wood'); the long vowels by *ā* for ـَا or آ (like *a* in 'father'); ī for ـِی or ـٖـ (like *ee* in 'deep'); *ai* for ـَی (like *i* in 'site'); *ū* for ـُو (like *oo* in 'root'); *au* for ـَو (resembling *ou* in 'sound').

The consonants not included in the above list have the same phonetic value as in the principal languages of Europe.

For quotes straight commas (straight quotes) are used to differentiate them from the curved commas used in the system of transliteration, ‘ for ع, and ’ for ء. Commas as punctuation marks are used according to the normal usage.

We have represented *tashdīd* ّ (shadd) by doubling the consonant having *tashdīd*, e.g., the word رَبّ in which the letter 'bā' has no *tashdīd* is written as '*ra bā*' while رَبَّ in which the letter 'bā' has a *tashdīd* on it is written as '*rabba*'.

The muffled sound of ن when و or ى with *tashdīd* follow the *tanwīn* has been represented by ñ.

As there are no capitals in Arabic, there are no capitals in transliteration, when the transliteration is not a part of the English text. We have followed the rules of English grammar (and have used capitals where applicable) when Arabic words or expressions appear in the English text.

بِسْمِ اللّٰهِ الرَّحْمٰنِ الرَّحِيْمِ

In the name of Allāh, the Gracious, the Merciful

THE HOLY PROPHET OF ISLĀM

ḤAḌRAT MUḤAMMAD MUṢṬAFĀ

(Peace and Blessings of Allāh be upon him)

INTRODUCTION

The life of the Holy Prophet of Islām[sa] is an open book, any part of which one may turn and see the details about his life. There is no other Prophet whose life is as well-recorded and accessible to study as that of the Holy Prophet of Islām[sa]. A large number of books have been written about the holy life and the excellent morals of the Holy Prophet[sa] by a variety of authors throughout the world. However, the life-story of the Holy Prophet of Islām[sa] is so open and so rich that it cannot be covered fully. Only glimpses of the life of the Holy Prophet[sa] have been presented in these books. The story is still incomplete and countless books will be written about the personality, excellent moral character and life of the Holy Prophet[sa].

This book is another humble effort to present the life and character of an excellent model for mankind whom God Almighty unequivocally has referred to in the Holy Qur'ān as *Al-Insān* (a perfect man) and who bore the trust (*Al-Amānat*) which the heavens, the earth and the mountains declined to bear:

إِنَّا عَرَضْنَا الْأَمَانَةَ عَلَى السَّمٰوٰتِ وَالْأَرْضِ وَالْجِبَالِ فَأَبَيْنَ أَنْ يَّحْمِلْنَهَا وَأَشْفَقْنَ مِنْهَا وَحَمَلَهَا الْإِنْسَانُ ط

innā 'araḍnal amānata 'alassamāwāti wal arḍi wal jibāli fa abaina añyyaḥmilnahā wa ashfaqna minhā wa ḥamalahal insānu

Verily, We offered the Trust to the heavens and the earth and the mountains, but they refused to bear it and were afraid of it. But man bore it. (33:73)

In the commentary of the above verse of the Holy Qur'ān it is stated:

Taking *al-Amānat* (trust) in the sense of the Law of the Qur'ān and *al-Insān* signifies the perfect man, i.e., the Holy Prophet[sa], the verse would mean that of all the denizens of the heavens and the earth, the Holy Prophet[sa] alone was found to be capable of being entrusted with the revelation of the most perfect and final Law - the Qur'ān, because no other man or being was endowed with those great qualities which were indispensable for the full and adequate discharge of this great responsibility.

(The Holy Qur'ān with English Translation and Short Commentary, Malik Ghulām Farīd, Islām International Publications, UK, 2002.)

The Holy Prophet[sa] was a Messenger for all mankind. Allāh says in the Holy Qur'ān:

قُلْ يٰٓأَيُّهَا النَّاسُ إِنِّىْ رَسُوْلُ اللّٰهِ إِلَيْكُمْ جَمِيْعًا نِ الَّذِىْ لَهٗ مُلْكُ السَّمٰوٰتِ وَ الْأَرْضِ ج

qul yā ayyu hannāsu innī rasūlullāhi ilaikum jamī'a nilladhī lahū

mulkussamāwāti walarḍ

Say, O mankind! truly I am a Messenger to you all from Allāh to Whom belongs the kingdom of the heavens and the earth. (7:159)

In the Holy Qur'ān the Holy Prophet[sa] is mentioned as *Ṭā Hā* (O Perfect Man) and in a *Ḥadīth-e-Qudsī* Allāh says about the Holy Prophet[sa]:

لَوْلَاكَ لَمَا خَلَقْتُ الْاَفْلَاكَ

lau lāka lamā khalaqtul aflāka

(O Muḥammad!) Had I not planned to create you, I would not have created the Universe

(Al-Fuwā'idul Majmū'ah, Muḥammad bin 'Alī Ashshaukānī, p. 346)

The Holy Prophet[sa] was a Messenger of Allāh but a human being. It is said in the Holy Qur'ān:

قُلْ سُبْحَانَ رَبِّيْ هَلْ كُنْتُ اِلاَّ بَشَرًا رَّسُوْلاً ۝

qul subḥāna rabbī hal kuntu illā basharar rasūlā

Say, 'Holy is my Lord! I am not but a man *sent as a* Messenger.' (17:94)

Thus, the Holy Prophet[sa] was an excellent model and example for mankind. He possessed and claimed no supernatural powers. As a human being, he was like other men: a son, a husband and a father. He was employed by Ḥaḍrat Khadījah[ra] before his marriage with her. He was first a citizen and then the chief executive of Medina, Mecca and pan Islāmica. He was a religious leader and guide for all mankind. He was a man of peace. For thirteen years he suffered all sorts of agony during his stay in

Mecca. He went to war to defend his community against threats from the enemies of Islām only when he was told to do so by God Almighty. In battle, he commanded his forces but did not personally kill anyone. He was a humble, kind-hearted and brave person.

God Almighty says in the Holy Qur'ān:

إِنَّ اللّٰهَ وَ مَلٰٓئِكَتَهٗ يُصَلُّوْنَ عَلَى النَّبِيِّ ؕ يٰٓاَيُّهَا الَّذِيْنَ اٰمَنُوْا صَلُّوْا عَلَيْهِ
وَسَلِّمُوْا تَسْلِيْمًا 0

innallāha wa malā'ikatahū yuṣallūna 'alannabiyyi yā ayyuhalladhīna āmanū ṣallū 'alaihi wa sallimū taslīmā

Allāh and His angels send blessings on the Prophet. O ye who believe! you *also* should invoke blessings on him and salute *him* with the salutation of peace. (33:57)

The Holy Prophet[sa] explained how to invoke *Durūd*. He[sa] said:

صَادِقًا مِّنْ نَّفْسِهٖ

ṣādiqamminnafsihī

(Send *Durūd*) with absolute sincerity

So we send *Durūd* with absolute sincerity of the heart:

اَللّٰهُمَّ صَلِّ عَلٰى مُحَمَّدٍ وَّ عَلٰى اٰلِ مُحَمَّدٍ كَمَا صَلَّيْتَ عَلٰى اِبْرَاهِيْمَ وَ
عَلٰى اٰلِ اِبْرَاهِيْمَ اِنَّكَ حَمِيْدٌ مَّجِيْدٌ

allāhumma ṣalli 'alā muḥammadiñwwa 'alā āli muḥammadin kamā

ṣallaita 'alā ibrāhīma wa 'alā āli ibrāhīma innaka ḥamīdummajīd

Bless O Allāh, Muḥammad and the people of Muḥammad as You did bless Abraham and the people of Abraham. You are indeed the Praiseworthy, the Glorious.

اَللّٰهُمَّ بَارِكْ عَلٰى مُحَمَّدٍ وَّ عَلٰى اٰلِ مُحَمَّدٍ كَمَا بَارَكْتَ عَلٰى اِبْرَاهِيْمَ وَ
عَلٰى اٰلِ اِبْرَاهِيْمَ اِنَّكَ حَمِيْدٌ مَّجِيْدٌ

allāhumma bārik 'alā muḥammadiñwwa 'alā āli muḥammadin kamā bārakta 'alā ibrāhīma wa 'alā āli ibrāhīma innaka ḥamīdummajīd

Prosper O Allāh, Muḥammad and the people of Muḥammad as You did prosper Abraham and the people of Abraham. You are indeed the Praiseworthy, the Glorious.

The Holy Qur'ān is the best source of information about the life of the Holy Prophet[sa]. Almost all the events which took place in the life of the Holy Prophet[sa] are mentioned in the Holy Qur'ān. Similarly, the traditions of the Holy Prophet[sa] present and explain vividly the various events which took place during the life of the Holy Prophet[sa]. In this book I have tried to use both sources of information -- the Holy Qur'ān and the traditions of the Holy Prophet[sa] -- to present the holy life of the Holy Prophet[sa].

It is a great honor and I am very pleased that Ḥaḍrat Khalīfatul Masīḥ V[aba] very graciously has written a preface for this book.

I dedicate this book to my parents, the late Soofi Khuda Bakhsh Zirvi and the late Amatul Karim Zirvi.

My father, Soofi Khuda Bakhsh Zirvi was the first one to join the fold of Aḥmadiyyat in his family. He acccpted Aḥmadiyyat when he was just 17 years old. He spent most of his life serving Aḥmadiyyat. He spent some time as a *Derwaish* in Qadian during 1947-1948 when Ḥaḍrat Muṣleḥ Mau'ūd[ra] asked for volunteers to go to Qadian at the time of the partition of the Indian subcontinent into India and Pakistan. Upon his return from Qadian in 1948 he devoted his life for the service of Aḥmadiyyat. In early 1949, he moved with his family to Rabwah, which at that time was an inhospitable barren land. He retired in 1992 as *Nā'ib Nāẓim Māl, Waqf-e-Jadīd*, Rabwah. He had the honor of working for almost 25 years with Ḥaḍrat Khalīfatul Masīḥ IV[rh] in *Waqf-e-Jadīd.* Upon his demise in 1998 at the age of 87 years, a letter of condolence from Ḥaḍrat Khalīfatul Masīḥ IV[rh] stated: "I am grieved to know about the sad demise of a long-serving servant of the *Jamā'at.* The deceased was a very sincere and revered person who was highly prayerful and devoted to supplications. I had an old acquaintance with him. He had served the *Jamā'at* selflessly. May God Almighty elevate his soul to high ranks in paradise."

My mother, Amatul Karim Zirvi, who was daughter of the late Babu Abdul Ghani Ambalvi, passed away suddenly at the young age of 37 years when I was 15 years old. May Allāh bless her soul. *Āmīn*

I am grateful to Maulāna Daud A. Hanif, Nā'ib Amīr and Missionary In-charge USA, Mr. Lutfur Rahman Mahmood, Maulāna Naseer A. Qamar, Additional Vakīl-e-Ishā'at, London, Maulāna Munir-ud-Din Shams, Additional Vakīlut Taṣnīf, London, Maulāna Hadi Ali Chaudhary, Professor, Jāmi'a Aḥmadiyya, Canada, Mr. Habibur Rehman Zirvi, Nā'ib Nāẓir Ishā'at, Rabwah and Dr. Naseer Ahmad for reviewing the manuscript and making excellent suggestions, which have been gladly incorporated. I appreciate Mr. Latif Ahmed's help in making the cover of the book. I also would like to acknowledge Dr. Monib Zirvi and Dr. Kaukab Zirvi for their help with editing the manuscript.

Karimullah Zirvi

September 2009

THE HOLY PROPHET OF ISLĀM

ḤAḌRAT MUḤAMMAD MUṢṬAFĀ

(Peace and Blessings of Allāh be upon him)

1

The World Before Islām

The world before Islām was quite different from what it is today. The two main powers at that time were the Roman Empire and the Persian Empire.

For many centuries the countries of the Mediterranean basin had been part of the Roman Empire. A settled countryside produced grain, fruits, wine and oil, and trade tarried along peaceful sea routes; in the great cities, a wealthy class of many origins shared the Greek and Latin culture of the empire. From the fourth century of the Christian era, the center of imperial power had moved eastwards. Constantinople replaced Rome as the capital city; there, the emperor was the focus of loyalty and the symbol of cohesion. Later on, in Germany, England, France, Spain and northern Italy, barbarian kings ruled, although the sense of belonging to the Roman Empire still existed; southern Italy, Sicily, the north African coast, Egypt, Syria, Anatolia and Greece remained under direct imperial rule from Constantinople. In this shrunken form, the empire was more Greek than

Roman. In its later phases it was more commonly called 'Byzantine' than Roman, after the former name of Constantinople, Byzantium.

Then a deeper change took place. The empire had become Christian, not just by formal decree of the ruler but by conversion at different levels. The majority of the population was Christian, although pagan philosophers taught in the school of Athens until the sixth century, Jewish communities lived in the cities, and memories of the pagan gods still haunted the temples turned into churches. Besides the official Orthodox Church, there sprouted others which differed from it in doctrine and practice and which gave expression to the loyalties and opposition to central authority of those whose language was other than Greek.

Over time, due to a dispute of authority there took place a division between the Church in the Byzantine territories, the Eastern Orthodox Church with its patriarchs as heads of its priesthood, and those in western Europe who accepted the supreme authority of the Pope in Rome.

To the east of the Byzantine Empire, across the Euphrates river, lay another great empire, that of the Sasanians, whose rule extended over what are now Iran and Iraq, and stretched into central Asia. The land now called Iran or Persia contained a number of regions of high culture and ancient cities inhabited by different ethnic groups, divided from each other by steppes or deserts, with no great rivers to give them easy communication. From time to time they had been united by strong and lasting dynasties; the latest was that of the Sasanians, whose original power lay among the Persian-speaking peoples of southern Iran. Theirs was a family state ruled through a hierarchy of officials, and they tried to provide a solid basis of unity and loyalty by reviving the ancient religion of Iran, traditionally associated with the teacher Zoroaster. For this religion, the universe was a battle-ground, beneath the supreme God, between good and evil spirits; the good would win, but men and women of virtue and ritual purity could hasten the victory.

The two empires included the main regions of settled life and high culture in the western half of the world, but further south, on either side of the Red Sea, lay two other societies with traditions of organized power and culture maintained by agriculture and by trade between the Indian Ocean and the Mediterranean. One was Ethiopia, an ancient kingdom with Christianity in its Coptic form as the official religion. The other was Yemen in south-western Arabia, a land of fertile mountain valleys and a point of transit for long-distance trade. At a certain stage its small local states had been incorporated in a larger kingdom, which had grown weak when trade declined in the early Christian era but revived later. Yemen had its own language, different from Arabic which was spoken elsewhere in Arabia, and its own religion: a multiplicity of gods were served by priests in temples which were places of pilgrimage, votive offerings and private, but not communal prayer, and also centers of great estates. In later centuries Christian and Jewish influences had come down from Syria on the trade-routes or across the sea from Ethiopia. In the sixth century, a center of Christianity had been destroyed by a king attracted to Judaism, but invasions from Ethiopia had restored some Christian influence; both the Byzantines and the Sasanians had been involved in these events.

Between the great empires of the north and the kingdoms of the Red Sea lay lands of a different kind. The greater part of the Arabian peninsula was steppe or desert, with isolated oases having enough water for regular cultivation. The inhabitants spoke various dialects of Arabic and followed different ways of life. Some of them were nomads who pastured camels, sheep or goats by using the scanty water resources of the desert; these have traditionally been known as 'Beduin'. Some were settled cultivators tending their grain or palm trees in the oases, or traders and craftsmen in small market towns; some combined more than one way of life. The balance between nomadic and sedentary peoples was precarious.

Although they were in the minority, it was the camel-nomads, mobile and carrying arms, who, together with merchant groups in the towns, dominated the cultivators and craftsmen. Their ethos of courage, hospitality, loyalty to family and pride of ancestry was also dominant. They were not controlled by a stable power of coercion, but were led by chiefs belonging to families around which there gathered lasting groups of supporters, expressing their cohesion and loyalty in the idiom of common ancestry; such groups are usually called tribes.

The power of tribal leaders was exercised from oases, where they had close links with merchants who organized trade through the territory controlled by the tribe. In the oases, however, other families were able to establish a different kind of power through the force of religion. The religion of pastoralists and cultivators seems to have had no clear shape. Local gods, identified with objects in the sky, were thought to be embodied in stones, trees and other natural things; good and evil spirits were believed to roam the world in the shape of animals; soothsayers claimed to speak with the tongue of some supernatural wisdom. It has been suggested, on the basis of modern practice in southern Arabia, that gods were thought of as dwelling in a sanctuary, a *haram*, a place or town set apart from tribal conflict, serving as a center of pilgrimage, sacrifice, meeting and arbitration, and watched over by a family under the protection of a neighboring tribe. Such a family could obtain power or influence by making skillful use of its religious prestige, its role as arbiter of tribal disputes, and its opportunities for trade.

Throughout this Near Eastern world, much was changing in the sixth and early seventh centuries. The Byzantine and Sasanian Empires were engaged in long wars, which lasted with intervals from 540 to 629. They were mainly fought in Syria and Iraq; for a moment the Sasanian armies came as far as the Mediterranean, occupying the great cities of Antioch and Alexandria as well as the holy city of Jerusalem, but in the 620s they were driven back by the Emperor Heraclius. For a time too Sasanian rule extended to south-western Arabia, where the kingdom of Yemen had lost much of its former power because of invasions from Ethiopia and a decline in agriculture. The settled societies ruled by the empires were very curious about the meaning of life and the way it should be lived, expressed in the idioms of the great religions.

The power and influence of the empires reached parts of the Arabian peninsula, and for many centuries Arab pastoral nomads from the north and center of the peninsula had been moving into the countryside of the area now often called the Fertile Crescent: the interior of Syria, the land lying west of the Euphrates in lower Iraq, and the region between Euphrates and Tigris in upper Iraq (the *Jazira*) were largely Arab in population. They brought with them their ethos and forms of social organization. Some of their tribal chiefs exercised leadership from oasis towns and were used by the imperial governments to keep other nomads away from the lands and to collect taxes. They were able therefore to create more stable political units, like that of the Lakhmids with its capital at Hira, in a region where the Sasanians did not exercise direct control, and that of the Ghassānids in a similar region of the Byzantine Empire. The people of these states acquired political and military knowledge, and were open to ideas and beliefs coming from the imperial lands; Hira was a Christian center. From these states, from Yemen, and also by the passage of traders along the trade routes, there came into Arabia some knowledge of the outside world and its culture, and some settlers from it. There were Jewish craftsmen, merchants and cultivators in the oases of Ḥijāz in western Arabia, and Christian monks and converts in central Arabia.

(A History of Arab Peoples, Albert Hourani, The Belknap Press of Harvard University Press, Cambridge, MA, 1991)

Europe was still largely pagan, devoted to the worship of Nordic, Teuton, and a host of other gods. In South Asia, Brahmanism and Buddhism had long passed their prime and had entered upon a placid and prolonged old age.

In the Far East, the homely philosophy of Confucius and the “way” of *Lao-Tze* pursued a sluggish and somnolent course. They had earlier been stirred by the advent of Buddhism into China, but had fallen back into passivity, along with Buddhism. Chinese scholars, feeling that a period of decline and decay had set in made sporadic efforts at revival.

The two great empires of Iran and Byzantium were interlocked in a struggle which ultimately resulted in death for both. The sudden end of one and the slow expiration of the other followed in due course, though the final blows in each case proceeded from a quarter entirely unexpected.

Religion, philosophy, and learning were at a low ebb. The spirit, the mind, and the intellect languished. Mankind had entered upon a decline. The earth seemed to be dying. It was the darkest period of the Dark Ages. There was only an occasional glimmer of light here and there.

As the Holy Qur'ān says:

ظَهَرَ الْفَسَادُ فِى الْبَرِّ وَ الْبَحْرِ بِمَا كَسَبَتْ اَيْدِى النَّاسِ

ẓaharal fasādu fil barri wal baḥri bimā kasabat aidinnāsi

Corruption has appeared on land and sea because of what men's hands have wrought. (30:42)

(The Excellent Exemplar - Muḥammad, Chaudhri Muḥammad Ẓafrullā Khān)

Arabian Peninsula Before Islām

Arabia is like an island which is surrounded by water on its three sides and land on the fourth side. Towards its West is the Red Sea, towards East is the Persian Gulf and Oman Sea, towards its South is Indian Ocean and towards the North there are Syria and Iraq. In area it is larger than all the other similar islands. According to some scholars the land is called Arabia because of the language spoken throughout this area which is Arabic. Other scholars think that since it was uninhabited desert land and the word 'Arab' means a desert, the place came to be known as Arabia. However, there was a time when the Arabian peninsula was lush green and densely populated. With the passage of time the area dried up and there was not enough water to support the inhabitants of the area. Therefore, groups of people started to migrate to areas where vegetation was plentiful. The migration started around 4,500 BC when some people migrated to Egypt. Then, some people migrated in 4,000 BC to the area now called Iraq where they lived under Akkadian rule for some time. Later on they established the kingdom of Babylon. Then another group of people migrated there and came to be known as Assyrians. The people who migrated around 2,000 BC were the people who wrote phonetically and were named Phoenicians by the Greeks. Around the same time the Aramites settled near Babylon and established Chaldean civilization. Some immigrants settled in Abyssinia and established the Abyssinan kingdom.

The Arabian peninsula can be divided into two parts, North and South, which are separated by a vast desert. The Arabs living in the Southern area traded with Syria, Iraq and Egypt. Aound 1,200 BC they established the first South Arabian kingdom known as the kingdom of Mainians. They controlled the trade routes. Mainians were succeeded by the Sabean kingdom. The Sabean kingdom, after achieving great riches from trade, went to ruins. Due to neglect in maintenance one of the large dams, the Dam of *Ma'rib*, was broken and it flooded and damaged the land to the extent that vegetation was not possible there anymore. Thus, the circumstances forced them to migrate. Some of them migrated in the vicinity of Medina while others migrated close to the borders of Syria and Iraq and settled there. These people were idol worshippers. Some of them worshipped the Sun, the Moon and the stars. During the first century AD some in the area became Jews and Christians and there was a struggle among the Christians and the Jews for control of the power. When the Abyssinians overran the kingdom of Yemen, the king of Yemen asked for support from the king of Persia against his enemies. Thus, Yemen became a protectorate of Persia and was governed through the viceroy of the king of Persia.

Mecca, the Birthplace of the Holy Prophet[sa]

Mecca stood about eighty kilometers from the coast. It was surrounded by mountains and had narrow passes for entry to the valley. There was no water in the area so there was very little life, if any. It is the place where Ḥaḍrat Ibrāhīm[as] left Ḥaḍrat Hājirah and their son Ḥaḍrat Ismāīl[as] under Divine Commandment. When water gushed out under the feet of Ḥaḍrat Ismāīl[as] under Divine intuition, Ḥaḍrat Hājirah saved the water by encircling the fountain with stones. She gave water to the passing tribes. Thus, soon some tribes settled there, and a town developed around the spring. *Banū Jurhum* was the first tribe to settle there. Ḥaḍrat Ismāīl[as] married the daughter of the chief of the *Jurhum* tribe, Muḍād ibn 'Amr. Twelve sons were born to Ḥaḍrat Ismāīl[as] from this marriage. These were the ancestors of the twelve tribes of Northern Arabs. Here, Ḥaḍrat Ibrāhīm[as] under Divine Commandment built the *Ka'bah*, the first house for the worship of Allāh with the help of Ḥaḍrat Ismāīl[as]. With the passage of time the residents of Mecca forgot the teachings of Ḥaḍrat Ibrāhīm[as] and Ḥaḍrat Ismāīl[as] and adopted idol-worshipping to such an extent that at the time of the birth of the Holy Prophet[sa] there were 360 idols in the *Ka'bah*, one idol for each day of the year.

Despite the fact that Yemen was the most advanced and most civilized part of the Arabian Peninsula due to its water resources and fertile land, it did not achieve the reputation achieved by Mecca. This was because Yemen never had a single center of pilgrimage as did Mecca in its *Ka'bah*. The *Ka'bah* was the pilgrimage center right from the beginning of the Arab history. Arabs sought to travel to it and its holy months were the source of joy and celebration for them.

The Holy Prophet[sa] was born on April 20, 571 AD (9 or 12 Rabī'ul Awwal, 52 BH) in Mecca. Mecca, where the Holy Prophet[sa] was born and lived part of his life is at present in Saudi Arabia which is part of Arabian peninsula. Arabia is still mostly desert with mountains found throughout the country. However, part of the country has rich soil and is green. Besides oil, there are silver and gold mines in abundance in the country. Its climate is hot and dry. There is little rainfall during the year. In summer it is very hot during the day time but the nights are quite cold. During winter it is a bit cold. Its main agricultural product is the date-palm of several different kinds. Date-palm used to be the major part of the diet of the Arabs. Where water is available there are date-palm gardens. During the rainy season there is a lot of rainfall in Ṭā'if. Therefore, Ṭā'if is famous for its gardens. Furthermore, due to the availability of plenty of agricultural land and grassy land Ṭā'if was used for raising animal herds and for growing agriculture products. The people of Arabia belonged to different tribes and each tribe had its own area assigned to them for grazing of their animals.

According to the traditions, at the time of the birth of the Holy

Prophet[sa], Arabs were primitive culturally and in their living style. People used to go out in the fields or to remote uninhabited areas to relieve themselves. Fighting among the people and the tribes over minor matters was common. Most people were idolators. The sanctuary, *Ka'bah,* was filled with idols placed there for worship. The largest idol named Hubal stood in the center of the *Ka'bah.*

Each tribe had its own leader. Their living style was very simple. Some people lived in cities while the others were nomadic. The Bedouin did not live in one place; they constantly moved to places wherever they would find water and greenery. Two coins, *'Dirham* and *Auqiyya'* were used as currency in those days. One *Auqiyya* was equivalent to forty *Dirhams.* For measuring purposes two units, *Madd* and *Ṣā'* were used. Most of the inhabitants were traders. Fairs were held at different locations which were attended by people coming to trade from far away areas. The majority of the people were illiterate. Only a few people could read and write. Idolatry was prevalent throughout Arabia. It is stated that the *Ka'bah* contained as many as three hundred and sixty idols. Other towns had their own major and minor gods and goddesses. It was an age of ignorance (*ayyāmul jāhiliyyah*) during which, generally speaking moral rectitude and the spiritual code had long been forgotten. Superstitious rites and dogmas had replaced the tenets of the Divine religion. Only a few *Quraishites* (the ancestors of the Holy Prophet[sa] and a handful of others) remained followers of the religion of Ibrāhīm[as], but they were an exception and were not able to exert any influence on others who were deeply submerged in pagan rites and beliefs. There were those who did not believe in God at all and thought that life was just a natural phenomenon. Some believed in God but not in the Day of Resurrection or reward and punishment.

It was customary to offer human sacrifices to the idols. Drinking, gambling and fornication were prevalent throughout the area. Marriage with two sisters was permissible and common. Similarly, upon on the death of his father, a man could marry the wife of his father who was his step-mother. There was no limit on the number of women one could marry. When girls were born, they often were buried alive. Women and slaves were treated cruelly. Fighting among the tribes over trivial issues was commonplace. Slavery was a familiar and widespread institution. In short, it was a period of extreme darkness. At that time, this darkness engulfed not only Arabia, but rather the whole world.

Prophethood in Ḥaḍrat Nūḥ's[as] (Noah) Progeny

About the prophethood of the Holy Prophet[sa] the following is stated in the Holy Qur'ān;

وَلَقَدْ اَرْسَلْنَا نُوْحًا وَّ اِبْرٰهِيْمَ وَ جَعَلْنَا فِيْ ذُرِّيَّتِهِمَا النُّبُوَّةَ وَ الْكِتٰبَ

walaqad arsalnā nūḥañwwa ibrāhīma wa ja'alnā fī dhurriyyatihi mannubuwwata walkitāba

And We did send Noah and Abraham, and We placed among thir seed prophethood and the Book. (57:27)

Ḥaḍrat Ibrāhīm[as] and Ḥaḍrat Ismā'īl[as]

Ḥaḍrat Ibrāhīm[as] was from the progeny of Ḥaḍrat Noah[as] and the Holy Prophet[sa] was from the progeny of Ḥaḍrat Ibrāhīm[as]. Ḥaḍrat Ibrāhīm[as] was originally from Iraq. Then, after living for sometime in Egypt, he settled in southern Palestine. Ḥaḍrat Ibrāhīm[as] married thrice. His first wife was Ḥaḍrat Sārah, the second wife was Ḥaḍrat Hājirah, and the third wife was Qaṭūrah. Ḥaḍrat Sārah was from the family of Ḥaḍrat Ibrāhīm[as] while Ḥaḍrat Hājirah, an Egyptian, was from outside the family of Ḥaḍrat Ibrāhīm[as]. Hadrat Ismā'īl[as] was born to Ḥaḍrat Hājirah while Ḥaḍrat Isḥāq[as] was born to Ḥaḍrat Sārah.

Ḥaḍrat Ismā'īl[as], the eldest son of Ḥaḍrat Ibrāhīm[as], was a small child when Ḥaḍrat Ibrāhīm[as] according to Allāh's design took Ḥaḍrat Ismā'īl[as] and Ḥaḍrat Hājirah with him and left them at a place where there was neither water nor any vegetation. As Ḥaḍrat Ibrāhīm[as] was leaving them, Ḥaḍrat Hājirah followed him and asked him why he was leaving them alone in such a desolate place. Ḥaḍrat Ibrāhīm[as] did not respond and kept walking. Then, Ḥaḍrat Hājirah told him to say something and asked him whether God Almighty had told him to do so. Ḥaḍrat Ibrāhīm replied in the affirmative and kept walking. Then, Ḥaḍrat Hājirah told him that he may leave as God Almighty would certainly take care of them and would not let them go to waste. Ḥaḍrat Ibrāhīm[as] prayed for them and begged God Almighty:

رَبَّنَآ اِنِّيٓ اَسْكَنْتُ مِنْ ذُرِّيَّتِيْ بِوَادٍ غَيْرِ ذِيْ زَرْعٍ عِنْدَ بَيْتِكَ الْمُحَرَّمِ ۙ
رَبَّنَا لِيُقِيْمُوا الصَّلٰوةَ فَاجْعَلْ اَفْئِدَةً مِّنَ النَّاسِ تَهْوِيْٓ اِلَيْهِمْ وَارْزُقْهُمْ
مِّنَ الثَّمَرٰتِ لَعَلَّهُمْ يَشْكُرُوْنَ 0

rabbanā innī askantu min dhurriyyatī biwādin ghairi dhī zar'in 'inda baitikal muḥarrami rabbanā liyuqīmuṣṣalāta faj'al af'idatamminannāsi tahwī ilaihim warzuqhumminaththamarāti la'allahum yashkurūn

Our Lord, I have settled some of my children in an uncultivable valley near Thy Sacred House -- our Lord -- that they may observe Prayer. So make men's hearts incline towards them and provide them with fruits, that they may be thankful. (14:38)

When the water and food supply which Ḥaḍrat Ibrāhīm[as] had given to Ḥaḍrat Hājirah and Ḥaḍrat Ismā'īl[as] were depleted, Ḥaḍrat Ismā'īl, a small child at that time, became extremely thirsty, started to toss around and restlessly kick his feet on the sandy ground. Ḥaḍrat Hājirah, seeing the suffering of her child, started to run in search of water back and forth between the two hills known as *Ṣafā* and *Marwah.* Sometimes she would run up to the *Ṣafā* hill and other times she would run up to the *Marwah* mountain. In this way she completed seven circuits of the two hills while crying and praying to God Almighty for help. Suddenly, she heard a voice saying, "O Hājirah, God Almighty has listened to you and your child's cries for help." When Ḥaḍrat Hājirah looked towards her son, she was overjoyed to see that water was gushing out of the place where her son was rubbing his feet. Ḥaḍrat Hājirah put sand and stones around the spring to contain the water. God Almighty made the race of Ḥaḍrat Hājirah between the two hills as part of the *Ḥajj* forever. This is known as '*Sa'ī*' i.e., running between *Ṣafā* and *Marwah.* This spring is famous as the '*Zamzam* Well'. When *Banū Jurhum* came to know about the water they asked Ḥaḍrat Hājirah for permission to settle close to the spring, which she happily granted. When Ḥaḍrat Ismā'īl[as] became a young man he married the daughter of the chief of *Banū Jurhum.*

The site of the well was later forgotten for a time, for it had been filled up with stones and a treasure trove by the *Jurhumites* who inhabited Mecca before the *Quraish.* Its site was rediscovered by the grandfather of the Holy Prophet[sa], 'Abdul Muṭṭalib. To drink the water of *Zamzam* is a rite of both the lesser and the greater pilgrimages. Today the well is not open at the surface; instead the water is led off to underground galleries reached by a flight of stairs where numerous faucets supply the water to scores of people at a time. The water supply is extremely copious, enough for thousands of people daily. The water is carried by pilgrims to all parts of the world as blessed water.

In the Holy Qur'ān performing the circuits in the memory of Ḥaḍrat Hājirah's desperate running between the two hills is described:

إِنَّ الصَّفَا وَالْمَرْوَةَ مِنْ شَعَآئِرِ اللّٰهِ ۚ فَمَنْ حَجَّ الْبَيْتَ اَوِ اعْتَمَرَ فَلَا جُنَاحَ
عَلَيْهِ اَنْ يَّطَّوَّفَ بِهِمَا ۗ وَمَنْ تَطَوَّعَ خَيْرًا فَاِنَّ اللّٰهَ ۙ شَاكِرٌ عَلِيْمٌ 0

innaṣṣafā wal marwata min sha'ā'irillāhi faman ḥajjal baita awi'tamara falā junāḥa 'alaihi añyyaṭawwafa bihima wa man taṭawwa'a khairan fa innallāha shākirun 'alīm

Surely, Al-Ṣafā and Al-Marwah are among the Signs of Allāh. It is, therefore, no sin for him who is on pilgrimage to the House, or performs 'Umra, to go round the two. And whoso does good beyond what is obligatory, surely then, Allāh is Appreciating, All-Knowing. (2:159)

After leaving Ḥaḍrat Hājirah and Ḥaḍrat Ismā'īl[as] at the barren valley of *Bakkah*, Ḥaḍrat Ibrāhīm[as] occasionally visited his wife and child. When Ḥaḍrat Ismā'īl[as] grew and became a young boy, Ḥaḍrat Ibrāhīm[as] saw in a dream that he was sacrificing Ismā'īl. Since it was not yet revealed to Ḥaḍrat Ibrāhīm[as] that sacrifice of humans is not permissible and it was a custom at that time to sacrifice human beings, Ḥaḍrat Ibrāhīm[as] wanted to fulfill his dream literally. Thus, to fulfill his dream Ḥaḍrat Ibrāhīm[as] decided to slaughter Ḥaḍrat Ismā'īl[as]. Accordingly, Ḥaḍrat Ibrāhīm[as] mentioned to Ḥaḍrat Ismā'īl[as] his dream and his desire to fulfill the dream literally.

This incident is mentioned in the Holy Qur'ān as:

فَلَمَّا بَلَغَ مَعَهُ السَّعْيَ قَالَ يٰبُنَيَّ اِنِّيْٓ اَرٰى فِى الْمَنَامِ اَنِّيْٓ اَذْبَحُكَ
فَانْظُرْ مَا ذَا تَرٰى ۗ قَالَ يٰٓاَبَتِ افْعَلْ مَا تُؤْمَرُ ز سَتَجِدُنِيْٓ اِنْ شَآءَ اللّٰهُ

مِنَ الصّٰبِرِيْنَ ٥

falammā balagha ma'ahussa'ya qāla yā bunayya innī arā filmanāmi annī adhbaḥuka fanẓur mā dhā tarā qāla yā abatif'al mā tu'maru satajidunī inshā Allāhu minaṣṣābirīn

And when he was old enough to work with him, he said, 'O my dear son, I have seen in a dream that I am slaughtering you. So consider, what you think *of it*!' He replied, 'O my father, do as you are commanded; you will find me, if Allāh please, of those who are patient.' (37:103)

Ḥaḍrat Ibrāhim[as] took Ḥaḍrat Ismā'īl[as] outside, away from his residence, and was about to slaughter him after making him lie down when God Almighty told Ḥaḍrat Ibrāhīm[as] to slaughter a sheep instead of Ḥaḍrat Ismā'īl[as].

It is mentioned in the Holy Qur'ān as:

فَلَمَّآ اَسْلَمَا وَ تَلَّهٗ لِلْجَبِيْنِ ٥ وَ نَادَيْنٰهُ اَنْ يّٰۤاِبْرٰهِيْمُ ٥ قَدْ صَدَّقْتَ الرُّءْيَا ۚ اِنَّا كَذٰلِكَ نَجْزِى الْمُحْسِنِيْنَ ٥ اِنَّ هٰذَا لَهُوَ الْبَلٰٓؤُا الْمُبِيْنُ وَفَدَيْنٰهُ بِذِبْحٍ عَظِيْمٍ ٥

falammā aslamā wa tallahū liljabīni wa nādaināhu añyyā ibrāhīmu qad ṣadaqtarru'yā innā kadhālika najzil muḥsinīna inna hādhā la huwal balā'ul mubīnu wa fadaināhu bi dhibḥin 'aẓīm

And when they both submitted *to the will of God* and he laid him *on the ground* face down, We called to him: 'O Abraham, You have indeed fulfilled the dream.' Thus indeed do We reward those who do good. That surely was a manifest trial.

And We ransomed him with a great sacrifice. (37:104-108)

Thus, Ḥaḍrat Ibrāhīm[as] did as commanded by Allāh. This is the sacrifice which is commemorated by the Muslims every year all over the world by slaughtering different animals such as goats, sheep, cows and camels at the occasion of *'Īdul Aḍḥiyya.*

'Īdul Aḍḥiyya is celebrated on the 10th of the month of *Dhul Ḥijjah* to commemorate the obedience of Ḥaḍrat Ibrāhīm[as] and his son Ḥaḍrat Ismā'īl[as].

Ḥaḍrat Ibrāhīm[as] visited Mecca when Ḥaḍrat Hājirah had passed away and Ḥaḍrat Ismā'īl[as] had bcome a young man. At this occasion, both Ḥaḍrat Ibrāhīm[as] and Ḥaḍrat Ismā'īl[as] under Divine Commandment rebuilt the *Ka'bah* by raising the walls at the original foundation site of the building so that people could come there to perform the rites of *Ḥajj.*

Ḥaḍrat Ibrāhīm[as] raised it from ruins that he discovered under Divine guidance. He[as] was commissioned by God to rebuild it with the help of his son Ḥaḍrat Ismā'īl[as]. It is the same place where he had left his wife Ḥaḍrat Hājirah and infant son Ismā'īl, again under Divine instructions. But work on the House of God awaited attention until Ḥaḍrat Ismā'īl[as] grew to an age where he could be of some help. So, both of them worked together to rebuild the house and to restart the institution of pilgrimage. In the Holy Qur'ān God Almighty says about the *Ka'bah:*

وَ اِذْ جَعَلْنَا الْبَيْتَ مَثَابَةً لِّلنَّاسِ وَاَمْنًا ؕ وَاتَّخِذُوْا مِنْ مَّقَامِ اِبْرٰهٖمَ
مُصَلًّى ؕ وَعَهِدْنَآ اِلٰٓى اِبْرٰهٖمَ وَ اِسْمٰعِيْلَ اَنْ طَهِّرَا بَيْتِىَ لِلطَّآئِفِيْنَ
وَالْعٰكِفِيْنَ وَالرُّكَّعِ السُّجُوْدِ ۝

wa idh ja'alnal baita mathābatallinnāsi wa amnā wattakhidhū mimmaqāmi ibrāhīma muṣalla wa 'ahidnā ilā ibrāhīma wa ismā'īla an ṭahhirā baitiya liṭṭā'ifina wal 'ākifina warrukka 'issujūd

And *remember the time* when We made the House a resort for mankind and *a place of* security; and take ye the station of Abraham as a place of Prayer. And We commanded Abraham and Ishmael, *saying,* 'Purify My House for those who perform the circuit and those who remain *therein* for devotion and those who bow down and fall prostrate *in Prayer.'* (2:126)

While raising the walls of the *Ka'bah* from the ruins Ḥaḍrat Ibrāhīm[as] prayed to God for the raising of a Messenger among his progeny:

رَبَّنَا وَاجْعَلْنَا مُسْلِمَيْنِ لَكَ وَ مِنْ ذُرِّيَّتِنَا اُمَّةً مُّسْلِمَةً لَّكَ

rabbanā waj'alnā muslimaini laka wa min dhurriyyatinā ummtammuslima tallaka

Our Lord, make us submissive to You and *make* of *our* offspring a people submissive to You. (2:129)

رَبَّنَا وَابْعَثْ فِيْهِمْ رَسُوْلاً مِّنْهُمْ يَتْلُوْا عَلَيْهِمْ اٰيٰتِكَ وَ يُعَلِّمُهُمُ الْكِتٰبَ وَالْحِكْمَةَ وَ يُزَكِّيْهِمْ

rabbanā wab'ath fihim rasūlamminhum yatlū 'alaihim āyātika wa yu'allimuhumul kitāba wal ḥikmata wa yuzakkīhim

And, Our Lord, raise up among us a Messenger from among themselves, who may recite to them Thy Signs and teach them the Book and Wisdom and may purify them. (2:130)

With the passing of time the progeny of Ḥaḍrat Ibrāhīm[as] and

Ḥaḍrat Ismā'īl[as] had spread throughout the Arabia. They were divided in different tribes. The *Quraish* to which the Holy Prophet[sa] belonged is one of the branches of the *'Adnānī* tribes. At the time of the birth of the Holy Prophet[sa] the *Quraish* had been divided into several sub-tribes.

Wāthilah ibn al-Asqa' narrated that the Holy Prophet[sa] said: "Verily Allāh chose Ismā'īl from the offspring of Ibrāhīm, and from the progeny of Ismā'īl, He chose *Banū Kinānah.* From *Banū Kinānah,* He chose the *Quraish,* and from the *Quraish,* He chose *Banū Hāshim,* and chose me from *Banū Hāshim.*"

(Jāmi' Tirmidhī, Vol. 2, p. 608, Ḥadīth # 3625))

The principle that the Prophet Muḥammad[sa] testifies to the truth of all previous revelations, furnishes a strong foundation for harmony among the various religions of the world, as well as for the unity of the human race. The fact that all of the foregoing Prophets testify to the truth of Prophet Muḥammad[sa] constitutes yet a stronger testimony to the truth of Islām and the unity of religions. The Prophets who lived thousands of years ago, and in countries distant from Arabia, all foretold the advent of the mighty Prophet of Islām. In fact, those very Prophets might well have impelled both Jews and Christians to settle down in Arabia; for the land of the Promised Prophet was specified by name in their Scriptures.

(Muḥammad[sa] in the Bible, Khalīl A. Nāṣir, Aḥmadiyya Movement in Islām, USA)

2

The Holy Prophet[sa] of Islām

Birth and Childhood

The Holy Prophet, Ḥaḍrat Muḥammad Muṣṭafā[sa], was born in Mecca on April 20, 571 AD (9 or 12 Rabī'ul Awwal, 52 BH) in the *Hāshimite* branch of the tribe of *Quraish.* His father's name was 'Abdullāh and his mother's name Āminah. His grandfather, 'Abdul Muṭṭalib, was the chief of Mecca at the time of Abraha's invasion. 'Abdullāh, who was the youngest son of 'Abdul Muṭṭalib was a very pious man. He was a healthy young man and used to write poems which were liked very much. He believed in One God and was not an idol worshipper which was the common practice in those days.

'Abdul Muṭṭalib was healthy and rich, and respected by his tribe. However, he was sad and worried because he had only one son to help him in carrying on the honorable duty of providing water to the people who visited *Ka'bah* every year. He, therefore, made a *nadhr* (vow) that should he be given ten sons and all of them reach manhood, he would sacrifice one of them to God near *Ka'bah.* His prayer was granted, and Allāh gave him eleven sons. When his sons reached manhood, 'Abdul Muṭṭalib decided to sacrifice one of them to fulfill his vow *(nadhr).* It was difficult for him to decide which one to sacrifice as all were dear to him. He decided to draw lots. The lot was drawn and 'Abdullāh's name came out. 'Abdullāh was the dearest to him, but he did not flinch from the decision of the fate. He took 'Abdullāh's hands and started towards the place where sacrifices were offered. His daughters started crying and begged him to sacrifice ten camels in place of 'Abdullāh. In fact, the whole *Quraish* insisted that 'Abdullāh be spared. At first 'Abdul Muṭṭalib refused. But when the pressure of the whole family and the whole tribe mounted, he agreed to cast a lot between 'Abdullāh and ten camels. Again the name of 'Abdullāh came out. On the suggestion of the people, the number of the camels was increased to twenty, again, the same result. Repeatedly, the number was increased to thirty, forty, fifty, sixty, seventy, eighty and ninety. But the result was always the same. At last the lot was cast between 100 camels and 'Abdullāh. Now the lot came out for the camels. The family was jubilant, but 'Abdul Muṭṭalib was not satisfied. He said: "Ten times the name of 'Abdullāh has come out. It is not fair to ignore those lots just for one lot." Three times more, he repeated the lot between 'Abdullāh and 100 camels, and every time the lot came out for the camels. Then 'Abdul Muṭṭalib sacrificed 100 camels and the life of 'Abdullāh was saved.

(Ibn Sa'd's Al-Ṭabaqāt Al-Kabīr, Vol. 1, p. 93)

'Abdullāh married a very honorable *Quraish* woman, Ḥaḍrat Āminah bint Wahb bin 'Abd Manāf bin Zuhra bin Quṣayy. Her mother's name was Barah bint 'Abdul 'Uzza. 'Abdullāh was twenty-five years old when he married Ḥaḍrat Āminah who was about twenty years old. After marriage they lived in the *Zaqāqul Muwallad* ward of Mecca. 'Abdullāh along with his father used to do business by making trade trips to neighboring areas. Shortly after his marriage, his father asked him to accompany him on a business trip to Syria to which he agreed. So before leaving for the trip he said farewell to his wife and this was the last time Ḥaḍrat Āminah saw her husband. On the way back from Syria, 'Abdullāh became ill. His maternal grandfather's family was living in *Yathrib,* so he stayed with them for a month for treatment. However, he died there a few months before Muḥammad, the Holy Prophet of Islām[sa] was born. The Holy Prophet[sa] was born in the *Sūqul Lail* ward of Mecca.

(Childhood of Ḥaḍrat Muḥammad Muṣṭafā[sa]*, Urdu, Amatul Bārī Nāṣir, p. 8, Lajna Imāillah, Karachi, Pakistan)*

The Holy Prophet's[sa] mother, Ḥaḍrat Āminah had seen a vision before his birth. In this vision, an angel proposed to her the name Muḥammad for her child, which literally means, the most praised one. As Ḥaḍrat Āminah was pregnant with him she saw a light come forth from her by which she could see the castles of Buṣrā in Syria. The Holy Prophet[sa] brought light from the heaven and himself was the light.

(The Life of Muḥammad[sa], Translation of Ibn Isḥāq's Sīrat Rasūlullāh[sa], A. Guilmore, p. 69, Oxford University Press, Oxford, UK, Printed in Pakistan, 2004)

He was a beautiful child with a bright broad face. His forehead and nose were elevated, eyes were black and bright with long eyebrows. He had a large head covered with black hair. His beauty was a reflection of the beauty of God Almighty. The Holy Prophet[sa] used to say:

اَوَّلُ مَا خَلَقَ اللّٰهُ نُوْرِیْ

awwalu mā khalaqallāhu nūrī

The first thing God Almighty created was my light.

(Al-Qastalānī in Al-Mawāhib Al-Ladunniyya, Vol. 1, pp, 5, 9, 10; Zurqānī, Sharḥ Mawāhib al-Ladunniyya, Vol. 1, p. 33)

His mother had seen a vision that the child was holding the keys to success, God's help and triumph.

In those days, it was a custom that the newborn children were sent to the tribes living in the Arabian desert to cultivate them, so that the open fresh air would make them healthy and strong, and also so that they would learn good Arabic language and oratory. Furthermore, they may learn the traits of hardwork and bravery from the Bedouin tribes. The tribes' women used to receive renumeration for taking care of the children. The year the Holy Prophet[sa] was born, ten women came to Mecca to take children with them for nursing. Often, these women looked for children from rich families to carry with them so that they could get more money for services. However, the Holy Prophet[sa] was an orphan. Therefore, most of the women picked children from rich families to carry with them and did not pay attention to the Holy Prophet's[sa] family. Only one woman was left who could not find a child from a rich family for grooming. Her name was Ḥalīmah and she belonged to the tribe of *Banū Sa'd*. She thought it better to take a child from a poor family than not to take a child at all. So she came to Ḥaḍrat Āminah and requested her to give her the child to carry with her for grooming. The Holy Prophet[sa] was one month old at that time. Ḥaḍrat Āminah gave the child to Ḥalīmah and prayed, "I give my child in the protection of God Almighty from the evil which develops in the mountains till I see him riding a camel, and that he treats others well and helps the poor and slaves."

(Raḥmatullil 'Ālamīn[sa]*, Vol. 2, p. 103, Sayyed Salmān Mansūrpūrī)*

Ḥalīmah was a poor lady and at the time she took the Holy Prophet[sa] in her care there was a drought causing a shortage of food for animals and humans. Due to the lack of food her milk also had dried up and her son, 'Abdullāh was often hungry. However, when carrying the Holy Prophet[sa] upon her return home, she realized that there was an unusual increase in her milk to the extent that both her own son, 'Abdullāh, and the Holy Prophet[sa] sucked the milk till they were full and still there was milk. Then she observed that her emaciated donkey suddenly gained such strength that it started to run fast and left all the others behind. Similarly, her goats started to produce much more milk than before. Ḥalīmah's daughter, Shīmā loved the Holy Prophet[sa] and used to carry him in her lap most of the time. The Holy Prophet[sa] started to talk in the language of the *Banū Sa'd* tribe of *Hawāzin* which he learned from Ḥalīmah and Shīmā. The Holy Prophet[sa] used to say, "I am the most eloquent Prophet because I belong to a *Quraish* family and I speak the language of *Banū Sa'd*."

(Ibn Sa'd's Al-Ṭabaqāt Al-Kabīr, Vol. 1, p. 71)

After raising the Holy Prophet[sa] for two years, Ḥalīmah brought him to Mecca to return him to his mother. She loved him very much and desired to keep him longer. So, she requested Ḥaḍrat Āminah to let him stay with her for a little longer. It happened so that in those days there was an epidemic in Mecca. So she had a good excuse to carry the child back with her. She told Ḥaḍrat Āminah that the child would get sick in Mecca so he should live with her a little longer. Ḥaḍrat Āminah concerned about the health of the child despite her earnest desire to keep the child with her agreed to Ḥalīmah's request. Thus Ḥalīmah took back the Holy Prophet[sa] with her. Ḥalīmah had four children. The Holy Prophet[sa] played with them and took care of the herd of goats along with them. He was a very brave child. Once, it so happened that he along with some other children took out the goats for grazing, some dacoits came and rounded up their goats to take with them. Though the Holy Prophet[sa] was only a child he stood with his arms spread in front of the dacoits and told them that he would not let them take the goats. The dacoits were astonished to see him standing like that in their way while usually people were frightened of them and ran away. The chief dacoit became furious and went to the Holy Prophet[sa]. Somehow he was impressed and realized he was not an ordinary child who is so bravely standing in their way. He asked the Holy Prophet[sa] what his name was? He said, "Muḥammad. 'Who is your father?' He replied, "Abdul Muṭṭalib.' " The chief of the dacoits understood that only a child belonging to the *Quraish* could be that brave. He let the herd go and left along with his comrades.

Another very interesting incident took place during his stay in the desert with Ḥalīmah. One day, when he was about four years old, he and his foster brother, ‘Abdullāh were tending goats not far from their house when strangers clad in white clothes appeared. They held in their hands a tray full of ice. They made the Holy Prophet[sa] lie down on the ground and dissected his chest. When ‘Abdullāh saw this he was so scared that he ran away to his parents and told them that someone had killed Muḥammad. Ḥalīmah and Ḥārith ran towards the place where Muḥammad was supposed to be. They did not see anyone besides Muḥammad who was terrified and pale due to fear. They comforted him and asked him what had happened. He told them that two men wearing white clothes came and had a golden tray filled with ice. "They were looking for something after opening my chest. They took out my heart, made a cut in it, took out a black piece and threw it out. Then they washed my heart and chest with the ice till they became clean and pure."

Ḥalīmah and Ḥārith looked around for the strangers. However, they did not find anyone or any part of the body. They thanked God Almighty that Muḥammad[sa] was safe. Ḥalīmah became worried about his safety and decided to return him to his mother soon. This incident is known as *Shaqq-e-Ṣadr* (i.e., the incident of cutting of the chest). It was a sort of a vision. It was the angels who had cleansed the chest of the Holy Prophet[sa].

(As-Sīratun Nabawiyyah libne Hishām, Vol. 1, p. 90; Sīrah Ibne Hishām, Biography of the Prophet[sa], Abridged by 'Abdus Salām Hārūn, pp. 23-24, Al-Falāḥ Foundation, Cairo, Egypt; Ṣaḥīḥ Muslim, Kitābul Īmān, Bāb al-Isrā'i bi rasūlillāhi[sa] ilassamāwāti wa farḍiṣṣalawāti)

When Ḥalīmah brought the Holy Prophet[sa] to Mecca to return him to his mother he became separated from Ḥalīmah and was lost. Ḥalīmah searched feverishly but could not find him. She went to 'Abdul Muṭṭalib and told him that she had lost Muḥammad and could not find him. 'Abdul Muṭṭalib went to the *Ka'bah* and prayed for his grandson. While he was praying a man from the *Quraish*, Waraqah bin Naufal, brought the child to 'Abdul Muṭṭalib. He thanked God and took him to Āminah.

(As-Sīratun Nabawiyyah libne Hishām, Vol. 1, p. 113)

It was in the sixth year of his life that Prophet Muḥammad[sa] was returned to the care of his mother. She along with her servant, Umm Aiman, took him to *Yathrib* to meet other relatives and pray at the grave of her husband. On the way back from *Yathrib* his mother fell ill and died. When she realized that she would not survive she prayed for her son, "O my dear son! May God bless you. I am certain that God Almighty who is the most Glorious and most Honored will appoint you towards His servants."

(Al-Mawāhib Al-Ladunniyya, Vol. 1, pp. 307-309; Zurqānī,Sharḥ Mawāhib al-Ladunniyya, pp. 308-312, Published by Dārul Kutab al-'Ilmiyyah, Beirut, Lebanon)

Ḥaḍrat Āminah passed away at a place called *Abwā'* and her grave is on a small hill in *Abwā'*.

(Musnad Aḥmad bin Ḥanbal, Vol. 5, p. 355)

Umm Aiman brought back to Mecca the child, who now at a very young age had neither a father nor mother. She brought him to his grandfather, 'Abdul Muṭṭalib. Prophet Muḥammad's[sa] grandfather, 'Abdul Muṭṭalib, was very fond of him and took him under his own care.

'Abdul Muṭṭalib had seen earlier in a dream a tree whose top reached the sky and whose branches were widespread to the East and the West. The tree was much brighter than the sun. A group of the *Quraish* was hanging on the branches of the tree while another group came forward to cut the branches of the tree. However, a beautiful young man from the *Quraish* whose body emitted a very pleasant smell dispelled the group which wanted to cut the branches. The dream was interpreted by the learned persons of the time that from his progeny that Prophet will appear whose appearance is mentioned in the earlier Holy Books. Imām Jalāluddīn Suyūṭī[rh] writes that when the Holy Prophet[sa] claimed to be the Messenger of Allāh, Abū Ṭālib used to say that the holy tree his father had seen in a dream, by God, that tree is Muḥammad.

(Khaṣā'iṣul Kubrā, Vol. 1, p. 99)

The guardianship of his grandfather lasted only two years and when the Prophet Muḥammad[sa] was eight years old, his grandfather also passed away at the age of 82 years (according to some traditions he was 100 years old when he passed away). On his deathbed, 'Abdul Muṭṭalib entrusted his grandson to the care of one of his sons, Abū Ṭālib. Thus, the Prophet Muḥammad[sa] was orphaned at a very young age. God Almighty says in the Holy Qur'ān

اَلَمْ يَجِدْكَ يَتِيْمًا فَاٰوٰى ٥

alam yajidka yatīman fa āwā

Did He not find you an orphan and give *you* shelter? (93:7)

Abū Ṭālib loved him very much. 'Abdul Muṭṭalib had several wives. He had two sons and two daughters from his wife, Fāṭimah bint 'Amr. The sons were 'Abdullāh and Abū Ṭālib and the daughters were Arwa and Umm Ḥakīm who was born as the twin sister with 'Abdullāh. Abū Ṭālib was older than 'Abdullāh.

When Muḥammad[sa] was 12 years old, he accompanied his uncle Abū Ṭālib on a business trip to Syria. When they reached Buṣrā, a town in the southern Syria, they met a Christian religious scholar by the name of Baḥīrah. When Baḥīrah saw the Holy Prophet[sa] he noticed that a small cloud was always making shade over him to protect him from the heat of the sun. He also saw in a vision that trees and stones were prostrating to the Holy Prophet[sa]. From these observations he became suspicious that the prophecy of the coming of the Promised Prophet which had been foretold seven generations ago may be fulfilled in this person. To observe the Holy Prophet[sa] closely, Baḥīrah invited Abū Ṭālib and his caravan to a dinner. Abū Ṭālib and his caravan had travelled to Syria several times before. This was the first time that the Christian priest had invited him to a dinner. All members of his caravan except Muḥammad[sa] went to Baḥīrah's house for dinner. Muḥammad[sa] was left behind to look after the camels and to safeguard the merchandise. However, Baḥīrah insisted that Muḥammad[sa] come to the dinner. So Muḥammad[sa] also joined the rest of the caravan at the dinner. At the dinner, Baḥīrah talked with Muḥammad[sa] and asked him several questions. After hearing the answers to his questions, Baḥīrah who had knowledge of the Bible was convinced that Muḥammad[sa] would be a Prophet when he grew up. He advised Abū Ṭālib to look after his nephew with great care. Abū Ṭālib took his advice to heart and left Buṣrā with his caravan immediately to return to Mecca.

Joined Ḥilful Fuḍūl Association During His Youth

When Muḥammad[sa] was 15 years old, a skirmish broke out between the *Quraish* and *Hawāzin* tribes at the occasion of a fair known as, "*'Ukāz Fair*". Despite the fact that war was prohibited during *Ḥajj*, this war not only started during the *Ḥajj* season, it continued for four years but with intervals. This war is known as the Battle of Fijār. The duration of this senseless war made people think of ways to stop it. A meeting was called by Az-Zubair, an uncle of Muḥammad[sa]. The concerned people gathered in the house of 'Abdullāh ibn Jud'ān, a wealthy resident of the town. In this meeting a society was formed to help the oppressed, the poor and the needy. The society was named, '*Ḥilful Fuḍūl*' after the common name, '*Faḍl*' of all its members. The members of this association took an oath to do the following:

"They will help those who were oppressed and will restore them their rights as long as the last drop of water remained in the sea. And if they do not do so, they will compensate the victims out of their own belongings."

Sincerely concerned about the conditions of the poor and needy, Muḥammad[sa] became a member of this society. Ṭalḥa bin 'Abdullāh narrated that the Holy Prophet[sa] said, "I witnessed in the house of 'Abdullāh ibn Jud'ān a covenant which I would not exchange for any number of fine camels: if I were invited to take part in it during Islām I should do so."

(The Life of Muḥammad[sa], Translation of Ibn Isḥāq's Sīrat Rasūlullāh[sa], A. Guilmore, p. 57, Oxford University Press, Oxford, UK, 2004)

As a Shepherd

While Muḥammad[sa] was still a boy, he took care of someone's animals and moved around with a flock of sheep, goats and camels in a wide area of the Arabian desert. About his experience as a shepherd, he used to say, "Allāh sent no Prophet who was not a shepherd. Moses was a shepherd and David was also a shepherd, and I was a shepherd. I grazed goats of my family at Ajyād (a pasture of Mecca)."

(Ibn Sa'd's Al-Ṭabaqāt Al-Kabīr, Translation by Mo'īnul Ḥaq, Kitāb Bhavan, New Delhi, India, Vol. 1, p. 141)

Marriage with Ḥaḍrat Khadījah[ra]

The Holy Prophet, Muḥammad[sa], grew into manhood exhibiting such sterling qualities of truthfulness, integrity, and piety that he became known throughout the land as the Truthful and the Trustworthy (*Al-Ṣādiq* and *Al-Amīn*). On hearing of Muḥammad's[sa] fame, a rich lady by the name of Khadījah[ra], who was twice widowed, invited him to her house and requested him to take charge of her business. Muḥammad[sa] travelled to Syria while in charge of Ḥaḍrat Khadījah's[ra] business. The expedition met with great success. Ḥaḍrat Khadījah[ra], the daughter of Khuwailid bin Asad bin 'Abdul 'Uzzā bin Quṣayy, was an intelligent and noble woman. She made a proposal of marriage to Muḥammad[sa] which was accepted. At the time of his marriage, Muḥammad[sa] was twenty-five years old while Ḥaḍrat

Khadījah[ra] was forty. They had six children - two boys and four girls. Both sons, Qāsim and 'Abdullāh had passed away before his prophethood but the daughters, Zainab[ra], Ruqayyah[ra], Ummi Kulthūm[ra] and Fāṭimah[ra] lived into Islām and embraced it.

(Sīrah Ibne Hishām, Biography of the Prophet[sa]*, Abridged by 'Abdus Salām Hārūn, pp. 37-38, Al-Falāḥ Foundation, Cairo, Egypt)*

Rebuilding of the Sacred House of Allāh (*Ka'bah*)

The *Ka'bah* had been damaged due to heavy rains and floods. It needed urgent repair. Four tribes of the *Quraish* divided the repair work among themselves. The walls were raised to the point where *Ḥajr-e-Aswad* was to be placed. The black stone was regarded as very sacred by the Meccans. Thus, it was considered a matter of pride and honor for a tribe to place the *Ḥajr-e-Aswad* in the *Ka'bah.* Therefore, the right to place the *Ḥajr-e-Aswad* in the *Ka'bah* became a bone of contention among the tribes who were involved in the reconstruction of the *Ka'bah.* To defuse the conflict and to avoid bloodshed, Abū Umayyah proposed that the first man who entered the gate of the *Ka'bah* the next morning suggest a solution to the dispute among the tribes. The next day, the first person to enter the gate of the *Ka'bah* was Muḥammad[sa]. Everyone was pleased to know that and shouted, "He is Muḥammad, he is *Al-Amīn* (the trustworthy)." So they asked Muḥammad[sa] to decide the matter.

Muḥammad[sa] said, "Give me a cloak." He spread the cloak on the ground and placed the *Ḥajr-e-Aswad* at the center of the cloak and said, "Let the elders of each clan hold on to one corner of the cloak and raise the cloak to the level where *Ḥajr-e-Aswad* is to be placed." When this was done, Muḥammad[sa] picked up the stone and placed it in its place in the wall of the *Ka'bah.* In this way, he defused a serious disagreement among the tribes and a bloody civil war was avoided.

3

The Beginning of Islām

Worship of Allāh in Solitude

After his marriage with Ḥaḍrat Khadījah[ra], the Holy Prophet[sa] became very contemplative. He used to retire to a cave on Mount *Ḥirā'* which was two miles north of Mecca, and spend his time in meditation and seclusion. He sometimes spent many nights in this cave and on one of these occasions he had an extraordinary experience.

Receiving the First Revelation

Ḥaḍrat 'Ā'ishah[ra] states that at first, the Holy Prophet[sa] began to have true dreams. Every dream would prove true like the break of the dawn. Then he became fond of seclusion. He used to go in seclusion in the cave *Ḥirā'* where he used to spend some nights in praying before returning to his family. He used to take some provisions with him. After exhausting the provisions, he would return to Khadījah[ra] and take a similar supply of provisions. This continued till the Truth was revealed to him. He was in the cave when an angel came to him and asked him to read. He said that he could not read. Then the angel held him so tightly and pressed him so hard that he could not bear it any more. After releasing him, the angel again asked him to read. He again replied that he could not read. For a second time the angel held the Holy Prophet[sa] so tightly and pressed him so hard that he could not bear it any more. After releasing him, the angel again asked him to read. The Holy Prophet[sa] again replied that he could not read. For a third time the angel held the Holy Prophet[sa] tightly and pressed him. After releasing him, the angel said to him:

اِقْرَاْ بِاسْمِ رَبِّكَ الَّذِىْ خَلَقَ ۝ خَلَقَ الْاِنْسَانَ مِنْ عَلَقٍ ۝ اِقْرَاْ وَ رَبُّكَ

الْاَكْرَمُ ۝ الَّذِىْ عَلَّمَ بِالْقَلَمِ ۝ عَلَّمَ الْاِنْسَانَ مَالَمْ يَعْلَمْ ۝

iqra' bismi rabbikalladhī khalaq khalaqal insāna min 'alaq iqra' wa rabbukal akramulladhī 'allama bil qalam 'allamal insāna mā lam ya'lam

Recite in the name of your Lord Who created, Created man from an adhesive clot. Recite! And your Lord is the Noblest. Who taught by the pen. Taught man what he knew not. (96:2-6)

After this incident, the Holy Prophet[sa] returned home. His heart was beating hard. He entered the house of Ḥaḍrat Khadījah[ra] bint Khuwailid and said, "Cover me up. Cover me up." She covered him with a blanket. After a while, when his fear subsided, he narrated the whole incident to Ḥaḍrat Khadījah[ra] and said that he was worried about himself. At this, Ḥaḍrat Khadījah[ra] said, "Never, By Allāh! Allāh Almighty will never disgrace you. Surely you take care of your kith and kin, help the oppressed, restore the lost virtues, honor the guest and help the needy." Then Ḥaḍrat Khadījah[ra] took the Holy Prophet[sa] to her cousin, Waraqah bin Naufal bin Asad bin 'Abdul 'Uzza, who had converted to Christianity during the days of ignorance. He knew Hebrew and could read and write the Hebrew Gospel, as long as Allāh wished that he writes. Waraqah bin Naufal was an old man and had lost his eyesight. Ḥaḍrat Khadījah[ra] said to him, "O my cousin! listen to your nephew." Waraqah bin Naufal said, "O my nephew! What did you see?" The Holy Prophet[sa] narrated to him all that he had seen. Waraqah bin Naufal told him that it was the same angel Gabriel who descended on Moses[as]. He told the Holy Prophet[sa] that he wished he could be alive and strong at the time when his people would expel him. The Holy Prophet[sa] asked Waraqah bin Naufal, "Will my people really expel me?" Waraqah bin Naufal replied that to whomsoever this status has been given has always been opposed. He said furthermore that if he were alive at the time (when people would oppose him), he would support him fully. However, soon after that Waraqah bin Naufal passed away.

(Ṣaḥīḥ Bukhārī, Kitāb Bad'ul Waḥyi Ilā Rasūlillāh[sa], Bāb Kaifa Kāna Bad'ul Waḥyi Ilā Rasūlillāh[sa])

The Pause in Revelation

The Holy Prophet[sa] felt that he needed Divine guidance to carry on the mission. However, after the first few revelations there was silence. Gabriel did not appear for some time. The Holy Prophet[sa] was a bit dismayed and frightened with the situation. He thought that maybe God Almighty was displeased with him. Even Ḥaḍrat Khadījah[ra] had similar thoughts about the pause in revelation. So the Holy Prophet[sa] went to the cave *Ḥirā'* to pray as was his practice. He prayed and begged God Almighty for guidance and help. His humble entreaties were accepted and clear and reassuring words were revealed to him by God Almighty:

مَا وَدَّعَكَ رَبُّكَ وَمَا قَلٰى ۝ وَلَلْاٰخِرَةُ خَيْرٌ لَّكَ مِنَ الْاُوْلٰى ۝ وَ لَسَوْفَ
يُعْطِيْكَ رَبُّكَ فَتَرْضٰى ۝ اَلَمْ يَجِدْكَ يَتِيْمًا فَاٰوٰى ۝ وَ وَجَدَكَ ضَآلًّا
فَهَدٰى ۝ وَ وَجَدَكَ عَآئِلًا فَاَغْنٰى ۝ فَاَمَّا الْيَتِيْمَ فَلَا تَقْهَرْ ۝

mā wadda'aka rabbuka wamā qalā wa lal-ākhiratu khairullaka minal ūlā wala saufa yu'ṭīka rabbuka fatarḍā alam yajidka yatīman fa āwā wa wajadaka ḍā allan fahadā wa wajadaka 'ā'ilan fa aghnā fa ammal yatīma falā taqhar

Your Lord has not forsaken you, nor is He displeased *with you.* Surely *every hour* that follows is better for you than *the one* that precedes.And Your Lord will soon give you and you will be well pleased. Did He not find you an orphan and give *you* shelter? And He found you wandering in search *for Him* and guided you *unto Himself.* And He found you in want and enriched *you.* So the orphan oppress not. (93:4-10)

The following was also revealed to the Holy Prophet[sa]:

إِنَّ فَضْلَهُ كَانَ عَلَيْكَ كَبِيْرًا ٥

inna faḍlahū kāna 'alaika kabīra

Surely, His grace towards you is great. (17:88)

4

Conveying the Message of Islām

It was the year 610 AD, when the angel Gabriel visited the Holy Prophet[sa] while he was meditating in the cave *Hirā'* and the first verses of the Holy Qur'ān were sent down to him by God Almighty. The Holy Prophet[sa] continued with his routine of meditation in the cave *Ḥirā'*. Then God Almighty revealed to him:

يٰٓأَيُّهَا الْمُدَّثِّرُ ۝ قُمْ فَأَنْذِرْ ۝ وَرَبَّكَ فَكَبِّرْ ۝

yā ayyuhal muddaththir, qum fa andhir, wa rabbaka fa kabbir

O you that has wrapped *yourself with your mantle*! Arise and warn, And your Lord do extol. (74:2-4)

The Holy Prophet[sa] was forty years old at the time of the first revelation which marks the beginning of his prophethood and the religion, Islām. The night of first revelation occurred towards the end of the month of *Ramaḍān*. When, he was called to prophethood by Allāh, he fully devoted his life to Allāh's service and to the universal spread of Islām. The Holy Prophet[sa] asked the people to give up idol-worship, and return to the worship of One God and be kind and charitable to the poor. Ḥaḍrat Khadījah[ra] was the first one to accept him as the Messenger of Allāh and the religion Islām. To begin with, Muḥammad preached the message of Allāh only to his friends, his closest relatives and those whom he could trust. Ḥaḍrat 'Alī[ra], the son of Abū Ṭālib who was just ten years old at that time, was the second and Ḥaḍrat Zaid[ra], the son of Ḥāritha was the third

Muslim. Among his friends, Ḥaḍrat Abū Bakr[ra] was the first to become a Muslim.

In the beginning, the Holy Prophet[sa] conveyed the message of Islām secretly to individuals. At the same time, Ḥaḍrat Abū Bakr[ra] also conveyed the message of Islām in the same way. They had some success in their efforts. A few young *Quraish* accepted Islām which included, Ḥaḍrat 'Uthmān bin 'Affān[ra], Ḥaḍrat 'Abdur Raḥmān bin 'Auf[ra], Ḥaḍrat Sa'd bin Abī Waqāṣ[ra], Ḥaḍrat Zubair bin al-'Awwām[ra] and Ḥaḍrat Ṭalḥa bin 'Abdullāh[ra]. At the same time, Ḥaḍrat Bilāl[ra] and some other slaves also accepted Islām.

After three years of preaching secretly to individuals, God Almighty commanded the Holy Prophet[sa] to spread the message of Islām openly:

فَاصْدَعْ بِمَا تُؤْمَرُ وَاَعْرِضْ عَنِ الْمُشْرِكِيْنَ ۝

fasda' bimā tu'maru wa a'riḍ 'anil mushrikīna

So declare openly that which you are commanded and turn aside from those who ascribe partners *to God.* (15:95)

At the same time the Holy Prophet[sa] was commanded by God Almighty to start conveying the message of Islām to his nearest kinsmen:

وَاَنْذِرْ عَشِيْرَتَكَ الْاَقْرَبِيْنَ ۝ وَاخْفِضْ جَنَاحَكَ لِمَنِ اتَّبَعَكَ مِنَ الْمُؤْمِنِيْنَ ۝

wa andhir 'ashīratakal aqrabīna wakhfiḍ janāḥaka lima nittaba'aka minal mu'minīna

And warn your nearest kinsmen. And lower your wing of *mercy* to the believers who follow you. (26:215-216)

The Holy Prophet[sa] once climbed to the top of Mount *Ṣafā* and announced to the people gathered close to the hill to see Muḥammad[sa], "O people of the *Quraish*, if I were to tell you that I see an army ready to attack on the other side of the mountain, would you believe me?" They answered, "Yes, certainly. We trust you and have never found you telling a lie." The Holy Prophet[sa] said, "Know then that I am a warner and I warn you of severe punishment. O *Banū 'Abdul Muṭṭalib*, *Banū 'Abd Manāf*, O *Banū Zuhrah*, O *Banū Taim*, O *Banū Makhzūm*, and O *Banū Asad*! Allāh has commanded me to inform you that I can assure you of good on this earth and in heaven if you declare that there is none worthy of worship except Allāh." Hearing this, Abū Lahab, his uncle, became extremely angry and cursed his nephew saying, "Did you gather us here to say this?" The spreading of the message openly by the Holy Prophet[sa] created severe opposition and hostility towards him and his followers.

Ḥaḍrat Ibn 'Abbās[ra] relates that when the verse, 'And warn your nearest kinsmen' was revealed, the Holy Prophet[sa] ascended the *Ṣafā* mountain and started calling various tribes of the *Quraish* by their name. Some *Quraish* Chiefs which included Abū Lahab came themselves while others sent their representatives. When they all gathered, the Holy Prophet[sa] said, "If I tell you that there is an enemy cavalary in the valley intending to attack you, would you believe me?" They said, "Yes we will believe you. You have always spoken the truth." The Holy Prophet[sa] then said, "I am a warner to you in face of a terrible punishment." Abū Lahab said to the Holy Prophet[sa], "May your hands perish this day. Is it for this purpose you have gathered us?"

Then the following verses were revealed to the Holy Prophet[sa]:

تَبَّتْ يَدَآ اَبِيْ لَهَبٍ وَّ تَبَّ ○ مَآ اَغْنٰى عَنْهُ مَالُهٗ وَمَا كَسَبَ ○ سَيَصْلٰى

نَارًا ذَاتَ لَهَبٍ ۝ وَّ امْرَاَتُهٗ ؕ حَمَّالَةَ الْحَطَبِ ۝ فِيْ جِيْدِهَا حَبْلٌ مِّنْ مَّسَدٍ ۝

tabbat yadā abī lahabiñwwa tabb mā aghnā 'anhu māluhū wamā kasab sayaslā nāran dhāta lahabiñwwamra atuhū hammā latal hatab fi jīdihā hablummimmasad

Perished be the two hands of Abū Lahab, and so perish he. His wealth and what he has earned shall avail him not. Soon shall he enter into a blazing fire; And his woman *too*, who goes around carrying the firewood. Round her neck shall be a halter of twisted palm-fiber. (111:1-6)

(Sahīh Bukhārī, Kitāb Tafsīrul Qur'ān, Bāb Sūrah "Tabbat yada abī lahabiñwwa tab")

Hadrat 'Alī[ra] relates that when the commandment to give the message to his near kinsmen was revealed, the Holy Prophet[sa] said, "At first he was fearful. He knew when he will preach to them, their response will not be good. So, for some time he kept quiet. Then Gabriel told him that if he did not proceed with the commandment then his Lord will seize him too."

The Holy Prophet[sa] told Hadrat 'Alī[ra] to arrange a feast where bread with mutton soup would be served and the entire clan of *Banī Muttalib* would be invited to the dinner. Hadrat 'Alī[ra] arranged the feast as directed by the Holy Prophet[sa] and invited at least forty members of the family of *Banī Muttalib* which included all the uncles of the Holy Prophet[sa], Abū Tālib, Hamzah, 'Abbās and Abū Lahab. The Holy Prophet[sa] himself poured the food in a large dish and told the guests to start eating. Everyone ate to his fill. When the Holy Prophet[sa] was about to talk with the guests, Abū Lahab started speaking before him. He said, "Your companion has mesmerized you." Hearing this people dispersed and the Holy Prophet[sa] could not convey his message to them.

The Holy Prophet[sa] told Ḥaḍrat 'Alī[ra] that because Abū Lahab started speaking he could not convey his message. He should arrange another such a feast where a selected forty people were to be invited. Ḥaḍrat 'Alī[ra] states that he organized a feast again. When everyone finished eating, the Holy Prophet[sa] said, "O Children of Abū Muṭṭalib! By God, none of the Arab youth has brought such a beautiful and glorious message for his people than that which I have brought to you. I have brought to you the goodness for this world and the hereafter. My Lord has commanded me that I call you towards Him. So, who will be my helper in this matter and establish the relationship of religious brotherhood with me?"

Everyone kept quiet. Ḥaḍrat 'Alī[ra] got up and said, "O Prophet[sa] of God! I will." Everyone laughed at it and left.

(Tārīkh Ṭabarī, Vol 2, p. 63, Istiqāmah Pulishers, Cairo, 1939)

The Holy Prophet[sa] conveyed the message of Islām to all sorts of people. He preached even to Rukānah, a famous wrestler of Mecca. While preaching to Rukānah the Holy Prophet[sa] asked him, "Would not you be afraid of Allāh and accept the message towards which I invite you? Rukānah said that if he is assured of the truth of his claim then he would accept his claim. The Holy Prophet[sa] asked him whether he would accept the truth of his claim were he to defeat him in wrestling. Rukānah said, "Yes". Thus the Holy Prophet[sa] challenged Rukānah to a wrestling bout which he accepted. In the wrestling match the Holy Prophet[sa] defeated Rukānah, the wrestler. Rukānah was surprised and asked the Holy Prophet[sa] to have another bout. Again the Holy Prophet[sa] defeated Rukānah. In this way three wrestling bouts took place and the Holy Prophet[sa] defeated Rukānah in all the three bouts. Rukānah said, "I am awestruck as to how he was able to defeat me." Later on Rukānah accepted Islām.

(As-Sīratun Nabawiyyah libne Hishām, Vol. 2, P. 31)

Invitation to Abū Jahl to Accept Islām

Besides giving the message of Islām to his nearest kinsmen as commanded by Allāh the Holy Prophet[sa] started to spread the message of Islām openly to other people. Despite severe opposition he kept on courageously spreading the message. The Holy Prophet[sa] conveyed the message of Islām to various Chiefs of the *Quraish.* The Holy Prophet[sa] personally gave the message of Islām to Abū Jahl (father of ignorance) who was a prominent enemy of Islām. Abū Jahl's hostility earned him the appellation of "father of ignorance" from the Muslims. His real name was 'Amr ibn Hishām.

Ḥaḍrat Mughīra bin Shi'ba[ra] relates that he met the Holy Prophet[sa] for the first time when he was walking through an alley along with Abū Jahl. The Holy Prophet[sa] said to Abū Jahl, "O Abul Ḥikam! Come to Allāh and his Messenger. I call you towards Allāh." Abū Jahl said, "O Muḥammad! Will you not restrain yourself from condemning our idols? If you desire that we be witness to it that you have conveyed the message to us then we affirm to it that you have conveyed the message. I swear that even if I come to know that what you proclaim is correct, I will not follow you." After hearing this, the Holy Prophet[sa] left. Then, Abū Jahl said to me, "I swear that I know he is rightful in what he proclaims. However, when his ancestors, the children of Quṣayy said that they are responsible for the management of the Covering of the *Ka'bah,* we accepted it. Then they said that the management of the *Majlis-e-Shūra* is also their responsibility and we could not repudiate it. Then they claimed to be the standard bearers of the Flag of the Arabs and we had to accept it. Then, they took the responsibility of serving water to pilgrims; again we kept quiet. However, in the matters of hospitality and almsgiving we competed with them shoulder to shoulder and both tribes became equal. Now they have claimed that the Prophet is from their tribe. I swear, I will never let this happen."

(Dalā'ilan-Nabuwwata li-Baihaqī, p. 198, Published by Dārul Kutab al-'Ilmiyya, Beirut, Lebanon)

Rejection of the Message by the Meccans

Despite the diligent effort by the Holy Prophet[sa] to give the message of Islām to the Meccans, they rejected the Holy Prophet's[sa] message and displayed considerable hostility to him and his followers. At first, they thought that it was a fantasy which would soon dissipate. However, when their own fantasy did not materialize and the message of Islām began to spread, they started to mistreat the Holy Prophet[sa] and his followers. At the same time, the Holy Prophet[sa] increased his efforts to convey the message of Islām. Thus a new ominous phase of trial in the life of the Holy Prophet[sa] and his Companions[ra], at the time when they were fully occupied in spreading the Message of Allāh, had begun.

Hostility Towards the Holy Prophet[sa] and His Companions[ra]

Meccans, who in the beginning did not take serious notice of the message and the movement, suddenly realized its consequences for them and became openly hostile to the Holy Prophet[sa] and his followers. The followers of the Holy Prophet[sa] were increasing in number day by day. This further worried the enemies of Islām.

At first, the *Quraish* asked Abū Ṭālib to withdraw his support from the Holy Prophet[sa]. They sent a delegation of influential people to talk to Abū Ṭālib in this regard. They went so far that they told Abū Ṭālib to tell Muḥammad that if he wants to marry a beautiful woman they would give him the most beautiful and rich woman to marry. Abū Ṭālib found himself in a difficult position. He asked the Holy Prophet[sa] not to annoy the *Quraish* too much by spreading his message as it put a lot of strain upon him as he was one of the leaders of the *Quraish*. The Holy Prophet[sa] was firm in his belief and considered it obligatory to spread the message of Islām and the worshipping of one God. So he said to his uncle, "By Allāh, if they place the sun on my right hand and the moon on my left hand and ask me to give up my mission, I shall not do so."

The opposition to the Holy Prophet[sa] and his message became violent. Once, the Holy Prophet[sa] was preaching in the area of *Ka'bah*, and idolators attacked and killed Ḥārith bin Abī Hālah while he was trying to pacify the opponents. He was the first Muslim to die in the cause of Islām. An Abyssinian slave, Bilāl bin Rabāḥ, was tortured by his master, Umayyah bin Khalaf, for accepting Islām. He was made to lie on his back on burning hot sand with a heavy stone placed on his chest. Despite the unbearable torture he suffered he remained steadfast in his belief in the Unity of God and repeatedly declared,

أَحَدْ ' أَحَدْ

Aḥad, Aḥad

Allāh is One, Allāh is One

(Usdul Ghābah, Vol. 1, p. 206)

Ḥaḍrat Abū Bakr[ra] arranged his freedom from his master. Later, when the Muslims settled in Medina and were able to live and worship in comparative peace, the Holy Prophet[sa] appointed Ḥaḍrat Bilāl[ra] as a *Mu'adhdhin* (the person who calls the worshippers to Prayers). There were many others who went through similar torture and these even included women. Zinnīra, a female slave, lost her eyes under the cruel treatment of the disbelievers. Abū Fukaih, a slave of Ṣafwān bin Umayyah was also laid down on hot sand while over his chest were placed heavy and hot stones, under pain of which his tongue dropped out.

The Holy Prophet[sa] himself was also accused, ridiculed and abused by the enemies of Islām. The Holy Prophet[sa] was called a sorcerer and accused of being possessed. The Holy Prophet[sa] was once almost strangled by an idolator while he was praying. Ḥaḍrat Abū Bakr[ra] rescued him. Umm Jamīl, the wife of Abū Lahab, used to throw rubbish and thorny bushes at the Holy Prophet's[sa] front door and obstruct the way to his house. All this did not slow or inhibit in any way the Holy Prophet[sa] in carrying out his mission. Rather, the Holy Prophet[sa] continued to preach with still more enthusiasm. Meccans did whatever they could do to stop him and his followers from spreading the message, without any success. The opposition to the Holy Prophet[sa] and hostility towards him further intensified. Despite this, Islām continued to flourish. During this period of turmoil, Ḥaḍrat Ḥamzah[ra], the uncle of the Holy Prophet[sa], accepted Islām. He was a brave man. His acceptance of Islām strengthened the mission of the Holy Prophet[sa] and the opposition was slightly muted.

'Utbah ibn Rābī'ah suggested to the Holy Prophet[sa] that if he wanted money it would be gathered for him to such an extent that he would become the richest person amongst them; if he wanted honor, he would be made their chief, if he wanted sovereignty, he would be made king so that he would decide all affairs. The Holy Prophet[sa] rejected his offer. 'Utbah returned to his cohorts and told them that no temptation would sway Muḥammad away from his mission.

When all the efforts of the idolators to dissuade the Holy Prophet[sa] from his mission failed, they came up with a proposal they thought might work. They proposed that if the Holy Prophet[sa] would adore their idols they would adore his God and as a result of this action the hostility would cease. The Holy Prophet[sa] rejected the proposal outright as in no way would he adore idols and mix truth with falsehood.

Migration of Muslims to Abyssinia (*Ḥabshah*)

With the failure of all their proposals to stop the Holy Prophet[sa] from spreading the message of Islām, the *Quraish* became frustrated and desperate. The threats of violence against the Holy Prophet[sa] and his Companions[ra] markedly increased. The Muslims were generally poor, were unsafe and vulnerable as they were surrounded by the idolators who were in the majority. Under these circumstances, the Holy Prophet[sa] advised his followers to migrate to Abyssinia, where the king (Negus) was a kind and noble person. Eighty-three adult Muslims and some children migrated to Abyssinia in groups. The first group which left Mecca for the sake of Allāh consisted of ten Muslims. the Holy Prophet[sa] appointed Ḥaḍrat 'Uthmān bin Maẓ'ūn[ra] as the leader of the first group which migrated to Abyssinia. This was the first migration (*Hijrah*) in Islām.

God Almighty says in the Holy Qur'ān:

وَالَّذِيْنَ هَاجَرُوْا فِى اللّٰهِ مِنْۢ بَعْدِ مَا ظُلِمُوْا لَنُبَوِّئَنَّهُمْ فِى الدُّنْيَا حَسَنَةً ؕ وَ لَاَجْرُ الْاٰخِرَةِ اَكْبَرُ ۘ لَوْ كَانُوْا يَعْلَمُوْنَ ۙ

walladhīna hājarū fillāhi mim ba'di mā ẓulimū lanubawwi'annahum fiddunyā ḥasanatan wa la ajrul ākhirati akbar lau kānū y'lamūn

And *as to* those who have left their homes for the sake of Allāh after they had been wronged, We will surely give them a goodly abode in this world; and truly the reward of the Hereafter is greater, if they but knew. (16:42)

The *Quraish* were not happy with the migration of the Muslims to Abyssinia. So a delegation comprised of two ambassadors, 'Amr bin al-'Ās and 'Abdullāh ibn Abū Rabī'ah, traveled to Abyssinia and tried to extradite the Muslims back to Mecca by bribing the courtiers of the king. They told the king that the emigrants follow a new religion of which no one had heard anything before. The king wanted to know more about these emigrants and their religion. So he gathered all the emigrants in his courtyard for a question and answer session. He asked what is the new religion they follow that they had to leave their country? Ḥaḍrat Ja'far bin Abū Ṭālib[ra] was the spokesperson for the Muslims. He responded to the question. He said, "O king! We were ignorant, worshipped idols, ate dead animals, committed all sorts of injustice. The strong amongst us exploited the weak, we broke ties and mistreated guests, and all sorts of immorality were prevalent in our society. Then Allāh sent a Prophet, who is one of us, whose lineage, truthfulness, trustworthiness and honesty were well known to us even before he claimed to be a Prophet. He told us to worship one God and to renounce the idol worship which is the practice we inherited from our forefathers. He commanded us to speak the truth, honor our promises, to be helpful to our relations, to be good to our neighbors, to abstain from bloodshed and to shun fornication. He commanded us not to give false witness, not to misappropriate an orphan's property or falsely accuse a married woman. He ordered us not to associate with Allāh. He commanded us to offer Prayers, keep the fast, pay *Zakāt.*

(Sīratul Ḥalabiyyah, 'Alī bin Burhanuddīn, Vol. 1, pp. 480-481, Bāb Hijratuththāniyya ilal Ḥabshah)

We believed in him and what he brought to us from Allāh. We do what he tells us to do and abstain from that which he tells us to abstain. All this was degrading and unacceptable to the non-believers. So they mistreated us, tortured some of us, and tried to force us to go back to idol-worshipping. This made our life in Mecca miserable. The way the non-believers treated us became unbearable and it became very difficult for us to live in Mecca, We have come to your country to seek protection and to live in justice and peace."

Upon hearing this, the king asked him to recite the Holy Qur'ān for him. Ḥaḍrat Ja'far[ra] recited to him *Sūrah Maryam.* While listening to it, Negus wept profusely and he said, "What you have just recited and that which was revealed to Moses[as] were from the same God. Go and live in my country. You will not be deported."

Ḥaḍrat Ḥamzah[ra] Accepts Islām

One day, during the sixth year of the prophethood of the Holy Prophet[sa], Abū Jahl behaved disrespectfully toward the Holy Prophet[sa] and insulted him. Ḥaḍrat Ḥamzah[ra] was an uncle of the Holy Prophet[sa] and he loved the Holy Prophet[sa] deeply. Ḥaḍrat Ḥamzah's[ra] bond-maid saw how Abū Jahl mistreated the Holy Prophet[sa]. When Ḥaḍrat Ḥamzah[ra] returned from hunting in the evening, his bond-maid told him about the mistreatment of the Holy Prophet[sa] by Abū Jahl. Ḥaḍrat Ḥamzah[ra] became very upset on hearing about the incident. He immediately went to Abū Jahl who was sitting in the *Ḥaram* area. Ḥaḍrat Ḥamzah[ra] hit Abū Jahl's head with his bow and said, "I have come to know that you have insulted Muḥammad. Listen, I have accepted Islām. If you have any courage then say something to me." After that Ḥaḍrat Ḥamzah[ra] went to the Holy Prophet[sa] and entered into the fold of Islām.

(As-Sīratun Nabawiyyah libne Hishām, Vol. 1, p. 90; Sīrah Ibne Hishām, Biography of the Prophet[sa], Abridged by 'Abdus Salām Hārūn, pp. 47-48, Al-Falāḥ Foundation, Cairo, Egypt)

Ḥaḍrat 'Umar[ra] Accepts Islām

Continuous propaganda against the Holy Prophet[sa] and Islām had created hatred for Islām in the minds of some people in Mecca which included Ḥaḍrat 'Umar[ra]. In his mind the hatred to the new religion had developed to such an extent that he once went with the intention to kill the Holy Prophet[sa]. On the way someone told Ḥaḍrat 'Umar[ra] that first he should worry about his sister (Fāṭimah, the daughter of Al-Khaṭṭāb) and her husband (Sa'īd ibn Zaid) who had accepted Islām. He was enraged to hear this and went straight to his sister's house. When he approached the house he heard the sound of recitation of the Holy Qur'ān coming from the house. Ḥaḍrat 'Umar[ra] entered the house without permission. He was furious and started hitting his brother-in-law, and accidentally injured his sister when she tried to protect her husband. Seeing blood flowing from injuries to his sister he mellowed and asked to see the sheets from which they were reciting the Holy Qur'ān. His sister told him to clean himself before he could see the sheets. Ḥaḍrat 'Umar[ra] cleaned himself and was given the sheets. He read the following verses of the Holy Qur'ān:

اِنَّنِیْ اَنَا اللّٰهُ لَاۤ اِلٰهَ اِلَّاۤ اَنَا فَاعْبُدْنِیْ وَاَقِمِ الصَّلٰوةَ لِذِكْرِیْ ۞ اِنَّ السَّاعَةَ اٰتِيَةٌ اَكَادُ اُخْفِيْهَا لِتُجْزٰی كُلُّ نَفْسٍ بِمَا تَسْعٰی ۞ فَلَا يَصُدَّنَّكَ عَنْهَا مَنْ لَّا يُؤْمِنُ بِهَا وَ اتَّبَعَ هَوٰىهُ فَتَرْدٰی ۞

innanī anallāhu lā ilāha illā anā fa'budnī wa aqimiṣṣalāta li dhikrī innassā'ata ātiyatun akādu ukhfihā li tujzā kullu nafsim bimā tas'ā falā yaṣuddannaka 'anhā mallā yu'minu bihā wattaba'a hawāhu fatardā

Verily, I am Allāh; there is no God beside Me. So serve Me, and observe Prayer for My remembrance. Surely, the Hour will come; I may reveal it, that every soul may be recompensed for its endeavor. So let not him who believes not therein and follows his own evil inclinations, turn you away therefrom, lest you perish. (20:15-17)

Ḥaḍrat 'Umar[ra] was moved by the depth of the contents of the verses of the Holy Qur'ān and decided to accept Islām. He told them to take him to the Holy Prophet[sa] so that he could accept Islām. Ḥaḍrat 'Umar[ra] was led to Arqam's[ra] house where the Holy Prophet[sa] was staying at that time. The Holy Prophet[sa] came to the gate of the house to welcome Ḥaḍrat 'Umar[ra] and asked him about his intentions. Ḥaḍrat 'Umar[ra] told him of his desire to accept Islām. The Holy Prophet[sa] was pleased to hear about his intention. Ḥaḍrat 'Umar's[ra] acceptance of Islām strengthened the will of the Muslims.

When the Holy Prophet[sa] started to deliver the message of Islām in Mecca, two chiefs of Mecca, 'Amr bin Hishām (Abū Jahl) and 'Umar bin Khaṭṭāb, were the most dangerous opponents of Islām and the Holy Prophet[sa]. The Holy Prophet[sa] prayed to God Almighty, "O Allāh, grant strength and respect to Islām through either one of the two, 'Amr bin Hishām (Abū Jahl) or 'Umar bin Khaṭṭāb (whosoever You like)."

(As-Sīratun Nabawiyyah libne Hishām, Urdu, Translation by 'Abdul Jalīl Siddiqī, Vol. 1, p. 379, I'tiqād Pulishing House, Delhi, India; Jāmi' Tirmidhī, Kitābul Manāqib, Bāb 'Umar bin Khaṭṭāb[ra])

Thus, acceptance of Islām by Ḥaḍrat 'Umar[ra] was the result of the acceptance of the prayers of the Holy Prophet[sa].

Confinement in Shi'bi Abī Ṭālib

The *Quraish* were full of anger on seeing the Muslim community flourish. They convened a large meeting in which they decided to impose a complete boycott of the Muslims. Their aim was to ostracize the *Banū Hāshim* and *Banū 'Abdul Muṭṭalib* clans and thus destroy them completely. They hatched a scheme and imposed a total boycott of the Holy Prophet[sa], his clan and tribe, *Banū Hāshim* and *Banū 'Abdul Muṭṭalib*, and all the Muslims. An agreement was signed to boycott which was written by Manṣūr ibn 'Ikrimah and was hung in the *Ka'bah*. The agreement stated: "They would neither take the daughters of the two clans (*Banū Hāshim* and *Banū 'Abdul Muṭṭalib*) nor will they give them their daughters in marriage; they would neither sell anything to them nor buy anything from them. Not only that, they would not have any contact with them nor even allow any food or drink to reach them.This boycott would continue till these clans agree to hand over Muḥammad to the *Quraish*."

Abū Ṭālib had no alternative but to take the two clans into the mountain trail called *Shi'bi Abī Ṭālib* which was his property. Thus, the Holy Prophet[sa], his family members and certain other people who were non-Muslims but had great regard for the Holy Prophet[sa] and his family were confined to a small lonely place.It was decided that the Meccans would not have normal dealings with the Muslims. They would neither buy from them nor sell them anything. They would not marry their daughters nor would give them their own daughters in marriage. They wrote down this covenant and hung it, like other proclamations, on the wall of the *Ka'bah*. Then the *Quraish* told the three men who were married to the three daughters of the Holy Prophet[sa] to divorce their wives. Two of the daughters of the Holy Prophet[sa] were married to the two sons of the Holy Prophet's[sa] uncle and bitter enemy, Abū Lahab. The third daughter, Ḥaḍrat Zainab[ra] was married to a cousin of Ḥaḍrat Khadījah[ra], Abū al-'Ās. Both sons of Abū Lahab divorced their wives. However, Abū al-'Āṣ refused to divorce his wife. The boycott continued for three years and during this confinement the clans of Hāshim and Muṭṭalib bore enormous difficulties and suffering. They were made to undergo the most extreme hardships and privations, so much so that at times they had nothing but tree leaves to sustain them. If any relative sent them any food, and the news leaked out, that relative was publicly insulted and put to shame. The *Quraish* used to express their pleasure on hearing the cries of the hungry children. Despite all that the Muslims remained steadfast in their beliefs. Then certain decent people from the enemies of Islām protested and revolted against the inhumane treatment of the people confined in *Shi'bi Abī Ṭālib.* At first, based on humanitarian grounds, Hishām ibn 'Amr and Zuhair ibn Abū Umayyah decided to revoke the pact of the boycott. Then they secretly asked others to do the same. They let it be known that they would invite the Holy Prophet[sa] and his Companions[ra] to come out of their place of retreat and go about their business as before. They met the confined people, talked with Abū Ṭālib and ended the boycott. Abū Jahl opposed it. However, he soon realized that there was a consensus to revoke the boycott pact and that would be foolish to oppose it. Thus, he stopped opposing them. One day the Holy Prophet[sa] said to Abū Ṭālib: "I have been informed by Allāh that the agreement of the *Quraish* has been eaten up by insects, and no writing has been left therein except the name of Allāh."

Al-Muṭ'am went to tear up the pact hanging on the wall of the *Ka'bah.* He was surprised to find out that insects had already devoured most of the pact except the beginning words, "In the name of Allāh." In this way the blockade was lifted. Although the boycott was revoked, still every obstruction was placed in the way of the Holy Prophet[sa] to prevent him from establishing contact with his fellow townsmen.

The Year of Sorrow and Grief: Death of Abū Ṭālib and Ḥaḍrat Khadījah[ra]

In his 10th year of prophethood, the Holy Prophet[sa] experienced several sorrowful events. The hardships endured by the Muslims during the blockade and confinement in *Shi'bi Abī Ṭālib* had gravely affected the health of both Ḥaḍrat Khadījah[ra] and the Holy Prophet's[sa] uncle, Abū Ṭālib. Ḥaḍrat Khadījah[ra] passed away within a few days of the lifting of the blockade, and Abū Ṭālib passed away a month thereafter. Thus the Holy Prophet[sa] lost his most faithful, loving and caring wife, Ḥaḍrat Khadījah[ra] and his uncle, Abū Ṭālib who at the critical time in his life gave him protection. The Holy Prophet[sa] patiently bore the grief due to all these tragedies.

Conveying the Message of Islām to the People of Ṭā'if

The opponents of the Holy Prophet[sa] had made it almost impossible for him to leave his house to carry his message to any section of the people of Mecca. Because of these circumstances the Holy Prophet[sa] decided to convey the message of Islām to the people of Ṭā'if, a city approximately forty miles to the east of Mecca. During this trip Zaid bin Ḥāritha accompanied him. First, the Holy Prophet[sa] met the important people of the town and conveyed to them the message of Islām. However, all of them refused to accept Islām and insulted him. Not only that, they asked the vagabonds and street thugs to follow him and force him lto eave the town. They followed him and pelted him with stones. His legs and feet were injured and blood filled his shoes. Thus, they forced him to leave the town.

Weary and sore, the Holy Prophet[sa] and his companion dragged themselves along a short distance, and when they were away from the town, they stopped in a vineyard belonging to two Meccans.

Ḥaḍrat 'Abdullāh bin Ja'far[ra] relates that after the sad demise of Abū Ṭālib, the Holy Prophet[sa] went to spread the message of Islām to the people of *Ṭā'if.* However, they did not accept him. The Holy Prophet[sa] offered two *rak'āt* prayer under the shade of a tree and most humbly supplicated to God Almighty in these words:

اَللّٰهُمَّ اِلَيْكَ اَشْكُوْ ضُعْفَ قُوَّتِيْ ' وَقِلَّةَ حِيْلَتِيْ وَهَوَانِيْ عَلَى النَّاسِ '
يَا اَرْحَمَ الرَّاحِمِيْنَ اِلٰى مَنْ تَكِلُنِيْ؟ اِلٰى عَدُوٍّ يَّتَجَهَّمُنِيْ اَمْ اِلٰى
قَرِيْبٍ مَّلَكْتَهُ ' اَمْرِيْ؟ اِنْ لَمْ تَكُنْ سَاخِطًا عَلَيَّ فَلَا اُبَالِيْ غَيْرَ اَنَّ
عَافِيَتَكَ اَوْسَعُ لِيْ اَعُوْذُ بِنُوْرِ وَجْهِكَ الْكَرِيْمِ الَّذِيْ ضَاءَتْ لَهُ
السَّمٰوٰتُ وَالْاَرْضُ ' وَاَشْرَقَتْ لَهُ الظُّلُمَاتُ ' وَصَلُحَ عَلَيْهِ اَمْرُ
الدُّنْيَا وَالْاٰخِرَةِ ' اَنْ تَحِلَّ عَلَيَّ غَضَبُكَ اَوْ تَنْزِلَ عَلَيَّ سُخْطُكَ '

وَلَكَ الْعُتْبٰى حَتّٰى تَرْضٰى وَلَاحَوْلَ وَلَا قُوَّةَ اِلَّا بِكَ -

allāhumma ilaika ashkū du'fa quwwatī, wa qillata ḥīlatī wa hawānī 'alannāsi, yā arḥamarrāḥimīna ilā man takilunī? ilā 'aduwwiñyyata jahhamunī am ilā qarībimmalaktahū amrī? in lam takun sākhiṭan 'alayya falā ubālī, ghaira anna 'āfiyataka ausa'u lī a'ūdhu bi nūri wajhikal karīmilladhī ḍa'at lahussamāwātu wal arḍu, wa ashraqat lahuẓẓulumātu, wa ṣaluḥa 'alaihi amruddunyā wal ākhirati, an taḥilla 'alayya ghaḍabuka au tanzila 'alayya sukhṭuka, walakal 'utbā ḥattā tarḍā walā ḥaula wa lā quwwata illā bika

O Allāh! To You I state my weakness and deficiencies in planning. I have become infamous among the people. O the Most beneficent among the beneficent people! To whom You will make in-charge of me. Will You entrust me to such an enemy who may destroy me or to some such a relative to whom You give full authority over my affairs? If You are not angry with me then I don't worry about anyone. However, I am certainly desirous of Your vast protection. I seek the protection of Your illuminating Countenance Which illuminates the earth and the heavens and which has illuminated the darkness and with which affairs of the world and the Hereafter are straightened. I seek Your protection from Your wrath that comes down upon me or Your displeasure with me. The future up till Your pleasure belongs to You. And all Power and Authority belongs to You.

(As-Sīratun Nabawiyyah libne Hishām, Vol. 2, pp. 61-62; Sīrah Ibne Hishām, Biography of the Prophet[sa], Abridged by 'Abdus Salām Hārūn, p. 90, Al-Falāḥ Foundation, Cairo, Egypt)

The owners of the vineyard, who happened to be in the vineyard at the time, had been among the Holy Prophet's[sa] persecutors in Mecca, but on this occasion they felt some sympathy toward their fellow townsman and permitted him to rest there a while. Soon, they sent him a tray of grapes by the hand of a Christian slave. This slave, Addas by name, belonged to Nineveh. The Holy Prophet[sa] took a grape, and before putting it into his mouth recited what has become the Muslim grace: "In the name of Allāh,

Ever Gracious, Most Merciful." This excited the curiosity of Addas who inquired about the identity of the stranger. The Holy Prophetsa told him about himself, and the conversation that ensued led Addas to declare his acceptance of Islām. So the Holy Prophet'ssa journey to Ṭā'if did not prove entirely fruitless. However, this was indeed one of the most difficult days of the Holy Prophet'ssa life. He rested for awhile in the garden and prayed there.

An angel descended upon him and asked for his permission to destroy the people of Ṭā'if who had mistreated him so badly. However, the Holy Prophetsa told the angel not to do so as he hoped that the good people among them may accept Islām and worship One God.

(Ṣaḥīḥ Bukhārī, Kitāb Bad'il Khalq, Bāb dhikril malā'ikati)

The incident is beautifully described in the following tradition:

Ḥaḍrat 'Urwah bin Zubairra relates that Ḥaḍrat 'Ā'ishahra said that she asked the Holy Prophetsa: "Did you experience a day harder than the day of the Battle of Uḥud" He answered: 'ndeed I experienced them at the hands of your people, and the hardest of them was the day of 'Aqabah when I presented myself to 'Abd Yalail bin 'Abd Kulāl and he made no response to that which I had desired. So I left grieved and depressed and felt no relief until I arrived at Qarn Tha'lib. Then I raised my head and saw a cloud that was shielding me from the sun in which I beheld Gabriel who called me and said: 'Allāh, the Most Honored and Glorious, has heard what your people have said to you and the response they have made to you and has sent the Angel of the Mountains to you so that you may direct him to do what you might wish to be done to them.' Then the Angel of the Mountains called to me, offered me the greeting of peace and said: 'Muḥammad, indeed Allāh has heard what thy people have said to you. I am the Angel of the Mountains, and my Lord has sent me to you, so that you might give me your direction concerning that which you would wish done to them. If you would so wish I would press down upon them the two great mountains.' " The Holy Prophetsa answered him: "Indeed not, I am hoping that Allāh will make out of their progeny such people as would worship Allāh, the One, not associating aught with Him."

(Ṣaḥīḥ Muslim, Kitābul Jihād, Bāb mā laqannabiyya[sa] *min idhil mushrikīna wal munāfiqīn)*

The Holy Prophet[sa] had now a difficult problem to resolve. He had left Mecca and he had been rejected by the people of Ṭā'if. Under Meccan custom, he could not go back to Mecca unless his re-entry was sponsored by some leading Meccan. There was nowhere else to go. The Holy Prophet[sa] prayed earnestly for light, guidance, and help from Allāh, and then set out with Zaid on the return journey to Mecca. He stopped on the way at a place called *Nakhla* for a few days and sent word to Muṭ'im bin 'Adī, a leading Meccan, asking whether he could be permitted to return to Mecca. Muṭ'im replied that he was prepared to sponsor his re-entry into Mecca, and when the Holy Prophet[sa] approached Mecca, Muṭ'im and his sons met him in the outskirts of Mecca and escorted him back into the town.

(The Excellent Exemplar, Muḥammad: Muḥammad Ẓafrullā Khān)

5

The Night Journey: Journey from Mecca to Jerusalem (*Isrā'*) and Ascension to Heaven (*Mi'rāj*)

One night, the Holy Prophet[sa] in a vision had made a trip from Mecca to Jerusalem which is commonly called *Isrā'*. At another occasion (2 BH) he made a journey to heaven which is commonly called *Mi'rāj* (the ascension). The Holy Prophet[sa] saw the first vision in the 5th year of the Call (7 BH).

Journey from Mecca to Jerusalem (*Isrā'*)

One night, when the Holy Prophet[sa] and the other present in the house of Ḥaḍrat Umm Hānī'[ra] went to sleep after offering their Prayer, the Holy Prophet[sa] was taken away by the angel Gabriel on a visit to *Aqṣā* Mosque in Jerusalem, and then to the seven heavens. In the morning the Holy Prophet[sa] said to them, "Last night I offered my evening Prayer with you, then I went to Jerusalem where I offered Prayer and now I am offering the dawn Prayer with you." Ḥaḍrat Umm Hānī'[ra], as Hind bint Abī Ṭālib was called, begged him not to tell the people, "Because they will regard you a liar and harm you." He said, "By God, I will tell them."

(As-Sīratun Nabawiyyah libne Hishām, Vol. 1, p. 267)

When the Holy Prophet[sa] told the *Quraish* that he had visited Jerusalem during the night the *Quraish* mocked him and mentioned it to Ḥaḍrat Abū Bakr[ra]. Ḥaḍrat Abū Bakr[ra] responded, "If he says so, then it is true." This earned Ḥaḍrat Abū Bakr[ra] the title of *Ṣiddique* (the truthful) from the Holy Prophet[sa].

(As-Sīratun Nabawiyyah libne Hishām,, Vol. 1, p. 399; Usdul Ghābah, Ibn Athīr, Vol. 3, p. 21 Dhikr 'Abdullāh bin Uthmān bin 'Āmir [Abū Bakr])

The journey of the Holy Prophet[sa] from Mecca to Jerusalem is called *Isrā'* and his ascension from Jerusalem to heaven is called the *Mi'rāj*. Both these events are known as the 'Night Journey'.

The extraordinary night journey of the Holy Prophet[sa] to Jerusalem is described in the Holy Qur'ān as follows:

سُبْحٰنَ الَّذِيٓ اَسْرٰى بِعَبْدِهٖ لَيْلاً مِّنَ الْمَسْجِدِ الْحَرَامِ اِلَى الْمَسْجِدِ الْاَقْصَا الَّذِيْ بٰرَكْنَا حَوْلَهٗ لِنُرِيَهٗ مِنْ اٰيٰتِنَا ۭ اِنَّهٗ هُوَ السَّمِيْعُ الْبَصِيْرُ 0

subḥānalladhī asrā bi 'abdihī lailamminal masjidil ḥarāmi ilal masjidil aqṣalladhī bāraknā ḥaulahū li nuriyahū min āyātina innahū huwassamī'ul baṣīr

Glory be to Him Who took His servant along by night from the Sacred Mosque to the Distant Mosque, the environs of which We have blessed, that We might show him *some* of Our Signs. Surely, He alone is the Hearing, the Seeing. (17:2)

"The Distant Mosque" refers to Prophet Solomon's[as] Temple at Jerusalem.

Ḥaḍrat Mirzā Bashīruddīn Maḥmūd Aḥmad, Khalīfatul Masīḥ II[ra] states that the above verse of the Holy Qur'ān which seems to mention a vision of the Holy Prophet[sa] is supposed by most Commentators of the Qur'ān to refer to his *Mi'rāj* (Spiritual Ascension). Contrary to popular opinion we are inclined to the view that the verse deals with the *Isrā'* (Spiritual Night Journey) of the Holy Prophet[sa] in a vision from Mecca to Jerusalem, while his *Mi'rāj* (Spiritual Ascension) has been dealt with at some length in *Sūrah Al-Najm.*

وَهُوَ بِا لْاُفُقِ الْاَعْلٰى 0 ثُمَّ دَنَا فَتَدَلّٰى 0 فَكَانَ قَابَ قَوْسَيْنِ اَوْاَدْنٰى 0 فَاَوْحٰى اِلٰى عَبْدِهٖ مَآ اَوْحٰى 0 مَا كَذَبَ الْفُؤَادُ مَا رَاٰى 0 اَفَتُمٰرُوْنَهٗ عَلٰى مَا يَرٰى 0 وَلَقَدْ رَاٰهُ نَزْلَةً اُخْرٰى 0 عِنْدَ سِدْرَةِ الْمُنْتَهٰى 0 عِنْدَهَا جَنَّةُ الْمَاْوٰى 0 اِذْ يَغْشَى السِّدْرَةَ مَا يَغْشٰى 0 مَا زَاغَ الْبَصَرُ وَمَا طَغٰى 0

wa huwa bil ufuqil a'lā thumma danā fatadallā fakāna qāba qausainin au adnā fa auḥā ilā 'abdihī mā auḥā mā kadhabal fu'ādu mā ra-ā afatumārūnahū 'alā mā yarā walaqad ra-āhu nazlatan ukhrā 'inda sidratil muntahā 'indahā jannatul ma'wā idh yaghshassidrata mā yaghshā mā zāghal baṣaru wamā ṭaghā

When he was at the loftiest horizon. Then he drew nearer *to God,* then he came down *to mankind.* So that he became, *as it were,* one chord to two bows or closer still. Then He revealed to His servant that which He revealed. The heart *of the Prophet* lied not regarding what he saw. Will you then dispute with him about what he saw? And certainly, he saw Him a second time *also.* Near the farthest lote-tree. Near which is the Garden of Eternal Abode. *This was* when that which covers covered the Lote-tree. The eye deviated not, nor did *it* wander. (53:8-18)

All the facts, mentioned in *Sūrah Al-Najm* which was revealed immediately after the Emigration to Abyssinia which took place in the month of *Rajab* in the 5th year of the Call, are to be found narrated in detail in the traditions which deal with the *Mi'rāj* of the Holy Prophet[sa]. The *Isrā'* or the Spiritual Night Journey of the Holy Prophet[sa] from Mecca to Jerusalem, with which the present verse deals, took place in the eleventh year of the Call, according to *Zurqānī*, and in the 12th year according to Muir and some other Christian writers. According to *Merdawaih* and *Ibn Sa'd*, however, the Isrā' took place on the 17th of *Rabī' Al-Awwal*, a year before *Hijrah.*

(Ibn Sa'd's Al-Ṭabaqāt Al-Kabīr, Translation by Mo'īnul Ḥaq, Kitāb Bhavan, New Delhi, India, Vol. 1, p. 247; Al-Khaṣāiṣ Al-Kubrā, Suyūṭī)

Baihaqī also relates that the *Isrā'* took place a year or six months before the *Hijrah.* Thus all relevant traditions go to show that the *Isrā'* took place a year or six months prior to *Hijrah* about the 12th year of the Call when after the death of Ḥaḍrat Khadījah[ra], which took place in the 10th year of the Call, the Holy Prophet[sa] was living with Ḥaḍrat Umm Hānī'[ra], his cousin. But the *Mi'rāj*, according to overwhelming scholarly opinion, took place about the 5th year of the Call. Thus, the two incidents are separated from each other by an interval of six or seven years and, therefore, cannot be identical; the one must be regarded as quite distinct and separate from the other. Moreover, the incidents which are mentioned in the Traditions to have taken place in the Prophet's[sa] *Mi'rāj*, are of quite a distinct nature from those which took place in his *Isrā'*.

Ascension to Heaven (*Mi'rāj*)

The ascension of the Holy Prophet[sa] to heaven (*Mi'raj*) is described in the following tradition of the Holy Prophet[sa]:

Anas bin Mālik[ra] from Mālik bin Sa'sa'a[ra] narrated that the Messenger[sa] of Allāh described to them his night journey saying, "While I was lying in *Al-Ḥaṭim* or *Al-Ḥijr*, suddenly someone came to me and cut my body open from here to here. I asked Al-Jārūd who was by my side, 'What does he mean?' He said: 'It means from his throat to his pubic area', or said, 'From the top of the chest.' The Holy Prophet[sa] further said, 'He then took out my heart. Then a gold tray full of Belief was brought to me and my heart was washed and was filled (with Belief) and then returned to its original place. Then a white animal which was smaller than a mule and bigger than a donkey was brought to me.' On this Al-Jārūd asked, 'Was it the *Burāq*, O Abū Ḥamzah?' Anas replied in the affirmative. The Holy Prophet[sa] said, 'The animal's step (was so wide that it) reached the farthest point within the reach of the animal's sight. I was carried on it, and Gabriel set out with me till we reached the nearest heaven. When he asked for the gate to be opened it was asked, 'Who is it?' Gabriel answered, 'Gabriel.' It was asked, 'Who is accompanying you?' Gabriel replied, 'Muḥammad'. It was asked, 'Has Muḥammad been called?' Gabriel replied in the affirmative. Then it was said, 'He is welcomed.' What an excellent visit his is! The gate was opened, and when I went over the first heaven, I saw Adam there. Gabriel said (to me), 'This is your father, Adam convey him your greetings.' So I greeted him and he returned the greeting to me and said, 'You are welcomed, O pious son and Prophet.' Then Gabriel ascended with me till we reached the second heaven. Gabriel asked for the gate to be opened. It was asked, Who is it?' Gabriel answered, 'Gabriel.' It was asked, 'Who is accompanying you?' Gabriel replied, 'Muḥammad.' It was asked, Has he been called?' Gabriel answered in the affirmative. Then it was said, 'He is welcomed.' What an excellent visit his is! The gate was opened. When I went over the second heaven, there I saw Yaḥyā (John) and 'Īsā (Jesus) who were cousins of each other. Gabriel said (to me), 'These are John and Jesus; convey them your greetings.' So I greeted them and both of them returned my greetings to me and said, 'You are welcomed, O pious brother and pious Prophet.' Then Gabriel ascended with me to the third heaven and asked for its gate to be opened. It was asked, 'Who is it?' Gabriel replied, 'Gabriel.' It was asked, 'Who is accompanying you?' Gabriel replied, 'Muḥammad.' It was asked, 'Has he been called?' Gabriel replied in the affirmative. Then it was said, 'He is welcomed.' What an excellent visit his is! The gate was opened, and when I went over the third heaven) there I saw Joseph. Gabriel said (to me), 'This is Joseph; convey him your greetings.' So I greeted him and he returned the greeting to me and said, 'You are welcomed, O pious brother and pious Prophet. Then Gabriel ascended with me to the fourth heaven and asked for its gate to be opened. It was asked, 'Who is it?' Gabriel replied, 'Gabriel.' It was asked, 'Who is accompanying you?' Gabriel replied, 'Muḥammad.' It was asked, 'Has he been called?' Gabriel replied in the affirmative. Then it was said, 'He is welcomed.' What an excellent visit his is! The gate was opened, and when I went over the fourth heaven, there I saw Idrīs. Gabriel said (to me), 'This is Idrīs; convey him your greetings.' So I greeted him and he returned the greeting to me and said, You are welcomed, O pious brother and pious Prophet. Then Gabriel ascended with me to the fifth heaven and asked for its gate to be opened. It was asked, 'Who is it?' Gabriel replied, 'Gabriel.' It was asked, Who is accompanying you?' Gabriel replied, 'Muḥammad.' It was asked, 'Has he been called?' Gabriel replied, in the affirmative. Then it was said, 'He is welcomed.' What an excellent visit his is! So when I went over the fifth heaven. There I saw Hārūn (i.e., Aaron). Gabriel said (to me), 'This is Aaron; pay him your greetings.' I greeted him and he returned greeting to me and said, 'You are welcomed, O pious brother and pious Prophet.' Then Gabriel ascended with me to the sixth heaven and asked for its gate to be opened. It was asked, 'Who is it?' Gabriel replied, 'Gabriel.' It was said, 'He is welcomed.'

What an excellent visit his is! When I went (over the sixth heaven), there I saw Moses. Gabriel said (to me), this is Moses pay him your greeting.' So I greeted him and he returned the greetings to me and said, 'You are welcomed, O pious brother and pious Prophet.' When I left him (i.e., Moses) he wept. Someone asked him, What makes you weep? Moses said, 'I weep because after me there has been sent (as Prophet) a young man whose followers will enter Paradise in greater number than my followers.' Then Gabriel ascended with me to the seventh heaven and asked for its gate to be opened. It was asked, 'Who is it?' Gabriel replied, Gabriel.' It was asked, 'Who is accompanying you?' Gabriel replied. 'Muḥammad'. I was asked, 'Has he been called?' Gabriel replied in the affirmative. Then it was said, 'He is welcomed.' What an excellent visit his is! So when I went (to the seventh heaven), there I saw Abraham. Gabriel said (to me), 'This is your father pay your greetings to him.' So I greeted him and he returned the greetings to me and said, 'You are welcomed, O pious son and pious Prophet.' Then I was made to ascend to *Sidratul Muntahā* (i.e., the Lote Tree of the farthest limit). Behold! Its fruits were like the jars of *Ḥajr* (a place near Medina) and its leaves were as big as the ears of elephants. Gabriel said, 'This is the Lote Tree of the farthest limit. Behold! There ran four rivers, two were hidden and two were visible. I asked, 'What are these two kinds of rivers, O Gabriel?' He replied, 'As for the hidden rivers, they are two rivers in Paradise, and the visible rivers are the Nile and the Euphrates.' Then *Al-Baitul Ma'mūr* (i.e., the Sacred House) was shown to me and a container full of wine and another full of milk and a third full of honey were brought to me. I took the milk. Gabriel remarked, 'This is the Islāmic religion which you and your followers are following. Then the prayers were enjoined on me: They were fifty prayers a day. When I returned, I passed by Moses who asked (me), 'What have you been ordered to do?' I replied, 'I have been ordered to offer fifty prayers a day.' Moses said, 'Your followers cannot bear fifty prayers a day, and by Allah, I have tested people before you, and I have tried my level best with Banī Israel (in vain). Go back to your Lord and ask for reducing your followers burden.' So I went back, and Allāh reduced ten prayers for me. Then again I came to Moses, but he repeated the same as he had said before. Then again I went back to Allāh and He reduced ten more prayers. When I came back to Moses he said the same, I went back to Allāh and He ordered me to observe ten prayers a day. When I came back to Moses, he repeated the same advice, so I went back to Allāh and was ordered to observe five prayers a day. When I came back to Moses, he said, 'What have you been ordered.' I replied, 'I have been ordered to observe five prayers a day.' He said, 'Your followers cannot bear five prayers a day, and no doubt, I have got an experience of the people before you, and I have tried my level best with Banī Isrā'īl, so go back to your Lord and ask for reducing your follower's burden.' I said, 'I have requested so much of my Lord that I feel ashamed, but I am satisfied now and surrender to Allāh's Order. When I left, I heard a voice saying, I have passed My Order and have reduced the burden of my Worshippers.' "

(Ṣaḥīḥ Bukhārī, Kitāb Manāqibul Anṣār, Bāb al-Mi'rāj; Ṣaḥīḥ Muslim, Kitābul Īmān, Bāb al-Isrā'i bi rasūlillāhi[sa] ilassamāwāti wa farḍiṣṣalawāti; Za'd al-Ma'ād, Vo. 2, p.49)

In addition to strong historical evidence, other relevant circumstances lend support to the view that the two incidents were quite distinct and separate from each other:

(a) The Qur'ān gives an account of the Holy Prophet's[sa] *Mi'rāj* (Spiritual Ascension) in Chapter 53, but makes no reference to his *Isrā'* (Night Journey to Jerusalem), while in the present *Sūrah* it speaks of his *Isrā'* but omits all allusion to his *Mi'rāj.*

(b) Ḥaḍrat Umm Hānī'[ra], the Holy Prophet's[sa] cousin with whom he was staying on the night when the *Isrā'* (Spiritual Night Journey to Jerusalem) took place speaks only of his visit to Jerusalem and makes no mention of his journey to the heavens. She was the first person whom the Holy

Prophet[sa] informed of his Night Journey to Jerusalem and at least seven collectors of Traditions have given her account of the incident on the authority of four different reporters who have reported the incident from her. All these four reporters concur in saying that the Holy Prophet[sa] went to Jerusalem and returned to Mecca the same night. If the Holy Prophet[sa] had spoken of his Ascension to the heavens also, Ḥaḍrat Umm Hānī'[ra] could not have failed to refer to it in one or other of her reports. But she does not do so in any of her reports, which conclusively shows that during the night in question the Holy Prophet[sa] made the *Isrā'* or the Spiritual Night Journey to Jerusalem only and that the *Mi'rāj* did not take place on that occasion. It seems that some reporters of Traditions mixed up the two accounts of the *Isrā'* and the *Mi'rāj*. The confusion appears to have arisen from the word *Isrā'* (Night Journey) having been used both for the *Isrā'* and the *Mi'rāj*; and the resemblance that existed in some of the details in the descriptions of the *Isrā'* and the *Mi'rāj* heightened and confirmed it.

(c) The Traditions which first give an account of the Holy Prophet's[sa] visit to Jerusalem and then of his transportation from Jerusalem to heaven also state that at Jerusalem he met the former Prophets, including Adam[as], Abraham[as], Moses[as] and Jesus[as], and that in the heavens he met the same Prophets again but did not recognize them. How did these Prophets whom he had met at Jerusalem reach the heavens before him and why could he not recognize them while he had seen them only a short while ago in the course of the same journey. It is inconceivable that he should have failed to recognize them when he had met them only a short while ago in the course of the same journey. For a detailed discussion of this important subject see: "*The Larger Edition of the Commentary of the Holy Qur'ān, pp. 1404-1409.*"

The Vision of the Holy Prophet[sa] referred to in the verse 17:2 of the Holy Qur'ān:

$$\text{سُبْحٰنَ الَّذِيْٓ اَسْرٰى بِعَبْدِهٖ لَيْلًا مِّنَ الْمَسْجِدِ الْحَرَامِ اِلَى الْمَسْجِدِ الْاَقْصَا الَّذِيْ بٰرَكْنَا حَوْلَهٗ لِنُرِيَهٗ مِنْ اٰيٰتِنَا ؕ اِنَّهٗ هُوَ السَّمِيْعُ الْبَصِيْرُ ۝}$$

subḥānalladhī asrā bi 'abdihī lailamminal masjidil ḥarāmi ilal masjidil aqsalladhī bāraknā ḥaulahū li nuriyahū min āyātina innahū huwassamī'ul baṣīr

implied a great prophecy. His journey to "The Distant Mosque" meant his Emigration to Medina where he was to build a Mosque which was destined to become later on the Central Mosque of Islām, and his seeing himself in the Vision that he was leading other Prophets of God in Prayers signified that the new faith, Islām was not to remain confined to the place of its birth but was to spread all over the world and the followers of all religions were to join its fold. His going to Jerusalem in the Vision may also be understood to mean that he was to be given dominion over the territory in which Jerusalem was situated. This prophecy was fulfilled during the Caliphate of Ḥaḍrat 'Umar[ra]. The Vision may also be taken as referring to a spiritual journey of the Holy Prophet[sa] to a distant land in some future time. It meant that when spiritual darkness would envelop the entire world, the Holy Prophet[sa] would appear in a spiritual sense a second time in the person of one of his followers, in a land far away from the scene of his First Advent. A pointed reference to this Second Advent of the Holy Prophet[sa] is to be found in 62:3-4:

هُوَ الَّذِيْ بَعَثَ فِى الْاُمِّيّٖنَ رَسُوْلًا مِّنْهُمْ يَتْلُوْا عَلَيْهِمْ اٰيٰتِهٖ
وَيُزَكِّيْهِمْ وَيُعَلِّمُهُمُ الْكِتٰبَ وَالْحِكْمَةَ ق وَ اِنْ كَانُوْا مِنْ قَبْلُ لَفِيْ
ضَلٰلٍ مُّبِيْنٍ 0 وَّ اٰخَرِيْنَ مِنْهُمْ لَمَّا يَلْحَقُوْا بِهِمْ ط وَهُوَ الْعَزِيْزُ
الْحَكِيْمُ 0

huwalladhī ba'atha fil ummiyyīna rasūlamminhum yatlū 'alaihim āyātihī wa yuzakkīhim wa yu'allimuhumul kitāba wal ḥikmata wa in kānū min qablu lafī ḍalālimmubīn wa ākharīna minhum lammā yalḥaqū bihim wa huwal 'azīzul ḥakīm

He it is Who has raised among the Unlettered *people* a Messenger from among themselves who recites unto them His Signs, and purifies them, and teaches them the Book and wisdom, although they had been, before, in manifest misguidance. And *among* others from among them who have not yet joined them. He is the Mighty, the Wise. (62:3-4)

(Short Commentary of the Holy Qur'ān by Ḥaḍrat Mirzā Bashīruddīn Maḥmūd Aḥmad, Khalīfatul Masīḥ II[ra]*)*

It may also be stated here that the two incidents were only spiritual phenomena and that the Holy Prophet[sa] did not physically go up to heaven or travel to Jerusalem.

Ḥaḍrat Ibn 'Abbās thinks the incidents were visions of the Holy Prophet[sa]:

عَنِ ابْنِ عَبَّاسٍ قَالَ رَأٰهُ بِفُؤَادِهٖ مَرَّتَيْنِ

‘anibni ‘abbāsin qāla ra-āhu bifu’ādihī marrataini

Ḥaḍrat Ibn ‘Abbās relates that the Holy Prophet[sa] saw God Almighty twice with his heart.

(Ṣaḥīḥ Muslim, Kitābul Īmān, Bāb ma‘nā qaulillāhi ‘azza wa jalla wa hall ra-annabiyyu[sa] *rabbahū lailatul isrā’a)*

Ḥaḍrat ‘Ā’ishah states:

مَنْ زَعَمَ اَنَّ مُحَمَّدًا ﷺ رَاٰی رَبَّهٗ فَقَدْ اَعْظَمَ عَلَى اللّٰهِ الْفِرْيَةَ

... اَوَلَمْ تَسْمَعْ اَنَّ اللّٰهَ عَزَّ وَجَلَّ يَقُوْلُ: لَاتُدْرِكُهُ الْاَبْصَارُ ز

وَهُوَ يُدْرِكُ الْاَبْصَارَ ج...

man za'ama anna muḥammadan ra-ā rabbahū faqad a‘ẓama ‘alallāhil firyata ... awalam tasma‘u annallāha ‘azza wa jalla yaqūlu lā tudrikuhul abṣāru wa huwa yudrikul abṣāra ...

The one who claims that the Holy Prophet[sa] saw his Lord, he would have forged a great lie against Allāh ... Did not you hear that God Almighty says, "Eyes (of the people) cannot reach Him but He reaches the eyes..." (6:104)

(Ṣaḥīḥ Muslim, Kitābul Īmān, Bāb ma‘nā qaulillāhi ‘azza wa jalla wa hall ra-annabiyyu[sa] *rabbahū lailatul isrā’a)*

The disbelievers of Mecca had demanded from the Holy Prophet[sa] that if he would go to the heaven and bring for them a Book only then will they believe in him. Upon this God Almighty told the Holy Prophet[sa] to say that Holy is He from such things. That is He has never taken anyone with a human body to the heavens and I am just a human being and a Messenger. This is stated in the Holy Qur'ān as:

اَوْ تَرْقٰى فِى السَّمَآءِ ؕ وَلَنْ نُّؤْمِنَ لِرُقِيِّكَ حَتّٰى تُنَزِّلَ عَلَيْنَا كِتَابًا نَّقْرَؤُهٗ ؕ قُلْ سُبْحَانَ رَبِّيْ هَلْ كُنْتُ اِلَّا بَشَرًا رَّسُوْلًا ۝

au tarqā fissamā'i wa lannu'mina liruqiyyika ḥattā tunazzila 'alainā kitābannnaqra'uhū qul subḥāna rabbī hal kuntu illā basharararrasūlā

Or you ascend up into heaven; and we will not believe in your ascension until you send down to us a book that we can read. Say, 'Holy is my Lord! I am not but a man *sent as a* Messenger.' (17:94)

The following *Ḥadīth* mentioned in *Ṣaḥīḥ Bukhārī* clearly shows that the whole experience was spiritual. In the beginning of the *Ḥadīth* it has been stated that the Holy Prophet[sa] was asleep in the *Masjidul Ḥarām.* His eyes were closed but his heart was awake. Then the *Ḥadīth* ends in the words that the Holy Prophet[sa] woke up and he was in the *Masjidul Ḥarām.* So it clearly proves that the whole vision was seen by his heart while his eyes were sleeping.

وَهُوَ نَائِمٌ فِى الْمَسْجِدِ الْحَرَامِ ... يَرٰى قَلْبُهٗ وَتَنَامُ عَيْنُهٗ وَلَا يَنَامُ قَلْبُهٗ ... وَاسْتَيْقَظَ وَهُوَ فِيْ مَسْجِدِ الْحَرَامِ -

wa huwa nā'imun fil masjidil ḥarāmi ... yarā qalbuhū wa tanāmu 'ainuhū wa lā yanāmu qalbuhū ... wastaiqaẓa wa huwa fil masjidil ḥarāmi

And he was sleeping in the sacred Mosque of the *Ka'bah* ... His heart was watching and his eyes were sleeping. And his heart was not sleeping ... When he woke up he was in the sacred Mosque of *the Ka'bah.*

(Ṣaḥīḥ Bukhārī, Kitābut Tauḥīd, Bāb qaulihī: wa kallamallāhu Mūsā taklīmā)

Ḥaḍrat 'Ā'ishah Ṣiddīqa[ra] says, "By God Almighty, The body of the Holy Prophet[sa] did not disappear during the ascension.

وَ اللّٰهِ مَا فُقِدَ جَسَدَ رَسُوْلِ اللّٰهِ ﷺ وَلٰكِنْ عُرِجَ بِرُوْحِهٖ

wallāhi mā fuqida jasada rasūlillāhi wa lākin 'urija bi rūḥihī

By Allāh! (During ascension) The body of the Holy Prophet[sa] did not disappear and his ascension was through his spirit.

(Tafsīr al-Kashshāf, Vol. 3, p. 416)

6

Migration to Medina

Migration of Early Muslims to Medina

The followers of the Holy Prophet[sa] had started moving from Mecca to Medina in large numbers before the migration of the Holy Prophet[sa]. When the hardships increased, the migration process slowly accelerated. Sometimes a whole lane of houses would be emptied in the course of a night. In the morning the Meccans would find out that the occupants of the houses had migrated to Medina.

After enduring thirteen years of unimaginable suffering at the hand of the fledgling religion's enemies, the Holy Prophet[sa] left Mecca under Divine guidance. He migrated to Medina, where the first Muslim community was already established by some of his followers who had migrated earlier.

Ḥaḍrat 'Ā'ishah[ra], wife of the Holy Prophet[sa] relates about her father, Ḥaḍrat Abū Bakr[ra]:

"Ever since I reached the age of discretion, I found my parents to be Muslim. There was not a day when the Holy Prophet[sa] did not visit our house, either in the morning or in the evening. When the Muslims experienced severe trials and oppressions by the infidels that had made the lives of the Muslims unbearable, like many others, Ḥaḍrat Abū Bakr[ra] also left his home with the intention to migrate to Abyssinia. When he reached a place called, *'Bark al-Ghimād'*, Ibn Daghinah, a leader of the *Qārah* tribe, met him. He asked, 'Abū Bakr[ra]! Where are you going?' Ḥaḍrat Abū Bakr[ra] responded, 'My people have expelled me. So, I wish to travel around the world and worship Allāh.' Ibn Daghinah said: 'O Abū Bakr! A person like you should neither leave the city nor be expelled by others. You try to reestablish lost virtues, strengthen the ties of kinship, help the poor and the weak; you are hospitable to guests, and you are always ready to help the people in need. I give you my protection. Go back to your home and worship Allāh.' Ḥaḍrat Abū Bakr[ra], therefore, returned home in the company of Ibn Daghinah. In the evening, Ibn Daghinah, roamed around the town and met elders and the revered people of the '*Quraish*'. He told them: 'Such a valuable person like Abū Bakr[ra] should not leave town. You are expelling a person who reestablishes lost virtues, strengthens the ties of kinship, helps the poor and the weak; he is hospitable to guests and is always ready to help people in need.' The *Quraish* did not belie what Ibn Daghinah had said about Ḥaḍrat Abū Bakr[ra] and accepted his guarantee of protection given to Ḥaḍrat Abū Bakr[ra]. However, they asked him to tell Ḥaḍrat Abū Bakr[ra] that he should worship, offer Prayers and recite whatever he likes in his home. He should not hurt their feelings with it, and should not do it in public. We fear that he may influence their women and children.

Accordingly, Ibn Daghinah told Ḥaḍrat Abū Bakr[ra] what the *Quraish* had said to him. Ḥaḍrat Abū Bakr[ra] worshipped Allāh at home and did not offer his Prayers in public and he did not recite the Holy Qur'ān outside his home. After sometime, Ḥaḍrat Abū Bakr[ra] reflected over the situation. He built a mosque in his home and started to offer Prayers and recite the Holy Qur'ān in his mosque. Soon women and children of the polytheists started to gather around him in large numbers. They were amazed to see him. As Ḥaḍrat Abū Bakr[ra] had no control over his emotions while reciting the Holy Qur'ān, he wept profusely. Seeing this, the leaders of the *Quraish* became nervous, and they talked with Ibn Daghinah about it. They told him: 'We had accepted your guarantee of protection to Ḥaḍrat Abū Bakr[ra] on the condition that he would worship, and offer Prayers and recite the Qur'ān in his house and not in public. However, he has failed to follow the conditions of the protection. He has built a mosque in his house and worships his Lord openly. We fear that our women and children will be affected by this. Ask him to refrain from worshipping in his mosque. If he agrees to worship within his house, he can stay under your protection. Otherwise, ask him to surrender your guarantee of protection to you. We do not want to disgrace the guarantee of protection given to him by you. At the same time, we cannot let Abū Bakr[ra] practice his beliefs openly.' Ḥaḍrat 'Ā'ishah[ra] says, 'Ibn Daghinah came to Abū Bakr[ra] and said, 'You know the conditions under which I had given you my protection. Either adhere to the conditions or surrender my protection, because I do not like people saying that my protection has been dishonored.' Ḥaḍrat Abū Bakr[ra] told him that he was surrendering his guarantee of protection and that he was happy to be under the protection and security of Allāh.

In those days, the Holy Prophet[sa] was in Mecca. He had told the Muslims that in his dream he had seen the place of migration. The place had date orchards and lay between two valleys. Thus, a few Companions[ra] of the Holy Prophet[sa] migrated to Medina and some of those who had migrated earlier to Abyssinia also moved to Medina. Ḥaḍrat Abū Bakr[ra] also started to prepare for migration to Medina. When the Holy Prophet[sa] came to know that Ḥaḍrat Abū Bakr[ra] intended to migrate to Medina, he told him to wait, because he thought he would also be given permission by God Almighty to migrate. Ḥaḍrat Abū Bakr[ra] said, 'May my father and mother be sacrificed for you! Do you really hope so?' The Holy Prophet[sa] said, 'Yes.' Thus, Ḥaḍrat Abū Bakr[ra] stopped making preparations for migration so that he could migrate along with the Holy Prophet[sa]. Furthermore, he made ready two camels in excellent condition for travelling by keeping them at home for four months and feeding them leaves of the acacia tree.' "

(Ibn Sa'd's Al-Ṭabaqāt Al-Kabīr, Translation by Mo'īnul Ḥaq, Kitāb Bhavan, New Delhi, India, Vol. 1, pp. 263-266; Ṣaḥīḥ Bukhārī, Kitābul Manāqibul Anṣār, Bāb Hijratun Nabī[sa] wa Aṣḥābihī ilal Medina)

The First Covenant of 'Aqabah

At the time of *Ḥajj*, while preaching, the Holy Prophet[sa] met a group of people who had come from Medina. He conveyed to them the message of Islām and asked them to accept it. They accepted his invitation and became Muslim. When they returned to Medina they conveyed the message of Islām to other members of their clan and urged them to accept the new faith.

In 621 AD, twelve people came from Medina at the time of *Ḥajj*. The Holy Prophet[sa] conveyed the message of Islām to them and entered into an agreement with them. The agreement took place at a place called 'Aqabah. Thus the agreement became to be known as the Covenant of 'Aqabah. In the agreement they agreed to worship one God and to obey His commandments. They further agreed not to steal, not to tell lies, not to commit adultery, kill their children, or commit any evil act and not to disobey the Holy Prophet[sa]. The Holy Prophet[sa] sent Ḥaḍrat Muṣ'ab ibn 'Umair[ra] with them to teach the Holy Qur'ān and the teachings of Islām. Soon the inhabitants of *Yathrib* started to accept Islām at his hand. The next year Ḥaḍrat Muṣ'ab[ra] came to Mecca and gave the good news that many people belonging to both the *Aus* and the *Khazraj* tribes had entered the fold of Islām and were eagerly learning the precepts of Islām.

(Sīrah Ibne Hishām, Biography of the Prophet[sa], Abridged by 'Abdus Salām Hārūn, pp. 84-85, Al-Falāḥ Foundation, Cairo, Egypt)

The Second Covenant of 'Aqabah

The next year, in 622 AD, a second covenat was signed at 'Aqabah with the people from Medina. This time 73 Muslims out of which 62 belonged to the *Khazraj* tribe and 11 to the *Aus* tribe came from Medina. The party included two women, Nuṣaybah, the daughter of Ka'b and 'Āṣma, the daughter of 'Amr. They had been taught Islām by Ḥaḍrat

Muṣ'ab[ra] and were full of faith and determination. They met the Holy Prophet[sa]. During the night they reached the appointed place and waited for the Holy Prophet[sa]. The Holy Prophet[sa] came with Ḥaḍrat 'Abbās[ra] who was the head of *Banū Hāshim* and *Banū 'Abd Manāf* at that time. They swore allegiance to the Holy Prophet[sa]. This was basically an extension of the earlier agreement. In this agreement they agreed to protect and help the Holy Prophet[sa] under all circumstances as they protect their own family members. All the drawbacks of signing this agreement were fully explained to them. They listened to all the drawbacks of the agreement to them and agreed to bear all the adverse consequences wholeheartedly. This covenant included clauses about wars they might have to face and that under all circumstances they would protect the Holy Prophet[sa]. The Holy Prophet[sa] told the party that he would go to Medina if they would hold Islām as dear as they hold their wives and children. All in the party with one voice said, 'Yes, Yes'.

Conditions of the Last Pledge of 'Aqabah

Ḥaḍrat 'Ubād ibn aṣ-Ṣāmit said, "We gave a pledge to the Holy Prophet[sa] that we would listen and obey in time of plenty as well as in scarcity, under favorable and unfavorable circumstances, and that we would not prefer ourselves to the other Muslims, and that we would not disagree with those who are in authority, and that we would speak the truth wherever we are, and that we would never fear the blame of the blamers."

(Sīrah Ibne Hishām, Biography of the Prophet[sa], Abridged by 'Abdus Salām Hārūn, pp. 85-89, Al-Falāḥ Foundation, Cairo, Egypt)
(For more information on the first and second Pledges of 'Aqabah, see: Sīrah Ibn Hishām, 2/54; Al-Ṭabarī, 2/355; Al-Kāmil fit-Tārīkh, 2/67; Al-Bidāyah wan-Nihāyah, 2/67; 'Uyūn Al-Aṯhat, 2/155)

Migration of the Holy Prophet[sa] to Medina

A Plan to Assassinate the Holy Prophet[sa]

When the *Quraish* realized that they could not stop the tide of conversion, and migration of the Muslims to Medina they became furious and their chiefs, such as Abū Jahl, Abū Lahab, Abū Sufyān, and 'Utbah gathered at *Darun-Nadwah* and, after rejecting suggestions to imprison or banish Muḥammad[sa], they planned to assassinate him. In order to escape the vendetta of *Banū Hāshim*, they decided that every clan would provide one man, and that they would collectively assault the Holy Prophet[sa]. God Almighty informed the Holy Prophet[sa] about their hideous plan. When the Holy Prophet[sa] learned of their evil intentions, he made a plan to leave the house at a time about which the enemy could not perceive. The Holy Prophet[sa] confided his plan to Ḥaḍrat 'Alī[ra] and made him cover himself with his mantle and told him to sleep in his place on the bed.

God Almighty states in the Holy Qur'ān:

وَ اِذْ يَمْكُرُ بِكَ الَّذِيْنَ كَفَرُوْا لِيُثْبِتُوْكَ اَوْ يَقْتُلُوْكَ اَوْ يُخْرِجُوْكَ ط وَ
يَمْكُرُوْنَ وَ يَمْكُرُ اللّٰهُ ط وَ اللّٰهُ خَيْرُ الْمٰكِرِيْنَ O

wa idh yamkuru bi kalladhīna kafarū liyuthbitūka au yaqtulūka au yukhrijūka wa yamkurūna wa yamkurullāhu wallāhu khairul mākirīn

And *remember the time* when the disbelievers plotted against you that they might imprison you or kill you or expel you. And they planned and Allāh also planned, and Allāh is the Best of planners. (8:31)

The *Quraish* men assigned to kill the Holy Prophet[sa] thought that the Holy Prophet[sa] was sleeping on the bed and kept an eye on the bed while looking for an opportune time to kill him. The Holy Prophet[sa] quietly slipped out of house in the secrecy of night just before dawn and on the way he picked Ḥaḍrat Abū Bakr[ra]. They both took shelter in a nearby cave called "*Thaur*". No one except the three children of Ḥaḍrat Abū Bakr[ra], Ḥaḍrat 'Abdullāh[ra], Ḥaḍrat 'Ā'ishah[ra] and Ḥaḍrat Aṣmā'[ra], knew about their hideout. For two days and two nights, the Holy Prophet[sa] and Ḥaḍrat Abū Bakr[ra] hid in the cave. On the third night, according to plan, the Holy Prophet[sa] continued his journey towards *Yathrib*, where the people were eagerly awaiting his arrival. When he reached *Yathrib*, he decided to stop for a while in Qubā*'*, a nearby village. He stayed in Qubā*'* for a few days and also laid down the foundation of the first mosque ever built by the Muslims. After ensuing the work on the Qubā*'* mosque, Holy Prophet[sa], finally arrived in Medina. The prospect of having to leave Mecca was very painful to the Holy Prophet[sa]. However, the anguish was softened by the Divine assurance that God Almighty would surely bring him back.

إِنَّ الَّذِيْ فَرَضَ عَلَيْكَ الْقُرْاٰنَ لَرَآدُّكَ اِلٰى مَعَادٍ ط

innalladhī faraḍa 'alaikal qur'āna larādduka ilā ma'ād

Most surely He Who had made *the teaching of* the Qur'ān binding on you will bring you back to *your* place of return. (28:86)

Ḥaḍrat 'Ā'ishah[ra] relates about the migration of the Holy Prophet[sa]:

"While we were at home, around noon-time, one day someone informed Ḥaḍrat Abū Bakr[ra] that the Holy Prophet[sa] was coming with his head covered with a sheet of cloth, whereas he never before came to our house at noon-time. Bewildered, Ḥaḍrat Abū Bakr[ra] arose saying, 'My father and mother be sacrificed for the Holy Prophet[sa]. By God! There must be something very important which has brought the Holy Prophet[sa] at this time.'

When the Holy Prophet[sa] arrived, he asked permission to enter. After getting permission, he entered the house and said to Ḥaḍrat Abū Bakr[ra], 'I have to talk to you about an important matter. Therefore, send the other people sitting here outside.' Ḥaḍrat Abū Bakr[ra] said: 'My father and mother be sacrificed for you[sa]! No one is an outsider. Everyone belongs to your household.' Anyhow, the Holy Prophet[sa] told Ḥaḍrat Abū Bakr[ra] that he had been granted permission by God Almighty to migrate. Ḥaḍrat Abū Bakr[ra] said, 'Will you please let me accompany you?' The Holy Prophet[sa] said, 'Yes.' Then Ḥaḍrat Abū Bakr[ra] said: 'My father and mother be sacrificed for you! Take one of these two camels.' The Holy Prophet[sa] said, 'Alright. However, I will pay for the camel.' "

Ḥaḍrat 'Ā'ishah[ra] says: "For the journey, we packed and provided provisions for both of them in a sack. My sister Asmā' tore a portion of her waist band and tied the mouth of the sack with it. That is why she came to be known as *'Dhātun Niṭāqain'.* Ḥaḍrat 'Ā'ishah[ra] says: 'Both the Holy Prophet[sa] and Ḥaḍrat Abū Bakr[ra], after leaving Mecca, hid in a cave in the *Thaur* mountain. They hid there for two to three nights. My brother 'Abdullāh[ra] was quite young, strong, and efficient at that time. He used to mix with the *Quraish* of Mecca and memorize whatever he heard. At night, he used to go to the cave and give all the news. Just before dawn, while it was still dark, he used to come back to Mecca, as if he was in Mecca throughout the night.

Ḥaḍrat Abū Bakr[ra] had a slave, 'Āmir bin Fuhairah, who used to take care of his goats. Around *'Ishā'* Prayer time he used to bring goats near the cave and give fresh milk to the Holy Prophet[sa] and Ḥaḍrat Abū Bakr[ra] for drinking. He also used to come back home just before the break of the dawn. He did so every night.

The Holy Prophet[sa] and Ḥaḍrat Abū Bakr[ra] hired a person belonging to the *'Banī ad-Dail'* tribe from the family of Banī 'Abd bin 'Adī as an expert guide. He was an expert in showing the way and knew every nook and cranny of the land, and he was in alliance with the family of Al-'Aṣ bin Wā'il As-Sahmī. Although he was on the religion of the infidels of *Quraish*, he was a reliable person. Therefore, both the Holy Prophet[sa] and Ḥaḍrat Abū Bakr[ra] charged their rides to him and told him to bring their rides near the cave of the mountain *Thaur*, early in the morning, after three days. Thus, The Holy Prophet[sa], Ḥaḍrat Abū Bakr[ra], 'Āmir bin Fuhairah, and the guide left the cave. The guide adopted the coastal route to travel. ' "

Ibn Shahāb relates that 'Abdur Raḥmān bin Mālik Mudlijī, nephew of Surāqah bin Mālik bin Ju'sham, told him that his father told him that he had heard from his brother, Surāqah: "Messengers from the infidels of *Quraish* came to us and told us that the *Quraish* had fixed a bounty (of 100 camels) each, for bringing back the Holy Prophet[sa] and Ḥaḍrat Abū Bakr[ra], dead or alive. Surāqah said: 'One day, I was sitting in the company of my people when a person came and said: 'O Surāqah! I have seen some people travelling along the coastal route. I think that they were Muḥammad and his Companions.' Surāqah stated that he realized that the travelers were the party of Muḥammad; however, as a decoy he said: 'They can't be Muḥammad and his party. You must have seen so and so who has just passed in front of us.' Anyway, I stayed for a short period of time in the company of my people and then silently slipped away to come to my home. I told my servant to bring my horse to the other side of the hillock and wait there till I come. Then I took my spear and left by the back door of my house dragging the lower end of the spear on the ground and keeping it low. Then I reached my horse. After mounting the horse I galloped swiftly. When I reached near the caravan of the Holy Prophet[sa], my horse slipped and I fell down in front of the horse. I got up fast, reached for my quiver, and picked an arrow as an omen whether I would be able to cause these people loss or not. However, I got the omen that I did not like. I did not accept the bad omen and mounted the horse again. The horse took me so near the caravan that I could hear the recitation of the Holy Qur'ān by the Holy Prophet[sa]. The Holy Prophet[sa] did not look back. However, Ḥaḍrat Abū Bakr[ra] repeatedly looked back towards me. In the meantime, both front feet of my horse sank up to the ankles in the ground. I got off the horse quickly and scolded the horse. The horse tried to get up and pull her feet out of the ground. When the horse pulled her feet out of the ground and stood up straight, a severe dust storm like rising smoke rose. At this, I again took an omen from my arrows. I picked the same arrow I had drawn the last time. At this, I called the caravan of the Holy Prophet[sa] with a loud voice, and I bade them peace and security. Hearing me, the caravan stopped. After mounting the horse, I reached near them. All that had happened to me while I was following the caravan had convinced me that the Holy Prophet[sa] would definitely succeed and gain power. So I told the Holy Prophet[sa] that his people had fixed a bounty for capturing and bringing him to them. I told the Holy Prophet[sa] other matters including the intentions of his people. I told them that I wished to offer them some provisions for the journey and other things. The Holy Prophet[sa] did not accept my offer. However, he asked me to continue meeting them secretly and not to tell anyone. At this occasion, I also requested the Holy Prophet[sa] to give an guarantee of peace and protection for me in writing. The Holy Prophet[sa] told 'Āmir bin Fuhairah to do so. He wrote a guarantee on a piece of leather. Then the Holy Prophet[sa] restarted travelling.' "

(Ṣaḥīḥ Bukhārī, Kitāb Faḍā'il Aṣḥābinnabī[ra]*, Bāb hijratun Nabī*[sa] *wa aṣḥābihī*[ra] *ilal Madīna)*

Stay in the Cave Thaur During Migration to Medina

In the evening, as soon as it became dark, the Holy Prophet[sa] left his house and went to the house of Ḥaḍrat Abū Bakr[ra]. The two then made their way out of Mecca and went up to one of the surrounding hills and took shelter in a cave called, "*Thaur*". The cave had an entrance so narrow that a person had to lie flat and crawl into it. During the course of the night the young men of *Quraish* who were assigned the task of killing the Holy Prophet[sa] discovered that the Holy Prophet[sa] was no longer in the house. In the morning, these young men decided to search for the Holy Prophet[sa] by following his footprints. Soon they realized that the Holy Prophet[sa] had company as there were tracks of two men. The tracks led the enemies of Holy Prophet[sa] to the mouth of the cave where the tracks suddenly disappeared. They were puzzled by the sudden disappearance of the marks and the leader of the group said, "The fugitives have not gone any farther; they have either sunk into the earth or ascended into the sky." The other possibility he suggested was their taking refuge in the cave. However, the possibility of their taking refuge in the cave was ruled out as they thought it would be certain death to go inside the cave as poisonous vipers abounded inside and at the mouth of the cave. The leader of the search party had reached close to the entrance of the cave but did not go inside the cave. The other members of the search party asked him why he did not go inside the cave to look for the Holy Prophet[sa]. He told them that the entrance was covered with cobwebs and there was a pigeon nest with a pair of pigeons and their eggs in it. No one could have gone inside the cave without destroying the cobweb and the pigeons' nest. Then, the party decided to leave the cave area.

Ḥaḍrat Abū Bakr[ra] relates, "I was with the Holy Prophet[sa] in the cave. When I raised my head, I saw the feet of the people. I said, 'O Allāh's Messenger! If some of them should look down, they will discover us.' The Holy Prophet[sa] said, 'O Abū Bakr! Be quiet. (For we are) two and Allāh is the Third One of them.' "

(Ṣaḥīḥ Bukhārī, Kitāb Faḍā'il Aṣḥābinnabī[ra]*, Bāb hijratun Nabī*[sa] *wa asḥabihī*[ra] *ilal Madīna)*

The incident is stated in the Holy Qur'ān:

اِلَّا تَنْصُرُوْهُ فَقَدْ نَصَرَهُ اللّٰهُ اِذْ اَخْرَجَهُ الَّذِيْنَ كَفَرُوْا ثَانِيَ اثْنَيْنِ

إِذْ هُمَا فِى الْغَارِ إِذْ يَقُوْلُ لِصَاحِبِهٖ لَا تَحْزَنْ إِنَّ اللّٰهَ مَعَنَا ۚ فَأَنْزَلَ اللّٰهُ سَكِيْنَتَهٗ عَلَيْهِ وَأَيَّدَهٗ بِجُنُوْدٍ لَّمْ تَرَوْهَا وَجَعَلَ كَلِمَةَ الَّذِيْنَ كَفَرُوا السُّفْلٰى ط

illā tanṣurūhu faqad naṣarahullāhu idh akhraja hulladhīna kafarū thāniyathnaini idh humā fil ghāri idh yaqūlu li ṣāḥibihī lā taḥzan innallāha ma'anā fa anzalallāhu sakīnatahū 'alaihi wa ayyadahū bi junūdillam tarauhā wa ja'ala kalimatalladhīna kafarussuflā

If you help him not, then *know that* Allāh helped him even when the disbelievers drove him forth while he was one of the two when they were both in the cave, when he said to his companion, 'Grieve not, for Allāh is with us.' Then Allāh sent down His peace on him, and strengthened him with hosts which you did not see, and humbled the word of those who disbelieved. (9:40)

After three nights in the cave of Thaur, they set off for Medina. The Holy Prophet[sa] looked back at Mecca, bidding it a heartfelt farewell, then said:

إِنِّيْ لَأُخْرَجُ مِنْكِ ، وَإِنِّيْ لَأَعْلَمُ أَنَّكِ أَحَبُّ بِلَادِ اللّٰهِ إِلَى اللّٰهِ ، وَأَكْرَمُهَا عَلَى اللّٰهِ تَعَالٰى ، وَلَوْ لَا أَنَّ أَهْلَكِ أَخْرَجُوْنِيْ مِنْكِ مَا خَرَجْتُ مِنْكِ ، اَللّٰهُمَّ إِنَّكَ تَعْلَمُ أَنَّهُمْ أَخْرَجُوْنِيْ مِنْ أَحَبِّ الْبِلَادِ إِلَيَّ ، فَأَسْكِنِّيْ أَحَبَّ الْبِلَادِ إِلَيْكَ

innī la ukhraju minki, wa innī la a'lamu annaki a-ḥabbu bilādillāhi ilallāhi, wa akramuhā 'alallāhi ta'ālā, wa lau lā anna ahlaki akhrajūnī minki mā karajtu minki, allāhumma innaka ta'lamu annahum akhrajūnī min a-ḥabbil bilādi ilayya, fa askinnī a-ḥabbil bilādi ilaika

"I am leaving you, but I know that you are the most beloved of the land of Allāh to Allāh, and the dearest to Allāh. Were it not that your people expelled me from you, I would not have left. O Allāh, You know that they drove me out from the land that is most beloved to you."

On 12th *Rabī'ul Awwal*, the Holy Prophet[sa] reached Qubā', where he stayed for four days, and established the first mosque to be built in Islām.

(As-Sīratun Nabawiyyah libne Hishām,, Vol. 2, p. 89; Ibn Sa'd's Al-Ṭabaqāt Al-Kabīr, Vol. 1, p. 277; Al-Kāmil fit-Tārīkh Vol. 2, p. 71)

Stop at the Camp of Umm Ma'bad

During migration while travelling from Mecca to Medina when the Holy Prophet[sa], Ḥaḍrat Abū Bakr[ra] and the guide reached the Caravan Camp of Umm Ma'bad, they asked her for some dates. However, at that time, she had none to offer them. Umm Ma'bad was a lady who used to offer water and food to travelers without any compensation. Then the Holy Prophet[sa] asked her for a little milk. She did not have even milk at that time to give to them. Her husband had taken all the healthy goats out to pasture. Only those goats which were too weak to walk and unable to give milk were left behind. The Holy Prophet[sa] asked Umm Ma'bd for permission to milk one of these goats. She said him to pick any one of the goats he liked. The Holy Prophet[sa] picked one of the goats, said, 'In the name of Allah', and started to milk the goat. Milk started to flow. The Holy Prophet[sa] gave the first bowl full of milk to Umm Ma'bd. He gave the second bowl to Ḥaḍrat Abū Bakr[ra] and the third bowl to the guide. The Holy Prophet[sa] was the last to drink. Then the Holy Prophet[sa] milked the second goat and gave many bowls full of milk to Umm Ma'bad. When the husband of Umm Ma'bad returned home he was amazed to see so many bowls full of milk while he had left home only those goats which were too weak to walk and also unable to give milk. He asked his wife, "Where did the milk come from?" She told him that a blessed man came with two of his friends. The face of the blessed man was luminous like a full moon. When he was quiet, he was very dignified. When he spoke his words were like pearls. His friends obeyed him and listened to him most obediently. Her husband said, "He is the man the *Quraish* are looking for. Had I been here when he visited I would have accepted Islām. Let us follow him and accept Islam." Thus, they followed the Holy Prophet[sa] to Medina and accepted Islām.

(Ibn Sa'd's Al-Ṭabaqāt Al-Kabīr, Translation by Mo'īnul Ḥaq, Kitāb Bhavan, New Delhi, India, Vol. 1, pp. 267-269; Baihiqī in his Dalā'il al-Nubuwwah 9/491)

Arrival of the Holy Prophet[sa] in Medina

Ibn Shahāb relates that 'Urwah bin Zubair told him: "During this journey, Ḥaḍrat Zubair[ra] who was coming back from Syria with a trade caravan also joined the Holy Prophet[sa]. Ḥaḍrat Zubair[ra] presented white clothes as a gift to the Holy Prophet[sa] and Ḥaḍrat Abū Bakr[ra], which they wore. Back in Medina, people had come to know that the Holy Prophet[sa] had left Mecca and was on his way to Medina where he was about to reach shortly. Therefore, every morning they came to Medina's high plane, an open space dotted with black stones called *'Ḥarrah'* and waited there for the Holy Prophet[sa]. They used to leave by noon. One day, they stayed at the open space for a long time before returning to their homes. They had just reached their homes when a Jew went to the top of a hillock for his own errand. He saw the Holy Prophet[sa] and his Companions[ra] who were wearing bright white clothes coming towards the town. Slowly, their faces became clear. Seeing them, the Jew shouted involuntarily, 'O Arabs! Here is he for whom you have been waiting for days.' As soon as the Muslims heard him, they ran with their armaments towards the Holy Prophet[sa] and received him with great enthusiasm in the center of the '*Ḥarrah*.' The Holy Prophet[sa] along with all the Muslims turned to the right and stayed at the house of Ḥaḍrat 'Umru bin 'Auf[ra]. It was the second of *Rabī'ul Awwal*. Ḥaḍrat Abū Bakr[ra] talked with the people, while the Holy Prophet[sa] sat silently, constantly thinking. Those *Anṣār* who had not seen the Holy Prophet[sa] thought Ḥaḍrat Abū Bakr[ra] was the Holy Prophet[sa]. When sunshine warmed the side where the Holy Prophet[sa] was sitting, Ḥaḍrat Abū Bakr[ra] provided shade over the Holy Prophet[sa] with a sheet of cloth. Then the people realized that the person protected from the heat with a sheet was the Holy Prophet[sa]. The Holy Prophet[sa] stayed at *Banū 'Amr bin 'Auf* for more than ten days and there, in Qubā', he laid the foundation of the first mosque to be built in Islām which is mentioned in the Holy Qur'ān:

لَمَسْجِدٌ اُسِّسَ عَلَى التَّقْوٰى

la masjidun ussisa 'alattaqwā

A mosque which was founded upon piety (9:108)

(As-Sīratun Nabawiyyah libne Hishām, Vol. 2, p. 89; Al-Ṭabarī, Vol. 2, p. 369; Ibn Sa'd's Ṭabaqāt Al-Kabīr Vol. 1, p.227)

Construction of Masjid Nabawī

The Holy Prophet[sa] led the Prayer in the first mosque for a few days. Then he mounted his camel and went to the town of Medina. His camel stopped and sat at the place where nowadays *'Masjid Nabawī'* (Mosque of the Holy Prophet[sa]) is located. The Muslims started offering their Prayers at this place temporarily. It belonged to two orphan brothers named Suhail and Sahl and was used as an open land for drying fresh dates. The orphaned brothers belonging to the *Banū Najjār* tribe were living under the supervision of Asad bin Zurārah.

Anyhow, when the camel of the Holy Prophet[sa] rested on the land, the Holy Prophet[sa] said: "This is our real destination." Then the Holy Prophet[sa] called both children to whom the land belonged and discussed the price of the land so that a mosque could be built there. Both children told the Holy Prophet[sa] that they presented the land to him as a gift. However, the Holy Prophet[sa] did not accept the gift. He bought the land by paying the price of the land and built a mosque there which is now known as *'Masjid Nabawī'.* During construction of the mosque, the Holy Prophet[sa], along with others, used to pick and carry bricks and recite the following couplet:

هٰذَا الْحِمَالُ لَا حِمَالَ خَيْبَر

هٰذَا اَبَرُّ رَبَّنَا وَ اَطْهَر

hādhal ḥimālu lā ḥimāla khaibar
hādhā abarru rabbanā wa aṭhar

This is not the load of trading material from Khaibar
Rather, this is the load of righteousness for our Lord's pleasure

And also:

اَللّٰهُمَّ اِنَّ الْاَجْرَ اَجْرُ الْاٰخِرَه

فَارْحَمِ الْاَ نْصَارَ وَالْمُهَاجِرَه

allāhumma innal ajra ajrul ākhirah
farḥamil anṣāra wal muhājirah

O Allāh! The real reward is the reward of the next life
Bestow Your Mercy on *Anṣār* and *Mutatisīn* "

(Ṣaḥīḥ Bukhārī, Kitābul Wā'il Al-Ḥatimī[ra], Bāb hijratun Nabī[sa] wa Al-Ḥātim ilal Medina)

The *'Masjid Nabawī'* was a modest structure made of mud and bricks. The roof was made from leaves and trunks of date palms. The dimensions of the Holy Prophet's[sa] mosque were as follows: Height, 10 feet; Length, 105 feet; Width, 90 feet.

Early Days of the Holy Prophet[sa] in Medina

The Muslims of Medina were extremely happy to receive the Holy Prophet[sa] and his Companions[ra]. This emigration of the Holy Prophet[sa] from Mecca to *Yathrib* is called the *Hijrah* and took place in September 10, 622 AD. The Islāmic Calendar (*Ḥijrī* Calendar) dates from this event. Also, after the arrival of the Holy Prophet[sa] the name *Yathrib* was changed to *Medinatun-Nabī* (The city of the Prophet[sa]) and later it was shortened to Medina. In Medina the Holy Prophet[sa] stayed at the home of Ḥaḍrat Abū Ayyūb Anṣārī[ra]. Ḥaḍrat Abū Ayyūb Anṣārī's[ra] house was double-storied. He offered to let the Holy Prophet[sa] have the upper storey. But the Holy Prophet[sa] preferred to have the lower storey for the convenience of his visitors. After his arrival in Medina the Holy Prophet[sa], first of all, bought a piece of land in Medina and laid the foundation of a mosque, called, *'Masjid Nabawī'* (The Holy Prophet's[sa] Mosque).

Establishment of Fraternity Among Anṣār and Muhājirīn

The faithful followers of the Holy Prophet[sa] who had left their homes and other worldly possessions in Mecca and had come to Medina for the sake of Islām, were known as *Muhājirīn* or Emigrants. The new converts at Medina, who helped the Prophet[sa] at a most difficult time, were called by him *Anṣār* or Helpers. The *Anṣār* belonged to the tribes of *'Aus* and *Khazraj*. Besides *Anṣār* and *Muhājirīn*, there were Jews from the tribes of *Banū Qainuqā'*, *Banū Naḍīr* and *Banū Quraiẓah* in Medina. Upon the arrival of the *Muhājirīn* in Medina, the Holy Prophet[sa] gathered the *Anṣār* and told them to become brothers of the *Muhājirīn*. The *Anṣār* decided to share their property and other belongings with their *Muhājirīn* brothers. They exhibited the real spirit of brotherhood.

God Almighty says in the Holy Qur'ān:

إِنَّ الَّذِيْنَ اٰمَنُوْا وَهَاجَرُوْا وَجٰهَدُوْا بِاَمْوَالِهِمْ وَ اَنْفُسِهِمْ فِيْ سَبِيْلِ اللّٰهِ
وَالَّذِيْنَ اٰوَوْا وَّ نَصَرُوْٓا اُولٰٓئِكَ بَعْضُهُمْ اَوْلِيَآءُ بَعْضٍ ۭ وَالَّذِيْنَ اٰمَنُوْا
وَلَمْ يُهَاجِرُوْا مَا لَكُمْ مِّنْ وَّ لَايَتِهِمْ مِّنْ شَيْءٍ حَتّٰى يُهَاجِرُوْا ۚ وَ اِنِ
اسْتَنْصَرُوْكُمْ فِى الدِّيْنِ فَعَلَيْكُمُ النَّصْرُ اِلَّا عَلٰى قَوْمٍۢ بَيْنَكُمْ
وَبَيْنَهُمْ مِيْثَاقٌ ۭ وَاللّٰهُ بِمَا تَعْمَلُوْنَ بَصِيْرٌ ٥

innalladhīna āmanū wa hajarū wa jāhadū bi amwālihim wa anfusihim fī sabīlillāhi walladhīna āwawwa naṣarū ulā'ika ba'ḍuhum auliyā'u ba'ḍ walladhīna āmanū wa lam yuhājirū mā

lakummiñwwa la yatihimmin shai'in ḥattā yuhājirū wa inistanṣarūkum fiddīni fa 'alaikumunnaṣru illā 'alā qaumim bainakum wa bainahum mīthāq wallāhu bimā ta'malūna baṣīr

Surely, those who have believed and left their homes and striven with their property and their persons for the cause of Allāh, and those who have given *them* shelter and help - are indeed mutual friends. But as for those who have believed but have not left their homes, you are not at all responsible for their protection untill they leave their homes. But if they seek your help in *the matter of* religion, then it is your duty to help them, except against a people between whom and yourselves there is a treaty. And Allāh sees what you do. (8:73)

Ḥaḍrat Anas bin Mālik[ra] relates, "At the time the Holy Prophet[sa] migrated from Mecca to Medina, the *Muhājrīn* came to the Holy Prophet[sa] and said, 'O Messenger[sa] of Allāh! We have never seen people more open-hearted and sympathetic than the people with whom we have settled with. If someone was wealthy he reserved a large portion of his wealth to spend upon us. If someone did not have money he found other extraordinary means of being sympathetic to us. They work hard to earn money and then spend equally upon us and themselves. We are worried that the *Anṣār* may not get all the reward and deprive us of the reward.' The Holy Prophet[sa] responded, 'As long as you will keep on praying for them to God Almighty and keep on praising them till then what you are worried about will not happen and you will get reward similar to them.' "

(Jāmi' Tirmidhī, Kitāb Ṣifatul Qiyāmah war Raqā'iq wal wara' an Rasūlullāh[sa])

The Holy Prophet[sa] became the leader of the city and Medina became the capital of the Islāmic state. After becoming the leader of Medina, the Holy Prophet[sa] took steps to secure internal peace and external security. To this effect, a treaty was signed with the Jews. The Muslims felt safe in Medina and became well organized under the leadership of the Holy Prophet[sa].

The Covenant of Medina

The covenant of Medina concluded between the *Muhājirīn* and *Anṣār* on one side and the Jews on the other, was dictated by the Holy Prophet Muḥammad[sa]. The following is the text of the document:

"In the Name of Allāh, the Compassionate, the Merciful. This is a covenant given by Muḥammad to the believers and the Muslims of *Quraish*, *Yathrib*, and those who followed them, joined them, and fought with them. They constitute one *Ummah* to the exclusion of all other men. As was their custom, the *Muhajirīn* from the *Quraish* are bound together and shall ransom their prisoners in kindness and justice as believers do. Following their own custom, *Banū 'Auf* are bound together as they have been before. Every clan of them shall ransom its prisoners with the kindness and justice common among believers. [The text here repeats the same injunction concerning every clan of the *Anṣār* and every house including *Banū al-Ḥārith*, *Banū Sāi'dah*, *Banū Jusham*, *Banū al-Najjār*, *Banū 'Amr bin 'Auf* and *Banū al-Nabit*.] The believers shall leave none of their members in destitution without giving him in kindness what he needs by way of ransom or bloodwit. No believer shall take as an ally a freedman of another Muslim without the permission of his previous master. All pious believers shall rise as one man against whosoever rebels or seeks to commit injustice, aggression, sin, or spread mutual enmity between the believers, even though he may be one of their sons. No believer shall slay a believer in retaliation for an disbeliever; neither shall he assist an disbeliever against a believer. Just as God's bond is one and indivisible, all believers shall stand behind the commitment of the least of them. All believers are bonded one to another to the exclusion of other men. Any Jew who follows us is entitled to our assistance and the same rights as any one of us, without injustice or partisanship. This Pax Islāmica is one and indivisible. No believer shall enter into a separate peace without all other believers whenever there is fighting in the cause of God, but will do so only on the basis of equality and justice to all others. In every military expedition we undertake our members shall be accompanied by others committed to the same objective. All believers shall avenge the blood of one another whenever any one of them falls fighting in the cause of God.

The pious believers follow the best and most upright guidance. No disbeliever shall be allowed to place under his protection against the interest of a believer, any wealth or person belonging to the *Quraish*. Whoever is convicted of killing a believer deliberately but without righteous cause, shall be held liable to the relatives of the killed. Until the latter are satisfied, the killer shall be subject to retaliation by each and every believer. The killer shall have no rights whatsoever until this right of the believers is satisfied. Whoever has entered into this covenant and believes in God and in the Last Day shall never protect or give shelter to a convict or a criminal; whoever does so shall be cursed by God and upon him shall the Divine wrath fall on the Day of Judgment. Neither repentance nor ransom shall be accepted from him. No object of contention among you may not be referred to God and to Muḥammad for judgment. As the Jews fight on the side of the believers, they shall spend of their wealth on equal par with the believers. For the Jews of *Banū Aus* are an *Ummah* alongside the believers. The Jews have their religion and the Muslims their religion. Both enjoy the security of their own populace and clients except the unjust and the criminal among them. The unjust or the criminal destroys only himself and his family. The Jews of *Banū al-Najjār*, *Banū al-Ḥarith*, *Banū Sāi'dah*, *Banū Jusharn*, *Banū al-Aus*, *Banū Tha'labah*, *Jafnah*, and *Banū al-Shutaibah* - all the same rights and privileges apply as to the Jews of *Banū Aus*. The clients of the tribe of *Tha'labah* enjoy the same rights and duties as the members of the tribe themselves. Likewise, the clients of the Jews, as the Jews themselves. None of the foregoing shall engage in war except with the permission of Muḥammad though none may be prevented from taking revenge for a wound inflicted upon him. Whoever murders anyone will have murdered himself and the members of his family, unless it be the case of a man suffering a wrong, for God will accept his action. The Jews shall bear their public expenses and so will the Muslims. Each shall assist the other against any violator of this covenant. Their relationship shall be one of mutual advice and consultation, and mutual assistance and charity rather than harm and aggression. However, no man is accountable for a crime committed by his ally. Assistance is due to the party suffering an injustice, not to one perpetrating it. Since the Jews fight on the side of the believers they shall spend their wealth on par with them. The town of *Yathrib* shall constitute a sanctuary for the parties of this covenant. Their neighbors shall be treated as themselves as long as they perpetrate no crime and commit no harm. No woman may be taken under protection without the consent of her family. Whatever difference or dispute between the parties to this covenant remains unsolved shall be referred to God and to Muḥammad, the Prophet of God. God is the guarantor of the piety and goodness that is embodied in this covenant. Neither the *Quraish* nor their allies shall be given any protection. The people of this covenant shall come to the assistance of one another against whoever attacks *Yathrib*. If they are called to cease hostilities and to enter into a truce, they shall be bound to do so in the interest of peace. If, on the other hand, they call upon the Muslims to cease hostilities and to enter into a truce, the Muslims shall be bound to do so and maintain the peace except when the war is against their religion. To every smaller group belongs the share which is their due as members of the larger group which is party to this covenant. The Jews of *al-Aus*, as well as their clients, are entitled to the same rights as this covenant has granted to its parties together with the goodness and charity of the latter. Charity and goodness are clearly distinguishable from crime and injury and there is no responsibility except for one's own deeds.

God is the guarantor of the truth and goodwill of this covenant. This covenant shall constitute no protection for the unjust or the criminal. Whoever goes out to fight as well as whoever stays at home shall be safe and secure in this city unless he has perpetrated an injustice or committed a crime. God grants His protection to whosoever acts in piety, charity and goodness."

The above political document, which the Holy Prophet[sa] wrote down fourteen centuries ago, establishes the freedom of faith and opinion, the inviolability of the city, human life, and property, and the forbiddance of crime. It certainly constitutes a breakthrough in the political and civil life of the world of that time. Though the Jews of *Banū Quraiẓah*, *Banū al-Naḍīr*, and *Banū Qainuqā'* did not sign this covenant at its conclusion, they did enter later on into similar pacts with the Holy Prophet[sa]. Thus Medina and all the territories surrounding it became inviolate to their peoples who were now bound to rise to their defense and protection together.

The Hypocrites of Medina

With the arrival of the Holy Prophet[sa] in Medina (622 AD), Islām began to spread rapidly among the two Arab tribes of the town. But as offen happens in a mass conversion, not all those who declare their allegiance were inspired by sincerity and high ideals. Some time before the Emigration, the *Aus* and *Khazraj* tribes, wearied by their prolonged mutual hostility, which had often erupted into fighting and had exacted a heavy toll of life, had decided to put an end to this state of affairs and to set up a form of administration in Medina which should have the support of both tribes and should also be acceptable to the three Jewish tribes. For this purpose it had been agreed that 'Abdullāh bin Ubayy bin Salūl, chief of the *Khazraj*, should be elected king of Medina. This plan had not yet been implemented when the Holy Prophet[sa] was invited to Medina. When he arrived it was generally felt that he was the most appropriate person to take on the responsibility of administering the affairs of Medina. Under his direction a covenant was drawn up which was accepted by both the Arabs and Jews. A common citizenship of Medina was established and conditions were prescribed to regulate the affairs of the town as well as to regulate its internal order and external security.

The principal conditions were that the internal affairs of each section would be regulated according to its own laws and customs, but that if the security of Medina were threatened from outside all sections would cooperate with each other in its defense. No section would enter into any separate treaty relations with any outside tribe; nor would any section be compelled to join in any fighting which should take place outside Medina. The final resolution of disputes would be determined by the Holy Prophet[sa], and his decision would be accepted and carried out. This became, as it were, the Charter of Medina. Thus was the Republic of Medina established.

'Abdullāh bin Ubayy was deeply chagrined at the loss of a crown, which, before the arrival of the Holy Prophet[sa], he had thought was assured for him. He became the leader of the disaffected party in Medina. This party was a source of constant worry and insecurity for the Holy Prophet[sa] and the Muslims. It is referred to in the Holy Qur'ān, at various places, as "the hypocrites."

It is stated in the Holy Qur'ān:

اِذَا جَآءَكَ الْمُنٰفِقُوْنَ قَالُوْا نَشْهَدُ اِنَّكَ لَرَسُوْلُ اللّٰهِ ۘ وَ اللّٰهُ يَعْلَمُ اِنَّكَ
لَرَسُوْلُهٗ ؕ وَ اللّٰهُ يَشْهَدُ اِنَّ الْمُنٰفِقِيْنَ لَكٰذِبُوْنَ ۚ

idhā jā'akal munāfiqūna qālū nash-hadu innaka larasūlullāh wallāhu ya'lamu innaka larasūluh wallāhu yash-hadu innal munāfiqīna la kādhibūn

When the hypocrites come to you, they say, 'We bear witness that you are indeed the Messenger of Allāh.' And Allāh knows that you are indeed His Messenger, but Allāh bears witness that the hypocrites are surely liars. (63:2)

(The Excellent Exemplar - Muḥammad, Chaudharī Muḥammad Ẓafrullā Khān)

Pact Among the Various Tribes of Medina

The Holy Prophet[sa] not only established brotherhood among the *Anṣār* and the *Muhājirīn*, but also instituted a covenant among all the inhabitants of Medina. In this way, the Arabs, the Jews and the Muslims were united into a common citizenship in Medina. The covenant was binding upon all three groups. The final agreement amongst the parties was as follows:

"Between the Prophet of God and the faithful on the one hand, and all those on the other, who voluntarily agree to enter. If any of the Meccan Muslims is killed, the Meccan Muslims will themselves be responsible. The responsibility for securing the release of their prisoners will also be theirs. The Muslim tribes of Medina similarly will be responsible for their own lives and their prisoners. Whoever rebels or promotes enmity and disorder will be considered a common enemy. It will be the duty of all the others to fight against him, even though he happens to be a son or a close relation. If a disbeliever is killed in battle by a believer, his Muslim relations will seek no revenge. Nor will they assist disbelievers against believers. The Jews who join this covenant will be helped by the Muslims. The Jews will not be put to any hardship. Their enemies will not be helped against them. No disbeliever will give quarter to anybody from Mecca. He will not act as a trustee for any Meccan property. In a war between Muslims and disbelievers he will take no part. If a believer is mistreated without cause, Muslims will have the right to fight against those who mistreat. If a common enemy attacks Medina, the Jews will side with the Muslims and share the expenses of the battle. The Jewish tribes in covenant with the other tribes of Medina will have rights similar to those of Muslims. The Jews will keep to their own faith, and the Muslims to their own. The rights enjoyed by the Jews will also be enjoyed by their followers. The citizens of Medina will not have the right to declare war without the sanction of the Prophet[sa]. But this will not prejudice the right of any individual to avenge an individual wrong. The Jews will bear the expenses of their own organization, and the Muslims their own. But in case of war, they will act with unity. The city of Medina will be regarded as sacred and inviolate by those who sign the covenant. Strangers who come under the protection of its citizens will be treated as citizens. But the people of Medina will not be allowed to admit a woman to its citizenship without the permission of her relation. All disputes will be referred for resolution to God and the Prophet[sa]. Parties to this covenant will not have the right to enter into any agreement with the Meccans or their allies. This is because parties to this covenant agree in resisting their common enemies. The parties will remain united in peace as in war. No party will enter into a separate peace. But no party will be obliged to take part in war. A party, however, which commits any excess will be liable to a penalty. Certainly God is the protector of the righteous and the faithful and Muḥammad is His Prophet."

(As-Sīratun Nabawiyyah libne Hishām, Vol. 2, pp. 147-150)

The First Written Constitution

It is the first written constitution of a state ever promulgated by a sovereign in history. It was endorsed from the first year of *Hijrah* (622 AD). The treaty stipulated a city-state in Medina, allowing independence to communities under the following terms:

1. In the name of Allāh (the One God), the Compassionate, the Merciful. This is a document from Muḥammad, the Prophet, governing the relation between the Believers from among the *Quraishites* (that is, Emigrants from Mecca) and *Yathribites* (i.e., the residents of Medina) and those who followed them and joined them and strived with them. They form one and the same community as against the rest of men.

2. No Believer shall oppose the client of another Believer. Whosoever is rebellious, or seeks to spread injustice, enmity or sedition among the Believers, the hand of every man shall be against him, even if he be a son of one of them. A Believer shall not kill a Believer in retaliation for an disbeliever, nor an disbeliever shall kill an disbeliever in retaliation for a Believer.

3. Whosoever among the Jews follows us shall have help and equality; they shall not be injured nor shall any enemy be aided against them... No separate peace will be made when the Believers are fighting in the way of Allāh... The Believers shall avenge the blood of one another shed in the way of Allāh... Whosoever kills a Believer wrongfully shall be liable to retaliation; all the Believers shall be against him as one man and they are bound to take action against him.

4. The Jews shall contribute (to the expenses of war) with the Believers so long as they are at war with a common enemy. The Jews of *Banū Najjār*, *Banū al-Ḥārith*, *Banū Sā'idah*, *Banū Jusham*, *Banū al-Aus*, *Banū Tha'labah*, *Jafnah*, and *Banū al-Shutaibah* shall enjoy the same rights and privileges as the Jews of *Banū Aus*.

5. The Jews shall adhere to their own religion and the Muslims to theirs. Loyalty is a protection against treachery. The close friends of Jews are as themselves. None of them shall go out on a military expedition except with the permission of Muḥammad[sa], but he shall not be prevented from taking revenge for a wound.

6. The Jews shall be responsible for their expenses and the Believers for theirs. Each, if attacked, shall come to the assistance of the other.

7. The valley of *Yathrib* (Medina) shall be sacred and inviolable for all that join this Treaty. Strangers, under protection, shall be treated on the same ground as their protectors; but no stranger shall be taken under protection except with consent of his tribe... No woman shall be taken under protection without the consent of her family.

8. Whatever difference or dispute between the parties to this covenant remains unsolved shall be referred to Allāh (The One God) and to Muḥammad, the Messenger of Allāh. Allāh is the Guarantor of the piety and goodness that is embodied in this covenant. Neither the *Quraish* nor their allies shall be given any protection.

9. Thc contracting partics arc bound to hclp onc anothcr against any attack on *Yathrib*. If they are called to cease hostilities and to enter into peace, they shall be bound to do so in the interest of peace; and if they make a similar demand on Muslims it must be carried out except when the war is against their religion.

10. Allāh (the One God) approves the truth and goodwill of this covenant. This treaty shall not protect the unjust or the criminal. Whoever goes out to fight as well as whoever stays at home shall be safe and secure in this city unless he has perpetrated an injustice or committed a crime... Allāh is the protector of the good and God-fearing people.

Facing the Ka'bah in Prayer

In Mecca, the Holy Prophet[sa] used to pray towards Jerusalem, with the *Ka'bah* in front of him. When the Holy Prophet[sa] migrated to Medina he continued praying towards Jerusalem. Sixteen months after emigration of the Holy Prophet[sa] from Mecca to Medina, God Almighty commanded him to change the direction while he was in Prayer towards the *Ka'bah*, the House built by Ḥaḍrat Ibrāhīm[as] and Ḥaḍrat Ismā'īl[as]. It was revealed to the Holy Prophet[sa]:

قَدْ نَرٰى تَقَلُّبَ وَجْهِكَ فِى السَّمَآءِ فَلَنُوَلِّيَنَّكَ قِبْلَةً تَرْضٰهَا فَوَلِّ وَجْهَكَ
شَطْرَ الْمَسْجِدِ الْحَرَامِ ط وَحَيْثُ مَا كُنْتُمْ فَوَلُّوْا وُجُوْهَكُمْ شَطْرَهٗ ط
وَاِنَّ الَّذِيْنَ اُوْتُوا الْكِتٰبَ لَيَعْلَمُوْنَ اَنَّهُ الْحَقُّ مِنْ رَّبِّهِمْ ط

qad narā taqalluba wajhika fissamā'i fala nuwalliyannaka qiblatan tarḍāhā fawalli wajhaka shaṭral masjidil ḥarāmi wa ḥaithu mā kuntum fawallū wujūhakum shaṭrah wa innalladhīna ūtul kitāba laya'lamūna annahul ḥaqqu mirrabbihim

Verily, We see you turning your face often to heaven; surely, then, will We make you turn to the Qiblah which you like. So, turn your faces towards the Sacred Mosque; and anywhere you be, turn your face towards it. And they to whom the Book has been given know that this is the truth from their Lord. (2:145)

Either during *Ẓuhr* or *'Aṣr* Prayer, the Holy Prophet[sa] had led his Companions[ra] in Praying two *Rak'āt*, then he was commanded by Allāh to face towards the *Ka'bah*, so he turned around towards the *Ka'bah*. The mosque where he offered this Prayer became known as, *'Masjid Al-Qiblatain'* (the mosque of the two *Qiblahs*).

(Ibn Sa'd 's Al-Ṭabaqāt Al-Kabīr, Vol. 1, p. 242)

Divine Protection for the Holy Prophet[sa]

Ḥaḍrat 'Ā'ishah[ra] relates that after migration to Medina, there was a night when the Holy Prophet[sa] was unable to sleep. In his anxiety, the Holy Prophet[sa] said to Ḥaḍrat 'Ā'ishah[ra]: "I wish some servant of God were on guard duty today. Ḥaḍrat 'Ā'ishah[ra] said that at the same time they heard the tinkling noise of armament. The Holy Prophet[sa] asked, 'Who is this?' Someone outside replied: 'I am Sa'd bin Abī Waqqās.' The Holy Prophet[sa] asked: 'Why did you come?' Sa'd bin Abī Waqqās said: 'I felt, in my heart, a premonition of danger regarding the Messenger[sa] of Allāh. Therefore, I have come to guard you[sa].' The Holy Prophet[sa] prayed for Sa'd bin Abī Waqqās and slept peacefully.' "

(Jāmi' Tirmidhī, Abwābul Manāqib, Manāqib Sa'd bin Abī Waqqāṣ[ra])

Ḥaḍrat 'Ā'ishah[ra] relates that people used to be on guard-duty at night to safeguard the Holy Prophet[sa]. However, on the night the verse

وَاللّٰهُ يَعْصِمُكَ مِنَ النَّاسِ

wallāhu ya'ṣimuka minannāsi

And Allāh will protect thee from men (5:68)

was revealed, the Holy Prophet[sa] looked out of his tent and said to the people guarding him, "Now you can go home because the Lord of Honor and Glory Himself has taken responsibility for my protection."

(Jāmi' Tirmidhī, Abwābut Tafsīr Sūrah Al-Mā'idah)

God Almighty says in the Holy Qur'ān about Divine protection of the Holy Prophet[sa]:

فَاِنَّكَ بِاَعْيُنِنَا

fa innaka bi a'yuninā

For assuredly you are before Our eyes. (52:49)

لَهٗ مُعَقِّبٰتٌ مِّنْۢ بَيْنِ يَدَيْهِ وَ مِنْ خَلْفِهٖ يَحْفَظُوْنَهٗ مِنْ اَمْرِ اللّٰهِ

lahū mu'aqqibātummim baini yadaihi wa min khalfihī yaḥfaẓūnahū min amrillāh

For him (the Messenger) is a succession *of angels* before him and behind him; they guard him by the command of Allāh. (13:12)

At the occasion of the conquest of Khaibar, Jews made a plan to kill the Holy Prophet[sa] by poisoning him. They prepared a large amount of roasted meat and added a large amount of deadly poison to the meat. They sent the meat to the Holy Prophet[sa] through Zainab, the wife of Salām bin Mushkam, as a present. When the meat was presented to the Holy Prophet[sa] he took just one bite and felt that the food was poisonous. So he did not swallow it. One of his Companions, Ḥaḍrat Bishr[ra] had already swallowed a morsel from the meat and he died after a short period of time due to eating the poisonous food. The Holy Prophet[sa] called the woman and other Jews and asked them why did they add poison in the food? The woman said: "We thought if you were not a true Prophet we will get rid of you and if you were a true Prophet the poison will do no harm to you." The Holy Prophet[sa] with a strong majestic voice told them that despite all their efforts to kill him God Almighty would never give them the power to kill him.

(Al-Sīratul Ḥalabiyyah, Vol. 3, pp, 78, 80; Ibn Sa'd's Al-Ṭabaqāt Al-Kabīr, Vol. 2, p. 249, S. Mo'īnul Ḥaq, Kitāb Bhavan, New Delhi, India; Al-Sīratul Ḥamdiyyah, p. 329)

The hypocrites of Medina were sure in their minds that the Muslims would be defeated in the expedition of Tabūk and the Holy Prophet[sa] would be killed. Thus, they were expecting soon to become the rulers of Medina. However, when they found out that the Holy Prophet[sa] was returning to Medina after great successes in the battle, they were very much disheartened and were fearful that now they would be punished for their conspiracies against the Muslims about which the Holy Prophet[sa] has come to know. To get out of this terrible situation they were facing, they conspired to kill the Holy Prophet[sa] on the way back to Medina. In fact, the scheme was hatched even before the Holy Prophet had left for the expedition of Tabūk and a few hypocrites were travelling as part of the Muslim army to carry out this plan, when necessary. At some distance from Medina the returning army had to pass through a narrow mountain pass. The passage was so narrow that one person could pass through it at a time. When the Holy Prophet[sa] and his Companions[ra] reached close to the narrow passage it was night time and it was dark. Taking advantage of the darkness, the hypocrites who were travelling with the Holy Prophet[sa] as part of the Muslim force rushed and went ahead towards the mountain pass and hid themselves close to the narrow passage. They had planned to kill the Holy Prophet[sa] in the narrow passage. God Almighty revealed to the Holy Prophet[sa] about the heinous plan of the hypocrites. The Holy Prophet[sa] sent Ḥaḍrat Ḥudhaifa bin Yamān[ra] to survey the area. When Ḥaḍrat Ḥudhaifa bin Yamān[ra] reached the narrow passage area he found a few men with faces covered hiding in the area. When they saw Ḥaḍrat Ḥudhaifa bin Yamān[ra] they ran away. The Holy Prophet[sa] did not like to pursue them so he let them go. God Almighty had informed the Holy Prophet[sa] the names of the hypocrites hiding near the narrow passage and planning to kill him. The Holy Prophet[sa] told Ḥaḍrat Ḥudhaifa bin Yamān[ra] the names of these people. Therefore, Ḥaḍrat Ḥudhaifa bin Yamān[ra] was known as:

صَاحِبُ سِرِّ رَسُوْلِ اللّٰهِ ﷺ فِى الْمُنَافِقِيْنَ

ṣāḥibu sirri rasūlillāh[sa] *fīl munāfiqīna*

The secret-keeper for the Holy Prophet[sa] about the hypocrites.

(Usdul Ghābah, Dhikr Ḥaḍrat Ḥudhaifah bin Yamān, Vol. 1, p.442, printed by Dārul Ma'rifa, Beirut, Lebanon; Ibn Kathīr, Ghazwah Tabūk)

On five occasions, the life of the Holy Prophet[sa] was in serious danger and had he not been a true Prophet of God, he would certainly have been destroyed. One was the occasion when the disbelieving *Quraish* had surrounded his house and had sworn that they would kill him that night. The second occasion was when pursuers had arrived with a large body of men at the entrance to the cave in which he had taken shelter along with Ḥaḍrat Abū Bakr[ra]. The third occasion was when he had been left alone in the Battle of Uḥud and the *Quraish* had surrounded him and attacked him in a body but whose plan was foiled. The fourth occasion was when a Jewish woman gave him meat to eat which had been saturated with a fatal poison. The fifth occasion was when Chosroes Pervaiz, Emperor of Persia, had made up his mind to destroy him and had sent his emissaries to arrest him. His delivery on all these dangerous occasions and his ultimate triumph over all his enemies is conclusive proof that he was righteous and God was with him.

(Chashma Ma'rifat, Rūḥānī Khazā'in, Vol. 23, pp. 263-264, footnote)

7

Battles of Badr, and Uḥud

Battle of Badr

The leaders of the non-believers in Mecca were furious due to the migration of the Holy Prophet[sa] to Medina. They were extremely disheartened due to the slipping away of the Holy Prophet[sa] from their hands while they had made extraordinary preparations to kill him. News of the peaceful living of the Muslims in Medina made them angrier. All their efforts to destroy or stall the progress of the mission of the Holy Prophet[sa] had failed miserably. They were unable to stem the progress of the new faith. Furthermore, their trade route to Syria was within reach of the Muslims.

So the Meccans continued to irritate and harass the Muslims. They instigated the non-Muslims of Medina against the Muslims and interfered with their right of pilgrimage. They started looking for causes to attack the Muslims and destroy them. It happened so that under the leadership of Abū Sufyān a caravan of 1000 camels laden with various types of goods including armaments was travelling from Syria to Mecca and had to pass close to Medina. Abū Sufyān informed the Meccans about his concern that the Muslims might attack the caravan. The Meccans immediately sent an army of 1000 war-ready men to Medina to attack the Muslims. When the Holy Prophet[sa] learned about the march of the Meccan army towards Medina, he consulted his Companions[ra]. After Ḥaḍrat Abū Bakr[ra] and Ḥaḍrat Umar[ra] presented their views, Ḥaḍrat al-Miqdād bin ‘Amr[ra] stood up and said, "O Messenger[sa] of Allāh, go ahead with what Allāh has commanded you. We are with you. By Allāh, we shall not say to you as the Jews said to Ḥaḍrat Moses[as], 'Go, you and your God fight the enemy, we will remain here behind.' We will fight to the right of you, to the left of you, in front of you and behind you.' "

(Ṣaḥīḥ, Bukhārī, Kitāb al-Maghāzī, Ghazwah Badr)

The trade caravan which had gone to Syria that year headed by Abū Sufyān was extraordinarily loaded with merchandise. It was decided by the *Quraish* that whatever the profit accrued that year, it would be spent on arms, horses, and other war material to fight the Muslims.

The trade caravan had reached Badr (200 miles from Mecca and 80 miles from Medina) when news came to the Meccan warriors who were just few miles away that the caravan had not encountered any attack from the Muslims. However, since the Meccans were so eager to fight the Holy Prophet[sa] and his followers, they decided to proceed to fight the Muslims anyway. So, they camped at the stream of Badr.

When the Muslims learned that the trade caravan was coming from Syria (on the north side) and that the Meccan army was marching towards Medina (from the South), they thought that they would be hard pressed to face these two enemy groups at the same time. The Muslims had two possible alternatives. Either fight the Meccans with all their resources or use the other option and fight the trade caravan returning from Syria which was led by Abū Sufyān with only 40 not so well-armed men. This course was the safest and many Muslims preferred it. However, the other alternative was adopted by the Holy Prophet[sa] in which the Muslims boldly faced the well-armed and well-equipped *Quraish* army of 1,000 men coming from Mecca.

This situation is described in the following verses of the Holy Qur'ān:

كَمَآ اَخْرَجَكَ رَبُّكَ مِنْۢ بَيْتِكَ بِالْحَقِّ ص وَ اِنَّ فَرِيْقًا مِّنَ الْمُؤْمِنِيْنَ
لَكٰرِهُوْنَ ۝ لا يُجَادِلُوْنَكَ فِى الْحَقِّ بَعْدَ مَا تَبَيَّنَ كَاَنَّمَا يُسَاقُوْنَ اِلَى
الْمَوْتِ وَهُمْ يَنْظُرُوْنَ ۝ ط وَ اِذْ يَعِدُكُمُ اللّٰهُ اِحْدَى الطَّآئِفَتَيْنِ اَنَّهَا لَكُمْ
وَ تَوَدُّوْنَ اَنَّ غَيْرَ ذَاتِ الشَّوْكَةِ تَكُوْنُ لَكُمْ وَ يُرِيْدُ اللّٰهُ اَنْ يُّحِقَّ الْحَقَّ
بِكَلِمٰتِهٖ وَ يَقْطَعَ دَابِرَ الْكٰفِرِيْنَ ۝ لا لِيُحِقَّ الْحَقَّ وَ يُبْطِلَ الْبَاطِلَ وَلَوْ كَرِهَ
الْمُجْرِمُوْنَ ۝ ع

kamā akhrajaka rabbuka mim baitika bilḥaqqi wa inna farīqamminal mu'minīna lakārihūna yujādilūnaka fil ḥaqqi ba'da mā tabayyana ka annamā yusāqūna ilal mauti wa hum yanẓurūn wa idh ya'idukumullāhu iḥdaṭṭā'ifataini annahā lakum wa tawaddūna anna ghaira dhātishshaukati takūna lakum wa yurīdullāhu añyyuḥiqqal ḥaqqa bi kalimātihī wa yaqṭa'a ḍābiral kāfirīna li yuḥiqqal ḥaqqa wa yubṭilal bāṭila wa lau karihal mujrimūn

As *it was* your Lord *Who* rightfully brought you forth from your house, while a party of the believers were averse, *therefore He helped you against your enemy.* They dispute with you concerning the truth after it has become manifest, as though they are being driven to death while they actually see it. And *remember the time* when Allāh promised you one of the two parties (i.e., the well-equipped Meccan army and the caravan which, only lightly armed, was proceeding to Mecca from the north) that it should be yours, and you wished that the one without sting should be yours, but Allah desired to establish the truth by His words and to cut off the root of the disbelievers. That He might establish the truth and bring to naught that which is false, although the guilty might dislike it. (8:6-9)

The Holy Prophet[sa] decided to face the Meccan army outside Medina. Accordingly, an army of 313 people which included some youth of the community was hastily prepared. The army was ill-equipped as far as arms were concerned. The army left Medina under the command of the Holy Prophet[sa] and camped at Badr, a place 80 miles from Medina. The Muslim army had only a few horses and a small quantity of arms. Abū Sufyān changed the course of his caravan and left the Muslim controlled area safely. However, the Meccans were determined to finish the Muslims once and for all. Therefore, they stayed there and soon an encounter between the two armies took place. A very small and poorly equipped Muslim army bravely fought the Meccan army and decisively defeated them. The Meccans left 70 dead and another 70 were taken prisoners by the Muslims. Defeat for the Muslims in this battle would have been disastrous. The Holy Prophet[sa] prayed fervently for the success over the infidels in the battle.

Ḥaḍrat Ibn 'Abbās[ra] relates: "During the Battle of Badr, the Holy Prophet[sa] was residing in a tent and was continuously supplicating: 'O Allāh! I cry for mercy reminding You of Your Promise. O My Allāh! If the Muslims are killed today, no one would be left to adhere to true *Tauḥīd* (unity of God) and Your worship.' Hearing this, Ḥaḍrat Abū Bakr[ra] held the hand of the Holy Prophet's[sa] and said: 'O Prophet[sa] of Allāh! It is enough. God Almighty will certainly accept your supplications.' At that time, the Holy Prophet[sa], who was wearing war gear came out of the hut in which he had been praying and gave the glad tidings to the Muslims: "The hosts will certainly be routed and will show their backs." These were the words revealed to the Holy Prophet[sa] while he was in Mecca which obviously referred to success in this battle.

سَيُهْزَمُ الْجَمْعُ وَيُوَلُّوْنَ الدُّبُرَ 0 بَلِ السَّاعَةُ مَوْعِدُهُمْ وَ السَّاعَةُ
أَدْهٰى وَأَمَرُّ 0

sa yuhzamul jam'u wa yu wallūnaddubura balissā'atu mau'iduhum wassa'atu ad-hā wa amarru

The hosts shall soon be routed and will turn their backs *in flight.* Aye, the Hour is their appointed time; and the Hour will be most calamitous and most bitter. (54:46-47)'"

(Ṣaḥīḥ Bukhārī, Kitābal Jihād, Bāb mā qul fī dara'nnabī[sa]*; aḥīḥ Bukhārī, Kitābal Maghāzī and Kitābuttafsīr)*

Ḥadrat Ibn 'Abbās[ra] relates that Ḥadrat 'Umar bin Khaṭṭāb[ra] said, "On the day of Badr, the Holy Prophet[sa] looked at the pagans who were one thousand -- whereas his Companions[ra] were three hundred and thirteen. Then the Holy Prophet[sa] supplicated the following:

اَللّٰهُمَّ اَنْجِزْ لِيْ مَا وَعَدْتَّنِيْ ' اَللّٰهُمَّ اٰتِنِيْ مَا وَعَدْتَّنِيْ ' اَللّٰهُمَّ اِنَّكَ
اِنْ تُهْلِكْ هٰذِهِ الْعِصَابَةَ مِنْ اَهْلِ الْاِسْلَامِ لَا تُعْبَدْ فِى الْاَرْضِ -

allāhumma anjizlī mā wa'attanī, allāhumma ātinī mā wa'attanī, allāhumma innaka in tuhlik hādhi hil 'iṣābata min ahlil islāmi lā tu'bad filarḍi

O Allāh! Give me what You promised me. O Allāh! grant me what You promised me. O Allāh! If this Muslim community is destroyed, none will worship You on the earth."

(Jāmi' Tirmidhī, Kitābut Tafsīr, Tafsīr Sūrah al-Anfāl)

At the beginning of the battle, the Holy Prophet[sa] threw a handful of gravel towards the Meccans, saying, "Abased be those faces." It produced amazing results and the enemy was badly defeated. God Almighty says in the Holy Qur'ān about it:

وَمَا رَمَيْتَ اِذْ رَمَيْتَ وَلٰكِنَّ اللّٰهَ رَمٰى ۚ

wamā ramitā idh ramaita wa lākinnallāha ramā

"And you threw not when you did throw, but it was Allāh who threw ..." (8:18)

The following is stated in the Holy Qur'ān about the success in the Battle of Badr:

اِذْ تَسْتَغِيْثُوْنَ رَبَّكُمْ فَاسْتَجَابَ لَكُمْ اَنِّيْ مُمِدُّكُمْ بِاَلْفٍ مِّنَ الْمَلٰٓئِكَةِ
مُرْدِفِيْنَ ۝ وَمَا جَعَلَهُ اللّٰهُ اِلَّا بُشْرٰى وَلِتَطْمَئِنَّ بِهٖ قُلُوْبُكُمْ ۚ وَمَا
النَّصْرُ اِلَّا مِنْ عِنْدِ اللّٰهِ ۗ اِنَّ اللّٰهَ عَزِيْزٌ حَكِيْمٌ ۝

idh tastaghīthūna rabbakum fastajāba lakum annī mumiddukum bi alfimminal malā'ikati murdifīn wamā ja'alahullāhu illā bushrā wa litaṭma'inna bihī qulūbukum wa mannaṣru illā min 'indillāhi innallāha 'azīzun ḥakīm

When you implored the assistance of your Lord, and He answered you, *saying*, 'I will assist you with a thousand of the angels, following one another. And Allāh made it only as glad tidings, and that your hearts might thereby be set at rest. But help comes from Allāh alone; surely, Allāh is Mighty, Wise. (8:10-11)

وَلَقَدْ نَصَرَكُمُ اللّٰهُ بِبَدْرٍ وَّ اَنْتُمْ اَذِلَّةٌ ۚ فَاتَّقُوا اللّٰهَ لَعَلَّكُمْ تَشْكُرُوْنَ ۝
اِذْ تَقُوْلُ لِلْمُؤْمِنِيْنَ اَلَنْ يَّكْفِيَكُمْ اَنْ يُّمِدَّكُمْ رَبُّكُمْ بِثَلٰثَةِ اٰلَافٍ مِّنَ
الْمَلٰٓئِكَةِ مُنْزَلِيْنَ ۝ بَلٰٓى ۙ اِنْ تَصْبِرُوْا وَ تَتَّقُوْا وَ يَاْتُوْكُمْ مِّنْ فَوْرِهِمْ هٰذَا
يُمْدِدْكُمْ رَبُّكُمْ بِخَمْسَةِ اٰلَافٍ مِّنَ الْمَلٰٓئِكَةِ مُسَوِّمِيْنَ ۝

walaqad naṣarakumullāhu bi badriñwwa antum adhillatun fattaqullāha la'allakum tashkurūn. Idh taqūlu lilmu'minīna alañyyakfiyakum añyyumiddakum rabbukum bi thalāthatin ālāfimminal malā'ikati munzalīn. balā in taṣbirū wa tattaqū wa ya'tū kummin faurihim hādhā yumdidkum rabbukum bi khamsati ālāfimminal malā'ikati musawwimīn.

And Allāh had *already* helped you at Badr when you were weak. So take Allāh for your Protector that you may be grateful. When you did say to the believers, 'Will it not suffice you that your Lord should help you with three thousand angels sent down *from on high*?' Yes, if you be steadfast and righteous and they come upon you immediately in hot haste, your Lord will help you with five thousand angels, attacking vehemently. (3:124-126)

Permission to take up arms in self-defense had been accorded in Divine revelations:

أُذِنَ لِلَّذِيْنَ يُقٰتَلُوْنَ بِاَنَّهُمْ ظُلِمُوْا ۭ وَاِنَّ اللّٰهَ عَلٰى نَصْرِهِمْ لَقَدِيْرُ ۨ ۙ

udhina lilladhīna yuqātalūna bi annahum ẓulimū wa innallāha 'alā naṣrihim laqadīr

Permission *to fight* is given to those against whom war is made, because they have been wronged - and Allāh indeed has power to help them. (22:40)

According to the consensus of scholarly opinion this is the first verse which gave the Muslims permission to take up arms in self-defense. The verse was revealed very early in Medina.

The next verse also lends support to this inference. It states that the permission to fight was given after the Muslims had been driven out of their hearths and homes. If, as some Commentators of the Qur'ān hold, the verse was revealed at Mecca, it must have been revealed immediately before *Hijra* when most of the Muslims had already emigrated to Medina and the Holy Prophet[sa] with only a very few Muslims had remained behind in Mecca and their cup of hardships and privations had become full to the brim. But the former view seems to be more akin to fact and reality.

The verse lays down principles according to which the Muslims can wage a defensive war, and clearly sets forth the reasons which led a handful of Muslims, without arms and other material means, to fight in self-defense after they had suffered at Mecca ceaseless persecution for years and had been pursued with relentless hatred to Medina and were harassed and harried there too. The first and foremost reason given is that "they had been wronged." The Muslims had suffered untold persecution and war was actually forced upon them. The verse incidentally shows that the Muslims were also very weak in numbers, means and material when the permission to fight in self-defense was granted to them as the comforting and encouraging words, "And Allāh indeed has power to help them," indicate. These words also implied a prophecy that though the Muslims were weak and their enemy was proud and powerful, yet as they were fighting in the cause of truth God would help them and they would be victorious.

اِلَّذِيْنَ اُخْرِجُوْا مِنْ دِيَارِهِمْ بِغَيْرِ حَقٍّ اِلَّآ اَنْ يَّقُوْلُوْا رَبُّنَا اللّٰهُ ۗ وَلَوْ لَا
دَفْعُ اللّٰهِ النَّاسَ بَعْضَهُمْ بِبَعْضٍ لَّهُدِّمَتْ صَوَامِعُ وَبِيَعٌ وَّ صَلَوٰتٌ وَّ
مَسٰجِدُ يُذْكَرُ فِيْهَا اسْمُ اللّٰهِ كَثِيْرًا ۗ وَلَيَنْصُرَنَّ اللّٰهُ مَنْ يَّنْصُرُهٗ ۗ اِنَّ
اللّٰهَ لَقَوِيٌّ عَزِيْزٌ ○

nilladhīna ukhrijū min diyārihim bighairi ḥaqqin illā añyyaqūlū rabbunallāh walau lā daf'ullā hinnāsa ba'ḍahum bi ba'ḍilla huddimat ṣawāmi'un wa biya'uñwwa ṣalawātuñwwa masājidu yudhkarufīhasmullāhi kathīrā wa layanṣurannallāhu mañyyanṣuruh

innallāha laqaviyyun 'azīz

Those who have been driven out from their homes unjustly, only because they said, 'Our Lord is Allāh' - "And if Allāh did not repel some men by means of others, there would surely have been pulled down cloisters and churches and synagogues and mosques, wherein the name of Allāh is oft commemorated. And Allāh will surely help one who helps Him. Allāh is indeed Powerful, Mighty. (22:41)

The verse gives the second reason which led the poor and weak Muslims to take up arms. It was that they were driven out from their hearths and homes without a just and legitimate cause -- their only crime being that they believed in one God. For years the Muslims were persecuted at Mecca, then they were driven out from it and were not left in peace even in their exile at Medina. They continued to be harassed there too. Islām was threatened with complete extirpation by a combined attack from the Arabian tribes around Medina, among whom the influence of the *Quraish*, on account of their being the custodians of the *Ka'bah*, was very great. Medina itself was honey-combed with sedition and treachery. The Jews, compact and united, were opposed to the Holy Prophet[sa]. 'Ahdullāh bin Ubayy, whose designs to become the crowned king of Medina had been upset by the Holy Prophet's[sa] arrival in that city, and the Hypocrites were an additional source of great danger to Islām. The *Quraish* held out a threat to 'Abdullāh bin Ubayy that if the people of Medina gave shelter to the Holy Prophet[sa] and did not make common cause with them against the Muslims they would attack Medina with all their powerful hosts and allies and would kill their men and carry their women to Mecca in captivity.

Thus Islām had to defend itself against much more powerful enemies at Medina than at Mecca. The position of the Muslims in the first few years of their life at Medina was decidedly much weaker than at Mecca and the Holy Prophet's[sa] difficulties instead of lessening had greatly increased. It was under these highly unfavorable circumstances that the Muslims had to take up arms to save themselves, their faith and their Holy Prophet[sa] from extermination. If ever a people had a legitimate cause to fight, it were the Holy Prophet Muhammad[sa] and his Companions[ra], and yet the unconscionable critics of Islām have accused him of waging aggressive wars to impose his faith on an unwilling people.

After having given reasons why the Muslims were obliged to take up arms, the verse proceeds to mention the object and purpose of the wars of Islām. The object was never to deprive anybody of his home and possessions or to deprive whole peoples of national freedom or compel them to submit to foreign yoke under the garb of making them civilized as Western nations do, on to explore new markets and get new colonies. It was to fight in self-defense and to save Islām from extermination and to establish freedom of conscience and liberty of thought. It was also to defend places of worship belonging to different religions against desecration or destruction. Having laid down the principle that all religions have their origin in Divine revelation and that the Founders of all religions were Divine Messengers and should therefore be equally respected (35: 25), the Holy Qur'ān in the present verse has enjoined upon the Muslims to defend, even with their lives, all the places of worship: the churches, the synagogues, the temples, the cloisters etc. This subject is echoed in the following verses of the Holy Qur'ān:

وَقٰتِلُوْهُمْ حَتّٰى لَا تَكُوْنَ فِتْنَةٌ وَّيَكُوْنَ الدِّيْنُ لِلّٰهِ ط

wa qātilūhum ḥattā lā takūna fitnatuñwwa yakūnaddīnu lillāhi

And fight them until there is no persecution and religion is *freely professed* for Allāh. (2:194)

فَمَنِ اعْتَدٰى عَلَيْكُمْ فَاعْتَدُوْا عَلَيْهِ بِمِثْلِ مَا اعْتَدٰى عَلَيْكُمْ

famani'tadā 'alaikum fa'tadū 'alaihi bi mithli ma'tadā 'alaikum

So, whoso transgresses against you, punish him for his transgression to the extent to which he has transgressed against you. (2:195)

لَآ اِكْرَاهَ فِی الدِّیْنِ ۙ قَدْتَّبَیَّنَ الرُّشْدُ مِنَ الْغَیِّ ۚ فَمَنْ یَّكْفُرْ بِالطَّاغُوْتِ وَ یُؤْمِنْۢ بِاللّٰهِ فَقَدِ اسْتَمْسَكَ بِالْعُرْوَةِ الْوُثْقٰی ۗ لَا انْفِصَامَ لَهَا ؕ وَاللّٰهُ سَمِیْعٌ عَلِیْمٌ 0

lā ikrāha fiddīni qattabayya narrushdu minal ghayyi famañyyakfur biṭṭāghūti wa yu'mim billāhi faqadistamsaka bil 'urwatil wuthqā lanfiṣāma lahā wallāhu samī'un 'alīm

There should be no compulsion in religion. Surely, right has become distinct from wrong; so whosoever refuses to be led by those who transgress, and believes in Allāh, has surely grasped a strong handle which knows no breaking. And Allāh is All-Hearing and All-Knowing. (2:257)

وَقَاتِلُوْهُمْ حَتّٰی لَا تَكُوْنَ فِتْنَةٌ وَّیَكُوْنَ الدِّیْنُ كُلُّهٗ لِلّٰهِ ۚ فَاِنِ انْتَهَوْا فَاِنَّ اللّٰهَ بِمَا یَعْمَلُوْنَ بَصِیْرٌ 0

wa qātilūhum ḥattā lā takūna fitnatuñwwa yakūnaddīnu kulluhū lillāhi fa inintahau fa innallāha bimā ya'malūna baṣīr

And fight them until there is no persecution and religion is wholly for Allāh. But if they desist, then surely Allāh is Watchful of what they do. (8:40)

Thus the first and foremost object of the wars of Islām was and will always be, to establish freedom of belief and worship and to fight in defense of country, honor and freedom against an unprovoked attack. Could there be a better cause to fight for than this? The Islāmic injunctions as embodied in the present verse did not remain merely pious principles. They were acted upon by the Muslims in their daily life. The Muslims in the hey-day of their power and glory always allowed complete freedom of belief and worship to people who accepted their protection and guardianship. To show the broad-mindedness and catholicity of Islāmic teaching in this respect, we give below only one of several charters of freedom which the Holy Prophet[sa] granted to the followers of other faith:

Charter of Freedom

"This is the document which Muḥammad, son of 'Abdullāh, God's Prophet, Warner and Bearer of glad-tidings, has caused to be written so that there should remain no excuse for those coming after. I have caused this document to be written for Christians of the East and the West, for those who live near, and for those of the distant lands, for the Christians living at present and for those who will come after, for those Christians who are known to us and for those as well whom we do not know. ... I promise that any monk or wayfarer who will seek my help on the mountains, in the forests, deserts or habitations, or in places of worship, I will repel his enemies with all my friends and helpers, with all my relatives and with all those who profess to follow me and will defend him, because they are my covenant. And I will defend the covenanted against the persecution, injury and embarrassment by their enemies in lieu of the poll-tax they have promised to pay. If they will prefer themselves to defend their properties and persons, they will be allowed to do so and will not be put to any inconvenience on that account. No bishop will be expelled from his bishopric, no monk from his monastery, no priest from his place of worship, and no pilgrim will be detained in his pilgrimage. None of their churches and other places of worship will be desolated or destroyed or demolished. No material of their churches will be used for building mosques or houses for the Muslims, any Muslim so doing will be regarded as recalcitrant to God and His Prophet. Monks and bishops will be subject to no tax or indemnity whether they live in forests or on the rivers, or in the East or West, North or South. I give them my word of honor. They are on my promise and covenant and will enjoy perfect immunity from all sorts of inconveniences, Every help shall be given them in the repair of their churches. They shall be absolved from wearing arms. They shall be protected by the Muslims. Let not this document be disobeyed till Judgement Day."

(Ḥaḍrat Mirzā Bashīruddīn Maḥmūd Aḥmad, the Holy Qur'ān Commentary, Vol. 4, pp. 1753-1756)

Murder of Ka'b bin Ashraf

Ka'b bin Ashraf, a Jewish chieftain of *Banū Naḍīr*, was a poet of considerable fame. Like so many others, he was bitterly hostile to Islām. With his fiery poems, he began to incite people to rise up against the Muslims. After the Battle of Badr, he composed a number of eulogies mourning the Meccan chiefs slain in the battle. He used to recite them at every gathering. When he learned about the death of the leaders of the *Quraish* he exclaimed, "Those were the nobles of Arabia, the kings of mankind. By God, if Muḥammad has vanquished these people, the interior of the earth is a better dwelling than the top of it." He contacted Abū Sufyān with a view to making a combined effort to wipe out the Muslims. He openly recited a number of poems derogatory to the Holy Prophet[sa]. As poetry had a high place in the life of the Arabs and could deepen influence and sway feelings, Ka'b bin Ashraf had become not only a nuisance but a serious menace. Ka'b plotted to kill the Holy Prophet[sa]. When the Holy Prophet[sa] came to know about the plot, he consulted his Companions[ra]. The Muslims were so irritated by Ka'b that they unanimously agreed to kill him. Abū Nā'ilah undertook this job and when he had the opportunity he and his companions killed Ka'b bin Ashraf.

Ghazwah Ghaṭafān (Ghazwah Qarqarat al-Kudr)

When the Holy Prophet[sa] learned that an army of *Banū Ghaṭafān* and *Banū Sulaim* tribesmen was travelling towards Medina to attack the Muslims, he led an expeditin of Muslim fighters to *Qarqarat al-Kudr* to meet them. However, the enemy gave up the idea when they learned about the march of the Holy Prophet[sa] and his Companions[ra] out of Medina to face them. When the Muslim force arrived at *Qarqarat al-Kudr*, they found camel traces but no men. The Muslims seized the camels they found in the area without battle. Later on the Holy Prophet[sa] learned that *Banī Tha'labah* and *Banī Muḥārib* tribesmen had gathered at *Dhū Amarr* to attack the Muslims. The Holy Prophet[sa] led a force of four hundred and fifty fighters to fight the enemy on their own grounds. However, when the enemy force learned of the arrival of the Muslim force they retreated to the mountains.

Ghazwah al-Sawīq

After defeat at Badr, Abū Sufyān took a vow that he would not touch his wives nor comb his hair till he had avenged the defeat. In order to fulfill this vow and to show that all was not lost to the Meccans and the *Quraish* were still strong, he mobilized two hundred Meccans and led them towards Medina. Sallām ibn Mishkam, Chief of the Jewish tribe of *Banū Naḍīr*, treated them to a feast and divulged the weak points of Medina's fortifications. On the next night, Abū Sufyān and his cohorts attacked a village called *al-'Urayd*. They martyred an Anṣār, Sa'd ibn 'Amr, and set fire to a number of houses and orchards. When this news reached the Holy Prophet[sa], the Muslims hotly pursued the raiders. Abū Sufyān and his party were frightened and they fled in a hurry, abandoning their provisions. The Muslims followed them and collected the provisions of wheat and barley left by them and returned home. This gave the raid its name, "*al-Sawīq*" (the battle of the flour). This raid by Abū Sufyān and his party did not increase the prestige of the *Quraish* as they had hoped. Rather, their fleeing instead of fighting the Muslims increased the prestige of the Muslims tremendously.

Battle of Uḥud

The Muslims, as a consequence of their success in the Battle of Badr had developed more confidence in themselves. They reorganized, consolidated their gains, and strengthened their community ties. However, the Meccans who had left the Battle of Badr defeated and humiliated were thirsty to take revenge for their defeat. They started preparations for taking revenge from the Muslims and were looking for an opportunity to do so. Ḥaḍrat 'Abbās[ra], an uncle of the Holy Prophet[sa] who was living in Mecca conveyed the information to the Holy Prophet[sa] about the intent of the Meccans.

When the Holy Prophet[sa] received news that an army of three thousand strongmen along with two hundred horsemen was marching towards Medina to attack the Muslims, he discussed the situation with the elders which included *Anṣār* and *Muhājirīn*. The elders favored defending themselves while remaining inside Medina, whereas, the young wanted to meet the enemy outside Medina and fight there.

When the Meccan army arrived and camped outside Medina, the Holy Prophet[sa] started to move towards Mount *Uḥud* with an army of 700 Muslims. When he reached Mount *Uḥud* he assigned an army brigade under the command of Ḥaḍrat 'Abdullāh bin Jubair[ra] to protect the mountain pass with strict orders not to leave the mountain pass under any circumstances. What happened during the war and how victory was almost lost is described in the following tradition:

Ḥaḍrat Abū Isḥāq narrates that he heard Ḥaḍrat Barā' bin 'Āzib[ra] say that in the Battle of Uḥud, the Holy Prophet[sa] appointed Ḥaḍrat 'Abdullāh bin Jubair[ra] as commander of a unit of fifty infantry men. Posting the army unit on a mountain pass, the Holy Prophet[sa] instructed them that even if you see that vultures are carrying us away and eating our flesh, do not leave the place (where I am posting you) till I send for you. Similarly, even if they notice that they have defeated the infidels and have crushed them they were not to leave the post until he told them through a messenger. Ḥaḍrat Barā'[ra] relates that they defeated them (the enemy). By Allāh! I saw infidel women running away from the battlefield showing their bare legs rolling up their dresses and ornaments. Seeing this, the brigade of Ḥaḍrat 'Abdullāh bin Jubair[ra] said: "Spoils of the war! O people! Spoils of the war. Your companions have become victorious. What are you now waiting for? Your companions have overcome the enemy, so what are you waiting for?" Ḥaḍrat 'Abdullāh bin Jubair[ra] said: "Have you forgetten what the Holy Prophet[sa] had told you?" They said: "By Allāh! We will go to the people and we will get the spoils." When they came to them, they were forced to turn back. The defeated enemy marched forward. That was the time when the Messenger[sa] of Allāh was calling them from the rear:

إِذْ يَدْعُوهُمُ الرَّسُولُ فِىٓ أُخْرَاهُمْ

idh yad'ūhumurrasūlu fī ukhrāhum

When the Messenger of Allāh was calling them from the rear.

when just twelve Companions[ra] of the Holy Prophet[sa] were left with him and about seventy Companions[ra] were martyred fighting the enemy. Whereas in the Battle of Badr, one hundred forty infidels were injured, seventy were imprisoned, and seventy were killed by the Muslims. During this incident, Abū Sufyān shouted three times: "Is Muḥammad with you?" The Holy Prophet[sa] told the Companions[ra] not to respond. Then Abū Sufyān shouted: "Is Abū Bakr bin Abū Quḥāfah with you?" Then he said three times: "Is 'Umar bin al-Khaṭṭāb with you?" When he did not hear a response to any of his inquiries, he turned to his army and said: "All of them have been killed." Ḥaḍrat 'Umar bin al-Khaṭṭāb[ra] was unable to bear Abū Sufyān's proclamation and said in loud voice: "O enemy of Allāh! By Allāh! All those about whom you have inquired are alive and there is nothing but disgrace for you." Then, Abū Sufyān said: "We have avenged our defeat in the Battle of Badr. A battle is like a bucket which tilts (sometimes to one side and sometimes to the other side). You might find some corpses mutilated. I did not tell them to do so. However, I do not feel remorse for this." Then, he shouted the slogan:

أُعْلُ هُبَلْ أُعْلُ هُبَلْ!

u'lu hubal, u'lu hubal!

O Hubal be high, O Hubal be high.

At this, the Holy Prophet[sa] said, "Why don't you respond?" The Companions[ra] said: "O Messenger[sa] of Allāh! What should we say?" The Holy Prophet[sa] told them to declare:

اَللّٰهُ اَعْلٰى وَ اَجَلُّ

allāhu a'lā wa ajall

Only God is the Supreme, there is none comparable to Him

In response to this, Abū Sufyān shouted the slogan:

لَنَا الْعُزّٰى وَلاَ عُزّٰى لَكُمْ

lanal 'uzzā wa lā 'uzzā lakum

We have the support of 'Uzza goddess, while you do not have 'Uzza

The Holy Prophet[sa] ordered: "Respond to the slogan." The Companions asked: "O Messenger[sa] of Allāh! What should we say?" He told them to proclaim:

اَللّٰهُ مَوْلَانَا وَ لَا مَوْلٰى لَكُمْ

allāhu maulānā wa lā maulā lakum

God is our Lord and our Master and you do not have such a Lord and Master who could help you.

(Ṣaḥīḥ Bukhārī, Kitāb al-Jihād Wassair, Bāb yakrah minattanāzi' wal ikhtilāf fil ḥarb)

In the Holy Qur'ān God Almighty states

وَلَقَدْ صَدَقَكُمُ اللّٰهُ وَعْدَهٗۤ اِذْ تَحُسُّوْنَهُمْ بِاِذْنِهٖ ۚ حَتّٰٓى اِذَا فَشِلْتُمْ
وَتَنَازَعْتُمْ فِى الْاَمْرِ وَعَصَيْتُمْ مِّنْۢ بَعْدِ مَآ اَرٰىكُمْ مَّا تُحِبُّوْنَ ؕ مِنْكُمْ
مَّنْ يُّرِيْدُ الدُّنْيَا وَ مِنْكُمْ مَّنْ يُّرِيْدُ الْاٰخِرَةَ ۚ ثُمَّ صَرَفَكُمْ عَنْهُمْ
لِيَبْتَلِيَكُمْ ۚ وَلَقَدْ عَفَا عَنْكُمْ ؕ

walaqad ṣadaqaku mullāhu wa'dahū idh taḥussūnahum bi idhnihī ḥattā idhā fashiltum wa tanāza'tum fil amri wa 'aṣaitummim ba'di mā arākummā tuḥibbūna minkummañyyurī duddunyā wa minkummañyyuridul ākhirata thumma ṣarafakum 'anhum li yabtaliyakum walaqad 'afā 'ankum

And Allāh had surely made good to you His promise when you were slaying and destroying them by His leave, until, when you faltered *concerning obedience to the Holy Prophet*[sa], and started arguing among yourselves regarding the true intent of the order and disobeyed after He had granted you your heart's desire *in the form of victory,* He *withdrew His help.* Among you were those who desired the present world, and among you were those who desired the next. Then He turned you away from them, that He might try you - and He has surely pardoned you. (3:153)

Due to the mistake made by some of the Muslim fighters, in a moment, there was confusion all around. The Holy Prophet[sa] was left with only a handful of Muslims to guard him. Most of these were killed by the arrows that rained down upon them. Ḥaḍrat Ṭalḥa bin 'Ubaidullāh[ra] stopped the arrows fired at the Holy Prophet[sa] by a sharp shooter called Mālik bin Zubair with his hands, as a result of which one of his hands was crippled. When his body was examined after the battle, there were more than seventy wounds on his body. Even as this took place, the Holy Prophet[sa] prayed for his enemies, "Lord, grant guidance to my people, for they know not what they do." While he was praying, he himself was hit in the cheek by a stone that drove two of the rings of his helmet into the flesh. He fell down, unconscious, among the heap of Muslims who had died fighting the enemy, others falling on top of him. This resulted in a rumor that the Holy Prophet[sa] had been martyred.

The rumor of the death of the Holy Prophet[sa] and the news of the dispersal of the Muslim army reached Medina. Women and children ran madly towards Uḥud. When they came to know that the Holy Prophet[sa] was alive and safe and sound, they returned to Medina.

Although, in this battle many Muslims were killed and many wounded, still the battle did not end in a defeat for the Muslims. In fact, the battle was a great victory for Muslims. However, the Meccans thought Uḥud was their first victory against Muslims. They spread the news of their victory all over Arabia and used the Battle of Uḥud to incite the Arab tribes against Islām and to persuade them that the Muslims were not invincible. The result of this propaganda was that hostility against Muslims began to gather strength. Under these circumstances it became necessary to keep an eye upon the activities of the enemy. For this reason the Holy Prophet[sa] sent a party of scouts to gather information about the plans of the enemy.

The Reconnaissance Mission Sent by the Holy Prophet[sa]

Ḥaḍrat Abū Hurairah[ra] relates that the Holy Prophet[sa] sent a party of ten scouts for espionage and appointed Ḥaḍrat 'Āṣim bin Thābit al-Anṣārī[ra] as its leader. When the party reached a place called *Hudā*, located between 'Usfān and Mecca, the *Banū Liḥyān* tribe of *Banū Hudhail* found out about the party. They sent one hundred archers in pursuit of the Muslim scouts, who traced the footsteps and drew near the scouts. When Ḥaḍrat 'Āṣim[ra] and his companions came to know about the pursuit, they took shelter on top of a hill. The pursuers surrounded the hill and told them to come down and surrender. They said that they pledged not to harm anyone. Ḥaḍrat 'Āṣim[ra] said: "By Allāh! I do not trust these infidels to surrender to them. Then Ḥaḍrat 'Āṣim[ra] supplicated: 'O My Lord! Please inform Your beloved Prophet about our situation.' Anyway, when the enemy felt that they were not coming down from the hill, they started to shoot the arrows heavily. Due to this, Ḥaḍrat 'Āṣim[ra] and some of his companions were martyred. Only three men trusting the enemy came down and surrendered themselves to them. These included Ḥaḍrat Khubaib[ra], Ḥaḍrat Zaid bin Dathinah[ra], and a third man whose name the narrator does not recall. When the enemy captured these men and started to tie them, the third man said to the enemy: 'This is your first betrayal and breach of promise. By God! I will not accompany you. These companions[ra] who have been martyred have set a good example for me. I will follow them.' The enemies dragged this Companion[ra] and tried to compel him to obey them by using force. But he refused to go with them. So, they martyred him. They took Khubaib[ra] and Zaid bin Dathinah[ra] with them and sold them (as slaves) to the Meccans. This event took place after the Battle of Badr. Ḥaḍrat Khubaib[ra] had killed a Meccan leader, Ḥārith, in the Battle of Badr. So in revenge, the sons of Ḥārith bought Ḥaḍrat Khubaib[ra]. They kept Ḥaḍrat Khubaib[ra] as a prisoner for a long time and then decided to kill him. It happened that in those days Ḥaḍrat Khubaib[ra] had borrowed a razor for his personal use from the daughter of Ḥārith. Ḥaḍrat Khubaib[ra] was holding the razor in his hand when a son of that woman crawled inside and sat in the lap of Ḥaḍrat Khubaib[ra]. When the daughter of Ḥārith saw her son sitting in the lap of Ḥaḍrat Khubaib[ra], she became extremely distraught. Ḥaḍrat Khubaib[ra] noticed her fear and said: 'Do you fear that I will kill him? Do not expect such a cowardly act from me.' Later on, while describing this incident, the daughter of Ḥārith said: 'By God! I did not see any prisoner better than Khubaib[ra]. By Allāh! One day, I saw him eating a bunch of grapes he was holding in his hands, while he was handcuffed with chains though it was not the season for grapes in Mecca. In fact, it was a provision provided by God Almighty to Khubaib[ra].' When the sons of Ḥārith took Khubaib[ra] out of the sacred zone to the place of execution, he asked them to let him offer two *rak'āt* of Prayer. They permitted him to do so. Khubaib[ra] finished offering two *rak'āt* of Prayer and said: 'By God! Had I not worried that you might think that I am afraid of being killed, I would have offered the Prayer a bit longer.' Khubaib[ra] supplicated: 'My Lord! Count them and kill each of them, one by one, disgracefully. Do not leave anyone of them.' Then Khubaib[ra] recited the following couplets:

فَلَسْتُ اُبَالِیْ حِیْنَ اُقْتَلُ مُسْلِمًا

falastu ubālī ḥīna uqtalu musliman

عَلٰی اَیِّ جَنْبٍ کَانَ لِلّٰہِ مَصْرَعِیْ

'alā ayyi janbin kāna lillāhi maṣra'ī

وَ ذٰلِكَ فِیْ ذَاتِ الْاِلٰہِ وَ اِنْ یَّشَأْ

wa dhālika fi dhātil ilāhi wa iñyyasha'

يُبَارِكْ عَلٰى اَوْصَالِ شِلْوٍ مُمَزَّعٖ

yubārik 'alā auṣāli shilvin mumazza'i

"Because, I am being killed as a Muslim and an innocent person, I mind not how I fall or die in the cause of Allāh. My death is for the sake of Allāh and to gain the pleasure of Allāh. If Allāh pleases He can shower His blessings on the amputated pieces of my body."

(As-Sīratun Nabawiyyah libne Hishām, Vol. 2, p. 170)

At the time, Ḥaḍrat Khubaib[ra] was being prepared to be killed by the offspring of the forty Meccan leaders who were killed in the Battle of Badr, he prayed, "O Allāh! There is no one here who could convey my *Salām* to the Holy Prophet[sa]. I request You to convey my *Salām* to the Holy Prophet[sa]." At that time the Holy Prophet[sa] was sitting in the company of his Companions[ra] 300 miles away in Medina. Suddenly, he went into the mode of receiving a revelation. Ḥaḍrat Usāma bin Zaid[ra] said that suddenly we heard the Holy Prophet[sa] say, *'Wa Alaikumussalām'.* When the Holy Prophet[sa] came out of the mode of receiving the revelation he said, "Gabriel came to convey Salām from Khubaib who has been martyred by the *Quraish.*"

(As-Sīratul Ḥalabiyyah, 'Alī bin Burhānuddīn, Vol. 3, P. 260, Printed in Beirut, Lebanon)

Ḥaḍrat Khubaib[ra] is the same Companion of the Holy Prophet[sa], who became instrumental for the *Sunnah* (practice) of offering funeral Prayer for the ones sentenced to death in captivity. After receiving information about this terrible incident from God Almighty on the day the Companions[ra] who had gone on the expedition were martyred, the Holy

Prophet[sa] told his Companions[ra] about it and offered the funeral Prayer. When the *Quraish* found out that Ḥaḍrat 'Āṣim[ra] had been martyred, some of them went to collect his body or a part of it. The reason was that Ḥaḍrat 'Āṣim[ra] had killed a prominent leader of the *Quraish* in the Battle of Badr, and they wanted to disgrace Ḥaḍrat 'Āṣim's[ra] body in revenge. However, to protect his body, God sent in a large hive of bees or swarm of wasps, like a shadow, which stung those who wanted to disgrace Ḥaḍrat 'Āṣim's[ra] body. They could not cut off anything from his flesh.

(Ṣaḥīḥ Bukhārī, Kitāb al-Mghāzī, Bāb ghazwatassarjī' wa ra'al wa dhakwān)

Martyrdom of Muslims at Bi'r Ma'ūnah

The Holy Prophet[sa] was saddened to learn about the martyrdom of his six Companions[ra] as a result of the treachery of *Hudhail*. During this period of anguish, Abū Barā' 'Āmir ibn Mālik came to see the Holy Prophet[sa]. The Holy Prophet[sa] preached to Abū Barā' and encouraged him to accept the message of Islām. However, Abū Barā' did not accept the message. At the same time, he requested the Holy Prophet[sa] to send some of his Companions[ra] to convey the message of Islām to the people of Najd. The Holy Prophet[sa] was reluctant to do so as he was worried that this may not be another treacherous scheme to harm Islām as was done earlier by the *Hudhail* tribe. However, Abū Barā' assured the Holy Prophet[sa] that he will be their guardian and protector. Abū Barā' being a notable person with strong influence among his people was a trustworthy person. Accordingly, the Holy Prophet[sa] sent with Abū Barā' around seventy *Ḥafiẓ-e-Qur'ān* (reciters) under the leadership of Mundhir ibn 'Amr. Most of them were *Anṣār*. The delagation left on their mission and reached the place known as, 'Bi'r Ma'ūnah', located close to the borders of *Banū 'Āmir* and *Banū Sulaim*. From there, they sent the message of the Holy Prophet[sa] through Ḥarām ibn Milḥān to 'Āmir ibn al-Ṭufail. 'Āmir ibn al-Ṭufail did not bother to read the Holy Prophet's[sa] letter and killed the messenger.

Furthermore, he incited the people of *Banū 'Āmir* against the Muslims and urged them to kill them. However, due to the protection given by Abū Barā', the tribesmen refused to do so. Then 'Āmir ibn al-Ṭufail contacted the people of other tribes to do the job. Some of them responded and killed the Muslims. Only, Ka'b ibn Zaid and 'Amr ibn Umayyah survived. Ka'b ibn Zaid was severely wounded and was left for dead. 'Amr ibn Umayyah was freed by 'Āmir ibn al-Ṭufail as an atonement to fulfill his mother's pledge to compensate for a man's life which she owed. Seventy *Ḥafiẓ-e-Qur'ān* Companions[ra] were martyred.

The martyrdom of Muslims at Bi'r Ma'ūnah was very painful and distressing for the Holy Prophet[sa]. All the Muslims were saddened to learn about the fate of their brethren. The Holy Prophet[sa] put the blame of this tragedy solely upon Abū Barā'. However, Abū Barā' was also saddened with the tragedy and wanted to take revenge from 'Āmir ibn al-Ṭufail for violating his protective agreement with the Muslims. Accordingly, he sent his own son, al-Rājī' to kill 'Āmir ibn al-Ṭufail.

(Sirah Al-Halabiyyah, Vol. 3, pp. 240-244; The Life of Muḥammad[sa], A Translation of Ibn Isḥāq's Sirat Rasūlullāh[sa], pp.433-436, A. Guillaume,, Oxford University Press,Reprinted in Pakistan, 2004)

8

Encounter with Banū Muṣṭaliq and Battle of Aḥzāb (Battle of the Ditch)

Encounter with Banū Muṣṭaliq

After the Battle of Uḥud, the Meccans faced severe famine. Despite the intense hostility of the Meccans towards the Holy Prophet[sa], the Holy Prophet[sa] collected funds to help the Meccans. However, this goodwill gesture by the Holy Prophet[sa] towards the Meccans was ignored by the Meccans and they continued their hostile attitude. Instead their hostility increased to the extent that previously neutral tribes also became hostile towards the Muslims. One such tribe was the tribe of *Banū Muṣṭaliq*. When the Holy Prophet[sa] learned that *Banū Muṣṭaliq* was preparing to attack Medina he sent a group of people towards *Banū Muṣṭaliq* to do reconnaissance and to determine their real intentions. The reconnaissance party confirmed that the *Banū Muṣṭaliq* tribe planned to attack Medina. The Holy Prophet[sa] decided to face the *Banū Muṣṭaliq* fighters in their own territory. Before the start of the fighting between the Muslim and the *Banū Muṣṭaliq* forces, the Holy Prophet[sa] tried to convince the leaders of the *Banū Muṣṭaliq* tribe to withdraw their forces without a fight. However, they did not accept the suggestion made by the Holy Prophet[sa] to avoid the bloodshed on both sides. Consequently, a fight pursued between the two forces and within a few hours the *Banū Muṣṭaliq* forces were defeated.

(al-Ṭabarī, Vol. 8, p. 51)

The hypocrites of Medina also had accompanied the Muslims to fight the *Banū Muṣṭaliq*. Their real intention was to create mischief among the Muslims. However, the fighting between the Muslim and the *Banū Muṣṭaliq* forces ended so fast that the hypocrites did not get the chance to act upon their plans. After defeating the *Banū Muṣṭaliq*, the Holy Prophet[sa] decided to stay in the area for a couple of days. During this period, it so happened that a Meccan Muslim (a *Muhājir*) had an argument with a Muslim from Medina (*a Nāṣir*) over drawing water from a well. The Medinite Muslim shouted for help from the *Anṣār* while the Meccan Muslim asked for help from the *Muhājirīn*. Both parties were ready to fight each other. 'Abdullāh bin Ubayy bin Salūl was one of the hypocrites who had accompanied the Muslim forces to create mischief. He thought it a golden opportunity to carry out his plan. So he made a speech with the intention to incite the Medinites against the Meccans. However, his tactics failed. The Medinites and Meccans resolved the issue peacefully. 'Abdullāh bin Ubayy bin Salūl was so sure, in his mind, that the argument amongst the *Anṣār* and the *Muhājirīn* will lead to a discord amongst the Muslims that in his speech he said, "When we return to Medina the most honored among the citizens will kick out the most despised." By the most honored, he meant himself and by the most despised he meant the Holy Prophet[sa]. Upon hearing such despicable comments, the Muslims realized that the hypocrites had come along with them just to create mischief. When the Holy Prophet[sa] learned about what 'Abdullāh bin Ubayy bin Salūl had said he sent for 'Abdullāh bin Ubayy bin Salūl and his companions and asked them about the comments. All of them denied making such a statement. The Holy Prophet[sa] said nothing to them. However, many people had heard 'Abdullāh bin Ubayy bin Salūl make the statement. So the comment started to reverberate. When 'Abdullāh bin Ubayy bin Salūl's son heard about the comments, he at once went to see the Holy Prophet[sa] and said, "O Messenger[sa] of Allāh! My father has insulted you. If you decide that death is his punishment, I would like to be the one who kills my father." The Holy Prophet[sa] told him that he did not intend to punish his father. Rather he will be compassionate to him. However, 'Abdullāh bin Ubayy bin Salūl's son was so full of anger against his father that when he returned to Medina he stopped his father on the way, and told him that he would not let him enter Medina until he repudiated what he had said about the Holy Prophet[sa]. He told his father that he must say, "The Holy Prophet[sa] is most honored and I am most despised." ‘Abdullāh bin Ubayy bin Salūl was astonished and frightened to see his son treating him like this. So, he agreed and said, "The Holy Prophet[sa] is most honored and I am most despised."

(As-Sīratun Nabawiyyah libne Hishām, Vol. 4, pp. 303-304; Miṣbāḥul Munīr fī Tahzīb-e-Tafsīr Ibn Kathīr (Abridged), Vol. 9, pp. 653-656; William Muir, The Life of Muḥammad, Vol. 3, Chapter 16)

Battle of Aḥzāb (Battle of the Ditch)

After repeatedly failing to destroy the new religion which was becoming stronger day by day, the Meccans tried to develop new strategies to annihilate the Muslims. They approached the Jews of Medina for help in destroying the Muslims. The Jewish tribe of *Banū Naḍīr* joined them, violating the pact they had made earlier with the Muslims. They intended to kill the Holy Prophet[sa] and thus annihilate the new religion, Islām. The Holy Prophet[sa] came to know of their intentions. The traitors were given the warning to stop their wrongdoing or they would be deported from Medina. They refused to accept the advice and continued committing treacherous acts. Due to their treachery, they were expelled from Medina. They moved to Khaibar which became a center of enmity against the Muslims. They encouraged the Meccans to launch a new offensive to finish the Muslims forever. Accordingly the Meccans made a plan to attack Medina. Thus, they were able to arouse general hostility against the Muslims throughout Arabia, and made agreements with most of the tribes under which they were obligated to raise an army against the Muslims. This army, known as the Confederates, was estimated at eighteen to twenty thousand men. When the news of the Meccans' intention to attack Medina reached the Holy Prophet[sa], he consulted his Companions[ra] to decide how to face the enemy in their latest offensive against them. Ḥaḍrat Salmān Fārisī[ra] suggested that trenches should be dug around the city to keep the enemy outside Medina. The Holy Prophet[sa] accepted his suggestion. Thus, a deep and wide trench was dug on the side of Medina which was open to the plain, and was the most probable side for attack by the enemy. On the other sides some security was offered by a range of hills, by the strongholds of the remaining Jewish tribe, and by some houses and groves which lay thickly together. The Jewish tribe was in alliance with the Muslims and was bound by the terms of the Charter of Medina to cooperate in the defense of the town. The Holy Prophet[sa] himself took part in the digging of the trench. The condition of the Holy Prophet[sa] and his Companions[ra] during the digging of the trench is well described in the following traditions:

Hadrat Jābir[ra] relates: "On the day of the Battle of the Ditch we were digging and encountered a big solid rock. They came to the Holy Prophet[sa] and said: 'There is a very hard piece of rock appearing across the Ditch. The Holy Prophet[sa] said: 'I shall descend into the ditch. He stood up and it was noticed that he had tied a piece of rock over his stomach for we had not eaten anything for three days. He took up a pick-axe and struck (the big solid rock) with it and it became like sand. I asked the Holy Prophet's[sa] permission to go home and said to my wife: 'I have seen the Holy Prophet[sa] in a condition that I am unable to endure. Do you have anything in the house?' She said: 'I have some barley and a she-goat.' I slaughtered the goat and ground down the barley and we put the meat in the cooking pot. The flour had been kneaded and the meat in the pot was nearly cooked, then I went to the Holy Prophet[sa]. I said to the Holy Prophet[sa]: 'I have some food, Messenger[sa] of Allāh, will you come with one or two?' He asked: 'How much food is there?' I told him everything in detail. He said: 'That is more than enough. Tell your wife not to take the pot off the fire nor remove the bread from the oven till I arrive.' Then he said to the *Muhājirīn* and the *Anṣār*: 'Get up.' They all got up.

I went to my wife and said: 'Bless you, the Holy Prophet[sa], the Emigrants, the Helpers and the whole company are coming over.' She said: 'Did he ask you (How much do we have)?' I said: 'Yes.' The Holy Prophet[sa] said to his Companions[ra]: 'Enter, but do not crowd.' Then he started breaking up the bread and putting meat on it. He would take a portion from the pot and the oven, then cover them up and approach his Companions[ra] and hand it over to them. He would then go back and uncover the pot and oven. He continued to break up the bread and putting meat on it till all had eaten to their fill and some was still left over. Then he said to my wife: 'Eat of it, and send it as a present, for people who have been afflicted with hunger.'

In another Hadīth it is related that Hadrat Jābir[ra] relates: "When the Ditch was being dug, I saw that the Holy Prophet[sa] was hungry. So I went to my wife and asked her whether she had anything? I have seen that the Holy Prophet[sa] is extremely hungry. She brought a bag to me which contained one *Sā'* of barley and we had a domestic ram. I slaughtered the ram and my wife grinded the barley. After grinding she came to me. I cut the meat into pieces and put it into a cooking pot . Then I returned to the Holy Prophet[sa]. My wife told me not to disgrace her in front of the Holy Prophet[sa] and his Companions[ra]. I came to the Holy Prophet[sa] and told him in low voice, 'Messenger[sa] of Allāh, we have slaughtered a ram and have grinded one *Sā'* of barley. Please come with a few Companions[ra].' The Holy Prophet[sa] said in loud voice, 'O the inhabitants of the Ditch, Jābir has invited us. Let us go.' The Holy Prophet[sa] told me not to remove the cooking pot from the fire and not to start making bread till he comes. I returned and Holy Prophet[sa] also came walking in front of the people. When I returned, my wife dubbed me as careless and neglectful. I told her that I did just as she had told. She brought the flour. The Holy Prophet[sa] blessed it by mixing his saliva in it. Then he[sa] went to our cooking pot and blessed it also by putting his saliva in it. Then he said, 'Call a lady-baker to help you in cooking the bread. Start serving the curry but do not remove the pot from the fire.' They were around one thousand. I swear by Allāh that all of them ate to their full while our cooking pot was still steaming and our dough was still being baked into breads.' "

(Sahīh Bukhārī, Kitābul Maghāzī, Bāb Ghazwah Khandaq)

During the Battle of Aḥzāb, the Holy Prophet[sa] used to do the following prayer for the defeat of the enemy:

Ḥaḍrat 'Abdullāh bin Abī Aufā[ra] relates a prayer of the Holy Prophet[sa] which he supplicated at the occasion of the Battle of Aḥzāb.

اَللّٰهُمَّ مُنْزِلَ الْكِتَابِ ، سَرِيْعَ الْحِسَابِ اِهْزِمِ الْاَحْزَابَ اَللّٰهُمَّ اهْزِمْهُمْ وَ زَلْزِلْهُمْ -

allāhumma munzilal kitābi, sarī'al ḥisābi, ihzimil aḥzāba allāhummahzimhum wa zalzilhum

O Allāh! The revealer of the Holy Book and swift in taking an account! Defeat the confederates. O Allāh! Defeat them and destroy them.

(Ṣaḥīḥ Bukhārī Kitābul Maghāzī, Bāb Ghazwatil Khandaqi wahyal Aḥzābu)

During the digging of the trenches when the Holy Prophet[sa] struck the big solid rock with his pick-axe, there appeared a bright flash of light and the Holy Prophet said, "*Allāhu Akbar*". He struck again. Again a light came out and again the Holy Prophet[sa] siad in a loud voice, "*Allāhu Akbar*". He struck the third time. Light came out again and the Holy Prophet[sa] again said, "*Allāhu Akbar*" and the rock shattered to pieces. The Companions[ra] asked the Holy Prophet[sa] about the significance of the light and why he said "*Allāhu Akbar*" each time there was the light. The Holy Prophet[sa] smiled and told them, "I struck the rock three times with the pick-axe, and three times I saw the scenes of the future glory of Islām. In the first spark I saw the Syrian palaces of the Roman Empire. I had the keys of those palaces given to me. The second time, I saw the palaces of Persia and *Madā'in*, and had the keys of Persian Empire given to me. The third time, I saw the gates of *Ṣan'ā* and I had the keys of the kingdom of Yemen given to me. These are the promises of Allāh and I trust you will put reliance in them. The enemy can do you no harm.

(Zurqānī, Sharḥ Mawāhib al-Ladunniyya, Vol. 3, pp. 31-32, Dārul Kutabul 'Ilmiyyah, Beirut, Lebanon; Al-Ṭabarī, Vol. 8, p. 12; Fatḥ al-Bārī, Ḥāfiz Ibni Ḥajar, Vol. 7; Muḥammad Al-Ghazālī, Fiqḥ-us-Sīrah, p. 308; Isḥāq, p. 451)

The Persian and Roman empires were the two main powers at that time. The Muslims were overjoyed to hear the prophecy. On the contrary, the Jews, the hypocrites and the idolators were amused and made fun of the prophecy of the Holy Prophet[sa]. Within a few years after the demise of the Holy Prophet[sa], his prophecy was fulfilled.

The Banū Quraiẓah Punished for Their Treachery

When the trench was dug on the plain side of Medina, the Muslim fighting force was spread all around to defend the city from inside. When the Meccan army which was close to ten thousand in number reached Medina they were surprised to see the trench and were unable to figure out why the trench has been dug and how to overcome the obstacle. So they decided to wait outside the city and plan to try to cross the trench. All their efforts to cross the trench were thwarted by the Muslims. The long stay had caused them to exhaust their supplies and the army's morale was waning. So they became worried and hatched a plot with the Jews of *Banū Quraiẓah* in Medina. Muslims were surrounded from all sides except the side where *Banū Quraiẓah* lived. Ḥuyyay bin Akhṭab, the Jewish Chief went to the leaders of *Banū Quraiẓah* to convince them to blockade the Muslims and cut their food and water supply. First they resisted following his plan. However, under consistant pressure from Ḥuyyay, the leaders of *Banū Quraiẓah* agreed to his suggestion of cutting the water and food supply to the Muslims. The Holy Prophet[sa] came to know of their treacherous plans and he conveyed the message to the Jews of *Banū Quraiẓah*. They were told to think of the consequences for them if the Meccans were defeated. The Holy Prophet[sa] sent a deputation of three men which included the heads of *Aus*, *Khazraj* tribes and an emigrant to talk with them and to assess the situation. They found the leaders of the *Banū Quraiẓah* very arrogant and in an evil mood. Sa'd ibn Mu'ādh, the head of the *Aus* tribe tried his best to convince them not to break their covenant and also warned them of the consequences of their treacherous behavior. However, they still supported the Meccans. Thus, they had broken their covenant with the Muslims. The deputation returned and told the Holy Prophet[sa] about the attitude of the *Banū Quraiẓah*. The enemy planned to attack Medina from three directions while the *Banū Quraiẓah* were asked to fight the Muslims from their side.

Relying on the loyalty of the Jews and their duty with respect to the defense of Medina, the Holy Prophet[sa] had posted no forces for the purpose of guarding the Muslim quarters of the town, and had left only a handful of watchmen to supervise the security of the women and children.

One day the enemy sent a spy to find out whether guards had been posted for the protection of the women and children, and, if so, in what strength. There was a special enclosure for families which the enemy regarded as their special target. The spy came and began to do surveillance around this enclosure. While he was doing so, Ḥaḍrat Ṣafiyyah[ra], an aunt of the Holy Prophet[sa] spotted him. Only one male adult happened to be on guard duty at the time and even he was ill. Ḥaḍrat Ṣafiyyah[ra] reported to the guard what she had seen and told him to catch him before he was able to give information to the enemy about the protection arrangements for the women and children in the area. The guard on duty refused to do anything. Upon which Ḥaḍrat Ṣafiyyah[ra] herself picked up a staff and began to fight the spy sent by the enemies. With the help of other women she was able to overpower and kill him. He turned out to be an agent of the *Banū Quraiẓah*.

When it became known to the Holy Prophet[sa] that the Confederates had won over the Jews to their side, he assigned two brigades of men, three hundred and two hundred strong respectively, to the Muslim quarters of the town to take measures for their defense against the Jews should they attempt an attack. This reduced the forces at his disposal at the trench facing the Confederate army to seven hundred and fifty men. Again, the disparity in numbers and in every other respect between the opposing forces was not only striking but pitiful. The plight of the Muslims is described in the Holy Qur'ān:

اِذْ جَآءُوْكُمْ مِّنْ فَوْقِكُمْ وَمِنْ اَسْفَلَ مِنْكُمْ وَ اِذْ زَاغَتِ
الْاَبْصَارُ وَبَلَغَتِ الْقُلُوْبُ الْحَنَاجِرَ وَ تَظُنُّوْنَ بِاللّٰهِ الظُّنُوْنَا 0
هُنَالِكَ ابْتُلِيَ الْمُؤْمِنُوْنَ وَزُلْزِلُوْا زِلْزَالاً شَدِيْدًا 0 وَ اِذْ يَقُوْلُ
الْمُنٰفِقُوْنَ وَالَّذِيْنَ فِيْ قُلُوْبِهِمْ مَرَضٌ مَّا وَعَدَنَا اللّٰهُ وَ رَسُوْلُهٗٓ
اِلاَّ غُرُوْرًا 0 وَ اِذْ قَالَتْ طَّآئِفَةٌ مِّنْهُمْ يٰٓاَهْلَ يَثْرِبَ لاَ مُقَامَ لَكُمْ
فَارْجِعُوْا ۚ وَ يَسْتَاْذِنُ فَرِيْقٌ مِّنْهُمُ النَّبِيَّ يَقُوْلُوْنَ اِنَّ بُيُوْتَنَا عَوْرَةٌ ط
وَمَا هِيَ بِعَوْرَةٍ ۚ اِنْ يُّرِيْدُوْنَ اِلاَّ فِرَارًا 0

idh jā'ūkummin fauqikum wa min asfala minkum wa idh zāgatil abṣāru wa balagatil qulūbul ḥanājira wa taẓunnūna billāhiẓẓunūna hunālikab tuliyal mu'minūna wa zulzilū zilzālan shadīda wa idh yaqūlul munāfiqūna walladhīna fī qulūbihim maraḍummā wa'adanallāhu wa rasūluhū illā ghurūra wa idh qālaṭṭā'ifa tumminhum yā ahla yathriba lā

muqāma lakum farji'ū wa yasta'dhinu farīqumminhu munnabiyya yaqūlūna inna buyūtanā 'aurah wamā hiya bi 'auratin iñyyurīdūna illā firārā

When they came upon you from above you, and from below you, and when *your* eyes became distracted, and *your* hearts leapt to *your* throats and you entertained wayward thoughts about Allāh. There *and then* were the believers *sorely* tried, and they were shaken with a violent shaking. And when the hypocrites and those in whose hearts was a desease said, "Allāh and His Messenger promised us nothing but a delusion.' And when a party of them said, 'O people of Yathrib, you have *possibly* no stand *against the enemy*, therefore turn back.' And a section of them even asked leave of the Prophet, saying, 'Our houses are exposed *and defenseless.*' And they were *in truth* not exposed. they only sought to flee away. (33:11-14)

Before the day decided upon for the joint assault by the Confederates and the Jews, relief came from an unexpected source: the weather. It was a stormy and turbulent night. The fierce wind caused great confusion in the Confederate camp. Further consternation arose when one of the tribal chiefs observed that the fire in front of his tent had gone out; according to Arab superstition, this portended death or defeat for him in the next day's fighting. To avoid this, the chief told his people to strike camp so that they could withdraw quietly into the desert for a day or two. This move was interpreted by both the Jew and Confederate as a device to secure safety against a feared night sortie by the Muslims. The alarm spread and there was general panic. Tents were hastily pulled down, and a disorderly retreat ensued. When morning came, the whole plain in front of the trench was empty. There was no trace of the Confederate forces. This is stated in the Holy Qur'ān as:

يٰٓأَيُّهَا الَّذِيْنَ اٰمَنُوا اذْكُرُوْا نِعْمَةَ اللّٰهِ عَلَيْكُمْ اِذْ جَآءَتْكُمْ جُنُوْدٌ

فَاَرْسَلْنَا عَلَيْهِمْ رِيْحًا وَّ جُنُوْدًا لَّمْ تَرَوْهَا ؕ وَكَانَ اللّٰهُ بِمَا تَعْمَلُوْنَ بَصِيْرًا ۚ۝

yā ayyuhalladhīna āmanudhkurū ni'matallāhi 'alaikum idh jā'atkum junūdun fa arsalnā 'alaihim rīḥañwwa junūdallam tarauhā wa kānallāhu bimā ta'malūna baṣīrā

O ye who believe! remember the favor of Allāh on you when there came down upon you hosts, and We sent against them a wind and hosts that you saw not. And Allāh sees what you. do. (33:10)

During one of the attacks, when a party of the Confederates had crossed the trench and were repulsed, a noted tribal chief was left dead on the Muslim side. His people, fearing that the Muslims would mutilate his dead body, as would have been their own procedure, offered a sum of ten thousand dirhems for the recovery of his body. They did not know that the Holy Prophet[sa] had abolished all barbaric customs and that their fears were unfounded. When their offer was conveyed to the Holy Prophet[sa] he declined to receive any payment, saying, "A corpse has no value for us. They can remove it whenever they like."

(The Excellent Exemplar - Muḥammad, Chaudharī Muḥammad Ẓafrullā Khān)

Thus, despite the pitiful condition of the Muslims the *Quraish* were unable to defeat the Muslims. They were disheartened and left for Mecca on foot, leaving behind their heavy armaments.

During the battle, the *Banū Quraiẓah* who had agreed with the Meccans to cut the food and water supply to the Muslims, started to threaten the women and children who were by themselves in the town as all their men had gone to the outskirts of Medina to fight the enemy forces. This had clearly shown that the *Banū Quraiẓah* were traitors and a threat to the Muslims from the inside. When the Muslims returned to Medina, the Holy Prophet[sa] told them to besiege the fort of the *Banū Quraiẓah.* The siege had gone for twenty-five days when the *Banū Quraiẓah* felt that there was no way out except to surrender to the Holy Prophet[sa] and make an agreement with him. The Holy Prophet[sa] told them that they had to accept his decision which would be made based on justice. They refused to accept a decision by the Holy Prophet[sa] and asked the Holy Prophet[sa] to send Abū Lubābah, an *Anṣārī* chief of the *Aus,* a tribe friendly to the Jews. They wanted to consult with him about a possible settlement. The Holy Prophet[sa] sent Abū Lubābah to them. They asked Abū Lubābah if they should lay down their arms and accept the decision of the Holy Prophet[sa]. Abū Lubābah told them that they should do so. However, they ignored Abū Lubābah's advice and refused to accept the Holy Prophet's[sa] award. Instead, they said they would accept the award of an arbiter from their allies, *Aus.* The Holy Prophet[sa] agreed to this and asked *Aus,* "Would you like one of you to be an arbiter between *Banū Quraiẓah* and me?" *Aus* replied, "Yes." The Holy Prophet[sa] said, "Then ask *Banū Quraiẓah* to choose one of you as an arbiter between themselves and me." The *Banū Quraiẓah* picked Sa‘d bin Mu‘ādh as an arbiter. They said that they would agree to the punishment proposed by Sa‘d bin Mu‘ādh. The Holy Prophet[sa] accepted their demand and asked Sa‘d bin Mu‘ādh to give his award on the Jewish breach of faith. Sa‘d bin Mu‘ādh got an agreement signed by both parties that they will be bound to accept his decision. The people of the *Aus* tribe presented the case of *Banū Quraiẓah* to Sa‘d bin Mu‘ādh and pleaded for permission for the same that was permitted to *Khazraj* earlier. After deliberations Sa‘d bin Mu‘ādh rendered his decision which was in accordance with the Jewish law in such cases (Deut. 20:10-18) and read it to the parties. His decision was as follows:

"All the fighting men of *Banū Quraiẓah* will be put to death and all their women and children will be made captives."

It was a terrible sentence. However, the Jews had brought it upon themselves. First by their treachery, next by their resistance to the Muslims and finally by preferring the judgement of Sa'd bin Mu'ādh by the application of their own religious law to their offense rather than throwing themselves upon the well-established mercy of the Holy Prophet[sa]. According to the teachings of the Bible, if the Jews had won and the Holy Prophet[sa] had lost, all Muslims - men, women and children - would have been put to death.

A dispute arose among the Jews. Some of them began to say that their people had really gone back on their agreement with the Muslims. The behavior of the Muslims, on the other hand, showed that they were true and honest and that their religion also was true. Those who thought in this way joined Islām. It was the moral duty of the Muslims to forgive men like these. Before being put to death, the men of the *Banū Quraiẓah* were offered to accept Islām, with an open mind. Thus, those who accepted Islām avoided their punishment for treason. Only four of them accepted Islām and they were spared. The rest of them refused and were put to death according to the decision of Sa'd bin Mu'ādh, the implementation of which was binding for both parties. The enemy was unsuccessful in its mission and thus was badly defeated and demoralized.

The Jews and other critics of Islām often refer to this incident and criticize the Holy Prophet[sa] that the treatment given to *Banū Quraiẓah* was unjust and cruel. They should consider the incident taking into consideration the following:

1. The Muslims were exposed to an attack by a well-equipped and huge fighting force. The *Banū Quraiẓah* had an agreement with the Muslims not to collaborate with the enemies of the Muslims. Based on this agreement Muslims

felt safe from the side where the *Banū Quraiẓah* lived and had sent all the fighting force to face the enemy. The collaboration of the *Banū Quraiẓah* with the Meccans was a treason. The Holy Prophet[sa] himself under the treaty could have punished the *Banū Quraiẓah* for their treason and offered to set the punishment.

2. However, the *Banū Quraiẓah* did not accept that a decision made by the Holy Prophet[sa] would have been based on justice and mercy. This was a mistake made by the *Banū Quraiẓah* which ultimately resulted in their severe punishment.

3. The decision to punish them by putting them to death was made by a person whom they themselves had picked as an arbiter and the decision was made according to the Jewish Law (Torah).

4. The arbiter had made both parties to sign that his decision will be final and accepted by both parties. Accordingly, the Holy Prophet[sa] was bound by the agreement to accept and implement the decision of the arbiter.

5. They were given the chance to accept Islām and avoid the punishment. Some of them did accept the offer and were spared. Only those who did not accept this offer were put to death according to the decision of the arbiter which they had appointed themselves.

A tradition about the incident is as follows:

Ḥaḍrat Ibn 'Umar relates, "*Banū Naḍīr* and *Banū Quraiẓah* fought against the Holy Prophet[sa] (violating their peace treaty). So the Holy Prophet[sa] exiled *Banū Naḍīr* and allowed *Banū Quraiẓah* to remain in their places (in Medina) taking nothing from them till they fought (again). He then killed their men and distributed their women, children and property among the Muslims, but some of them came to the Holy Prophet[sa] and he granted them safety, and they embraced Islām. He exiled all the Jews from Medina. They were the Jews of *Banū Qainuqā'*; the tribe of 'Abdullāh bin Salām and the Jews of *Banū Ḥāritha* and all of the other Jews."

(Ṣaḥīḥ Bukhārī, Kitāb al-Maghāzī, Bāb Ḥadīth Banū Naḍīr wa Ghadrihim bi Rasūlillah[sa]*)*

Until the expulsion of *Banū Naḍīr* from Medina, a Jew did all the correspondence for the Holy Prophet[sa] as he could write letters in Hebrew, Syriac and Arabic. When *Banū Naḍīr* and *Banū Quraiẓah* fought against the Holy Prophet[sa] (violating their peace treaty) the Holy Prophet[sa] no longer trusted a non-Muslim to write letters for him. Accordingly, the Holy Prophet[sa] told Ḥaḍrat Zaid bin Thābit[ra] to learn the Hebrew and Syriac languages and assigned him the job of writing letters for him. This is stated in the following tradition:

Ḥaḍrat Zaid bin Thābit[ra] relates that the Holy Prophet[sa] told him to learn the Syriac language.

Another version is that the Holy Prophet[sa] told him to learn the language which the Jews use for correspondence, as he had no confidence in what the Jews said or wrote about him. Ḥaḍrat Zaid bin Thābit[ra] further relates that within fifteen days he learned to read and write the Syriac language. After this, whenever the Holy Prophet[sa] needed to write anything to the Jews he dictated it to me and whenever he received any correspondence from the Jews, he read it to him.

(Jāmi' Tirmidhī, Abwābul Adab, Bāb mā jā'a fī ta'līmul siryāniyyah)

9

Ḥudaibiyyah Pact (*Ṣulḥ Ḥudaibiyyah*)

The Holy Prophet[sa] saw in a dream that he along with his Companions[ra] was performing the *Ṭawāf* of the Holy *Ka'bah.* Accordingly, in the sixth year of *Hijrah,* the Holy Prophet[sa] announced his intention to perform *'Umrah.* The Muslims were happy and enthusiastic to go to Mecca to perform *'Umrah.* The Holy Prophet[sa] left for Mecca with 1,400 of his Companions[ra]. They were strictly told not to carry any kind of weapons except their swords as they were going for *'Umrah.* The *Quraish* of Mecca did not want the Muslims to enter Mecca. They decided to stop the Muslims from entering Mecca with the use of force. Their top generals, Khālid bin Walīd and 'Ikrimah had prepared their army and were ready to stop the Holy Prophet[sa] and his Companions[ra] from entering Mecca. The Muslim caravan continued to travel towards Mecca. When the Muslims reached a place called *Ḥudaibiyyah,* they stopped to determine the mood and intentions of the Meccans. Soon they found out that Meccans were ready to fight to stop them from entering Mecca.

Envoys were sent by each side to the other side. Muslim envoys made it crystal clear to the *Quraish* that they have come to perform *'Umrah.* However, the *Quraish* mistreated the Muslim envoy and threatened to attack the Muslims. They were in no mood to allow the Muslims to enter Mecca even for *'Umrah.* They made it a matter of pride for themselves while the Muslims considered the refusal to enter Mecca by the *Quraish* humiliation. The Muslims became testy as they thought they could teach a lesson to the *Quraish.* However, they were prohibited to enter Mecca with force, by the Holy Prophet[sa], and they were obedient to the Holy Prophet[sa].

Budail bin Warqā' of the *Khuzā'* tribe conveyed the message of the Holy Prophet[sa] to the *Quraish* that they had come to perform *'Umrah* and not to have a fight with Meccans. The *Quraish* sent 'Urwah to the Holy Prophet[sa] with the message that under no circumstances would they let them enter Mecca. 'Urwah conveyed the message to the Holy Prophet[sa]. Upon returning to Mecca he told the *Quraish* leaders that he had seen the courts of Heraclius, Chosroes and *Najjāshī*, but nowhere seen such obedience to a leader as he had seen in the court of Muḥammad. When he talks there is complete silence and when he is performing *wuḍū'* his Companions[ra] do not let the water fall on the ground. Rather, they collect the water in their hands and rub it on their hands and face.

The Oath of Riḍwān *(Bai'at-e-Riḍwān)*

Since nothing was decided during 'Urwah's visit, the Holy Prophet[sa] sent Ḥaḍrat Kharāsh bin Umayyah to the *Quraish*. The *Quraish*, in anger, killed the mount of Kharāsh bin Umayyah and tried to kill him also. However, he was able to escape from the place and return safely. Then, the Holy Prophet[sa] sent Ḥaḍrat 'Uthmān with a message to the *Quraish*. The *Quraish* detained him. Meanwhile the rumor spread in the area that Ḥaḍrat 'Uthmān had been killed by the *Quraish*. When this news reached the Holy Prophet[sa] he said that they must take revenge of 'Uthmān's death. At that time, the Holy Prophet[sa] took an oath of allegiance under an acacia tree and this oath is called the "*Bai'at-e-Riḍwān* (Oath of *Riḍwān*)".

The *Quraish* of Mecca after gathering information about the strength of the Muslim caravan had come to the conclusion that the Muslims had no other intention to come to Mecca than to perform *'Umrah*. The *Quraish* sent Suhail bin 'Amr as their envoy to talk with the Holy Prophet[sa]. The Holy Prophet[sa] asked Ḥaḍrat 'Alī[ra] to write an agreement with Suhail. When Ḥaḍrat 'Alī[ra] started to write the agreement and wrote,

'In the name of Allāh, the Gracious, the Merciful', Suhail bin 'Amr objected to it and siad that instead of it '*bi ismkallahum*' should be written. The Holy Prophet[sa] told Ḥaḍrat 'Alī[ra] to write as suggested by Suhail. Then, with the name, Muḥammad', Ḥaḍrat 'Alī[ra] wrote the 'Messenger of Allāh'. Again Suhail objected to it and insisted that as is the custom in Arabs the name of the father should be written with 'Muḥammad' instead of the 'Messenger of Allāh'. The Holy Prophet[sa] said, "By Allāh! I am the Prophet of God. However, write as Suhail desires." Ḥaḍrat 'Alī[ra] showed hesitance to delete the word '*Rasūlullāh*'. At this the Holy Prophet[sa] asked Ḥaḍrat 'Alī[ra] to point to him where the word, '*Rasūlullāh*' is written so that he could erase it. Ḥaḍrat 'Alī[ra] obliged and the Holy Prophet[sa] himself erased the word, '*Rasūlullāh*' in the written agreement.

After negotiations an agreement was signed between the two parties which was acceptable to both and it is called the 'Pact of *Ḥudaibiyyah*'. The conditions laid down in the agreement were as follows:

In the name of Allāh. These are the conditions of peace between Muḥammad, son of 'Abdullāh and Suhail ibn 'Amr, the envoy of Mecca. There will be no fighting for ten years. Anyone who wishes to join Muḥammad and to enter into any agreement with him is free to do so. Anyone who wishes to join the *Quraish* and to enter into an agreement with them is also free to do so. A young man, or one whose father is alive, if he goes to Muḥammad without permission from his father or guardian, will be returned to his father or guardian. But should anyone go to the *Quraish*, he will not be returned. This year Muḥammad will go back without entering Mecca. But next year he and his followers can enter Mecca, spend three days and perform the circuit. During these three days the *Quraish* will withdraw to the surrounding hills. When Muḥammad and his followers enter Mecca, they will be unarmed except for the sheathed swords which wayfarers in Arabia always have with them.

(The Life of Muḥammad[sa]*, A Translation of Ibn Isḥāq's Sīrat Rasūlullāh*[sa]*, p.504, A. Guillaume,, Oxford University Press,Reprinted in Pakistan, 2004)*

Thus, the salient features of the agreemet were:

1. The Muslims will not enter Mecca this year.

2. The Muslims can enter Mecca next year. However, they will go back to Medina after three days' stay in Mecca.

3. The Meccans taking refuge with the Holy Prophet[sa] would be handed over to the *Quraish*, but the Muslims taking refuge in Mecca would not be handed over to the Muslims.

4. There will be peace between the two parties for ten years. The Muslims could go to Mecca and Ṭā'if and the *Quraish* could go to Syria through the Muslim areas.

5. Each party will not take part if there is a war between one of the parties and a third party.

6. Any tribe wishing to sign an agreement with any of the two parties (Muslims and *Quraish*) could do so.

(As-Sīratun Nabawiyyah libne Hishām, Vol. 2, p.180)

At the time this agreement was being written, Ḥaḍrat Abū Jandal, the son of Suhail who was in chains and wounded somehow reached the Holy Prophet[sa]. The Holy Prophet[sa] told Suhail to let Abū Jandal stay with him. However, Suhail did not agree. The Muslims felt real pain seeing the situation of Abū Jandal. The Holy Prophet[sa] said to Abū Jandal, "Be patient, God Almighty will certainly make a way for you and others who are being mistreated to come to us." Now an agreement has been signed and I cannot disregard the agreement. Thus, Abū Jandal who was in chains and wounded was returned to the *Quraish.*

The terms and conditions of the agreement appeared to be unfavorable to the Muslims. Initially, the Muslims were not happy with the terms and conditions of the agreement as it appeared to them a one-sided agreement. However, in the long run the terms and conditions turned out to be good for the Muslims. God Almighty gave them the glad tiding about the agreement:

إِنَّا فَتَحْنَا لَكَ فَتْحًا مُّبِينًا ۙ

innā fataḥnā laka fatḥammubīnā

Verily, We have granted you a clear victory. (48:2)

(Ṣaḥīḥ Bukhārī, Kitābul Maghāzī, Bāb Ghazwahtil Ḥudaibiyyah wa Qaulillāh Ta.'ālā)

In fact, the agreement was a victory for the Muslims as it gave them the opportunity to communicate with the other party and live a little at ease due to the decrease in tension between the two parties. Meccans now could come to Medina which provided the opportunity for the Muslims to convey the message of Islām to them. In fact, the number of Meccans accepting Islām after the pact increased dramatically and Meccans of great fame such as, Khālid bin Walīd[ra] and 'Amr bin 'Āṣ[ra] accepted Islām during this time. It also helped the Muslims in Mecca to escape to Medina when the extradition clause of the agreement was abolished later on.

After signing the agreement with the *Quraish*, the Holy Prophet[sa] told the Companions[ra] to sacrifice their animals at *Ḥudaibiyyah.* However, the Companions[ra] were so heart-broken that no one got up to sacrifice his animal. The Holy Prophet[sa] came back to his tent and told about the incident to Ḥaḍrat Ummi Salamah[ra] who was accompanying the Holy Prophet[sa]. Ḥaḍrat Ummi Salamah[ra] was a very intelligent lady. She told the Holy Prophet[sa] that he should go out and sacrifice his animal, remove *Iḥrām* and get his head shaved. When the Holy Prophet[sa] sacrificed his animal the Muslims rushed to sacrifice their animals in such a hurry that it was worried that they may not accidentally hurt each other. The Companions[ra] after performing the sacrifice removed their *Iḥrām* and shaved their head.

After the signing of the *Ḥudaibiyyah* pact, the Muslims started to travel to Mecca which attracted many good-natured people in Mecca towards Islām and they accepted Islām. The notable amongst them were Ḥaḍrat Khālid bin Walīd and Ḥaḍrat 'Amr bin 'Āṣ. Sometime after the *Ḥudaibiyyah* agreement, a strange incident took place which resulted in the removal of the clause in the agreement that the Muslims leaving Mecca for Medina must be returned to Mecca. What happened was that Ḥaḍrat 'Utbah bin Usaid[ra] ran away from Mecca and reached Medina. The *Quraish* sent two men to the Holy Prophet[sa] to ask for the return of 'Utbah bin Usaid[ra] fulfilling one of the clauses of the agreement. The Holy Prophet[sa] followed the agreement and gave the custody of Ḥaḍrat 'Utbah[ra] to the two *Quraish* who had come from Mecca to take him back. When the three of them reached a place called, *Dhul Ḥulaifah*, Ḥaḍrat 'Utbah[ra] killed one of the *Quraish* who were taking him back to Mecca. The other got scared and ran away, leaving Ḥaḍrat 'Utbah[ra] free to live wherever he wanted. Ḥaḍrat 'Utbah[ra] decided not to go to Medina and started to live close to *Dhumarwah* near the sea. When the other Muslims who were being mistreated in Mecca came to know about the place where Ḥaḍrat 'Utbah[ra] had gone to live, they also started to come and settle there. This process continued and when a large number of Muslims settled there they started to attack the business caravans of the *Quraish* who had to pass through the area to go to Syria for business. Since the *Quraish's* survival totally depended upon business and they were having difficulties in travelling to Syria for business, they wrote to the Holy Prophet[sa] to abolish the clause in the agreement which prohibits the Muslims of Mecca from going to Medina. Anyone could go and live in Medina. When the Muslims in Mecca came to know about the removal of the clause concerning travel to Medina they migrated to Medina in large numbers which included Abū Jandal and settled there.

Ghazwah Dhī Qarad (Ghazwah Ghābah)

Ghābah is a valley having many springs about five miles from

Medina towards Syria. Since the battle started at Ghābah and ended at Dhī Qarad the battle is known as the *Ghazwah Dhī Qarad* and *Ghazwah Ghābah.* The battle started soon after the Holy Prophet's[sa] return to Medina after *Ṣulḥ Ḥudaibiyyah.* The background of this battle is as follows:

Some camels belonging to the Holy Prophet[sa] used to graze in the Ghābah area under the supervision of Ḥaḍrat Abū Dharr Ghaffārī[ra]. One night, 'Uyainah bin Ḥiṣn, the chief of *Banū Fazārah*, a branch of the tribes of Ghaṭafān, attacked with 40 of his colleagues to steel the camels. In the attack the son of Ḥaḍrat Abū Dharr Ghaffārī[ra] was martyred while the wife of Ḥaḍrat Abū Dharr Ghaffārī[ra] was captured by the enemy. However, Ḥaḍrat Abū Dharr Ghaffārī[ra] was successful in escaping from the attack. The attackers rounded up all the camels and began moving them towards their homeland. In the morning, Ḥaḍrat Salamah bin al-Akwa' who was on surveillance duty, by chance, reached the area and saw that the camels of the Holy Prophet[sa] were being stolen. Rabāḥ[ra], the servant of the Holy Prophet[sa] was also riding with Ḥaḍrat Salamah bin al-Akwa'[ra]. Ḥaḍrat Salamah bin al-Akwa'[ra] sent Rabāh[ra] to the Holy Prophet[sa] to inform him that his camels have been stolen by Fazārī dacoits, while he himself followed the Fazārī dacoits. As soon as the Holy Prophet[ra] learned about the incident he called his Companions[ra] to come to him with their military gears. As soon as the Companions[ra] heard the announcement they immediately gathered close to the Holy Prophet[sa]. The Holy Prophet[sa] appointed Ḥaḍrat Sa'd bin Zaid[ra] as commander of the force. Soon the Companions[ra] from all around the area started to gether there. The Holy Prophet[sa] appointed Ḥaḍrat Ibn Ummi Maktūm[ra] as *Amīr* (in-charge) of Medina and left three hundred fighters in Medina underr the command of Ḥaḍrat Sa'd bin 'Ubādah[ra] for the protection of the civilian residents of Medina.

Ḥaḍrat Salamah bin al-Akwa'[ra] who was a brave fighter with extraordinary running ability pursued the Fazārī dacoits and attacked them so fiercely and with such confidence that the dacoits became helpless against his attacks. He kept on attacking the dacoits and single-handedly was able to get all the camels stolen by the dacoits freed. Thus he kept the enemy bewildered and at bay till he saw the Holy Prophet[sa] and his Companions[ra] approaching near to him. Then the Holy Prophet[sa] sent an advance party of eight fighters to attack the enemy. One of them, Ḥaḍrat Maḥraz bin Naḍlah[ra], reached close to Abdur Raḥmān, the son of 'Uyainah bin Ḥiṣn and seriously injured his horse. However, Abdur Raḥmān was able to injure Ḥaḍrat Maḥraz bin Naḍlah[ra] with his spear. The injury became fatal for him. In the meantime, Ḥaḍrat Abū Qatādah[ra] attacked Abdur Raḥmān and killed him and then he also killed Ḥabīb bin 'Uyainah. While the Holy Prophet[sa] along with his fighters was pursuing the enemy, Ḥaḍrat Salamah bin al-Akwa'[ra] went so far away in pursuit of the dacoits that he became invisible to the Muslim force. Ḥaḍrat Salamah bin al-Akwa'[ra] did not let the dacoits rest or eat and drink throughout his pursuit. They became so disorganized and disoriented with continuous relentless pursuit of them by Ḥaḍrat Salamah bin al-Akwa'[ra] that they ran away and left their horses behind. Ḥaḍrat Salamah bin al-Akwa'[ra] brought these horses to the Holy Prophet[sa].

After the defeat of the enemy, the Holy Prophet[sa] and his Companions[ra] arrived at the spring in the valley of *Dhī Qarad* where his camels used to graze. He had collected most of his camels after getting them freed from the dacoits. Moreover, all the war booty the enemy had left was also collected and brought here. Ḥaḍrat Bilāl[ra] slaughtered a camel and the meat was used to arrange dinner for the Holy Prophet[sa] and his Companions[ra].

(Ṣaḥīḥ Muslim, Kitābul Jihād wal-Yusr, Bāb Ghazwah Dhī Qarad)

10

Invitations Sent to Various Rulers to Accept Islām

After the *Ḥudaibiyyah* Pact, the Holy Prophet[sa] sent letters to Heraclius, the Roman Emperor, Chosroes, the king of Persia, Negus, the king of Abyssinia, the ruler of Egypt and other Arab leaders inviting them to accept the message of Islām.

Letter Sent to Heraclius, the Roman Emperor

When Heraclius received the letter of the Holy Prophet[sa] he made an inquiry about the new religion which is stated in the following tradition:

Ḥaḍrat Ibn 'Abbās[ra] relates that Ḥaḍrat Abū Sufyān[ra] stated this to him: "During the days when the *Ḥudaibiyyah* treaty was signed between us and the Holy Prophet[sa], I went on a business trip to Syria. I was still in Syria when a letter from the Holy Prophet[sa] reached Heraclius, the Roman Emperor. The letter was brought by Diḥyah al-Kalbī. When the letter reached Heraclius, he asked his people, 'Is there anyone here from the people of the Arab who claims to be a Prophet?' They said, 'Yes.' Thus, along with the party of *Quraish*, I was also called to see Heraclius. When we arrived in the royal court of Heraclius, we were made to sit facing Heraclius. Heraclius said: 'Is anyone here a near-relative of the Arab who claims to be a Prophet?' Abū Sufyān[ra] said, 'I am his near-relative.' Thus, I was seated right in front of Heraclius, while the rest of the members of the group were seated behind me. Heraclius called an interpreter and told him to tell the people sitting behind me that he will ask Abū Sufyān[ra] about the Arab who has claimed to be a Prophet. If he tells a lie, you let me know through a gesture that he is telling a lie. Abū Sufyān[ra] said, 'By God! If I was not scared that the people, sitting behind me would let Heraclius know that I am telling a lie, I definitely would have told lies. Anyway, Heraclius asked us through his interpreter, 'What is the lineage of your Messenger?' Abū Sufyān[ra] said that he responded, 'He belongs to a very noble family.' Then Heraclius said, 'Has there been any king in his forefathers?' I told him, 'No.' Then he said, 'Did you ever notice him telling a lie before claiming to be a Messenger?' I replied, 'No.' Then he said, 'Did the rich and the powerful accept his claim or the poor?' I replied, 'The poor and the weak have accepted his claim.' Then he asked, 'Are his followers increasing or decreasing in number?' I replied, 'They are increasing.' Then he asked, 'Did anyone renounce his faith after becoming a Muslim, considering it a bad religion?' I replied, 'No.' Then he asked, 'Did you ever fight a battle with him? I told him,'Yes.' He asked, 'What was the result of the battle?' I responded, 'Sometimes they had the upper hand and the other times we had the upper hand. Sometimes we were successful while other times they were successful.' Then he asked, 'Did he ever break an agreement or deal treacherously?' I said, 'Until now he has neither broken an agreement nor has he dealt treacherously. However, we have just entered into a treaty with him, and I don't know how he will behave regarding the treaty.' Abū Sufyān[ra] said, 'By God! Throughout the conversation, except this last statement, I did not get any chance to say anything against the Holy Prophet[sa]. Then he asked, 'Did anyone else make such a claim before him in his people?' I replied, 'No.' The king told his interpreter to tell me the following: 'When I asked you about the lineage of the claimant of the Prophethood, you stated that he belongs to a very noble family. Messengers always belong to noble families. I asked you if there has been a king in his forefathers? You responded no. From this, I concluded that had there been a king in his forefathers, he might be desirous of regaining the kingdom of his forefathers. I asked you about his followers, whether they are rich and powerful? You replied they are weak and poor. In the beginning, always the poor and weak accept the Messengers. I asked you, Did you ever blame him for telling a lie before he claimed to be a Prophet? You said, 'No.' I was convinced that the one who does not tell a lie to the people, how can he tell a lie about God? Then I asked you, Did any one of his followers apostatize after accepting Islām due to disliking Islām? You said, 'No.' This is the case with a true faith. When someone accepts a faith with clarity of mind, it is very difficult for him to turn away from that faith. I asked you, Whether they are increasing or decreasing in number? You said, 'They are increasing in number and also in steadfastness.' This is always the case with true faiths. I asked you, Did you ever fight a battle with him? You said, 'We have fought several battles. Sometimes they had the upper hand in the battle and other times we had the upper hand. Sometimes we were successful while the other times they were successful.' This is the case with the Messengers of God. In the beginning, they went through many trials but ultimately they were triumphant. I asked you, did he ever break an agreement or deal treacherously? You said, 'No.' Such is the high status of the Prophets. They never break an agreement. Then I asked, Has anyone among your people claimed to be a Prophet before him? You said, 'No.' From this, I concluded that since there had not been a Prophet in his people he is not imitating anyone. Abū Sufyān[ra] said that then, Heraclius asked him, 'What did he (i.e., the Holy Prophet[sa]) command you to do?' I said, 'He commanded us to observe Prayer, pay *Zakāt*, strengthen the ties of kinship, tell the truth, be pious and chaste.' Hearing this Heraclius said, 'If everything you have told is true, then definitely he is a Prophet. I was expecting the coming of a Prophet. However, I did not know that the Prophet would be commissioned from among your people. Had the circumstances permitted me, I certainly would have gone to see this Prophet. Had I visited him, I would have washed his feet.

The kingdom of this Prophet will reach the land where I stand.' Abū Sufyān[ra] said, 'Heraclius asked for the letter of the Holy Prophet[sa] in which the following was written: 'I begin with the name of Allāh, the most Gracious, the most Merciful. This letter is from the Prophet of Allāh, Muḥammad[sa], to the king of Rome, Heraclius. Peace be upon him who follows the true guidance. I invite you to accept Islām. Accept Islām and be at peace. If you accept Islām you will have double reward from God. However, if you reject it and do not accept me then you will bear the sins of all the inhabitants of Rome. In the letter the following verse was also written:

قُلْ يٰٓاَهْلَ الْكِتٰبِ تَعَالَوْا اِلٰى كَلِمَةٍ سَوَآءٍۢ بَيْنَنَا وَ بَيْنَكُمْ اَلَّا نَعْبُدَ اِلَّا اللّٰهَ وَ لَا نُشْرِكَ بِهٖ شَيْئًا وَّ لَا يَتَّخِذَ بَعْضُنَا بَعْضًا اَرْبَابًا مِّنْ دُوْنِ اللّٰهِ ؕ فَاِنْ تَوَلَّوْا فَقُوْلُوْا اشْهَدُوْا بِاَنَّا مُسْلِمُوْنَ ۝

qul yā ahlal kitābi ta'ālau ilā kalimatin sawā'im bainanā wa bainakum allā na'budu ilallāha wa lā nushrika bihī shai'añwwa lā yattakhidha ba'ḍunā ba'ḍan arbābammin dūnillāh fa in tawallau faqūlush hadū bi annā muslimūn

Say, 'O People of the Book! come to a word equal between us and you --- that we worship none but Allāh, and that we associate no partner with Him, and that some of us take not others for Lords beside Allāh.' But if they turn away, then say, 'Bear witness that we have submitted *to God.*' (3:65)

When Heraclius finished reading the letter, the people in the court became very agitated and started to speculate widely. Therefore, the king ordered us to leave the court, and we were made to leave the court. After coming out of the court, I said to my Companions[ra], 'Ibn Abī Kabsha has excelled drastically in status. What a high status he has that even the king of Rome fears him.' So

I was convinced that the Holy Prophet[sa] would definitely succeed. Later on, God Almighty made me also accept Islām.' "

(Ṣaḥīḥ Bukhārī, Kitāb Bad'ul Waḥyi ilā rasūlillah[sa]*, Bāb kaifa bad'ul waḥyi ilā rasulillah*[sa]*)*

Ḥaḍrat Imām Ẓuhrī[ra], the narrator of this tradition, relates: "When Heraclius received the letter of the Holy Prophet[sa], he made a thorough inquiry about the situation, and then called his cabinet to the court and said, 'O Leaders of the Nation! If you wish to be successful and rightly-guided, and you wish that your government remains established, then you should accept this Prophet.' After hearing this, the courtiers stampeded toward the doors like wild asses run when they are scared. However, the doors were closed. Heraclius asked them to come back and said, 'I was testing the firmness of your belief in your religion. Now I know how firmly you are attached to your religious beliefs.' Hearing this, all the court members prostrated to the king and became happy with the king.' "

(Ṣaḥīḥ Bukhārī, Kitābut Tafsīr Sūrah Āl-e-'Imrān qul yā ahlal kitābi ta'ālau ilā kalimah)

Letter Sent to the King of Persia

The letter to Chosroes, the king of Iran was sent through Ḥaḍrat 'Abdullāh bin Ḥudhāfa[ra]. The text of the letter was as follows:

"In the name of Allāh, the Gracious, the Merciful. This letter is from Muḥammad, the Messenger of God, to Chosroes, the Chief of Iran. Whoever submits to a perfect guidance, and believes in Allāh, and bears witness that Allāh is One, and has no equal or partner, and that Muḥammad is His Servant and Messenger, on him be peace. O king, under the command of God, I invite you to Islām. For I have been sent by God as His Messenger to all mankind, so that I may warn all living men and complete my Message for all disbelievers. Accept Islām and protect yourself from all afflictions. If you reject this invitation, then the sin of the denial of all your people will rest on your head."

> *(Ibn Sa'd's Al-Ṭabaqāt Al-Kbīr, Vol. 1, p. 360; Tārīkh-i-Ṭabarī, Vol. 2, pp. 295 & 296; Tārīkh-i-Kāmil, Vol. 2, p. 81; Biḥārul Anwār, Vol. 20, p. 389; Tārīkh Al-Khamīs FīiAḥwāl Anfa Nafīs, Vol. 2, p. 34, Ḥusain bin Muḥammad a-Diyār Bakrī)*

At the time of the birth of the Holy Prophet[sa], control over Yemen was exercised by Ethiopia, from across the Red Sea. The year the Holy Prophet[sa] was born (571 AD) Abraha, Ethiopia's Viceroy in Yemen, had led an expedition against Mecca, with the declared intention of destroying the *Ka'bah*.

When news of the advance of Abraha's army came, the Arabian tribes of *Quraish, Kinānah, Khuzā'ah and Hudhayl* joined together to defend the *Ka'bah*. Abraha sent a small contingent towards Mecca. The contingent captured many animals, including two hundred camels belonging to 'Abdul Muṭṭalib.

'Abdul Muṭṭalib, with 'Amr ibn Lu'āba and some other prominent leaders, went to see Abraha. Abraha was informed before hand of the prestige and position of 'Abdul Muṭṭalib. Also the personality of 'Abdul Muṭṭalib was very impressive and awe-inspiring. When he entered Abraha's tent, the latter rose from his throne, warmly welcomed him, and seated him beside him on the carpet. During the conversation, 'Abdul Muṭṭalib requested him to release his camels. Abraha was astonished. He said: "When my eyes fell upon you, I was so impressed by you that had you requested me to withdraw my army and go back to Yemen, I would have granted that request. But now, I have no respect for you. Why? Here I have come to demolish the House which is the religious center of yours and of your forefathers and the foundation of your prestige and respect in Arabia, and you say nothing to save it; instead, you ask me to return your few camels back to you."

'Abdul Muṭṭalib said: "I am the owner of the camels, (therefore, I tried to save them), and this House has its own Owner Who will surely protect it." Abraha was stunned by this reply. He ordered the camels to be released, and the deputation of *Quraish* returned.

On the second day, Abraha issued orders to his army to enter Mecca. 'Abdul Muṭṭalib told the Meccans to leave the city and to seek refuge in the surrounding hills. But he, together with some leading members of the *Quraish*, remained within the precincts of the *Ka'bah*. Abraha sent someone to warn them to vacate the building. When the messenger came, he asked the people who their leader was. All fingers pointed towards 'Abdul Muṭṭalib. He was again invited to go to Abraha where he had a talk with him. When he came out, he was heard saying: "The Owner of this House is its Defender, and I am sure He will save it from the attack of the adversaries and will not dishonor the servants of His House."

Then he, too, went to the summit of the hill, Abū Qubais. Abraha advanced with his army. Seeing the walls of the *Ka'bah*, he ordered its demolition. No sooner had the army reached near the *Ka'bah* when an army of Allāh appeared from the western side. A dark cloud of small birds (known in Arabic as *Abābīl*) overshadowed the entire army of Abraha. The expedition proved an utter failure. Abraha's forces, which included elephants, were struck by a virulent epidemic that destroyed large numbers of them during their encampment in a valley a few miles outside Mecca. The remainder of the group retired in confusion and terror. The event is the subject matter of a brief Chapter in the Holy Qur'ān:

بِسْمِ اللّٰهِ الرَّحْمٰنِ الرَّحِيْمِ

اَلَمْ تَرَ كَيْفَ فَعَلَ رَبُّكَ بِاَصْحٰبِ الْفِيْلِ ۝ اَلَمْ يَجْعَلْ كَيْدَهُمْ

فِيْ تَضْلِيْلٍ ۝ وَّ اَرْسَلَ عَلَيْهِمْ طَيْرًا اَبَابِيْلَ ۝ تَرْمِيْهِمْ بِحِجَارَةٍ مِّنْ سِجِّيْلٍ ۝ فَجَعَلَهُمْ كَعَصْفٍ مَّاْكُوْلٍ ۝

alam tara kaifa fa'ala rabbuka bi aṣḥābil fīl alam yaj'al kaidahum fī taḍlīliñwwa arsala 'alaihim ṭairan abābīl tarmīhim bi ḥijāratimmin sijjīl faja'alahum ka'aṣfimma'kūl

Have you not seen how your Lord dealt with the People of Elephant (Abraha, the Christian viceroy in Yemen of the king of Abyssinia)? Did He not cause their plan to miscarry? And He sent against them swarms of birds. *Which ate their carrion*, striking them against stones of clay. And *thus* made them like broken straw, eaten up. (105:1-6)

Some years later Yemen appears to have passed under the sovereignty of Iran. When the king of Iran received the letter of the Holy Prophet[sa] and noticed that the letter starts with the name of Allāh and the name of the Holy Prophet[sa] instead of the name of the king which was the Iranian custom to address the king, he was enraged. He considered this way of addressing an insult to him and tore down the letter into pieces. Furthermore, he ordered Bādhān, the Governor of Yemen to imprison this claimant of the new religion and present to him in his court. Bādhān sent his two messengers to Medina who told the Holy Prophet[sa] that Chosroes has asked him to come to his court. The Holy Prophet[sa] told them to wait for a short while for his response. After a couple of days the Holy Prophet[sa] told the emissaries of the Governor of Yemen to go back as his Lord has killed their lord. When the representatives of the Governor of Yemen returned to him they received the news that Sherawiyyah had assassinated his father Chosroes Pervaiz, the king of Persia and has cancelled all the decrees and orders issued by his father.

(Al-Ṭabarī, Vol. 3, pp. 1583-1584; Fatḥ Al-Bārī, 8/127,128)

Letter Sent to the Negus, the King of Abyssinia

The letter to Negus, the king of Abyssinia (Aṣḥama ibn Abjar), was carried by Ḥaḍrat 'Amr bin Umayya al-Ḍamrī[ra]. It stated:

"In the name of Allāh, the Gracious, the Merciful, Muḥammad, the Messenger of God, writes to the Negus, king of Abyssinia. O king, peace of God be upon you. I praise before you the One and Only God. None else is worthy of worship. He is the king of kings, the source of all excellences, free from all defects, He provides peace to all His servants and protects His creatures. I bear witness that Jesus, son of Mary was a Messenger of God, who came in fulfillment of promises made to Mary by God. Mary had consecrated her life to God. I invite you to join with me in attaching ourselves to the One and Only God and in obeying Him. I invite you also to follow me and believe in the God Who has sent me. I am His Messenger. I invite you and your armies to join the faith of the Almighty God. I discharge my duty hereby. I have delivered to you the Message of God, and made clear to you the meaning of this Message. I have done so in all sincerity and I trust you will value the sincerity which has prompted this message. He who obeys the guidance of God becomes heir to the blessings of God."

(Sīrah-i-Ḥalabī, Vol. 3, p. 279; Ibn Sa'd's Al-Ṭabaqāt Al-Kabīr, Vol. 1, p.259; Zurqānī, Sharḥ Mawāhib al-Ladunniyya, Vol. 3, pp. 343-344)

When Negus, the king of Abyssinia, received the letter of the Holy Prophet[sa], he treated the letter with great respect. He held it up to his eyes, descended from the throne and ordered an ivory box for it. Then he deposited it in the box and said, "While this letter is safe, my kingdom is safe." What he said proved true. For one thousand years Muslim armies were out on their career of conquest. They went in all directions, and passed by Abyssinia on all sides, but they did not touch this small kingdom of the Negus;

and this, out of regard for two memorable acts of the Negus: the protection he afforded the refugees of early Islām and the reverence he showed to the Prophet's[sa] letter.

The day the Negus died God Almighty revealed to the Holy Prophet[sa] about his death. The Holy Prophet[sa] informed his Companions[ra] about the demise of the Negus. He said, "Today a pious person has died.

اَسْتَغْفِرُوْا لِاَخِيْكُمْ

astaghfirū li akhīkum

Pray for forgiveness of your brother."

Then the Holy Prophet[sa] told his Companions[ra] to gather at the place of Prayer, where he led funeral Prayer in absentia for the Negus. This was for the first time that a funeral Prayer in absentia was offered for anyone in Islām. The Holy Prophet[sa] exclaimed four times: "Allāh is the Greatest" for An-Najāshī's funeral Prayer.

(Ṣaḥīḥ Bukhārī, Kitābul Janāi'z, Bāb At-Takbīr 'alal janāzati arba'an; Masnad aṣ-Ṣaḥābah fil kutubatissa'ata, Vol. 2, p. 110; Usdul Ghābah fi Ma'rafatiṣ-Ṣaḥābah, Vol. 1, p. 252, Ibn Athīr)

Letter Sent to Muqawqis, the King of Egypt

The letter to Muqawqis was carried by Ḥaḍrat Ḥāṭib bin Abī Balta'ah[ra]. The text of this letter was exactly the same as that to the Roman Emperor. The letter to the Roman Emperor said that the sin of the denial of the Roman subjects would he on his head. The letter to the Muqawqis said that the sin of the denial of the Copts would be on the head of the ruler. The text of the letter was as follows:

"In the name of Allāh, the Gracious, the Merciful. This letter is from Muḥammad, the Messenger of Allāh, to Muqawqis the Chief of the Copts. Peace be upon him who follows the path of rectitude. I invite you to accept the Message of Islām. Believe and you will be saved and your reward will be twofold. If you disbelieved, the sin of the denial of the Copts will also be on your head. Say, "O People of the Book come to a word equal between us and you that we worship none but Allāh, and that we associate no partner with Him, and that some of us take not others for lords beside Allāh. But if they turn away, then say, 'Bear witness that we have submitted to God."

(As-Sīratul Ḥalabiyyah, Vol. 3, p. 275, 'Alī bin Burhānuddīn al-Ḥilmī al-Shāfi'; Durr-i-Manthūr, Vol. 1, p.40; A'ayan--Shi'ah, Vol. 1, p. 142)

When Ḥaḍrat Ḥāṭib[ra] reached Egypt, he did not find Muqawqis in the capital. Ḥaḍrat Ḥāṭib[ra] followed him to Alexandria, where he was holding court near the sea. The king paid a tribute to Ḥaḍrat Ḥāṭib[ra] and said he was a wise envoy of a wise man. He had answered well the questions put to him. Ḥaḍrat Ḥāṭib[ra] advised Muqawqis: "Show no pride. Believe in this Prophet of God. Now that a Prophet has appeared in your time it is your duty to believe in him and follow him."

Upon hearing this, Muqawqis sent for an ivory box and placed the letter of the Holy Prophet[sa] in it, sealed it and handed it over to a servant girl for safekeeping. He also wrote a letter in reply to the Holy Prophet[sa]. The text of this letter is as follows:

"In the name of Allāh, the Gracious, the Merciful. From Muqawqis, king of the Copts, to Muḥammad, son of 'Abdullāh. Peace be on you. After this, I say that I have read your letter and pondered over its contents and over the beliefs to which you invite mc. I am aware that the Hebrew Prophets have foretold the advent of a Prophet in our time. But I thought he was going to appear in Syria. I have received your envoy, and made a present of one thousand *Dinars* to him and I sent two Egyptian girls as a present to you. My people, the Copts, hold these girls in great esteem. One of them is Mariah and the other Sīrīn. I also send you twenty garments made of Egyptian linen of high quality. I also send you a mule for riding. In the end I pray again that you may have peace from God."

(Al-Ṭabaqāt Al-Kabīr, Vol. I, p.260; Tārīkh Al-Rusul wal Malūk, Abū Ja'far Muḥammad bin Jarīr al-Ṭabarī)

Although, the king of Egypt did not accept Islām, however, he treated the message and the messenger of the Holy Prophet[sa] with great respect. He sent several gifts to the Holy Prophet[sa] which included two noble Christian sisters, Mariah al-Qibṭiyyah[ra] who became the wife of the Holy Prophet[sa] and Sīrīn[ra] who was married to the famous poet, Ḥaḍrat Ḥassān bin Thābit[ra].

(Ibn Kathīr, al-Bidāya, Vol. 7, p. 272; Zurqānī, Sharḥ Mawāhib al-Ladunniyya, Vol. 5, p. 33; Narrative of Ḥaḍrat Mariah al-Qibtiyyah; Usdul Ghāba, Narrative of Ḥaḍrat Mariah and Sīrīn)

Letters Sent to Various Tribal Chiefs

The Holy Prophet[sa] sent a letter to Mundhir bin Sāwā al-'Abdī, Chief of Baḥrain. This letter was carried by 'Ala ibn Ḥaḍramī. The text of this letter has been lost. When it reached this Chief, he believed, and wrote back to the Holy Prophet[sa] saying that he and many of his friends and followers had decided to join Islām. Some, however, had decided to stay outside. He also said that there were some Jews and Magians living under him. What was he supposed to do about them? The Holy Prophet[sa] wrote again to this Chief:

"I am glad at your acceptance of Islām. Your duty is to obey the delegates and messengers whom I should send to you. Whoever obeys them, obeys me. The messenger who took my letter to you praised you to me, and assured me of the sincerity of your belief. I have prayed to God for your people. Try, therefore, to teach them the ways and practices of Islām. Protect their property. Do not let anyone have more than four wives. The sins of the past are forgiven. As long as you are good and virtuous you will continue to rule over your people. As for the Jews and Magians, they have only to pay a tax. Do not, therefore, make any other demands on them. As for the general population, those who do not have land enough to maintain them should have four *Dirhams* each, and some cloth to wear."

(Zurqānī, Sharḥ Sharḥ Mawāhib al-Ladunniyya, Vol. 5, pp. 34,-36 & 66; Zād Al-Ma'ad, Vol. 3, pp. 61-62).

The Holy Prophet[sa] also wrote to the king of Oman, the Chief of *Yamāmah*, the king of *Ghassān*, the Chief of *Banī Nahd*, a tribe of Yemen, the Chief of *Hamdān*, another tribe of Yemen, the Chief of *Banī 'Alīm* and the Chief of the *Ḥaḍramī* tribe. Most of them became Muslims.

When the Arab chiefs received the letters of the Holy Prophet[sa] inviting them to Islām, some of them accepted Islām at once. Others treated the letters respectfully, but did not accept Islām. Still some treated the letter with ordinary courtesy and others showed contempt and pride.

It had been agreed upon by the Meccan leaders in the *Ḥudaibiyyah* Pact that the Holy Prophet[sa] could come to Mecca for the circuits a year after the signing of the pact. Accordingly, the Holy Prophet[sa] left for Mecca with his 2,000 Companions[ra]. When the party reached *Marr al-Zahrān*, the Holy Prophet[sa] ordered his followers to remove their armaments which were collected in one place. This was in conformity with the agreement signed at *Ḥudaibiyyah*. The Holy Prophet[sa] and his Companions[ra] entered the Sacred Place carrying just sheathed swords which was a custom in those days. They were overjoyed and thankful to God Almighty for the chance to perform circuits of the *Ka'bah* peacefully after seven years. The Muslims were full of zeal. The Meccans came out of their houses and went on top of the hills to see the Muslims. They were dumbfounded to see the party of Muslims entering Mecca. After circuiting the *Ka'bah* and running between the hills of *Ṣafā* and *Marwah*, the Holy Prophet[sa] and his Companions[ra] stayed in Mecca for three days. On the fourth day, the Holy Prophet[sa] asked his followers to start leaving Mecca to return to Medina. This historic trip of the Holy Prophet[sa] and his Companions[ra] to Mecca was a fulfillment of the vision of the Holy Prophet[sa]:

Soon after the circuits of the *Ka'bah*, two renowned generals of the Meccan army joined Islām. One was, Ḥaḍrat Khālid bin Walīd[ra] under whose leadership country after country was added to the Muslim Empire, and the other was Ḥaḍrat 'Amr bin al-'Āṣ[ra], the conquerer of Egypt.

11

The Jews of Medina

At the time, the Muslims and the Holy Prophet[sa] migrated to Medina, three powerful tribes of Jews were living in Medina: *Banū Naḍīr*, *Banū Quraiẓah* and *Banū Qainuqā'*. The Jews were not happy with the migration of the Muslims to Medina who were now dominating the city. The Jews of Medina were always plotting and looking for the chances to harm the believers in Islām and to destroy the new religion. With the arrival of the Holy Prophet[sa] the balance of power had shifted towards the Muslims. The Holy Prophet[sa] made treaties with the Jews granting them security and peace so that both communities could live together peacefully and in harmoniously. However, the Jews were not happy seeing the new religion progressing rapidly and were particularly annoyed when the Muslims returned to Mecca victorious. This led to an increase in their animosity towards the Muslims and they started to plot feverishly against the Holy Prophet[sa] and the Muslim community. The Jews of Medina colluded with the hypocrites in Medina and with the infidels of Mecca against the Muslims. The people of the tribe of *Banū Naḍīr* were always plotting to kill the Holy Prophet[sa].

Once, the Holy Prophet[sa] in the company of few of his Companions[ra] went to the Jewish tribe of *Banū Naḍīr* to discuss payment of blood money for the killing of two men mistakenly, who belonged to the *Banū 'Āmir*. The people of *Banū Naḍīr* received the Holy Prophet[sa] cordially. However, at the same time, they planned to kill him by throwing a large rock at his head while he was sitting to discuss with them the matter of the blood money. The Holy Prophet[sa] sat with them for a short period of time and then suddenly left.

The Holy Prophet[sa] had come to know about their secret plan which they were concealing under the guile of showing extraordinary hospitality to the Holy Prophet[sa] and his Companions[ra]. The *Banū Naḍīr* were shocked to find out that the Holy Prophet[sa] knew of their secret plans. The Holy Prophet[sa] sent a message to *Banū Naḍīr* that they must leave the town within ten days which is the punishment for their breaking the covenant by planning to kill him. However, their leader, Ḥuyyay bin Akhṭab responded that they would not leave their houses and possessions. When the ultimatum of ten days passed without any action taken by the *Banū Naḍīr* with regards to leaving the town, the Muslims besieged them. Soon, the *Banū Naḍīr* realized that they could not break the siege and defeat the Muslims. Accordingly, they sent a message to the Holy Prophet[sa] agreeing to surrender and requesting safe-passage to leave. The request was accepted by the Holy Prophet[sa]. Each individual was allowed to carry one camel load of possessions with them. They left for Khaibar where many Jews were already living.

Banū Qainuqā' was one of the three largest Jewish tribes of Medina. Like other tribes they also had signed an agreement with the Muslims which had granted them freedom and security. Despite that they plotted to harm the Muslims. The Holy Prophet[sa] sent a deputation to their leaders reminding them of their obligations under the agreement they had made with the Muslims and told them to stop provoking the Muslims. Instead of accepting the plea of curtailing their annoying activities they behaved more arrogantly. This left no choice for the Holy Prophet[sa] but to meet the challenge head on. Accordingly, the Muslims besieged the fort of *Banū Qainuqā'*. The siege lasted for fifteen days. Then, they surrendered to the Muslims. After their defeat, the Muslims had two options: either to enslave them or to have mercy on them and let them live like before. It was decided that they should be deported without their weapons. When it was announced, they obeyed the order and left Medina and moved to another town.

Fall of Khaibar

With the signing of the treaty of *Ḥudaibiyyah* the south of Medina became relatively safe. However, in the North of Medina there lived powerful Jewish tribes. The Jewish tribes which due to one reason or the other were deported from Medina also had migrated and joined the Jewish tribes living in Khaibar, in the North of Medina. The residents of Khaibar were arrogant and posed a continuous threat to the Muslims. They were continuously inflaming the Christian and the Jewish tribes living in Iraq against the Muslims. There was no way to establish peace with them because whenever an agreement was made with them by the Muslims, they always broke it when they thought to do so advantageous to them. The only alternative left for the Muslims was to fight with them and force them to become submissive. Accordingly, the Holy Prophet[sa] led a force of fifteen hundred men and marched towards Khaibar. They covered a distance of approximately one hundred and fifty miles in three nights. The Jews were holding themselves and their treasure in four different forts. In one of the forts there were 10,000 warriors ready to fight, while in the other forts there were their women, children and treasure. The Holy Prophet[sa] divided his warriors into five divisions and made them face the fort in such a way that it appeared as if a large army was ready to attack and fight. The Muslims concentrated their efforts to defeat the Jews by surrounding the fort where the Jewish warriors were stationed. Fierce fighting took place between the two armies. Fifty Muslim warriors were killed on the first day of the fighting. The Jews also lost a significant number of their warriors including their leader on the first day of fighting. In the next two days, The Muslims made several attempts to break the entrance to the Fort. The forces were sent first under the command of Ḥaḍrat Abū Bakr[ra] and later on under the command of Ḥaḍrat 'Umar[ra]. However, both times the forces were unsuccessful in their mission. Both parties, the Jews and the Muslims, fought bravely for three days. Then, the Holy Prophet[sa] received a revelation that Khaibar will fall at the hands of Ḥaḍrat 'Alī[ra].

Ḥaḍrat Sahl bin Sa'd[ra] narrates that he heard the Holy Prophet[sa] on the day of the Battle of Khaibar saying:

"I will give the flag to a person at whose hands Allāh will grant victory."

So the Companions[ra] of the Holy Prophet[sa] stood up, to see to whom the flag would be given. Everyone wished eagerly that the flag be given to himself. The Holy Prophet[sa] asked for Ḥaḍrat 'Alī[ra]. Someone informed him that he was suffering from an eye disease. The Holy Prophet[sa] asked them to bring Ḥaḍrat 'Alī[ra] to him. The Holy Prophet[sa] rubbed his saliva on Ḥaḍrat 'Alī's[ra] eyes and his eyes were cured immediately as if he never had an eye problem.

(Ṣaḥīḥ Bukhārī, Kitābul Maghāzī, Bāb Ghazwah Khaibar)

So, the Holy Prophet[sa] sent the Muslim warriors under the command of Ḥaḍrat 'Alī[ra] to fight the Jews and told him to keep on fighting till Allāh makes the door of the fort open for him. Ḥaḍrat 'Alī[ra] kept on fighting till the fort was conquered and the Jews of Khaibar were defeated. After their defeat the Jews desired to stay and cultivate the land which was now owned by the Muslims. They explained to the Muslims and convinced them that they had extensive experience in cultivation of the palm trees. Taking into consideration the appeal of the Jews, the Holy Prophet[sa] made an agreement with them according to which they could stay to take care of the palm trees and also they could take half of the harvest. However, they had to leave the place, if due to any reason the Muslims desired that they must leave. The Jews of Fadak and Taymā' did not fight with the Muslims and were granted an agreement similar to the agreement with the Jews of Khaibar. Fadak and Taymā' are the places about which God Almighty has stated in the Holy Qur'ān:

وَ اَوْرَثَكُمْ اَرْضَهُمْ وَ دِيَارَهُمْ وَ اَمْوَالَهُمْ وَ اَرْضًا لَّمْ تَطَئُوْهَا ؕ

wa aurathakum arḍahum wa diyārahum wa amwālahum wa arḍallam taṭa'ūhā

And He made you inherit their land and their houses and their wealth, and a land on which you had never set foot. (33:28)

However, the Jews of the *Wādī al-Qurā* fought with the Muslims and upon their defeat they were also granted a similar agreement. Thus, within three months of the *Ḥudaibiyyah* agreement, the Muslims were able to conquer Khaibar. The conquest of Khaibar made the Jews powerless in the Arabian Peninsula.

In the Battle of Khaibar, it was for the first time ever that women accompanied the warriors in a war. They were assigned the duty of providing drinking water and first aid to the wounded and to look after them.

Peace Agreement With the Inhabitants of Fadak

Fadak was a Jewish town located in Ḥijāz near Khaibar towards Syria from Medina. Like the Jews of Khaibar the Jews of Fadak were also rich and always hatching conspiracies against Islam. When the Holy Prophet[sa] came to know that the Jews of Khaibar in Fadak along with the *Banū Sa'd* tribe were planning to attack Medina, he sent Ḥaḍrat 'Alī[ra] to Fadak with a squadron. Ḥaḍrat 'Alī[ra] made the *Banū Sa'd* run away.

While travelling for the Battle of Khaibar, the Holy Prophet[sa] sent Ḥaḍrat Muḥayyiṣah bin Mas'ūd[ra] to Fadak to convey the message of Islām and that they should agree to live obediently and peacefully under Islām. If they do not accept the proposal then due to their constant conspiracies against Islām we will fight with them just like we are going to fight with the people of Khaibar. However, they did not give importance to the message of the Holy Prophet[sa] and did not even care to respond to the message. Ḥaḍrat Muḥayyiṣah bin Mas'ūd[ra] stayed there for two days. On the third day of his stay when the news of the victory in the Battle of Khaibar reached Fadak, the people of Fadak were terrified. They immediately requested Ḥaḍrat Muḥayyiṣah bin Mas'ūd[ra] to stay a bit longer so that they could consult their leaders regarding their response to the letter. So Ḥaḍrat Muḥayyiṣah bin Mas'ūd[ra] delayed his departure. They decided to send one of their leaders, Nūn bin Yūsha', with Ḥaḍrat Muḥayyiṣah bin Mas'ūd[ra] to present an offer of peace and submission to the Holy Prophet[sa]. After discussion with Nūn bin Yūsha' the Holy Prophet[sa] decided not to fight with the people of Fadak. It was further agreed upon that the people of Fadak would not be expelled from their land and also that they could keep their wealth with them. However, the Muslims would own half of their land and half of the land would remain with the Jews.

(Tārīkh al-Khamīs, Fatḥ Fadak, Vol. 2, p. 58; The Life of Muḥammad[sa], A Translation of Ibn Isḥāq's Sirat Rasūlullāh[sa], p. 515-523, A. Guillaume,, Oxford University Press,Reprinted in Pakistan , 2004)

Ghazwah Wādī al-Qurā

After the fall of Khaibar, the Holy Prophet[sa] left the area and stayed for three days at *Sahbā*. Then he left for *Wadī al-Qurā* where within a day the Muslims were successful and had an agreement made between the Muslims and the people of *Wadī al-Qurā*. Since the valley contained several settlements the valley became to be known as the *Wadī al-Qurā*. These settlements were located at the middle of Medina and Khaibar. When the Holy Prophet[sa] reached *Wadī al-Qurā* the Jews were ready to face him militarily and they welcomed the Muslims by throwing arrows towards them. The Holy Prophet[sa] did not expect such a response. A servant of the Holy Prophet[sa], Mid'am, who was unloading the baggage from the mount of the Holy Prophet[sa] was hit by an arrow, probably just by chance, and he was killed. The Holy Prophet[sa] ordered his forces to get battle-ready. He gave the main battle-flag to Ḥaḍrat Sa'd bin 'Ubādah[ra] and gave three smaller flags to Ḥaḍrat Ḥubāb bin Mundhir[ra], Ḥaḍrat Sahl bin Ḥunaif[ra] and Ḥaḍrat 'Abbād bin Bishar[ra] in order. The Holy Prophet[sa] sent the message to leaders of the *Wadī al-Qurā* that they should obey the Muslims and thus live peacefully. The message further stated that if they accept the offer and do not fight the Muslims they and their properties would be safe. However, instead of accepting the invitation of peace from the Holy Prophet[sa], they sent their fighters out to battle. In response to this, amongst the Muslims Ḥaḍrat Zubair came forward and killed the enemy fighter. Then another man came forward from the enemies. Ḥaḍrat Zubair[ra] killed him also. When the third person came out to fight, Ḥaḍrat 'Alī[ra] killed him. The fourth and the fifth enemy fighters were killed by Ḥaḍrat Abū Dujānah[ra]. In this way within a short period of time, the enemy lost eleven of their fighters fighting Muslim fighters individually. The Holy Prophet[sa] again conveyed to them the message of peace and submission to Muslims. However, they again refused to accept the offer and kept on fighting the Muslims. Due to their obstinacy the Holy Prophet[sa] had to fight with them. The fighting continued for whole day and then the next day they offered to live in peace and submission to Muslims. The Holy Prophet[sa] accepted their plea. This way the whole valley of *Wadī al-Qurā* was conquered by the Muslims in a short period of time. The Holy Prophet[sa] stayed in the area for four days and during this time he distributed amongst his Companions[ra] the war booty, which he had received in large amount. The land and the gardens belonging to the Jews were left with the Jews and an administrator was appointed to look after the matters.

(Zurqānī, Sharaḥ Sharḥ Mawāhib al-Ladunniyya, Fatḥ Wādī al-Qurā, Vol. 3, pp. 301-303; Zād al-Ma'ād, 2/148-147; The Life of Muḥammad[sa], A Translation of Ibn Isḥāq's Sirat Rasūlullāh[sa], p.516, A. Guillaume,, Oxford University Press, Reprinted in Pakistan, 2004)

Ghazwah Taymā'

After staying for four days in the area of Wadī al-Qurā the Holy Prophet[sa] moved towards Taymā'. Taymā' was also a settlement of Jews near Wadī al-Qurā towards Syria. When the people of came to know about the arrival of the Holy Prophet[sa] they requested to submit to him with the condition that they will pay *Jizyah*. The Holy Prophet[sa] accepted their offer and appointed Ḥaḍrat Yazīd bin Sufyān[ra] who had accepted Islām on that very day as their keeper (Governor).

(Zurqānī, Sharḥ Mawāhib al-Ladunniyya, Fatḥ Wādī al-Qurā, Taymā')

Ghazwah Dhātur Riqā'

When the Holy Prophet[sa] was returning after the conquest of Khaibar he learned that the *Banū Tha'lbah* tribe of Ghaṭafān in Najd and their branch of Maḥārib were planing to attack the Muslims. The Holy Prophet[sa] prepared a force of a few hundred of his Companions[ra] and left Medina towards Najd. In his absence he appointed Ḥaḍrat 'Uthmān as *Amīr* of Medina. While the *Banū Tha'lbah* were still making preparations to attack the Muslims, the Holy Prophet[sa] decided to make a preemptive strike. However, when the Muslims reached a place called, *'Nakhal'*, a large number of disbelievers challenged the Muslim force. Both forces arrayed facing each other to fight. Before the fighting started, the *Ghaṭafānī* fighters became scared of the Muslim force and left the field. They scattered in the surrounding mountains. When the Holy Prophet[sa] saw that the enemy force had run away and disappeared, he decided to return to Medina. While returning to Medina they stayed overnight in a valley. Since their was always a chance of a surprise attack by the *Ghaṭafānī* fighters the Holy Prophet[sa] asked the Companions[ra] who would like to be on surveillance duty during the night? In response, Ḥaḍrat

'Ammār bin Yāsir[ra] from the *Muhājirīn* and Ḥaḍrat 'Ayād bin Bishr[ra] from the *Anṣār* offered themselves for the duty. Thus both of them did the surveillance duty while the Holy Prophet[sa] and the rest of the force stayed in the valley.

There are several explanations given for naming this Ghazwah as Ghazwah *Dhātur Riqā'*. One of these is that there is a mountain in the valley the stones of which have prominent streaks of black, red and white colors, that is why the Ghazwah is called Ghazwah *Dhātur Riqā'*. Another explanation which is given by Ḥaḍrat Abū Mūsā Ash'arī[ra] is as follows:

In this battle, the Companions[ra] of the Holy Prophet[sa] had very few mounts to ride. He himself was one of six fighters who had only one mount to ride. Thus most of the fighters had to walk on foot. The area was mountainous. The feet of the Companions[ra] were badly injured from walking on sharp stones and they had wrapped them with torn pieces of cloth to walk. Since in Arabic the bandages made of cloth are called, "*ar-Riqā'*" that is why the *Ghazwah* became to be known as *Ghazwah Dhātur Riqā'*.

In the Ghazwah *Dhātur Riqā'*, when the time of Prayer came, the Muslims feared that they would be attacked, so the Holy Prophet[sa] offered the *Ṣalātul Khauf* (Prayers of fear) which was the first Prayer of fear. The Prayer was offered by parties alternately. Muslims confronting the enemy divided themselves into two parties. One of them offered one *rak'at* with the *Imām* and then took position against the enemy, and the party which had been facing the enemy came to offer the Prayer with the *Imām*, and offered one *rak'at*.

(As-Sīratun Nabawiyyah libne Hishām, Vol. 4, p. 214 Sabab Tasmiyatihā bi Dhāturriqā'; Ibn Sa'd's Al-Ṭabaqāt Al-Kabīr, Ghazwah Dhāturriqā', Vol. 2, pp. 74-75; Abū Dāwūd, Kitābuṭ Ṭahārat, Bāb al-Wuḍū''Aniddam; Ṣaḥīḥ Bukhārī, Kitāb al-Maghāzī, Ghazwah Dhāturriqā')

12

Battle of Mu'tah

Upon his return from the *Ka'bah*, the Holy Prophet[sa] began to receive reports that Christian tribes on the Syrian border, instigated by Jews and pagans, were preparing for an attack upon Medina. He, therefore, dispatched a party of fifteen to find out the truth. They saw an army amassing on the Syrian border. Instead of returning at once they started to give the message of Islām to the enemy. Instead of listening to the exposition, the enemy started raining arrows on this party of fifteen. However, they stood firm, fifteen against thousands, and fell fighting.

The Holy Prophet[sa] planned an expedition to punish the Syrians for this wanton cruelty, but in the meantime he had reports that the forces which had been concentrating on the border had dispersed. He, therefore, postponed his plans. The Holy Prophet[sa], however, wrote a letter to the Emperor of Rome (or to the Chief of the *Ghassān* tribe who ruled Buṣrā in the name of Rome). The letter was carried by Ḥaḍrat al-Ḥārth bin 'Umair al-Azdī[ra]. He stopped *en route* at Mu'tah where he met Shuraḥbīl, a *Ghassān* chief acting as a Roman official. He asked Ḥaḍrat al-Ḥārth[ra], "Are you a messenger of Muḥammad?" On being told "Yes", he arrested Ḥaḍrat al-Ḥārth[ra], tied him up and belaboured him to death. Perhaps he was afraid that he may have to answer to the Byzantine Emperor about what had happened to the party of fifteen Muslims killed earlier. The Holy Prophet[sa] came to know of the murder of Ḥaḍrat Al-Ḥarth[ra]. To avenge this and the earlier murders, he raised a force of three thousand and dispatched it to Syria under the command of Ḥaḍrat Zaid bin Ḥāritha[ra], the freed slave of the Holy Prophet[sa].

(Zād al-Ma'ād, 2/155; Ibn Ḥajar Asqalānī, Fatḥ al-Bārī 7/511)

The Holy Prophet[sa] nominated Ja'far bin Abū Ṭālib as the successor of Zaid, should Zaid die, and 'Abdullāh bin Rawāḥah, should Ja'far die. Should 'Abdullāh bin Rawāḥah also die, the Muslims were to choose their own commander. A Jew who heard this exclaimed,

"O Abul Qāsim, if thou art a true Prophet, these three officers whom thou has named are sure to die; for God fulfills the words of a Prophet."

Turning to Zaid, he said, "Take it from me, if Muḥammad is true you will not return alive." Zaid, the true believer that he was, said in reply, "I may return alive or not, but Muḥammad is a true Prophet of God."

(As-Sīratul Ḥalabiyyah, Vol. 3, p. 75, 'Alī Bin Burhānuddīn).

The following morning the Muslim army set out on its long march. The Holy Prophet[sa] and the Companions[ra] went some distance with the Muslim army. A large and important expedition such as this had never before gone without the Holy Prophet[sa] commanding it in person. As the Holy Prophet[sa] walked along to bid the expedition farewell, he counselled and instructed. When they reached the spot where the people of Medina generally bade farewell to friends and relations going to Syria, the Holy Prophet[sa] stopped and said:

"I urge you to fear God and to deal justly with the Muslims who go with you. Go to war in the name of Allāh and fight the enemy in Syria, who is your enemy, as well as Allāh's. When you are in Syria, you will meet those who remember God much in their houses of worship. You should have no dispute with them, and give no trouble to them. In the enemy country do not kill any women or children, nor the blind or the old; do not cut down any tree, nor pull down any building."

(As-Sīratul Ḥalabiyyah, Vol. 3, Alī Bin Burhānuddīn)

It was the first Muslim army sent to fight the Christians. When the Muslims reached the Syrian border, they heard that the Byzantine Emperor himself had taken the field with one hundred thousand of his own soldiers and another hundred thousand recruited from the Christian tribes of Arabia. Confronted by such large enemy numbers, half of the Muslim army wanted to stop on the way and send word to the Holy Prophet[sa] about the strength of the enemy force as he might be able to reinforce their numbers or wish to send fresh instructions. When the army leaders took counsel, Ḥaḍrat ʻAbdullāh bin Rawāḥah[ra] made a fiery speech: "My people, you set out from your homes to die as martyrs in the way of God, and now when martyrdom is in sight you seem to flinch. We have not fought so far because we were better equipped than the enemy in men or material. Our mainstay was our faith. If the enemy is so many times superior to us in numbers or equipment, what does it matter? One reward out of two we must have. We either win, or die as martyrs in the way of God."

The army heard Ḥaḍrat ibn Rawāḥah[ra] and was much impressed. Thus, the army marched on. As they marched, they saw the Roman army advancing towards them. So at Mu'tah the Muslims took up their positions and the battle began. Soon Ḥaḍrat Zaid[ra], the Muslim commander, was killed and the Holy Prophet's[sa] cousin Ḥaḍrat Jaʻfar bin Abū Ṭālib[ra] received the standard and the command of the army. When he saw that enemy pressure was increasing and the Muslims, because of utter physical inferiority, were not holding their own, he dismounted from his horse and cut its legs. The action meant that at least he was not going to flee; he would prefer death to flight. Ḥaḍrat Jaʻfar[ra] lost his right hand, but held the standard in his left. He lost his left hand also and then held the standard between the two stumps pressed to his chest. True to his promise, he fell down fighting. Then Ḥaḍrat ʻAbdullāh bin Rawāḥah[ra], as the Holy Prophet[sa] had ordered, grasped the standard and took over the command. He also fell fighting. The order of the Holy Prophet[sa] now was for the Muslims to take counsel together and elect a commander. But there was no time to hold an election. The Muslims might well have yielded to the vastly superior numbers of the enemy. But Ḥaḍrat Khālid bin Walīd[ra], accepting the suggestion of a friend, took the standard and went on fighting until evening came. The following day Ḥaḍrat Khālid[ra] took the field again with his crippled and tired force but employed a brilliant strategy. He changed the positions of his men. Those in front changed with those in the rear and those on the right flank changed with those on the left. They also raised some slogans. The enemy thought the Muslims had received reinforcements overnight and withdrew in fear. Ḥaḍrat Khālid[ra] saved his remaining army and returned to Medina. The Holy Prophet[sa] had been informed of these events through a revelation. He collected the Muslims in the mosque. As he rose to address them his eyes were wet with tears. He said,

"I wish to tell you about the army which left here for the Syrian border. It stood against the enemy and fought. First Zaid, then Ja'far and then 'Abdullāh bin Rawāḥah held the standard. All three fell, one after the other, fighting bravely. Pray for them all. After them the standard was held by Khālid bin Walīd. He appointed himself. He is a sword among the swords of God. So he saved the Muslim army and returned."

(Zurqānī, Sharḥ Mawāhib al-Ladunniyya, Vol. 3, pp. 341-348; Zād al-Ma'ād, Vol. I; Fatḥ al-Barī, 7/513)

It was a battle in which the Muslims were neither champions nor losers. On Ḥaḍrat Khālid bin Walīd's[ra] return with the Muslim army, some Muslims of Medina described the returning soldiers as defeated and lacking in spirit. The general criticism was that they should all have died fighting. The Holy Prophet[sa] chided the critics: "Khālid and his soldiers were not defeatist or lacking in spirit, he said. They were soldiers who returned again and again to the attack."

(Life of Muḥammad by Ḥaḍrat Mirzā Bashīruddīn Maḥmūd Aḥmad, Khalīfatul Masīḥ II[ra]*, pp. 129-133)*

13

The Conquest of Mecca

The Holy Prophet's[sa] enemies continued their efforts to wipe out the new faith and its adherents. They fought many battles with Muslims to wipe out Islām, but were completely unsuccessful in thwarting the spread of Islām. Islām spread rapidly, and when the Holy Prophet[sa] returned to Mecca in January 630 AD, it was in triumph with ten thousand followers.

He asked the residents of Mecca what they expected from him and how did they thought he would treat them now that he had come to Mecca as a conquerer. They said;

"We expect from you goodness. We request you to do goodness to us. You are our revered cousin and now have all the power to do whatever you like."

The Holy Prophet[sa] said, "I will say the same to you which my brother Yūsuf had said to his brothers:

لَا تَثْرِيبَ عَلَيْكُمُ الْيَوْمَ اِذْهَبُوْا فَاَنْتُمُ الطُّلَقَاءُ

lā tathrība 'alaikumul yauma idh habū fa antumuṭṭulaqā'u

No blame *shall lie* on you this day. (12:93) Go forth, you are free today.

(Al-Sīrat Ḥalabiyyah, Vol. 3, p. 141; Dalā'il An-Nabuwwata lil Baihaqī, Vol. 5, p. 79; As-Sīratun Nabawiyyah libne Hishām, Ghazwah Fateḥ Mecca)

The Holy Prophet[sa] also said to the inhabitants of Mecca:

"May Allāh forgive you. He is the Most Forgiving and the Most Compasionate."

(Tafsīr Durr-e-Manthūr, Sūrah Yūsuf)

Abū Quḥāfah, father of Ḥaḍrat Abu Bakr[ra], who was an old blind man at the time of the conquest of Mecca had gone with the help of his daughter on the mount of Abū Qubais to find out what was happening before the Muslims entered the city. Ḥaḍrat Abū Bakr[ra] brought his father to the Holy Prophet[sa]. The Holy Prophet[sa] told Ḥaḍrat Abū Bakr[ra] that he should not have brought his father to him. Rather he would have gone to his father. Ḥaḍrat Abū Bakr[ra] said, "It was his father's duty to come to the Holy Prophet[sa] and not vice versa." The Holy Prophet[sa] made Abū Quḥāfah sit next to him, cleaned his face and invited him to accept Islām. Abū Quḥāfah accepted Islām and became an ardent defender of Islām.

Ḥaḍrat Sa'd[ra] relates that on the "Conquest of Mecca", the Holy Prophet[sa] forgave everyone except for four people. To inform everyone, the Holy Prophet[sa] announced the names of these people. One of them, Ibn Abī Saraḥ, hid himself with Ḥaḍrat 'Uthmān[ra]. When the Holy Prophet[sa] took the initiation, Ḥaḍrat 'Uthmān[ra] brought Ibn Abī Saraḥ with him to the Holy Prophet[sa] and requested him to take the initiation of Ibn Abī Saraḥ. The Holy Prophet[sa] raised his eyes three times and looked towards Ibn Abī Saraḥ. Each time, he looked at him in such a manner as if he did not want to take his initiation. When Ḥaḍrat 'Uthmān[ra] requested the third time, the Holy Prophet[sa] took Ibn Abī Saraḥ's initiation. Then, addressing the Companions[ra] the Holy Prophet[sa] said: "None of you were wise and intelligent enough to kill Ibn Abī Saraḥ when I was hesitating to take his initiation. The Companions[ra] said: 'O Messenger[sa] of Allāh! We did not know what was in your mind. If you had blinked your eyes, we would have killed him.' The Holy Prophet[sa] said: 'It is not proper for a Prophet to have eyes that are deceiving.' "

(Sunan Abū Dāwūd, Kitābul Jihād, bāb fīl asīr yuqtal wa lā ya'raḍ 'alaihil islām)

When the Holy Prophet[sa] entered Mecca as a triumphant leader after bearing all sort of oppression and cruelties for two decades, he was so thankful to God Almighty and so humbled that due to bending downward his head had touched his camel. His heart was full of praise of God Almighty. God's words as regards to victory over the infidels of Mecca as stated in the following verse of the Holy Qur'ān had been fulfilled beautifully:

لَقَدْ صَدَقَ اللّٰهُ رَسُوْلَهُ الرُّءْيَا بِالْحَقِّ ۚ لَتَدْخُلُنَّ الْمَسْجِدَ الْحَرَامَ اِنْ شَآءَ اللّٰهُ اٰمِنِيْنَ ۙ مُحَلِّقِيْنَ رُءُوْسَكُمْ وَ مُقَصِّرِيْنَ لَا تَخَافُوْنَ ؕ فَعَلِمَ مَا لَمْ تَعْلَمُوْا فَجَعَلَ مِنْ دُوْنِ ذٰلِكَ فَتْحًا قَرِيْبًا ۝

laqad ṣadaqallāhu rasūlahurru'yā bil ḥaqqi latadkhulunnal masjidal ḥarāma inshā 'allāhu āminīna muḥalliqīna ru'ūsakum wa muqaṣṣirīna lā takhāfūna fa'alima mā lam ta'lamū faja'ala min dūn dhālika fatḥan qarība

Surely has Allāh in truth fulfilled for His Messenger the Vision. You will certainly enter the Sacred Mosque, if Allāh will, in security, *some* having *their* heads shaven, and *others* having *their* hair cut short; *and* you will have no fear. But He knew what you knew not. He has in fact ordained for you, besides that, a victory near at hand. (48:28)

The migration of the Holy Prophet[sa] and the successful and honorable re-entry to Mecca were foretold by God Almighty to the Holy

Prophet[sa] in the following verse of the Holy Qur'ān:

وَقُلْ رَّبِّ اَدْخِلْنِىْ مُدْخَلَ صِدْقٍ وَّ اَخْرِجْنِىْ مُخْرَجَ صِدْقٍ وَّ اجْعَلْ لِّيْ مِنْ لَّدُنْكَ سُلْطٰنًا نَّصِيْرًا ۝

wa qurrabbi adkhilnī mudkhala ṣidqiñwwa akhrijnī mukhraja ṣidqiñwwaj'allī milladunka sulṭanannaṣīrā

And say, O my Lord, make my entry a good entry and *then* make me come forth with a good forthcoming. And grant me from Thyself a helping power. (17:81)

The House of Allāh (*Ka'bah*) Cleared of the Idols

The Holy Prophet[sa] was sitting on his camel when he went round the house (*Ka'bah*), which had been built by Ḥaḍrat Ibrāhīm[as] and his son, Ḥaḍrat Ishmā'īl[as] for the worship of One and the Only God, but which now had become a sanctuary for idols. The Holy Prophet[sa] smote one by one three hundred and sixty idols which were placed by the idol-worshippers in the House. As an idol fell the Holy Prophet[sa] would recite:

وَقُلْ جَآءَ الْحَقُّ وَزَهَقَ الْبَاطِلُ ؕ اِنَّ الْبَاطِلَ كَانَ زَهُوْقًا ۝

wa qul jā'al ḥaqqu wa zahaqal bāṭilu innal bāṭila kāna zahūqā

And say, 'Truth has come and falsehood has vanished away, Falsehood does indeed vanish away *fast.*' (17:82)

Thus, within a short time, all the idols including the famous idols placed inside the *Ka'bah* by the idol worshippers such as, Hubal and other idols were turned into pieces with the strikes of the Holy Prophet[sa]. The clearance of *Ka'bah* of the idols by the Holy Prophet[sa] was a magnificent sign of the acceptance of Ḥaḍrat Ibrāhīm's[as] prayer:

رَبِّ اجْعَلْ هٰذَا الْبَلَدَ اٰمِنًا وَّاجْنُبْنِيْ وَبَنِيَّ اَنْ نَّعْبُدَ الْاَصْنَامَ 0

rabbij'al hādhal balada āminañwwaj nubnī wa baniyya anna'budal aṣnām

My Lord, make this city *a city* of peace, and keep me and my children away from worshipping idols. (14:36)

The *Ka'bah* was restored to its true purpose, the worship of the One God, as was intended by Ḥaḍrat Ibrāhīm[as].

After breaking all the idols and thus purifying the *Ka'bah*, the Holy Prophet[sa] offered two *rak'āt* of Prayer at the *'Muqām-e-Ibrāhīm'.* Then he called Ḥaḍrat 'Uthmān bin Ṭalḥa[ra] who had the key to the Sacred Mosque of the *Ka'bah.* The Holy Prophet[sa] took the key from him and opened the *Ka'bah* and then returned the key to Ḥaḍrat 'Uthmān bin Ṭalḥa and told him, "From now on the key to *Ka'bah* will remain forever with Ḥaḍrat 'Uthmān bin Ṭalḥa and his progeny."

The Holy Prophet[sa] stayed for fifteen days in Mecca during which besides organizing its affairs and instructing its people in Islām, he wiped out all the traces of paganism in the city. Thus, *Umm al-Qurā* (Mecca) embraced Islām and raised high the torch of genuine monotheism.

The Holy Prophet's[sa] Dream Regarding Migration and Future Successes

Ḥaḍrat Abū Mūsā[ra] relates that the Holy Prophet[sa] said: "I saw in a dream that I migrated from Mecca to a place where there were many palm trees. I have interpreted the dream that this is either the area of *Yamāmah* or *Ḥajar*. However, the events taken place since then have shown that it meant *Yathrib* (i.e., Medina). Then, I saw in the dream that I had shaken my sword and its front part had broken. Its interpretation was manifested when many Muslims were martyred in the Battle of Uḥud. I saw also in the dream that I shook the sword again and it became better than before. Its interpretation was manifested in that God Almighty granted the Muslims a great victory in the form of the conquest of Mecca, and then through His blessings gathered all the Muslims together. I saw a few cows in my dream and saw also some blessings. The cows referred to the faithful who were martyred in the Battle of Uḥud and the blessings referred to the reward which God gave in different ways after the Battle of Badr."

(Ṣaḥīḥ Bukhārī, Kitābul Manāqib, Bāb 'Alāmātinnabuwwah fil Islām;, Muslim , Kitābarru'yā', Ru'yā' an-Nabī[sa])

After the conquest of Mecca the Holy Prophet[sa] felt that the people of Medina might be thinking that he would take up his residence in Mecca, which was not his intention. So the Holy Prophet[sa] called the leaders of Medina and informed them, "I have no intention of taking up residence in Mecca. Although Mecca is very dear to me, but I will stay with the people who accepted and supported me when the Meccans had rejected me." The people of Medina were delighted to get this extremely pleasing news.

14

Battles of Ḥunain and Auṭās

Battles of Ḥunain

At the time of the conquest of Mecca, many Arab tribes had accepted Islām. However, there were several tribes who due to being proud of their bravery and heritage were opposed to Islām. Specially, the *Banū Hawāzin* the tribe of *Ṭā'if* and their branch, the *Banū Thaqīf* who were strong and experienced fighters and also were extremely proud of their strength and bravery. Most of the tribes around Mecca came to know of the conquest of Mecca much after its happening. With the conquest of Mecca by the Muslims the tribes around Mecca felt threatened. To face this challenge they started to prepare their forces and appointed Mālik bin 'Auf Naṣry as leader of their forces. The *Banū Sa'd, Banū Bakr, Jatham,* and *Naṣr* branches of the *Banū Hawāzin* joined the *Banū Thaqīf* in their expedition. However, the *Banū Kalab* and *Banū Ka'b* did not join them. When the people of *Hawāzin* and *Thaqīf* marched to attack Mecca, their leader Mālik bin 'Auf ordered them to take their family and cattle along with them. He thought that due to the company of their family and cattle his fighters would not run back. They encamped at Auṭās which was a valley close to *Ḥunain* between Mecca and *Ṭā'if.* The place was most suitable for fighting as the attacking army had to pass through a particular pathway and they could be ambushed by the opposing fighters. The Muslim army of 12,000 strong included 10, 000 fighters who took part in the conquest of Mecca and 2,000 Meccans who willingly had joined the Muslim Army. Some of them were new converts and a few were non-Muslims.

The enemy had hidden their archers on the narrow passage through which the Muslim army had to go through to attack the opponent. When the Muslim army went through the narrow pathway and faced the enemy the hidden archers attacked the Muslim forces from the back. The new recruits who were not tested in the battles as were the others started to run back towards Mecca while they were riding their horses and camels. Their horses and camels were also frightened with this sudden shooting by the archers from the back and also an attack from the front. This created chaos and panic in the experienced Muslim army and their mounts were also frightened. Thus, they ran back towards Mecca. Some of them tried their best to turn back their mounts towards the Holy Prophet[sa] who was still in the battlefield. However, their mounts were so frightened that they were unsuccessful in forcing their mounts to turn back towards the battlefield. The Holy Prophet[sa] and about a hundred of his Companions[ra] faced the enemy courageously. However, there were only ten Companions[ra] who were close to the Holy Prophet[sa]. The rest were at a distance from him. They all were exposed to a volley of arrows coming from three directions. The only way to protect from the arrows was to pass through the narrow passage through which only a few people could pass at a time. Ḥaḍrat Abū Bakr[ra] suggested to the Holy Prophet[sa] to wait till the Muslim forces regroup. However, the Holy Prophet[sa] did not accept his suggestion. He spurred his mule towards the narrow passage where the volleys of arrows were flying from different directions. While moving fast the Holy Prophet[sa] was saying in loud but majestic voice:

أَنَا النَّبِيُّ لَا كَذِبْ أَنَا ابْنُ عَبْدُ الْمُطَّلِبْ

annannabiyyu lā kadhibun, anabnu 'abdul muṭṭalib

I am a Prophet, (I am) not a liar. I am son of 'Abdul Muṭṭalib

And he was praying

اَللّٰهُمَّ نَزِّلْ نَصْرَكَ

allāhumma nazzil naṣraka

O Allāh! Send your help.

(Ṣaḥīḥ Muslim, Kitābul Jihād, Bāb Conquest of Mecca)

After announcing that he was a Prophet of God and a human being, the Holy Prophet[sa] called Ḥaḍrat 'Abbās[ra]. He told Ḥaḍrat 'Abbās[ra] to call those who had taken a pledge under the tree at the occasion *Ḥudaibiyyah* agreement and those who had accepted Islām in the early days at the time of the revelation of *Sūrah Al-Baqarah* and tell them that the Prophet[sa] of God was calling them. When Ḥaḍrat 'Abbās[ra] called the Companions[ra] in loud voice as was directed by the Holy Prophet[sa], the Companions[ra] as soon as they heard the call returned to the Holy Prophet[sa]. Some of them even left their mounts which were not turning back towards the battlefield. Thus, within a very short period of time the Companions[ra] gathered around the Holy Prophet[sa]. Ḥaḍrat Abū Sufyān[ra] took responsibility for the safety of the Holy Prophet[sa] and held the stirrup of the mule of the Holy Prophet[sa]. The Holy Prophet[sa] alighted from his mount, picked up some sand from the ground and threw it towards the enemy and said:

شَاهَتِ الْوُجُوْهُ

shāhatil wujūhu

May the faces of the enemy be defaced

Attack the enemy forcefully and decisively.

Upon hearing this, the Companions[ra] attacked the enemy so forcefully and bravely that the enemy was routed. Ultimately, the enemy forces ran away leaving behind a large number of prisoners and other spoils of the war. The Battle of Ḥunain is described in the following tradition:

Ḥaḍrat 'Abbās bin 'Abdul Muṭṭalib[ra] relates: "I was with the Holy Prophet[sa] on the day of Ḥunain. My nephew, Abū Sufyān bin Ḥārith bin 'Abdul Muṭṭalib[ra] and I remained close to the Holy Prophet[sa] throughout and never left the Holy Prophet[sa] alone. He[sa] was riding on his white mule, when the Muslims and the pagans encountered each other. The Muslims turned back. The Holy Prophet[sa] urged his mule towards the pagans. I was holding the bridle of his mule trying to restrain it from going too fast, and Ḥaḍrat Abū Sufyān[ra] was holding the Holy Prophet's[sa] stirrup. The Holy Prophet[sa] said to me, 'Abbās, call out to those who have made the covenant at *Samurah*. I called out in my loudest voice: "Where are those of the Covenant of *Samurah*?" My voice is naturally far-reaching and as soon as they heard my voice they turned towards the Holy Prophet[sa], like a cow turning towards her calf, shouting, 'At your service, At your service' and started to fight the infidels. Then the Holy Prophet[sa] told me to call the *Anṣār*. *O Anṣār*! *O Anṣār!* the Messenger[sa] of Allāh is calling you. Then Holy Prophet[sa] asked for, '*Banī Ḥārith bin Khazraj*.' The Holy Prophet[sa] raised his head from his seat on his mule, observed the fighting and said, 'The battle is heating up.' Then the Holy Prophet[sa] threw some pebbles at the pagans and said, 'By the Lord of Muḥammad, they will be defeated.' I noticed that as soon as the Holy Prophet[sa] threw the pebbles, all the fierceness of the enemy was subdued, and they started running away.' "

(Ṣaḥīḥ Muslim, Kitābul Jihād, Bāb Ghazwah Ḥunain)

The prisoners of war in the Battle of Ḥunain included Shīmā who was a daughter of Ḥaḍrat Ḥalīma and thus a foster sister of the Holy Prophet[sa]. Shīmā told the Muslims that she is the foster sister of the Holy Prophet[sa]. Her claim was mentioned to the Holy Prophet[sa]. The Holy Prophet[sa] told the messenger to bring Shīmā to him. When she came, the Holy Prophet[sa] talked with her and recognized her as being his foster sister. The Holy Prophet[sa] gave her due respect and gave her the option of either living with him or going back to her family. She preferred to go back to her family. Accordingly, the Holy Prophet[sa] gave her some presents and sent her back to her family respectfully.

Ḥaḍrat Ṭufail[ra] relates that one day when the Holy Prophet[sa] was distributing meat in Ji'rānah, a woman came and the Holy Prophet[sa] spread a sheet on the floor for her to sit. I asked who is this woman whom the Holy Prophet[sa] has treated so respectfully? The people told me that she was foster mother of the Holy Prophet[sa]. Thus both the foster mother and the foster sister of the Holy Prophet[sa] were the prisoners of war in the Battle of Ḥunain.

(Sunan Abū Dāwūd, Kitābul Adab, Bāb fil-bir)

Divine Help in the Battle of Ḥunain

The Holy Qur'ān states about the Battle of Ḥunain:

لَقَدْ نَصَرَكُمُ اللّٰهُ فِيْ مَوَاطِنَ كَثِيْرَةٍ ۙ وَّيَوْمَ حُنَيْنٍ ۙ اِذْ اَعْجَبَتْكُمْ كَثْرَتُكُمْ فَلَمْ تُغْنِ عَنْكُمْ شَيْئًا وَّ ضَاقَتْ عَلَيْكُمُ الْاَرْضُ بِمَا رَحُبَتْ ثُمَّ وَلَّيْتُمْ مُّدْبِرِيْنَ ۚ ثُمَّ اَنْزَلَ اللّٰهُ سَكِيْنَتَهٗ عَلٰى رَسُوْلِهٖ وَعَلَى الْمُؤْمِنِيْنَ وَاَنْزَلَ جُنُوْدًا لَّمْ تَرَوْهَا وَعَذَّبَ الَّذِيْنَ كَفَرُوْا ؕ وَذٰلِكَ جَزَآءُ الْكٰفِرِيْنَ ۝

laqad naṣarakumullāhu fī mawāṭina kathīratiñwwa yauma Ḥunainin idh a'jabatkum kathratukum falam tughni 'ankum shsai'añwwa ḍāqat 'alaikumul arḍu bimā raḥubat thumma wallaitummud birīn thumma anzalallāhu sakīnatahū 'alā

rasūlihī wa 'alal mu'minīna wa anzala junūdallam tarauhā wa 'adhdhaballadhīna kafarū wa dhālika jazā'ul kāfirīn

Surely, Allāh had helped you on many a battlefield, and on the Day of Ḥunain, when your great numbers made you proud, but they availed you nought, and the earth, with *all* its vastness, became straitened for you, *and* then you turned your backs retreating. Then Allāh caused tranquility to descend upon His Messenger and upon the believers, and He sent down hosts which you did not see, and He punished those who disbelieved. And this is the reward of the disbelievers. (9:25-26)

Battle of Auṭās

A part of the *Banū Hawāzin* army, after their defeat in the Battle of Ḥunain, marched towards *Auṭās.* The Holy Prophet[sa] sent a small force under the command of Ḥaḍrat Abū 'Āmir Ash'arī[ra], the uncle of Ḥaḍrat Abū Mūsā Ash'arī[ra], to follow and destroy them. The Muslim army, which included Ḥaḍrat Abū Mūsā Ash'arī[ra] and Ḥaḍrat Salamah bin Al-Akwa'[ra] caught the enemy forces in *Auṭās.* Although, the *Banū Ḥawāzin* forces were defeated in the Battle of Ḥunain, the part of their force which has gathered at *Auṭās* was ready to fight the Muslim army. Thus, a battle between the two forces ensued. The blind leader of the *Banū Hawāzin,* from the enemy forces, Durayd ibn al-Ṣimmah came first to fight. Ḥaḍrat Rabī'ah bin Rafī'[ra] killed him. Ḥaḍrat Abū 'Āmir[ra] invited nine soldiers, individually, to accept Islām. However, all of them refused the invitation and kept on fighting. Ḥaḍrat Rabī'a bin Rafī'[ra] killed all of them. When Ḥaḍrat Abū 'Āmir[ra] invited the tenth person to accept Islām. He accepted Islām and remained steadfast in Islām throughout his life. Salamah, son of Durayd ibn al-Ṣimmah, shot an arrow towards Ḥaḍrat Abū 'Āmir Ash'arī[ra] which hit his knee. When Ḥaḍrat Abū Mūsā Ash'arī[ra] saw this, he attacked Salamah and killed him, and kept the Muslim Flag in his control. Thus, a large part of the *Banū Hawāzin* force was destroyed here also. The remaining force was defeated and they ran away.

Distribution of the Spoils of the Battles of Ḥunain and Auṭās

Ji'rānah is a town located between *Ṭā'if* and Mecca on the road to Iraq. It is around 12 miles from Mecca. After the Battle of Ḥunain, the Holy Prophet[sa] left the prisonors of the *Banū Hawāzin* and the war-booty at Ji'rānah and went for the siege of *Ṭā'if.* After the end of the siege of *Ṭā'if* the Holy Prophet[sa] came back to Ji'rānah so that war booty, etc. could be divided. Already three weeks had passed since ending the battle and the booty had not yet been distributed. However, the Holy Prophet[sa] delayed the distribution for another few days in order to wait for the people of *Hawāzin* and to talk with them about the captives and other war booty before distribution. When people from *Hawāzin* did not show up, the Holy Prophet[sa] started distribution of the war booty. The spoils of the war collected by the Muslims were as follows:

> Prisoners: 6,000; Camels: 24,000; Goats: 40,000; Silver: 4,000 *Auqiyyas.*

The Holy Prophet[sa] divided the booty into five parts. One part was kept for *Baitul Māl* and the rest was divided between the Muslim fighters. The Holy Prophet[sa] appointed Ḥaḍrat Zaid bin Thābit[ra] to count the soldiers and do the distribution.

In this battle many new Muslims and some rich people of Mecca who had just basic knowledge of Islām had taken part. In order to win their hearts towards Islām the Holy Prophet[sa] gave to many of them extra from the *Baitul Māl* portion of the spoils. Some amongst the *Anṣār* saw this distribution as if favor had been done to the *Quraish* of Mecca who were the people of the Holy Prophet[sa], over them. Accordingly, some of them openly said that the Holy Prophet[sa] had given extra booty to the Meccans while he had ignored them. The Holy Prophet[sa] was saddened to hear such remarks. The incident is mentioned in detail in the following tradition:

Ḥaḍrat Abū Saʿīd al-Khudrī[ra] relates that when the Holy Prophet[sa] distributed the spoils of the conquests of *Hawāzin* and *Ḥunain* amongst the Arab tribes, the *Anṣār* were not given anything. At this, the *Anṣār* were displeased and felt heavy-hearted to the extent that they started talking a lot about the distribution of the goods. Someone said that the Holy Prophet[sa] had sided with his own people. From the *Anṣār*, Ḥaḍrat Saʿd bin ʿUbādah[ra] came to the Holy Prophet[sa] and said, "Messenger[sa] of Allāh, your distribution of goods has created confusion in the minds of some *Anṣār*. While you have bestowed huge endowments out of the spoils of the wars to the people of your tribe, you did not give anything to the *Anṣār*. The Holy Prophet[sa] said, 'O Saʿd! Where were you at that time?' Ḥaḍrat Saʿd bin ʿUbādah[ra] said, 'Messenger[sa] of Allāh! I am also one of the *Anṣār*. They do not care about my explanation.' The Holy Prophet[sa] told Ḥaḍrat Saʿd bin ʿUbādah[ra] to gather his people in a pavilion so that he could address them. Ḥaḍrat Saʿd bin ʿUbādah[ra] gathered his people. Some of the Emigrants were also allowed to come in while the rest of them were asked to leave. When all the *Anṣār* gathered in the pavilion, the Holy Prophet[sa] was notified. Ḥaḍrat Abū Saʿīd al-Khudrī[ra] relates that the Holy Prophet[sa] came to the pavilion. After praising Allāh, he said, 'O *Anṣār*! I have come to know about your complaints. O *Anṣār*! If you think that I came to you when you were misguided and through me, God Almighty has guided you. You were destitute and through me, God made you rich and wealthy. You were the enemy of one another and through me, God made you brothers. Is not all this true?' The *Anṣār* said, 'Certainly, it is a great blessing of God and His Messenger[sa] upon us.' The Holy Prophet[sa] said, 'O *Anṣār*! Why do you not respond to what I have told you? The *Anṣār* said, 'What should we say? We are indebted to God and His Messenger[sa].' The Holy Prophet[sa] said, 'If you like, you can respond like this and it will be a correct response: 'You came to us at a time when your people had rejected you and we accepted you. You came to us in a miserable state and we helped you. You came to us homeless and we gave you shelter. You came when you were destitute and without any support, and we took care of your needs and gave you support.

O *Anṣār*! Do you feel heavy-hearted and displeased because of the glittering wordly goods, which I have given to the *Quraish* and the new Muslims from the Arab tribes to console and solace them. O *Anṣār*! Are you not happy that people take with them goats and camels and you take the Messenger[sa] of Allāh with you? By God, Who has control over my life! If I had not migrated, I would have been one of the *Anṣār*. If all the people go towards a valley using the same way and the *Anṣār* use another way, I will accompany the *Anṣār*.

O Allāh! Have Mercy upon the *Anṣār*, have Mercy on their children, have Mercy on their children's children.

Upon hearing this address of the Holy Prophet[sa], the *Anṣār* wept bitterly with great remorse, to the extent that their beards were soaked with tears and they said, 'Messenger[sa] of Allāh! We are pleased with you and with your distribution of the goods.' "

(Sīrah Ḥalabiyyah, Bāb Dhikr Maghāziyyah, Vol. 3, pp. 176-177; Al-Musanna Li Ibn Abī Shaiba, the Book on al-Maghāzī, the Battle of Ḥunain, Ḥadīth # 36986, Vol. 7, p. 419, Dār ul Kutab al-'Ilmiyyah)

According to another tradition, the Holy Prophet[sa] asked, "O *Anṣār*! What did you say? They replied, 'There were a few ignorant people who made those unsuitable and unpleasant remarks that God have mercy upon the Holy Prophet[sa]. He gives to the *Quraish* leaving us out while it is our swords which shed the blood of the enemy. However, the serious elderly *Anṣār* were disgusted with what happened.' Anyhow, after the problem was resolved, the Holy Prophet[sa] left for his residence and the rest of the people also went to their places.' "

(Sīrah Ḥalabiyyah, Vol. 3, pp. 176-177)

15

The Expedition of Tabūk

Abū 'Āmir Madanī who belonged to the *Khazraj* tribe had developed the habit of silent meditation and of repeating the names of God. Because of this habit, he was generally known as Abū 'Āmir, the Hermit. When the Holy Prophet[sa] migrated to Medina, Abū 'Āmir moved from Medina to Mecca. After the conquest of Mecca, he started different sorts of intrigues against Islām. He changed his name, came back from Mecca and settled down in Qubā', a village near Medina. As he had been away for a long time the people of Medina did not recognize him. He contacted the hypocrites of Medina and with their help made a plan to go to Syria and excite and provoke the Christian rulers and Christian Arabs into attacking Medina. At the same time, he had planned to spread discord in Medina and rumors that Medina was going to be attacked by Roman forces. He hoped that as a result of this strategy Muslims and Syrian Christians would go to war or at least the Muslims would themselves be provoked into attacking Syria. After completing his plans, he went to Syria. While he was away the hypocrites at Medina according to the plan began to spread rumors that caravans had been sighted which were coming to attack Medina. When no caravan appeared, they issued some kind of explanation.

These rumors became so persistent, that the Holy Prophet[sa] thought it necessary to lead in person a Muslim army against Syria. These were difficult times. Arabia was in the grip of a famine. It was late September or early October when the Holy Prophet[sa] set out on this mission. The hypocrites knew that the rumors were their own inventions. Their goal was to create a conflict between the great Roman Empire and the Muslims so that the Romans could destroy the Muslims. While the hypocrites were busy spreading rumors about the Roman attack on the Muslims, they also made every effort to strike fear in the minds of the Muslims. Their plan was, on the one hand, to provoke the Muslims into attacking Syria and, on the other, to discourage them from going in large numbers. They wanted the Muslims to go to war against Syria and meet with certain defeat. But as soon as the Holy Prophet[sa] announced his intention of leading this new expedition, enthusiasm ran high among the Muslims. Individual Muslims vied with one another in the spirit of sacrifice for the sake of their faith. The poor Muslims were also provided with riding animals, swords and lances. There was at Medina at the time a party of Muslims who had migrated from Yemen. They were very poor. Some of them went to the Holy Prophet[sa] and offered their services for this expedition. They said, "O Prophet of God, take us with you. We want nothing beyond the means of going." The Qur'ān makes a reference to these Muslims and their offers in the following words:

وَّ لَا عَلَى الَّذِيْنَ اِذَا مَآ اَتَوْكَ لِتَحْمِلَهُمْ قُلْتَ لَآ اَجِدُ مَآ اَحْمِلُكُمْ عَلَيْهِ
ص تَوَلَّوْا وَّ اَعْيُنُهُمْ تَفِيْضُ مِنَ الدَّمْعِ حَزَنًا اَلَّا يَجِدُوْا مَا يُنْفِقُوْنَ ۝

wa lā 'alalladhīna idhā mā atauka li taḥmilahum qulta lā ajidu mā aḥmilukum 'alaihi tawallawwa a'yunuhum tafiḍu minaddam'i ḥazanan allā yajidū mā yunfiqūn

Nor against those to whom, when they came to you that you should mount them, thou did say, 'I cannot find whereon I can mount you'; they turned back, their eyes overflowing with tears, out of grief that they could not find what they might spend (9:92).

Abū Mūsā[ra] was the leader of this group. When asked what they had asked for? He said, "We did not ask for camels or horses. We only said we did not have shoes and could not cover the long journey bare-footed. If we only had shoes, we would have gone on foot and taken part in the war alongside with our Muslim brethren."

The disbelievers and the hypocrites had probably thought that the Holy Prophet[sa] acting upon the rumors spread by them would attack the Syrian armies without a thought. When the Holy Prophet[sa] reached close to Syria, he stopped and sent his men in different directions for reconnaissance. The men returned and reported there were no Syrian concentrations anywhere. The Holy Prophet[sa] decided to return, but stayed for a few days during which he signed agreements with some of the tribes on the border. There was no war and no fighting in this trip. The journey took the Holy Prophet[sa] about two and a half months. When the hypocrites at Medina found out that their scheme for inciting war between Muslims and Syrians had failed and that the Prophet[sa] was returning safe and sound, they began to fear that their plot had been exposed. They were afraid of the punishment which was now their due. But they did not halt their sinister plans. They equipped a party and posted it on the two sides of a narrow pass at some distance from Medina. The pass was so narrow that only a single file could go through it. When the Holy Prophet[sa] and the Muslim army approached the spot, the Holy Prophet[sa] received a warning by revelation that the enemy was lying in ambush on both sides of the narrow pass. The Holy Prophet[sa] ordered his Companions[ra] to check out the area. When they reached the spot near the passage they saw men in hiding with the obvious intent to attack. However, they fled as soon as they saw this reconnaissance party. The Holy Prophet[sa] decided not to pursue them. When the Holy Prophet[sa] reached Medina, the hypocrites who had kept out of this battle began to make lame excuses. The Holy Prophet[sa] accepted their excuses. At the same time he felt that the time had come to expose their hypocrisy. He had a command from God that the mosque at Qubā', which the hypocrites had built in order to be able to hold their meetings in secret, should be demolished. The hypocrites were compelled to say their Prayers with other Muslims. No other penalty was imposed. Upon returning from Tabūk, the Holy Prophet[sa] found that the people of Ṭā'if also had submitted. After this the other tribes of Arabia applied for admission to Islām. In a short time the whole of Arabia was under the flag of Islām.

(Life of Muḥammad[sa]*, Ḥaḍrat Mirzā Bashīruddīn Maḥmūd Aḥmad, p. 156-160)*

At the time of the expedition of Tabūk, there was a group of people who did not want to take part in the battle. In fact, they were hypocrites. Privately, they ridiculed the call to arms for the battle, and the timing and the strategy of the battle. They consulted one another to find ways to stay out of the battle and offered lame excuses to the Holy Prophet[sa] for not taking part in the battle. God Almighty revealed at that time:

فَرِحَ الْمُخَلَّفُوْنَ بِمَقْعَدِهِمْ خِلٰفَ رَسُوْلِ اللّٰهِ وَكَرِهُوْٓا اَنْ يُّجَاهِدُوْا
بِاَمْوَالِهِمْ وَاَنْفُسِهِمْ فِيْ سَبِيْلِ اللّٰهِ وَقَالُوْا لَا تَنْفِرُوْا فِى الْحَرِّ ؕ قُلْ نَارُ
جَهَنَّمَ اَشَدُّ حَرًّا ؕ لَوْ كَانُوْا يَفْقَهُوْنَ ۝

fariḥal mukhallafūna bi maq'adihim khilāfa rasūlillāhi wa karihū añyyujāhidū bi amwālihim wa anfusihim fī sabīlillāhi wa qālū lā tanfirū fil ḥarri qul nāru jahannama ashaddu ḥarran lau kānū yafqahūn

Those *who contrived to be* left behind rejoiced at their staying back in contradiction to the Messenger of Allāh, and were averse to striving with their property and their persons in the cause of Allāh. And they said, 'Go not forth in the heat.' Say, 'The fire of Hell is more intense in heat.' Could they but understand! (9:81)

The Case of the Three Companions[ra] of the Holy Prophet[sa] Who Remained Behind in the Expidition of Tabūk

Ḥaḍrat 'Abdullāh bin Ka'b[ra] relates that he had heard from his father, Ka'b bin Mālik a full account of the incident of his remaining behind the Holy Prophet[sa] when he proceeded on the campaign of Tabūk. Ka'b said: "I did not remain behind the Messenger[sa] of Allāh in any battle except the Battle of Tabūk, and I failed to take part in the Battle of Badr, and in that case there was no question of any penalty for anyone who had not participated in it, for in fact, the Holy Prophet[sa] and the Muslims had gone out in search of the caravan of *Quraish*, but Allāh brought about a confrontation between them and their enemies unexpectedly. I was present with the Messenger[sa] of Allāh the night of 'Aqabah, when we pledged for Islām. I would not exchange 'Aqabah with Badr, forall the fame of Badr as compared with 'Aqabah. My failure to accompany the Holy Prophet[sa] in the campaign of Tabūk fell out in this wise. I was stronger and more affluent at the time of this campaign than at any other time. I had then two riding camels, and never before did I have two. Whenever the Holy Prophet[sa] decided on a campaign he would not disclose his real objective till the last moment. In this case, as the season was one of intense heat, the journey was long across the desert and the enemy was in great strength; he warned the Muslims clearly and told them his objective so that they should be fully prepared. A large number of Companions[ra] were ready to accompany the Messenger[sa] of Allāh. No register would have sufficed for setting down the particulars of all of them. Most of those who were minded to keep away imagined that they would get away with it, unless their defection was disclosed through Divine revelation. Also the fruit on the trees had ripened and their shade was thick and this too occupied my mind.

The Messenger[sa] of Allāh and the Muslims who were to accompany him occupied themselves with their preparations and I would go out in the morning meaning to do the same along with him but would return without settling anything, saying to myself: 'There is plenty of time. I can get ready whenever I wish.' This went on and the Muslims completed their preparations, and one day the Messenger[sa] of Allāh started with them on his march, and I had not yet done anything to prepare myself. I still continued in my state of indecision, without settling anything, while the Muslims continued on the march. I thought I would go forth alone and overtake them. How I wish I had done it, but it was not to be. Now when I went about in the town it grieved me to observe that among those who were still at home like me were only those who were either suspected of hypocrisy or were excused on account of age or the like.

The Holy Prophet[sa] made no mention of me till after he had arrived at Tabūk. There while sitting among the people he inquired, 'What had happened to Ka'b?' Someone from among the *Banī Salimah* said: 'Messenger[sa] of Allāh, he has been hindered by his two cloaks and his habit of admiring his finery.' On this Mu'adh bin Jabal admonished him. The Holy Prophet[sa] said nothing. At this time he observed someone at a distance in the desert clad in white and exclaimed: May it be Abū Khaisamah; and so he proved to be. He was the one who was taunted by the hypocrites when he gave away a quantity of dates in charity.

When I learned that the Messenger[sa] of Allāh was on his way back from Tabūk I was much distressed and began to condider false excuses in my mind that might serve to shield me from his anger. I also consulted those members of my family whose judgment I trusted. When I heard that the Holy Prophet[sa] was approaching I realized that no false excuse would avail me and I resolved to stick to the truth. He arrived the next morning. It was his custom that when he returned from a journey he first entered the mosque and offered two *rak'āt* of Prayer and then sat facing the people. He did the same on this occasion and those who had remained behind from the campaign came up and began to put forward their excuses on oath. There were well over eighty. The Holy Prophet[sa] accepted their verbal declarations, renewed their covenants, prayed for forgiveness for them and committed to Allāh whatever was in their minds. When it came to my turn and I saluted him, he smiled, but it was the smile of someone angry, and said: 'Come forward.' So, I stepped forward and sat down before him. He asked: 'What kept you back? Had you not purchased your mount?' I replied: 'Messenger[sa] of Allāh, were I confronted by someone other than yourself, a man of the world, I could easily escape his displeasure by some excuse, for I am gifted with skill in argument, but I know that if I were to spin before you a false tale today, which might even convince you, most certainly will Allāh soon rouse your anger against me over something. On the other hand, if I tell you the truth and you are wroth with me, I might still hope for a good end from Allāh, the Exalted, the Glorious. I have no excuse. I was never stronger and more affluent than when I held back from accompanying you.' The Holy Prophet[sa] said: 'This one has told the truth. Now withdraw, till Allāh issues His decree concerning you.' Some men of *Banī Salimah* followed me out of the mosque and said: 'We have not known you to commit a fault before this, then why did you not put forward an excuse before the Holy Prophet[sa] like the others who had held back from the campaign? Your fault would have found its forgiveness through the prayer of the Holy Prophet[sa] for your forgiveness.' They kept on reproaching me so severely that I made up my mind to go back to the Holy Prophet[sa] and to retract my confession. Then I asked them: 'Is anyone else in similar situation as mine?' They said: 'Yes. Two persons met him (the Holy Prophet[sa]) who explained to him the same as you have. They were told as you have been told.' He said: 'Who were those?' They said: 'Murārah bin Ar-Rabī‘ Al-‘Amrī and Hilāl bin Umayyah Al-Wāqifī.' Thus, they mentioned two such persons who were righteous, had participated in the Battle of Badr, and in whom there was an example for me. So I did not change my mind when they mentioned them to me.

The Holy Prophet[sa] directed the Muslims to stop speaking to the three of us. People kept away from us, as if we were strangers, and it seemed to me that I was in a strange land which I could not recognize. This continued for fifty days. My two companions in misery were resigned and took to keeping inside their homes. But I being the youngest of the three and the toughest used to go out and join the Muslims in Prayer and walked the streets but nobody would talk to me. I would attend upon the Holy Prophet[sa] when he sat in the mosque after Prayer and would salute him and wonder whether he had moved his lips in returning my salutation. I would stand in Prayer near him and I noticed that he would look in my direction when I was occupied with the Prayer and would look away when I looked in his direction. Being oppressed by the hardness of the Muslims towards me I went one day and vaulted over the garden wall of my cousin Abū Qatādah of whom I was very fond, and saluted him, but he did not return my salutation. I said to him: 'O Abū Qatādah, I adjure you in the name of Allāh! Do you not know that I love Allāh and His Messenger?' But he said nothing. I repeated my adjuration. Still he did not reply. Then I asked him again. He said: 'Allāh and His Messenger know best.' At this my eyes burst into tears and I returned and jumped over the wall.

Ka'b[ra] added: 'One day I was sauntering in the market-place of Medina when I heard a peasant from Syria, who had brought a quantity of corn for sale, say: 'Would someone direct me to Ka'b bin Mālik?' People pointed in my direction. He came to me and handed me a letter from the king of Ghassān. Being literate myself I read it. Its message was: 'We have heard that your master has treated you harshly. God has not made you to be humiliated and mistreated. Come over to us and we shall receive you graciously.' Having read it, I said to myself: 'This is another trial; and I went to the oven and threw my letter in it.'

When forty days had elapsed without any indication in the revelation concerning us, a messenger of the Holy Prophet[sa] came to me and said: 'The Messenger[sa] of Allāh directs you to keep away from your wife.' I inquired: 'Shall I divorce her or what?' He said: 'No. Only do not associate with her.' I understood that my two companions had been directed likewise. So I told my wife: 'Go to your parents and remain with them till Allāh determines this matter.' Hilāl bin Umayyah's wife went to the Holy Prophet[sa] and said: 'Messenger[sa] of Allāh, Hilāl bin Umayyah is old and is not able to look after himself, nor has he a servant. Would it displease you if I were to serve him?' He said: 'No. But he should not associate with you.' She said: 'He has no desire for me; since this incident he is occupied only with weeping.' Some of my people said to me: 'You should also seek the permission of the Holy Prophet[sa] that your wife should look after you as the wife of Hilāl bin Umayyah looks after him.' I told them: 'I shall not ask the Holy Prophet[sa] for permission for I do not know what he might say. Besides, I am young.'

Ten more days passed like this and on the fifty-first morning, after communication with us had been outlawed, when, after the dawn Prayer at home, I was sitting in a melancholy state and the wide world, as Allāh the Exalted, has described it, seemed to close in on me, I suddenly heard someone shout at the top of his lungs from the crest of Mount *Sal'*: 'O Ka'b bin Mālik, good news!' I immediately fell into prostration and realized that relief had come. It seems that the Holy Prophet[sa] had informed the people at the time of the dawn Prayer that Allāh the Most Honored and Glorious, had turned to us in mercy, and several people had set out to convey the good news to us. Some went to my two companions. One spurred his horse in the direction of my home. A man belonging to the tribe of *Aslam* ran up to the mount and his voice reached me before the arrival of the cavalier. When the one whose voice I had heard arrived to greet me, I took off my garments and made him wear them. I had no other garments for my own wearing and borrowed a pair to put on and set out to present myself before the Holy Prophet[sa]. On the way I encountered crowds of people who congratulated me, saying: 'Blessed be the acceptance by Allāh of thy repentance.' When I entered the mosque I found the Holy Prophet[sa] seated surrounded by people. Of them, Ṭalḥa bin 'Ubaidullāh got up and sprang towards me and, shaking my hand, congratulated me. He was the only one out of the Emigrants who got up and Ka'b never forgot Ṭalḥa for this.

When I saluted the Holy Prophet[sa] his face was aglow with joy and he said: 'Be happy with the best one of all your days that have passed since your mother gave you birth.' I said: 'Messenger of Allāh, is this from you or from Allāh?' He answered: 'It is indeed from Allāh.' It was usual with him that his happy face glowed as if it were a segment of the moon, which we took as a signal that he was pleased. I then submitted to him: 'Messenger[sa] of Allāh, to complete my repentance I would like to give up all my possessions as charity in the cause of Allāh and His Messenger.' He said: 'Hold back part of it; that would be better for you.' On which I said: 'I shall hold back that portion which is in Khaibar.' Then I submitted: 'Messenger[sa] of Allāh! Allāh the Exalted, has delivered me only because I adhered to the truth, and it is part of my repentance that for the rest of my days I shall speak nothing but the truth.' Ever since I declared this before the Holy Prophet[sa], Allāh the Exalted, has not tried anyone so well in the matter of telling the truth as He has tried me. To this day, since my declaration, I have never had any inclination to tell a lie, and I hope that Allāh will continue to safeguard me against it during the rest of my days.

Allāh the Exalted revealed:

لَقَدْ تَّابَ اللّٰهُ عَلَى النَّبِيِّ وَالْمُهٰجِرِيْنَ وَالْاَنْصَارِ الَّذِيْنَ اتَّبَعُوْهُ
فِيْ سَاعَةِ الْعُسْرَةِ مِنْۢ بَعْدِ مَا كَادَ يَزِيْغُ قُلُوْبُ فَرِيْقٍ مِّنْهُمْ ثُمَّ
تَابَ عَلَيْهِمْ ؕ اِنَّهٗ بِهِمْ رَءُوْفٌ رَّحِيْمٌ ۝ وَّ عَلَى الثَّلٰثَةِ الَّذِيْنَ
خُلِّفُوْا ؕ حَتّٰٓى اِذَا ضَاقَتْ عَلَيْهِمُ الْاَرْضُ بِمَا رَحُبَتْ وَضَاقَتْ
عَلَيْهِمْ اَنْفُسُهُمْ وَ ظَنُّوْٓا اَنْ لَّا مَلْجَاَ مِنَ اللّٰهِ اِلَّآ اِلَيْهِ ؕ ثُمَّ تَابَ
عَلَيْهِمْ لِيَتُوْبُوْا ؕ اِنَّ اللّٰهَ هُوَ التَّوَّابُ الرَّحِيْمُ ۝ يٰٓاَيُّهَا الَّذِيْنَ

اٰمَنُوا اتَّقُوا اللّٰهَ وَ كُوْنُوْا مَعَ الصّٰدِقِيْنَ ۝

laqattābāllāhu 'alannabiyyi walmūhājirīna wal anṣārilla dhīnattaba'ūhu fī sā'atil'usrati mim ba'di mā kāda yazīghu qulūbu farīqimminhum thumma tāba 'alaihim innahū bihim ra'ūfurraḥīmunwwa 'alaththalātha tilladhīna khullifū ḥattā idhā ḍaqat 'alaihim ul arḍu bimā raḥubat wa ḍaqat 'alaihim anfusuhum wa ẓannū allā malja-ā minallāhi illā ilaihi thumma tāba 'alaihim li-yatūbū innallāha huwattawwāburraḥīm yā ayyu halladhīna āmanuttaqullāha wa kūnū ma'aṣṣādiqīn

Allāh has certainly turned with mercy to the Prophet and *to* the Emigrants and the Helpers who followed him in the hour of distress after the hearts of a party of them had well-nigh swerved. He again turned to them with mercy. Surely, He is to them Compassionate, Merciful. And the three *who remained* behind, until the earth seemed too narrow for them despite *all* its vastness, and their souls were *also* straitened for them, and they became convinced that there was no refuge from Allāh save unto Himself. Then He turned to them with mercy that they might turn to *Him*. Surely, it is Allāh Who is Oft-Returning *with compassion and is* Merciful. O ye who believe! fear Allāh and be with the truthful. (9:117-119).

Ka'b continued: 'After Allāh had guided me to Islām. His greatest bounty in my estimation, that He bestowed upon me, was my telling the truth to the Holy Prophet[sa], and not lying to him and ruining myself as were ruined those who did tell lies to him. In His revelation Allāh had said concerning those who told lies worse than He said concerning anyone:

سَيَحْلِفُوْنَ بِاللّٰهِ لَكُمْ اِذَا انْقَلَبْتُمْ اِلَيْهِمْ لِتُعْرِضُوْا عَنْهُمْ ؕ

فَاَعْرِضُوْا عَنْهُمْ ؕ اِنَّهُمْ رِجْسٌ ز وَّ مَاْوٰهُمْ جَهَنَّمُ ۚ جَزَآءًۢ بِمَا

كَانُوْا يَكْسِبُوْنَ ۝ يَحْلِفُوْنَ لَكُمْ لِتَرْضَوْا عَنْهُمْ ۚ فَإِنَّ اللّٰهَ لَا يَرْضٰى عَنِ الْقَوْمِ الْفٰسِقِيْنَ ۝

sa yaḥlifūna billāhi lakum idhanqalabtum ilaihim li tu'riḍū 'anhum fa a'riḍū 'anhum innahum rijsuñwwa ma'wāhum jahannam jazā-am bimā kānū yaksibūn yaḥlifūna lakum litarḍau 'anhum fa innallāha lā yarḍā 'anil qaumil fāsiqīn

They will swear to you by Allāh, when you return to them, that you may leave them alone. So leave them alone. Surely, they are foul, and their abode is Hell -- a *fit* recompense for that which they used to earn. They will swear to you that you may be pleased with them. But *even* if you be pleased with them, Allāh will not be pleased with the rebellious people. (9:95-96)

Our matter had been left pending, of the three of us, apart from the matter of those who had made excuses on oath before the Holy Prophet[sa] which he accepted, and whose covenants he renewed and for whom he prayed for forgiveness. The Holy Prophet[sa] kept our matter pending till Allāh determined it with: 'He has also turned with mercy to the three whose matter was deferred.' The reference here is not to our holding back from the campaign, but to his deferring our matter and keeping it pending beyond the matter of those who made their excuses on oath which the Holy Prophet[sa] accepted.

(As-Sīratun Nabawiyyah libne Hishām, Vol. 4, p. 175)

One version adds: The Holy Prophet[sa] set out for Tabūk on Thursday. He preferred setting out on a Thursday. He always returned from a journey in the early forenoon and went directly to the mosque where he offered two *rak'āt* Prayer, thereafter he sat down for sometime and then left for home."

(Ṣaḥīḥ Bukhārī, Ka'b bin Mālik[ra])

Establishment of Mosques

During his trip from Medina to Tabūk wherever the Holy Prophet[sa] encamped or stayed overnight he established a mosque for offering Prayers. Thus during this trip the Holy Prophet[sa] established seventeen mosques at following locations: *Tabūk, Thanītah Madrān, Dhātazzarāb, al-Akhḍar, Dhātil Khaṭmā, al-Abā', Dhanb Kawākib near al-Batrā', al-Shaqq, Dhil Jaifah, Ṣadr Ḥauḍī, al-Ḥajar, al-Ṣa'īd, al-Wādīul Qurā, Shaqta Banī 'Uzrah, Dhil-Marwah, al-Faifā'* and *Dhī Khushab.*

(As-Sīratun Nabawiyyah libne Hishām, Vol. 4, pp. 174-175; Sīrah Ibne Hishām, Urdu, Translation by 'Abdul Jalīl Siddiqī, Vol. 2, p. 636, I'tiqād Publishing House, Delhi, India, 1982)

16

Demolition of the Conspiracy Centers

Demolition of the Mosque Built by Hypocrites (Ḍirār Mosque)

When the Holy Prophet[sa] migrated from Mecca to Medina, before entering Medina he stayed at Qubā'. During his stay in Qubā', the Holy Prophet[sa] laid the foundation of a mosque there. This mosque was located in the area belonging to the *Banū 'Amr bin 'Auf.* This gave high status and respect to the *Banū 'Amr bin 'Auf. Banū Ghanam bin 'Auf* who were always competing with the *Banū 'Amr bin 'Auf* who had also accepted Islām. However, due to the construction of the mosque by *Banū 'Amr bin 'Auf* they became jealous of the *Banū 'Amr bin 'Auf.* The hypocrites exploited the situation and by showing sympathy to the *Banū Ghanam bin 'Auf* they developed a close relationship with them. Abū 'Āmir, a Christian Priest, had already settled in Qubā' to conspire and to develop strategies to damage Islām. He incited the *Banū Ghanam* and advised them to safeguard their interests by building a mosque to compete with the *Banū 'Amr.* He also told them to collect and store armament in the mosque, so that, when the Roman army attacks Medina, with their help, he would make the Holy Prophet[sa] leave Medina. After planning this scheme, he himself left for Syria to incite and encourage Heraclius to attack Medina. In his absence, the hypocrites and many new Muslims who had poor understanding of Islām started to come to the mosque built by the *Banū Ghanam.* In the mosque they used to meet to hatch schemes and plan strategies to damage Islām. Furthermore, they would pick out faults with and conspire against the Holy Prophet[sa] and Islām. One of the strategies they used to damage Islām was the misrepresentation and interpretation of the Holy Qur'ān to the people. They also started to spread rumors and false propaganda about the Holy Prophet[sa] and Islām. Thus, the mosque became a center for sowing discord among the Muslims. At the same time, the Holy Prophet[sa] was very busy in making preparations for the expedition of Tabūk. Before he left for the expedition of Tabūk the hypocrites even asked the Holy Prophet[sa] to come to their mosque and bless it by offering Prayer there. Their intention was to establish the mosque as a legitimate mosque. Due to lack of time the Holy Prophet[sa] was unable to go to the mosque. However, he promised them to come to the mosque sometime later on. God Almighty revealed to the Holy Prophet[sa] the true nature of the mosque in the following verses:

وَالَّذِيْنَ اتَّخَذُوْا مَسْجِدًا ضِرَارًا وَّ كُفْرًا وَّ تَفْرِيْقًا بَيْنَ الْمُؤْمِنِيْنَ وَ
اِرْصَادًا لِّمَنْ حَارَبَ اللّٰهَ وَ رَسُوْلَهٗ مِنْ قَبْلُ ؕ وَلَيَحْلِفُنَّ اِنْ اَرَدْنَاۤ اِلَّا
الْحُسْنٰى ؕ وَاللّٰهُ يَشْهَدُ اِنَّهُمْ لَكٰذِبُوْنَ 0 لَاتَقُمْ فِيْهِ اَبَدًا ؕ لَمَسْجِدٌ اُسِّسَ
عَلَى التَّقْوٰى مِنْ اَوَّلِ يَوْمٍ اَحَقُّ اَنْ تَقُوْمَ فِيْهِ ؕ فِيْهِ رِجَالٌ يُّحِبُّوْنَ اَنْ
يَّتَطَهَّرُوْا ؕ وَاللّٰهُ يُحِبُّ الْمُطَّهِّرِيْنَ 0 اَفَمَنْ اَسَّسَ بُنْيَانَهٗ عَلٰى تَقْوٰى مِنَ
اللّٰهِ وَ رِضْوَانٍ خَيْرٌ اَمْ مَّنْ اَسَّسَ بُنْيَانَهٗ عَلٰى شَفَا جُرُفٍ هَارٍ فَانْهَارَ بِهٖ
فِيْ نَارِ جَهَنَّمَ ؕ وَاللّٰهُ لَا يَهْدِى الْقَوْمَ الظّٰلِمِيْنَ 0 لَا يَزَالُ بُنْيَانُهُمُ الَّذِيْ
بَنَوْا رِيْبَةً فِيْ قُلُوْبِهِمْ اِلَّاۤ اَنْ تَقَطَّعَ قُلُوْبُهُمْ ؕ وَاللّٰهُ عَلِيْمٌ حَكِيْمٌ 0

walladhī nattakhadhū masjidan ḍirārañwwa kufrañwwa tafrīqam bainal mu'minīna wa irṣādalliman ḥārabal-lāha wa rasūlahū min qablu wala yaḥlifunna in aradnā illal ḥusnā wallāhu yash-hadu

innahum la kādhibūn lā taqum fīhi abadā la masjidun ussisa 'alattaqwā min awwali yaumin aḥaqqu an taqūma fīhi fīhi rijālunyyu ḥibbūna anyyataṭahharū wallāhu yuḥibbul muṭṭahhirīn afaman assasa bunyānahū 'alā taqwā minallāhi wa riḍwānin khairun amman assasa bunyānahū 'alā shafā jurufin hādin fanhāra bihī fī nāri jahannama wallāhu lā yahdil qaumaẓẓālimīn lā yazālu bunyānu humulladhī banau rībatan fī qulūbihim illā an taqaṭṭa'a qulūbuhum wallāhu 'alīmun ḥakīm

And *among the hypocrites are* those who have built a mosque in order to injure *Islām* and *help* disbelief and cause division among the believers, and to provide a place of hiding for those who have already waged war against Allāh and His Messenger before *this*. And they will surely swear: 'We meant nothing but good', but Allāh bears witnes that they are certainly liars. Never stand to *pray* therein. A mosque which was founded upon piety from the *very* first day is surely more worthy that you should stand *to pray* therein. In it are men who love to become purified, and Allāh loves those who purify themselves. Is he, then, who laid his foundation on fear of Allāh and His pleasure better or he who laid his foundation on the brink of a tottering water-worn bank which tumbled down with him into the fire of Hell? And Allāh does not guide a people who transgress. *This* building of theirs, they have raised, will ever be a source of disquiet and uncertainty in their hearts, until their hearts split and are torn to pieces. And Allāh is All-Knowing, Wise. (9:107-110)

While returning from the expedition of Tabūk, when the Holy Prophet[sa] reached a place called *Dhū Awān*, he sent Ḥaḍrat Mālik bin al-Dukhshum[ra], Ḥaḍrat Ma'n bin 'Adī[ra], Ḥaḍrat 'Āṣim bin 'Adī[ra], Ḥaḍrat 'Āmir bin al-Sakn[ra] and Ḥaḍrat Waḥshī[ra] to Medina and said to them, "The founders of this mosque are very cruel. Burn the mosque while they are watching it." All of them left for Qubā' to implement the order of the Holy Prophet[sa]. They burnt the mosque to ashes during the time between *Maghrib* and *'Ishā'* Prayers. Thus, the mosque which had become a central gathering-place for the enemies of Islām was permanently destroyed. Since this mosque was built to harm the Muslims, that is why, in Islāmic literature the mosque is mentioned as '*Ḍirār Mosque*'. With the destruction of their gathering-place, the hypocrites were scared and went into hiding.

(As-Sīratun Nabawiyyah libne Hishām, Vol. 4, p. 174; The Life of the Prophet Muḥammad, Ibn Kathīr, al-Sīrah al-Nabawiyya, Vol. 4, pp. 26-28, Translated by Trevor Le Gassik, 2000; The History of al-Ṭabarī, Vol. 9, pp. 60-61, Translated by Isma'īl Poonawāla, Los Angeles, CA, 1987)

Demolition of the House Used by the Hypocrites to Conspire Against the Muslims

Some of the Jews who had lived in Medina, due to their animosity towards the Holy Prophet[sa], used to conspire against the Holy Prophet[sa] and Islām. One such Jew by the name of Suwailam was living in the part of Medina called 'Jāsūm'. His house was used by the hypocrites as a center to meet and conspire. They used to gather there, create damaging stories about the expedition of Tabūk and then spread these stories among the Companions[ra] of the Holy Prophet[sa] to discourage them from taking part in the expedition. When the Holy Prophet[sa] came to know about these Jews and their evil plans he sent Ḥaḍrat 'Ammār bin Yāsir[ra] to tell them that the Holy Prophet[sa] knew about their evil designs. When they found out that the Holy Prophet[sa] knew about their activities they came to the Holy Prophet[sa] and apologized for their activities. God Almighty revealed the following concerning them:

يَحْذَرُ الْمُنٰفِقُوْنَ اَنْ تُنَزَّلَ عَلَيْهِمْ سُوْرَةٌ تُنَبِّئُهُمْ بِمَا فِيْ قُلُوْبِهِمْ ؕ قُلِ
اسْتَهْزِءُوْا ۚ اِنَّ اللّٰهَ مُخْرِجٌ مَّا تَحْذَرُوْنَ 0 وَلَئِنْ سَاَلْتَهُمْ لَيَقُوْلُنَّ اِنَّمَا كُنَّا
نَخُوْضُ وَنَلْعَبُ ؕ قُلْ اَبِاللّٰهِ وَاٰيٰتِهٖ وَرَسُوْلِهٖ كُنْتُمْ تَسْتَهْزِءُوْنَ 0 لَا

تَعْتَذِرُوْا قَدْ كَفَرْتُمْ بَعْدَ اِيْمَانِكُمْ ط اِنْ نَّعْفُ عَنْ طَآئِفَةٍ مِّنْكُمْ نُعَذِّبْ طَآئِفَةً م بِاَنَّهُمْ كَانُوْا مُجْرِمِيْنَ ٥

yaḥdharul munāfiqūna an tunazzala 'alaihim sūratun tunabbi'uhum bimā fi qulūbihim qulistahzi'ū innallāha mukhrijummā taḥdharūn wa la'in sa-altahum layaqūlunna innamā kunnā nakhūḍu wa nal'abu qul a-billāhi wa āyātihī wa rasūlihī kuntum tastahzi'ūn lā ta'tadhirū qad kafartum ba'da īmānikum inna'fu 'an ṭā'ifa timminkum nu'adhdhib ṭā'ifatambi annahum kānū mujrimīn

The hypocrites fear lest a Sūrah should be revealed against them, informing them of what is in their hearts. Say, 'Mock ye! surely, Allāh will bring to light what you fear.' And if you question them, they will most surely say, 'We were only talking idly and jesting.' Say, 'Was it Allāh and His Signs and His Messenger that you mocked at? 'Offer no excuse. You have certainly disbelieved after your believing, If We forgive a party from among you, a party shall We punish, for they have been guilty.' (9:64-66)

When the Holy Prophet[sa] got confirmation that the house was being used as a center for conspiracies against Islām, he ordered Ḥaḍrat Ṭalḥa bin 'Ubaidullāh to destroy the center. Ḥaḍrat Ṭalḥa bin 'Ubaidullāh took a few Companions[ra] with him to Suwailum's house and set it on fire. Thus, at least temporarily, the center was destroyed.

(Sīrah Ibne Hishām, Urdu, Translated by 'Abdul Jalīl Siddiqī, Vol. 2, p. 622, I'tiqād Publishing House, Delhi, India, 1982).

Death of 'Abdullāh bin Ubayy bin Salūl

'Abdullāh bin Ubayy bin Salūl, the leader of the hypocrites fell ill after the Expedition of Tabūk and died within two months of his illness. He had developed a strong hatred for the Holy Prophet[sa] due to the emigration of the Holy Prophet[sa] to Medina. Despite that the Holy Prophet[sa] was compassionate to him and made sure that the Muslims did not harm him.

When Ḥaḍrat 'Abbās[ra], the uncle of the Holy Prophet[sa], was captured in the Battle of Badr, none of the shirts available at that time fitted Ḥaḍrat 'Abbās[ra]. He was quite a tall man and the shirts were of standard size. However, 'Abdullāh bin Ubayy bin Salūl's shirt fitted Ḥaḍrat 'Abbās[ra] as he was also a tall man. 'Abdullāh bin Ubayy bin Salūl removed his shirt and gave it to Ḥaḍrat 'Abbās[ra]. When 'Abdullāh bin Ubayy bin Salūl died, the Holy Prophet[sa] returned the favor by giving his own shirt to use as a shroud for his burial and prayed for him. He also led his funeral Prayer despite strong opposition from Ḥaḍrat 'Umar[ra].

Ḥaḍrat 'Umar[sa] states that he said: "Messenger[sa] of Allāh, will you pray over one of the enemies of Allāh?" The Holy Prophet[sa] smiled and did not say anything. I kept on mentioning the evil acts 'Abdullāh bin Ubayy bin Salūl had committed against the Holy Prophet[sa] and the Muslims. The Holy Prophet[sa] said, "I was given a choice. I was told to plead forgiveness for the hypocrites or not. Even if I plead for them seventy times Allāh will not forgive them. If I knew that if I exceeded seventy times, He would forgive them, I would do so." The Holy Prophet[sa] was referring to the following verse of the Holy Qur'ān:

اِسْتَغْفِرْ لَهُمْ اَوْ لَا تَسْتَغْفِرْ لَهُمْ ؕ اِنْ تَسْتَغْفِرْ لَهُمْ سَبْعِيْنَ مَرَّةً فَلَنْ
يَّغْفِرَ اللّٰهُ لَهُمْ ؕ ذٰلِكَ بِاَنَّهُمْ كَفَرُوْا بِاللّٰهِ وَ رَسُوْلِهٖ ؕ وَاللّٰهُ لَا يَهْدِى
الْقَوْمَ الْفٰسِقِيْنَ ۟

istaghfir lahum au lā tastaghfir lahum in tastaghfir lahum sab'īna marratan falañyyaghfirallāhu lahum dhālika bi annahum kafarū

billāhi wa rasūlihī wallāhu lā yahdil qaumal fāsiqīn

Ask you forgiveness for them, or ask you not forgiveness for them; even if you ask forgiveness for them seventy times, Allāh will never forgive them. That is because they disbelieved in Allāh and His Messenger. And Allāh guides not the perfidious people. (9:80)

When the Holy Prophet[sa] returned from the graveyard after burial of 'Abdullāh bin Ubayy bin Salūl, God Almighty revealed the following to the Holy Prophet[sa]:

وَلَا تُصَلِّ عَلٰٓى اَحَدٍ مِّنْهُمْ مَّاتَ اَبَدًا وَّ لَا تَقُمْ عَلٰى قَبْرِهٖ ؕ اِنَّهُمْ كَفَرُوْا
بِاللّٰهِ وَ رَسُوْلِهٖ وَمَاتُوْا وَهُمْ فٰسِقُوْنَ 0 وَلَا تُعْجِبْكَ اَمْوَالُهُمْ
وَاَوْلَادُهُمْ ؕ اِنَّمَا يُرِيْدُ اللّٰهُ اَنْ يُّعَذِّبَهُمْ بِهَا فِى الدُّنْيَا وَتَزْهَقَ اَنْفُسُهُمْ
وَهُمْ كٰفِرُوْنَ 0

wa lā tuṣalli 'alā aḥadimminhummāta abadañwwa lā taqum 'alā qabrihī innahum kafarū billāhi wa rasūlihī wa mātū wa hum fāsiqūn wa lā tu'jibka amwāluhum wa aulāduhum innamā yurīdullāhu añyyu'adhdhibahum bihā fiddunyā wa tazhaqa anfusuhum wa hum kāfirūn

Never say prayer over any of them when he dies, nor stand by his grave *to pray*, for they disbelieved in Allāh and His Messenger and died while they were disobedient. And their possessions and their children should not excite your wonder; Allāh only intends to punish them therewith in this world and that their souls may depart while they are disbelievers. (9:84-85)

(The Life of the Prophet Muḥammad, Ibn Kathīr (al-Sīrah al-Nabawiyya), Vol. 4, pp. 45-47, Translation by Trevor Le Gassik, 2000)

17

Basic Teachings of Islām

The Five Fundamentals of Islām

Islām has five basic duties which a Muslim has to perform. They are known as the Five Fundamentals of Islām or the Five Pillars of Islām.

The pillars of Islām are mentioned in the following *Ḥadīth* of the Holy Prophet[sa]:

بُنِيَ الْاِسْلَامُ عَلٰى خَمْسٍ شَهَادَةِ اَنْ لَّآ اِلٰهَ اِلَّا اللّٰهُ وَ اَنَّ مُحَمَّدًا رَّسُوْلُ اللّٰهِ ' وَ اِقَامِ الصَّلٰوةِ ' وَ اِيْتَآءِ الزَّكٰوةِ ' وَ حَجِّ الْبَيْتِ ' وَصَوْمِ رَمَضَانَ 0

buniyal islāmu 'alā khamsin; shahādati 'allā ilāha illallāhu wa anna muḥammadar rasūlullāhi, wa iqāmiṣṣalāti, wa 'ītā'izzakāti, wa ḥajjil baiti, wa ṣaumi ramaḍān.

Islām is based on five (pillars):

1) Bearing witness that there is none worthy of worship but Allāh, and Muḥammad is His servant and His messenger (*Declaration of Faith*)

2) Observance of *Ṣalāt* (Daily Prayers)

3) Paying of *Zakāt*

4) Pilgrimage to the House of Allāh *(The Ka'bah)*

5) Fasting during *Ramaḍān*

(Ṣaḥīḥ Bukhārī, Kitābul Īmān, Bāb qaulannabī[sa] *'Buniyal Islāmu 'alā khamsīn').*

The ***first*** and the foremost pillar of Islām is called *Shahādah*, the declaration of Islāmic faith. The belief in the Oneness of God is the basic requirement of believing in Islām.

The ***second*** pillar is called *Ṣalāt*, i.e., to perform Prayer in a prescribed form. Prayer is the basic and most important means by which man communicates with Allāh and draws himself near to Him.

The ***third*** pillar is called *Ṣaum*, i.e., to keep fast in the month of *Ramaḍān*. By fasting, a Muslim can purify himself spiritually, elevate his soul and obtain nearness to Allāh. To fast is to abstain from food, drink, smoking and conjugal relations from dawn to dusk. It was the month during which revelation of the Holy Qur'ān to the Holy Prophet[sa] began.

The Holy Qur'ān allows exemption from fasting to the elderly, the chronically sick and children. However, they are required to feed or pay to feed the poor for the whole month of *Ramaḍān* in order to make up for fasts they could not keep. Temporary exemption is permitted to those travelling, the sick, pregnant and nursing or menstruating women. They are expected to make up the fasts at a later time before the start of the next month of fasting.

The ***fourth*** pillar is called *Zakāt*. It is a form of levy which Muslims of means pay annually in cash or kind, and is spent for good causes mentioned in the Holy Qur'ān. Thus it is given for the purpose of purification of wealth. *Zakāt* is used for the upkeep of the poor, the destitute, travelers in need, for those serving in the way of Islām, for those fighting in the way of Allāh, for slaves to buy their freedom, and for benevolent works. *Zakāt* can be levied on land produce, livestock, and liquid assets, e.g., gold, silver, and savings in the bank left for more than one year.

The ***fifth*** pillar is called *Ḥajj*, i.e., to perform pilgrimage to the *Ka'bah* (*Baitullāh*) in Mecca, at least once in the lifetime of a Muslim when the person is able bodied and has the means to go for *Ḥajj*. The *Ḥajj* ceremony involves a series of religious rites which extend over several days, performed at the Holy *Ka'bah* in Mecca and other special holy sites near it. The *Ka'bah* is believed by Muslims to be the first house built for the worship of One God. It was rebuilt by Prophet Abraham[as] and his son Ishmael[as], and later on by the Holy Prophet[sa].

The *Ḥajj* serves as a striking reminder of the Oneness of Allāh and it emphasizes the brotherhood and equality of human beings, as well as the importance of man's willingness to sacrifice himself for the sake of his Creator.

The above mentioned five pillars of Islām must be professed by everyone who desires to become a Muslim. Although Muslims are already divided into many sects -- like all other religions -- on this issue there are no two opinions. By whatever title the sects are recognized, be they *Sunnīs* or *Shī'ites*, all believe in these five fundamental pillars.

Shahādah (Declaration of Faith)

The ***first*** and the foremost pillar of Islām is called *Shahādah*, the declaration of Islāmic faith, i.e.,

اَشْهَدُ اَنْ لاَّ اِلٰهَ اِلاَّ اللّٰهُ وَحْدَهٗ لاَ شَرِيْكَ لَهٗ وَ اَشْهَدُ اَنَّ

مُحَمَّدًا عَبْدُهٗ وَ رَسُوْلُهٗ

ash hadu allā ilāha illallāhu waḥdahū lā sharīkalahū wa ash hadu anna muḥammadan 'abduhū wa rasūluh

I bear witness that there is none worthy of worship except Allāh. He is One; (and) Has no partner, and I bear witness that Muḥammad is His servant and messenger.

Ṣalāt (Daily Prayers)

In every religion Prayer is regarded as the pivot on which rests man's Communion with God. God prescribed Prayer as the second pillar of His everlasting religion Islām.

Of all religious obligations, Islām has laid the greatest emphasis on the institution of Prayer (*Ṣalāt).* It is enjoined upon every Muslim to pray five times a day. Besides the five obligatory Prayers, there are other types of prayers which are optional.

Ḥaḍrat Jābir[ra] relates that the angel Gabriel visited the Holy Prophet[sa] and said: "Arise and offer Prayer." Accordingly, the Holy Prophet[sa] offered *Ẓuhr* Prayer at the declining of the sun, then he came to him at the time of *'Aṣr* Prayer and said: 'Arise and offer Prayer.' So the Holy Prophet[sa] offered *'Aṣr* Prayer when the shadow of objects was equal to their size, then he came to him at the *Maghrib* time and said: 'Arise and offer Prayer.' So the Holy Prophet[sa] offered *Maghrib* Prayer after the sunset, then he came to him at the time of *'Ishā'* Prayer and said: 'Arise and offer Prayer.' So the Holy Prophet[sa] offered *Ishā'* Prayer when light in the horizon had disappeared, then he came to him at the time of *Fajr* Prayer and said: 'Arise and offer Prayer.' So the Holy Prophet[sa] offered the *Fajr* Prayer at the beginning of the dawn.

The next day, Gabriel again visited the Holy Prophet[sa] at the time of *Ẓuhr* Prayer and said: 'Arise and offer Prayer.' So he (the Holy Prophet[sa]), offered *Ẓuhr* Prayer when the shadow of objects corresponded to their size, then he came to him at the time of *'Aṣr* Prayer and said: 'Arise and offer Prayer.' So the holy Prophet[sa] offered *'Aṣr* Prayer when the shadow of things was twice their size, then he came to him at the *Maghrib* Prayer time which was the same time as that of the previous day, then he came to him at the *'Ishā'* Prayer time after passing of either half or one-third of the night, then he came to him for *Fajr* Prayer when the light had spread fully, then he said: 'Arise and offer Prayer.' So he offered *Fajr* Prayer.

After that Gabriel said: "The time to offer the Prayers in between the two times (prescribed)."

(Musnad Aḥmad, p. 330/3)

ṢAUM (Fasting of Ramaḍān)

Fasting is another form of worship found universally in the world religions. Although there are vast differences regarding the mode of fasting and the conditions applied to it, the central idea of fasting is present everywhere. Fasting in Islām is a highly developed institution. There are two types of injunctions with regards to fasting. One relates to obligatory fasting and the other to optional. Obligatory fasting is further divided into following two categories:

1. There is one full month (*Ramaḍān*) in every year in which fasting is prescribed for Muslims all over the world. As the month is a lunar month, so it keeps changing around the year according to the solar months.

   Fasting in Islām begins everywhere at the first appearance of dawn, and ends with sunset. During this period one is expected to abstain from all food and drink, and conjugal relations, completely. Furthermore, a greater part of the night is spent in spiritual exercises such as recitation of the Holy Qur'ān and offering of the *Tahajjud* Prayers, which is very essence of fasting. During the month of fasting, Muslims are required to redouble their efforts in alms-giving and care for the destitute.

2. Other obligatory fasting is most often related to seeking forgiveness of God for sins. This includes violation of the obligatory fasts.

The Holy Qur'ān says:

يٰٓاَيُّهَا الَّذِيْنَ اٰمَنُوْا كُتِبَ عَلَيْكُمُ الصِّيَامُ كَمَا كُتِبَ عَلَى الَّذِيْنَ
مِنْ قَبْلِكُمْ لَعَلَّكُمْ تَتَّقُوْنَ ۙ

yā ayyuhalladhīna āmanū kutiba 'alaikumuṣṣiyāmu kamā kutiba 'alalladhīna min qablikum la'allakum tattaqūn

O Ye who believe! fasting is prescribed for you, as it was prescribed for those before you, so that you may become righteous. (2:184)

Zakāt (Alms Giving)

Zakāt is a kind of worship prescribed in order to bring about equitable economic adjustment in society. The Arabic word *Zakāt* literally means to purify something. In this context a mandatory payment of a fixed portion of the wealth would mean that the residual wealth after the deduction of *Zakāt* has been rendered pure and lawful for the believers.

The Holy Qur'ān commands:

وَ اَقِيْمُوا الصَّلٰوةَ وَ اٰتُوا الزَّكٰوةَ وَ اَطِيْعُوا الرَّسُوْلَ لَعَلَّكُمْ تُرْحَمُوْنَ ۝

wa aqīmuṣṣalāta wa ātuzzakāta wa aṭī'urrasūla la'allakum turḥamūn

And observe Prayer and give the Zakāt and obey the Messenger, that you may be shown mercy (24:57)

The Holy Qur'ān further says about *Zakāt*:

وَمَآ اٰتَيْتُمْ مِّنْ زَكٰوةٍ تُرِيْدُوْنَ وَجْهَ اللّٰهِ فَاُولٰٓئِكَ هُمُ الْمُضْعِفُوْنَ ۝

wa mā ātaitummin zakātin turīdūna wajhallāhi fa ulā'ika humul muḍ'ifūn

But whatever you give in Zakāt seeking the favor of Allāh -- it is these who will increase *their wealth* manifold (30:40)

Apart from meeting the demands of the State, this collection is intended to meet the needs of the poor. It is collected from Muslims possessing a certain amount of money or property, and is spent on the poor, the needy, the orphans, widows and wayfarers, etc. It is normally levied at 2.5% on disposable assets above specific thresholds which have remained in the hands of owners beyond one year. One of the many benefits of *Zakāt* is that due to the fear that any idle capital would be gradually eroded away through the imposition of *Zakāt*, every one with surplus savings would be encouraged to employ it in earning profit to off-set the effect of *Zakāt*.

The Holy Qur'ān says that in the wealth is a share of those who are unable to meet their basic needs and are considered deprived in their environment.

وَفِيْٓ اَمْوَالِهِمْ حَقٌّ لِّلسَّآئِلِ وَالْمَحْرُوْمِ ٥

wa fi amwālihim ḥaqqullissā'ili walmaḥrūm

And in their wealth is a share belonging to the beggar and the destitute. (51:20)

وَالَّذِيْنَ فِيْٓ اَمْوَالِهِمْ حَقٌّ مَّعْلُوْمٌ ۙ٥ لِّلسَّآئِلِ وَالْمَحْرُوْمِ ۙ٥

walladhīna fi amwālihim ḥaqquma'lūmullissā'ili walmaḥrūm

And those in whose wealth there is a recognized right for the beggar and the destitute who begs not. (70:25-26)

This clearly establishes that it is the right of every person to have certain basic necessities of life provided to him in every land and society, and those made responsible for meeting this obligation are the ones who possess more than their basic needs, leaving it to the State to decide upon the *modus operandi*, to ensure that the system is fair, just and equitable and adequately fulfills its basic purpose.

A tradition of the Holy Prophet[sa] regarding *Zakāt* is as follows:

عَنِ الْحَسَنِ قَالَ قَالَ رَسُوْلُ اللّٰهِ ﷺ: حَصِّنُوْا اَمْوَالَكُمْ

بِالزَّكٰوةِ وَ دَاوُوْا مَرْضَاكُمْ بِا لصَّدَقَةِ وَاسْتَقْبِلُوْا اَمْوَاجَ الْبَلَاءِ

بِالدُّعَاءِ وَ التَّضَرُّعِ

'anil ḥasani[ra] qāla qāla rasūlullāhi[sa]: ḥaṣṣinū amwālakum bizzakāti wa dāwū marḍākum biṣṣadaqati wastaqbalū amwājal balā'i biddu'ā'i wattaḍarru'i

Ḥasan[ra] relates that the Holy Prophet[sa] said: "Fortify your property by paying *Zakāt*, cure the sick by giving charity and defend yourself against the undulations of calamities through invocations and humble entreaties.

(Murāsīl Abū Dāwūd, Bāb fiṣṣā'im yuṣību ahlihī)

Ḥajj (Pilgrimage)

To perform a pilgrimage of the *"Ka'bah"*, which is also called *"Baitullāh"*, in Mecca, Saudi Arabia, is called *Ḥajj*.

Like the month of fasting, the time appointed for the pilgrimage, ten weeks after the Festival of the breaking of the fast *('Īdul fiṭr)* is fixed according to the lunar calendar, and rotates throughout the year. The pilgrimage thus falls in all seasons of the year.

God Almighty says in the Holy Qur'ān:

وَ لِلّٰهِ عَلَى النَّاسِ حِجُّ الْبَيْتِ مَنِ اسْتَطَاعَ اِلَيْهِ سَبِيْلًا

wa lillāhi 'alannāsi ḥijjulbaiti manistaṭā'a ilaihi sabīlā

And pilgrimage to the House (House of Allāh) is a duty which men -- those who can find a way thither -- owe to Allāh. (3:98)

One finds the institution of pilgrimage in all religions of the world, but the sites for pilgrimage are scattered at different places in one or more countries. One does not find a single central place, which all the followers of a religion must visit at least once in the lifetime. In Islām, Mecca is such a place, where Muslims from all over the world are expected to gather and spend about ten days entirely dedicated to the memory of God. The pilgrims come from all countries, all nations, all races and all ages. Men, women and children all gather once a year for *Ḥajj*, running into millions.

(An Elementary Study of Islām, Ḥaḍrat Mirzā Ṭāhir Aḥmad, p. 37)

Ḥaḍrat 'Umar bin Al-Khaṭṭāb[ra] relates: "We were sitting one day with the Holy Prophet[sa] when a man appeared among us whose clothes were of an intense whiteness, whose hair was jet black, who bore no mark of travel and who was not known to any of us. He sat down in front of the Holy Prophet[sa], their knees touching, and placing his hands on his thighs he said: 'Muḥammad, tell me about Islām.' The Holy Prophet said: 'Islām is that you should bear witness that there is none worthy of worship except Allāh and Muḥammad is His Messenger, and that you should observe Prayer, pay the *Zakāt*, observe the fast during *Ramaḍān*, and perform the Pilgrimage to the House if you can afford the journey thither.' The man said: 'That is right.' We were surprised that he inquired and also confirmed the correctness of the answer. He then said: 'Tell me about faith.' The Holy Prophet[sa] said: 'That you should believe in Allāh, His Angels, His Books, His Messengers, the Last Day, and that you should believe that He determines the measure of good and evil.' The man said: 'That is right. Now tell me about the due performance of obligations.' The Holy Prophet[sa] said: 'That you should worship Allāh as if you are beholding Him, and if not then remaining conscious that He is watching you.' The man said: 'Now tell me about the Hour of Judgment.' The Holy Prophet[sa] said: 'He who is being asked knows no more about it than the one who asks.' The man then said: 'Well, tell me some of the signs of its approach.' The Holy Prophet[sa] answered: 'The slave-girl would give birth to her master and that barefooted, bare bodied, penurious goat-herders would be seen building great mansions.' Then the man departed, and I remained a while. The Holy Prophet[sa] said to me: "Umar, do you know who the questioner was?' I said: 'Allāh and His Messenger know best.' He said: 'It was Gabriel who came to instruct you in your faith.' "

(Ṣaḥīḥ Bukhārī, Kitābul Īmān, Bāb Jibrīlannabiyyu 'anil Īmāni wal-Islām; Jāmi' Tirmidhī, Kitābul Īmān, Bāb fī waṣaf Jibrīlunnabī al-īmān wal-islām; Ṣaḥīḥ Muslim,, Kitābul Īmān)

Compilation of the Holy Qur'ān

God Almighty appointed the Chief of mankind, Pride of the Prophets, *Khātamun Nabiyyīn* (the Seal of the Prophets), Ḥaḍrat Muḥammad Muṣṭafā[sa] , as a Prophet at the age of forty, and revealed to him His Word recorded as the Holy Qur'ān. Thus the Holy Qur'ān is the record of the verbal revelations in Arabic from God Almighty to the Holy Prophet Muhammad[sa], over a period of about 23 years (610-632 AD). The word Qur'ān means that which is often read or recited. It contains a complete code of teaching and laws suitable to the needs of every age and provides the means for the spiritual and moral development of all mankind. The Holy Qur'ān also contains numerous prophecies for the future. The Holy Qur'ān calls itself a reminder to the worlds:

إِنْ هُوَ إِلَّا ذِكْرٌ لِّلْعٰلَمِيْنَ ۝

in huwa illā dhikrullil 'ālamīn

It is nothing but a Reminder unto all the worlds. (81:28)

The revelation of the Holy Qur'ān and its preservation was a very important and delicate responsibility of the Holy Prophet[sa]. He had to devote a large part of his time to this. Whenever he received the revelation, whether at home or in the company of his Companions[ra], he would pass through an extraordinary condition which would cause him to sweat profusely. Immediately after receiving the revelation he would call for one of the scribes and dictate the revelation to him.

The Divine revelations were committed to memory and also written down by scribes appointed by the Holy Prophet[sa]. He himself indicated the arrangement of verses and chapters in the Qur'ān, as we find it today. So the entire text of the Holy Qur'ān was written on bark, leaves, bones, etc., during the lifetime of the Holy Prophet[sa].

As soon as a revelation was received by the Holy Prophet[sa] it was recorded in writing from his dictation. A number of persons are known to have been employed by the Holy Prophet[sa] for this purpose. Of these the names of the following fifteen have been mentioned in the traditions.

(Fatḥ al-Bārī, Ḥafīẓ Ibni Ḥajr, Vol. 9, p. 19):

1. Zaid bin Thābit
2. Ubayy ibn Ka'b
3. 'Abdullāh bin Sa'd bin Abī Sarḥ
4. Zubair bin al-'Awwām
5. Khālid bin Sa'īd bin al-'Ās
6. Abān bin Sa'īd bin al-'Ās
7. Hanẓalā bin al-Rabī' al-Asadī
8. Mu'aiqīb bin Abī Fāṭimah
9. 'Abdullāh bin Arqam al-Zuhrī
10. Shuraḥbīl bin Ḥasana
11. 'Abdullāh bin Rawāḥah
12. Abū Bakr
13. 'Umar
14. 'Uthmān
15. 'Alī

Whenever the Holy Prophet[sa] received a revelation, he would send for one of these persons and dictate to him the text of the revelation he had received. A very distinctive feature of the Holy Qur'ān is that it contains a Divine guarantee for its perpetual preservation. God Almighty says in the Holy Qur'ān:

إِنَّا نَحْنُ نَزَّلْنَا الذِّكْرَ وَ إِنَّا لَهٗ لَحٰفِظُوْنَ 0

innā naḥnu nazzalnadhdhikra wa innā lahū la ḥāfiẓūn

Verily, We Ourself have sent down this Exhortation, and most surely We will its Guardian. (15:10)

As a result of this guarantee, the text of the Holy Qur'ān has remained unchanged for more than fourteen hundred years.

The Holy Prophet[sa] had two tasks: The first was to convey the message of God Almighty as indicated in the following verse of the Holy Qur'ān:

يٰٓاَيُّهَا الرَّسُوْلُ بَلِّغْ مَآ اُنْزِلَ اِلَيْكَ مِنْ رَّبِّكَ ط وَ اِنْ لَّمْ تَفْعَلْ فَمَا بَلَّغْتَ رِسَالَتَهٗ ط

yā ayyu harrasūlu balligh mā unzila ilaika mirrabika wa illam taf'al famā ballaghta risālatah

O Messenger! convey *to the people* what has been revealed to you from your Lord; and if you do it not, you have not conveyed His Message *at all.* (5:68)

The second task of the Holy Prophet[sa] was to expound on the Holy Qur'ān and give a commentary on it. This is encompassed in the form of

Sunnah and *Ḥadīth* of the Holy Prophet[sa] and is well known as such amongst the followers of the Holy Prophet of Islām[sa]. This task of the Holy Prophet[sa] has been explained in the following verse of the Holy Qur'ān:

وَ اَنْزَلْنَآ اِلَيْكَ الذِّكْرَ لِتُبَيِّنَ لِلنَّاسِ مَا نُزِّلَ اِلَيْهِمْ وَ لَعَلَّهُمْ يَتَفَكَّرُوْنَ ٥

wa anzalnā ilaikadhdhikra li-tubayyina linnāsi mā nuzzila ilaihim wa la'allahum yatafakkarūn

And We have sent down to you the reminder that you may explain to mankind that which has been sent down to them, and that they may reflect. (16:45)

Thus along with the recitation of the Holy Qur'ān, the explanation and commentary of the Holy Qur'ān through the sayings and actions of the Holy Prophet[sa] is as essential for Muslims to obey and follow as it is to follow and obey the Holy Qur'ān, as stated by God Almighty in the Holy Qur'ān:

وَمَآ اٰتٰكُمُ الرَّسُوْلُ فَخُذُوْهُ ۚ وَمَا نَهٰكُمْ عَنْهُ فَانْتَهُوْا ۚ

wa mā ātākumurrasūlu fa khudhūhu wamā nahākum 'anhu fantahū

And whatsoever the Messenger gives you, take it; and whatsoever he forbids you, abstain from *that.* (59:8)

18

The Exalted Status of the Holy Prophet[sa]

As Stated in the Holy Qur'ān

In the Holy Qur'ān God Almighty has given the following titles to the Holy Prophet[sa]:

طٰهٰ	Ṭā Hā (20:2)	(O Perfect man)
يٰسٓ	Yā Sīn (36:2)	(O Perfect Leader)
اَلْاِنْسَانُ	Al-Insān (33:73)	(The Perfect man)
عَبْدُ اللّٰهِ	'Abdullāh 72:20:	(The Servant of Allāh)
اَلْمُزَّمِّلُ	Al-Muzzammil (73:2)	(O you who has wrapped *himself* in a robe!)
اَلْمُدَّثِّرُ	Al-Mudaththir (74:2)	(O you that has wrapped *yourself with your mantle*!)

God Almighty says about the Holy Prophet[sa] in a *Ḥadīth-e-Qudsī*:

لَوْلَاكَ لَمَا خَلَقْتُ الْاَفْلَاكَ

lau lāka lamā khalaqtul aflāka

(O Muḥammad!) Had I not planned to create you, I would not have created the Universe

(Al-Fuwā'idul Majmū'ah, Muḥammad bin 'Alī Ashshaukānī, p. 346)

In the Holy Qur'ān, God Almighty has mentioned many praiseworthy and exalted attributes of the Holy Prophet[sa]. Some of which are as follows:

1. His coming was as if God Himself came

وَمَا رَمَيْتَ إِذْ رَمَيْتَ وَلٰكِنَّ اللّٰهَ رَمٰى ۚ

wamā ramita idh ramaita wa lākinnallāha ramā

"And you threw not when you did throw, but it was Allāh who threw ..." (8:18)

2. His pure heart is the throne of Allāh

فَكَانَ قَابَ قَوْسَيْنِ اَوْ اَدْنٰى ۚ ۝

fa kāna qāba qausaini au adnā

"So that he became, *as it were*, one chord to two bows or closer still." (53:10)

3. Allāh and His angels send blessings on him

إِنَّ اللّٰهَ وَ مَلٰٓئِكَتَهٗ يُصَلُّوْنَ عَلَى النَّبِيِّ ؕ يٰٓاَيُّهَا الَّذِيْنَ اٰمَنُوْا صَلُّوْا

عَلَيْهِ وَسَلِّمُوْا تَسْلِيْمًا 0

innallāha wa malā'ikatahū yuṣallūna 'alannabiyyi yā ayyuhalladhīna āmanū ṣallū 'alaihi wa sallimū taslīmā

Allāh and His angels send blessings on the Prophet. O ye who believe! you *also* should invoke blessings on him and salute *him* with the salutation of peace. (33:57)

4. Allāh has sent down to him the Book (the Holy Qur'ān:

وَاَنْزَلَ اللّٰهُ عَلَيْكَ الْكِتٰبَ وَالْحِكْمَةَ وَعَلَّمَكَ مَا لَمْ تَكُنْ تَعْلَمُ ؕ

وَكَانَ فَضْلُ اللّٰهِ عَلَيْكَ عَظِيْمًا 0

wa anzalallāhu 'alaikal kitāba wal ḥikmata wa 'allamaka mā lam takun ta'lam wa kāna faḍlullāhi 'alaika 'aẓīmā

Allāh has sent down to you the Book and Wisdom and has taught you what you knew not; and great is Allāh's Grace on you. (4:114)

وَاِنَّكَ لَتُلَقَّى الْقُرْاٰنَ مِنْ لَّدُنْ حَكِيْمٍ عَلِيْمٍ 0

wa innaka latulaqqal qur'āna milladun ḥakīmin 'alīm

Verily, you have been given the Qur'ān from the presence of One Wise, All-Knowing. (27:7)

5. Allegiance to him was allegiance to Allāh:

إِنَّ الَّذِيْنَ يُبَايِعُوْنَكَ إِنَّمَا يُبَايِعُوْنَ اللّٰهَ ط يَدُ اللّٰهِ فَوْقَ أَيْدِيْهِمْ ج

innalladhīna yubāyi'ūnaka innamā yubāyi'ūnallāha yadullāhi fauqa aidīhim

"Verily, those who swear allegiance to you indeed swear allegiance to Allāh. The hand of Allāh is over their hands." (48:11)

6. If you love Allāh, follow the Holy Prophet[sa], then will Allāh love you:

قُلْ إِنْ كُنْتُمْ تُحِبُّوْنَ اللّٰهَ فَاتَّبِعُوْنِيْ يُحْبِبْكُمُ اللّٰهُ وَيَغْفِرْلَكُمْ

ذُنُوْبَكُمْ ط وَاللّٰهُ غَفُوْرٌ رَّحِيْمٌ 0 قُلْ أَطِيْعُوا اللّٰهَ وَالرَّسُوْلَ ج فَإِنْ

تَوَلَّوْا فَإِنَّ اللّٰهَ لَايُحِبُّ الْكَافِرِيْنَ 0

qul in kuntum tuhibbūnallāha fattabi'ūnī yuhbibkumullāhu wa yaghfirlakum dhunūbakum wallāhu ghafūrurrahīm qul atī'ullāha warrasūla fa in tawallau fa innallāha lā yuhibbul kāfirīn

Say, 'If you love Allāh, follow me: *then* will Allāh love you and forgive you your faults. And Allāh is most Forgiving and Merciful.' Say, 'Obey

Allāh and the Messenger:' but if they turn away, then *remember that* Allāh loves not the disbelievers. (3:32-33)

In the Holy Qur'ān, the commandment to follow the Holy Prophet[sa]:

أَطِيْعُوا اللّٰهَ وَ أَطِيْعُوا الرَّسُوْلَ

aṭī'ullāha wa aṭī'urrasūl

is mentioned several times.

7. Obedience to him was obedience to Allāh

مَنْ يُّطِعِ الرَّسُوْلَ فَقَدْ أَطَاعَ اللّٰهَ ۚ وَمَنْ تَوَلّٰى فَمَآ أَرْسَلْنٰكَ عَلَيْهِمْ حَفِيْظًا ۝

wa mañyyuṭ'irrasūla faqad aṭā'allāha wa man tawallā famā arsalnāka 'alaihim ḥafīẓā

"Whoso obeys the Messenger obeys Allāh indeed; and whoso turns away, then We have not sent you as a keeper over them." (4:81)

8. Allāh is sufficient for him and his followers:

يٰٓأَيُّهَا النَّبِيُّ حَسْبُكَ اللّٰهُ وَمَنِ اتَّبَعَكَ مِنَ الْمُؤْمِنِيْنَ ۝

yā ayyuhannabiyyu ḥasbukallāhu wama nittaba'aka minal mu'minīna

O Prophet, Allāh is sufficient for you and for those who follow you of the believers. (8:65)

9. His prayers are a source of tranquility

وَصَلِّ عَلَيْهِمْ إِنَّ صَلٰوتَكَ سَكَنٌ لَّهُمْ

wa ṣalli 'alaihim inna ṣalātaka sakanullahum

And pray for them; your prayer is indeed a *source of* tranquility for them. (9:103)

10. Respond to Allāh and the Holy Prophet[sa] that he may give you life

يٰٓاَيُّهَا الَّذِيْنَ اٰمَنُوْا اسْتَجِيْبُوْا لِلّٰهِ وَلِلرَّسُوْلِ اِذَا دَعَاكُمْ لِمَا يُحْيِيْكُمْ

yā ayyu halladhīna āmanustajībū lillāhi wa lirrasūli idhā da'ākum limā yuḥyīkum

O ye who believe! respond to Allāh, and the Messenger when he calls you that he may give you life. (8:25)

11. Allah gives a double share of His Mercy upon believing in Him and His Messenger

يٰۤاَيُّهَا الَّذِيْنَ اٰمَنُوا اتَّقُوا اللّٰهَ وَ اٰمِنُوْا بِرَسُوْلِهٖ يُؤْتِكُمْ كِفْلَيْنِ مِنْ
رَّحْمَتِهٖ وَيَجْعَلْ لَّكُمْ نُوْرًا تَمْشُوْنَ بِهٖ وَيَغْفِرْ لَكُمْ ؕ وَاللّٰهُ غَفُوْرٌ
رَّحِيْمٌ ۚۙ O

yā ayyuhalladhīna āmanttaqullāha wa āminū birasūlihī yu'tikum kiflaini mirraḥmatihī wa yaj'allakum nūran tamshūna bihī wa yaghfirlakum wallāhu ghafūrurraḥīm

O ye who believe! fear Allāh and believe in His Messenger; He will give you a double share of His mercy, and will provide for you a light wherein you will walk, and will grant you forgiveness - and verily Allāh is Most Forgiving, Merciful. (57:29)

12. He was fully a perfect light

يٰۤاَيُّهَا النَّاسُ قَدْ جَآءَكُمْ بُرْهَانٌ مِّنْ رَّبِّكُمْ وَاَنْزَلْنَآ اِلَيْكُمْ نُوْرًا
مُّبِيْنًا O

yā ayyu-hannāsu qad jā'akum burhānummirrabbikum wa anzalnā ilaikum nūrammubīnā

"O ye people, a manifest proof has indeed come to you from your Lord, and We have sent down to you a clear light." (4:175)

13. He was the manifestation of the Light of Allāh

اَللّٰهُ نُوْرُ السَّمٰوٰتِ وَالْاَرْضِ ؕ مَثَلُ نُوْرِهٖ كَمِشْكٰوةٍ فِيْهَا مِصْبَاحٌ ؕ
اَلْمِصْبَاحُ فِيْ زُجَاجَةٍ ؕ اَلزُّجَاجَةُ كَاَنَّهَا كَوْكَبٌ دُرِّيٌّ يُّوْقَدُ مِنْ
شَجَرَةٍ مُّبٰرَكَةٍ زَيْتُوْنَةٍ لَّا شَرْقِيَّةٍ وَّلَا غَرْبِيَّةٍ ۙ يَّكَادُ زَيْتُهَا يُضِيْٓءُ
وَلَوْ لَمْ تَمْسَسْهُ نَارٌ ؕ نُوْرٌ عَلٰى نُوْرٍ ؕ يَهْدِى اللّٰهُ لِنُوْرِهٖ مَنْ يَّشَآءُ ؕ

allāhu nūrussamāwāti wal-arḍ mathalu nūrihī kamishkātin fīhā miṣbāḥun al-miṣbāḥu fī zujājatin azzujājatu ka annahā kaukabun durriñyyuñyūqadu min shajaratimmubārakatin zaitūnatillā sharqiyya tiñwwa lā gharbiyyatiñyyakādu zaituhā yuḍī'u walau lam tamsashu nārun nūrun 'alā nūr yahdillāhu li nūrihī mñyyashā'

Allāh is the Light of the heavens and the earth. The similitude of His light is as a lustrous niche, wherein is a lamp. The lamp is in a glass. The glass is as it were a glittering star. It is lit from a blessed tree--an olive--neither of the east nor of the west, whose oil would well-nigh glow forth even though fire touched it not. Light upon light! Allāh guides to His Light whomsoever He wills (24:36)

14. He was the bright sun

يٰۤاَيُّهَا النَّبِيُّ اِنَّآ اَرْسَلْنٰكَ شَاهِدًا وَّمُبَشِّرًا وَّنَذِيْرًا ۙ۝ وَّدَاعِيًا اِلَى
اللّٰهِ بِاِذْنِهٖ وَسِرَاجًا مُّنِيْرًا ۝

yā ayyu hannabiyyu innā arsalnāka shāhidañwwa mubashshirañwwa nadhīrañwwa dā'iyan ilallāhi bi idhnihī wa sirājammunīrā

O Prophet, truly We have sent you as a Witness, and a Bearer of glad tidings, and a Warner. And as a Summoner to Allāh by His command, and as a radiant Lamp. (33:46-47)

15. He unfolds what is hidden of the book

يَٰٓأَهْلَ الْكِتٰبِ قَدْ جَآءَكُمْ رَسُوْلُنَا يُبَيِّنُ لَكُمْ كَثِيْرًا مِّمَّا كُنْتُمْ
تُخْفُوْنَ مِنَ الْكِتٰبِ وَ يَعْفُوْا عَنْ كَثِيْرٍ ط قَدْ جَآءَكُمْ مِّنَ اللّٰهِ
نُوْرٌ وَّ كِتٰبٌ مُّبِيْنٌ لا ٥

yā ahlalkitābi qad jā'akum rasūlunā yubayyinu lakum kathīrammimmā kuntum tukhfūna minalkitābi wa ya'fū 'an kathīr qad jā'akumminallāhi nūruñwwa kitābummubīn

O People of the Book! there has come to you Our Messenger who unfolds to you much of what you had kept hidden of the Book and passes over much. There has come to you indeed from Allāh a Light and a clear Book. (5:16)

16. He had an exalted status

وَمِنَ الَّيْلِ فَتَهَجَّدْ بِهٖ نَافِلَةً لَّكَ ط عَسٰٓى اَنْ يَّبْعَثَكَ رَبُّكَ مَقَامًا
مَّحْمُوْدًا ٥

waminallaili fata-hajjad bihī nāfilatallaka 'asā añyyab'athaka rabbuka maqāmammaḥmūdā

"And wake up for it (the Qur'ān) in *the latter part of* the night as a supererogatory service for you. It may be that your Lord will raise you to an exalted station." (17:80)

17. He was *Khātamun Nabiyyīn* (Seal of the Prophets)

مَا كَانَ مُحَمَّدٌ اَبَآ اَحَدٍمِّنْ رِّجَالِكُمْ وَلٰكِنْ رَّسُوْلَ اللّٰهِ وَخَاتَمَ النَّبِيّٖنَ ۭ وَكَانَ اللّٰهُ بِكُلِّ شَىْءٍ عَلِيْمًا 0

mā kāna Muḥammadun abā aḥadimmirrijālikum wa lākirrasūlallāhi wa khātamannabiyyīn wa kānallāhu bi kulli shai'in 'alīmā

"Muḥammad is not the father of any of your men, but *he is* the Messenger of Allāh and the Seal of the Prophets; and Allāh has full knowledge of all things." (33:41)

The Holy Prophet[sa] once said:

كُنْتُ مَكْتُوْبًا عِنْدَ اللّٰهِ خَاتَمَ النَّبِيّٖنَ وَاَنَّ اٰدمَ لَمُنْجَدِلٌ فِيْ طِيْنِهٖ

kuntu maktūban 'indallāhi khātamannabiyyīna wa anna ādama lamunjadilun fī ṭīnihī

(In the sight of Allāh, I was *Khātamun-Nabiyyīn* since the time Adam was in the early stages of creation from clay and water."

(Musnad Aḥmad, p 127/4, Kanzul 'Ummāl, p. 112/6; Al-Khaṣā'sa al-Kubrā, Vol. 1, p.4)

Ḥaḍrat Zuhrī relates that he heard Jubair bin Muṭ'im[ra] say what he had heard from his father that the Holy Prophet[sa] said: "I am Muḥammad and Aḥmad; I am an obliterator. I will obliterate infidelity. I am a resurrector. People will be resurrected after me, and I am the last one to come. Therefore, no (independent and Law bearing) Prophet will come after me."

(Ṣaḥīḥ Muslim, Kitābul Faḍāi'l, Bāb fī asmāi' ṣalallāhu 'alaihi wasallam[sa])

18. He was a means to achieve nearness to Allāh

يَآيُّهَا الَّذِيْنَ اٰمَنُوْا اتَّقُوا اللّٰهَ وَابْتَغُوْٓا اِلَيهِ الْوَسِيْلَةَ وَجَاهِدُوْا فِيْ سَبِيْلِهٖ لَعَلَّكُمْ تُفْلِحُوْنَ 0

yā ayyuhalladhīna āmanuttaqullāha wabtaghū ilaihil wasīlata wa jāhidū fī sabīlihī la'allakum tufliḥūn

"O ye who believe! fear Allāh and seek the waý of approach unto Him and strive in His way that you may prosper." (5:36)

19. He will be a witness on the Day of Judgement

فَكَيْفَ اِذَا جِئْنَا مِنْ كُلِّ اُمَّةٍۭ بِشَهِيْدٍ وَّ جِئْنَا بِكَ عَلٰى هٰٓؤُلَآءِ

شَهِيْدًا 0 يَوْمَئِذٍ يَّوَدُّ الَّذِيْنَ كَفَرُوْا وَعَصَوُا الرَّسُوْلَ لَوْ تُسَوّٰى
بِهِمُ الْاَرْضُ ۗ وَلَا يَكْتُمُوْنَ اللّٰهَ حَدِيْثًا 0

fa kaifa idhā ji'nā min kulli ummatim bishahīdiñwwa ji'nā bika 'alā hā-'ulā'i shahīdā yauma'idhiñyya waddulladhīna kafarū wa 'aṣawurrasūla lau tusawwā bihimul arḍu walā yaktumūnallāha ḥadīthā

And how *will it fare with them* when We shall bring a witness from every people, and shall bring you as a witness against these! On that day those who disbelieved and disobeyed the Messenger will wish that the earth were made level with them, and they shall not *be able to* conceal anything from Allāh. (4:42-43)

20. He was the chief of all the Prophets and mercy for mankind

وَمَآ اَرْسَلْنٰكَ اِلَّا رَحْمَةً لِّلْعٰلَمِيْنَ 0

wa mā arsalnāka illā raḥmatallil 'ālamīn

"And We have sent you not but as a mercy for all peoples." (21:108)

21. He was a warner to all the worlds

تَبٰرَكَ الَّذِيْ نَزَّلَ الْفُرْقَانَ عَلٰى عَبْدِهٖ لِيَكُوْنَ لِلْعٰلَمِيْنَ نَذِيْرًا ۙ 0

tabārakalladhī nazzalal furqāna 'alā 'abdihī liyakūna lil 'ālamīna nadhīrā

Blessed is He Who has sent down the Discrimination (distinction between truth and falsehood) to His servant, that he may be a Warner to *all* the wolds. (25:2)

22. His heart was right regarding what he saw

فَاَوْحٰۤى اِلٰى عَبْدِهٖ مَاۤ اَوْحٰى ۝ط مَا كَذَبَ الْفُؤَادُ مَا رَاٰى ۝

fa auḥā ilā 'abdihī mā auḥā mā kadhabal fu'ādu mā ra-ā

"Then He revealed to His servant that which He revealed. The heart *of* the Prophet lied not regarding what he saw." (53:11-12)

23. Those who follow the Prophet, shall prosper

اَلَّذِيْنَ يَتَّبِعُوْنَ الرَّسُوْلَ النَّبِيَّ الْاُمِّيَّ الَّذِيْ يَجِدُوْنَهٗ مَكْتُوْبًا
عِنْدَهُمْ فِى التَّوْرٰىةِ وَالْاِنْجِيْلِ ز يَاْمُرُهُمْ بِالْمَعْرُوْفِ وَيَنْهٰهُمْ
عَنِ الْمُنْكَرِ وَيُحِلُّ لَهُمُ الطَّيِّبٰتِ وَيُحَرِّمُ عَلَيْهِمُ الْخَبٰٓئِثَ
وَيَضَعُ عَنْهُمْ اِصْرَهُمْ وَالْاَغْلٰلَ الَّتِيْ كَانَتْ عَلَيْهِمْ ط فَالَّذِيْنَ
اٰمَنُوْا بِهٖ وَعَزَّرُوْهُ وَنَصَرُوْهُ وَاتَّبَعُوا النُّوْرَ الَّذِيْٓ اُنْزِلَ مَعَهٗٓ لا
اُولٰٓئِكَ هُمُ الْمُفْلِحُوْنَ ۝ط

alladhīna yattabi'ūnarrasūlannabiyyal ummiyyalladhī yajidūnahū maktūban 'indahum fittaurāti wal injīli ya'muruhum bil ma'rūfi wa yanhāhum 'anil munkari wa yuḥillu lahumuṭṭayyibāti wa yuḥarrimu 'alaihimul khabā'itha wa yaḍa'u 'anhum iṣrahum wal aghlālallatī kānat 'alaihim falladhīna āmanū bihī wa 'azzarūhu wa naṣarūhu wattaba'unnūralladhī unzila ma'ahū ulā'ika humul mufliḥūn

Those who follow the Messenger, the Prophet, the unlettered one, whom they find mentioned in the Torah and the Gospel *which are* with them. He enjoins on them good and forbids them evil, and makes lawful for them the good things and forbids them the bad, and removes from them their burden and the shackles that were upon them. So those who shall believe in him, and honor and support him, and help him, and follow the light that has been sent down with him - these shall prosper. (7:158)

24. He possessed high moral excellences

وَإِنَّكَ لَعَلٰى خُلُقٍ عَظِيْمٍ 0

wa innaka la'alā khuluqin 'aẓīm

"And you do surely possess high moral excellences." (68:5)

25. He was kind-hearted and gentle in his conduct

فَبِمَا رَحْمَةٍ مِّنَ اللّٰهِ لِنْتَ لَهُمْ ۚ وَلَوْ كُنْتَ فَظًّا غَلِيْظَ الْقَلْبِ

لَانْفَضُّوْا مِنْ حَوْلِكَ ص

fabimā raḥmatimminallāhi linta lahum walau kunta faẓẓan ghalīẓal qalbi lanfaḍḍū min ḥaulika

"And it is by the *great* mercy of Allāh that you are kind towards them, and if you had been rough *and* hard-hearted, they would surely have dispersed from around you." (3:160)

26. He occupied a position of manifest knowledge

قُلْ هٰذِهٖ سَبِيْلِيْٓ اَدْعُوْٓا اِلَى اللّٰهِ قف عَلٰى بَصِيْرَةٍ اَنَا وَ مَنِ اتَّبَعَنِيْ ط

qul hādhihī sabīlī ad'ū ilallāh 'alā baṣīratin anā wa manittaba'anī

Say, "This is my way: I call unto Allāh. I occupy a position of manifest knowledge, and also those who follow me. (12:109)

27. He was compassionate and merciful

لَقَدْ جَآءَكُمْ رَسُوْلٌ مِّنْ اَنْفُسِكُمْ عَزِيْزٌ عَلَيْهِ مَا عَنِتُّمْ
حَرِيْصٌ عَلَيْكُمْ بِالْمُؤْمِنِيْنَ رَءُوْفٌ رَّحِيْمٌ 0

laqad jā'akum rasūlummin anfusikum 'azīzun 'alaihi mā 'anittum ḥarīṣun 'alaikum bil mu'minīna ra'ūfurraḥīm

"Surely, a Messenger has come unto you from among yourselves; grievous to him is that you should fall into trouble; *he is* ardently desirous of your *welfare*, *and* to the believers *he is* compassionate, merciful." (9:128)

28. His heart was full of kindness for the humanity

فَلَعَلَّكَ بَاخِعٌ نَّفْسَكَ عَلٰٓى اٰثَارِهِمْ اِنْ لَّمْ يُؤْمِنُوْا بِهٰذَا الْحَدِيْثِ
اَسَفًا 0

fala'allaka bākhi'unnafsaka 'alā āthārihim illam yu'minū bihādhal ḥadīthi asafā

"So haply thou will grieve yourself to death for sorrow after them if they believe not in this discourse. (18:7)

29. He sought Allāh's forgiveness even for the hypocrites

سَوَآءٌ عَلَيْهِمْ اَسْتَغْفَرْتَ لَهُمْ اَمْ لَمْ تَسْتَغْفِرْ لَهُمْ ط لَنْ
يَّغْفِرَ اللّٰهُ لَهُمْ ط اِنَّ اللّٰهَ لَا يَهْدِى الْقَوْمَ الْفٰسِقِيْنَ 0

sawā'un 'alaihim astaghfarta lahum am lam tastaghfir lahum lañyyaghfirallāhu lahum innallāha lā yahdil qaumal fāsiqīn

It is equal to them whether you ask forgiveness for them or ask not forgiveness for them, Allāh will never forgive them. Surely Allāh guides not the rebellious people. (63:7)

30. Each moment of his life was better than what preceded

وَلَلْاٰخِرَةُ خَيْرٌ لَّكَ مِنَ الْاُوْلٰى 0

walal-ākhiratu khairullaka minal ūlā

Surely *every hour* that follows is better for you than *the one* that precedes." (93:5)

31. He was abundantly bestowed with knowledge of the unseen

ذٰلِكَ مِنْ اَنْۢبَآءِ الْغَيْبِ نُوْحِيْهِ اِلَيْكَ ۚ وَمَا كُنْتَ لَدَيْهِمْ اِذْ اَجْمَعُوْٓا اَمْرَهُمْ وَهُمْ يَمْكُرُوْنَ ۝

dhālika min ambā'il ghaibi nūḥīhi ilaika wamā kunta ladaihim idh ajma'ū amrahum wa hum yamkurūn

That is of the tidings of the unseen, *which* We reveal to you. And you were not with them when they agreed upon their plan while they were plotting. (12:103)

32. He never spoke out of his own desires

وَمَا يَنْطِقُ عَنِ الْهَوٰى ۝ اِنْ هُوَ اِلَّا وَحْيٌ يُّوْحٰى ۝

wamā yanṭiqu 'anilhawā in huwa illā waḥyuñyyūḥā

"Nor does he speak out of *his own* desire. It is nothing but *pure* revelation *that has been* revealed *by God*." (53:4-5)

33. He was a perfect and an exemplary servant of Allāh

وَّ اَنَّهٗ لَمَّا قَامَ عَبْدُ اللّٰهِ يَدْعُوْهُ كَادُوْا يَكُوْنُوْنَ عَلَيْهِ لِبَدًا ٥

wa annahū lammā qāma 'abdullāhi yad'ūhu kādū yakūnūna 'alaihi libadā

"And when the Servant of Allāh stands up praying to Him, they crowd upon him, well nigh suffocating him. (72:20).

عَبْدًا اِذَا صَلّٰى ٥

'abdan idhā ṣallā

A servant *of Ours* when he prays?" (96:11)

34. He was a true servant of Allāh

قُلْ اِنَّ صَلَاتِيْ وَنُسُكِيْ وَمَحْيَايَ وَمَمَاتِيْ لِلّٰهِ رَبِّ الْعٰلَمِيْنَ ٥

qul inna ṣalātī wa nusukī wa maḥyāya wa mamātī lillāhi rabbil 'ālamīn

Say, 'My Prayer and my sacrifice and my life and my death are *all* for Allāh, the Lord of the worlds.' (6:163)

35. He was a Messenger to all mankind

قُلْ يٰٓاَيُّهَا النَّاسُ اِنِّيْ رَسُوْلُ اللّٰهِ اِلَيْكُمْ جَمِيْعًا الَّذِيْ لَهٗ

مُلْكُ السَّمٰوٰتِ وَالْاَرْضِ ۚ لَآ اِلٰهَ اِلَّا هُوَ يُحْيٖ وَيُمِيْتُ ۖ

فَاٰمِنُوْا بِاللّٰهِ وَرَسُوْلِهِ النَّبِيِّ الْاُمِّيِّ الَّذِيْ يُؤْمِنُ بِاللّٰهِ وَكَلِمٰتِهٖ

وَاتَّبِعُوْهُ لَعَلَّكُمْ تَهْتَدُوْنَ 0

qul yā ayyu hannāsu innī rasūlullāhi ilaikum jamī'a nilladhī lahū mulkussamāwāti walarḍ, lā ilāha illā huwa yuḥyī wa yumītu fa āminū billāhi wa rasūlihinnabiyyil ummiyyilladhī yu'minu billāhi wa kalimātihī wattabi'ūhu la'allakum tahtadūn

Say, 'O mankind! truly I am a Messenger to you all from Allāh to Whom belongs the kingdom of the heavens and the earth. There is no God but He. He gives life, and He causes death. So believe in Allāh and His Messenger, the Prophet, the Immaculate one, who believes in Allāh and His words; and follow him that you may be rightly guided.' (7:159)

36. He was a means to achieve Allāh's Mercy

وَ اَطِيْعُوا الرَّسُوْلَ لَعَلَّكُمْ تُرْحَمُوْنَ 0

wa aṭī'urrasūla la'allakum turḥamūn

And obey the Messenger, that you may be shown mercy. (24:57)

37. He was a means to attain success

وَمَنْ يُّطِعِ اللّٰهَ وَ رَسُوْلَهٗ فَقَدْ فَازَ فَوْزًا عَظِيْمًا 0

wa mañyyuṭi‘illāha wa rasūlahū faqad fāza fauzan ‘aẓīmā

And whoso obeys Allāh and HIs Messenger, shall surely attain a mighty success. (33:72)

38. He was a means to obtain great Blessings of Allāh

وَمَنْ يُّطِعِ اللّٰهَ وَالرَّسُوْلَ فَاُولٰٓئِكَ مَعَ الَّذِيْنَ اَنْعَمَ اللّٰهُ عَلَيْهِمْ مِّنَ
النَّبِيّٖنَ وَالصِّدِّيْقِيْنَ وَالشُّهَدَآءِ وَالصّٰلِحِيْنَ ۚ وَحَسُنَ اُولٰٓئِكَ رَفِيْقًا ۝

wa mañyyuṭi ‘illāha warrasūla fa ‘ulā’ika ma‘alladhīna an‘amallāhu ‘alaihimmi nannabiyyīna waṣṣiddīqīna washshuhadā’i waṣṣāliḥīna wa ḥasuna ‘ulā’ika rafīqā

And whoso obeys Allāh and this Messenger *of His* shall be among those on whom Allāh has bestowed His blessings, namely, the Prophets, the Truthful, the Martyrs, and the Righteous. And excellent companions are these. (4:70)

39. He was a bearer of glad tidings and a warner

وَمَآ اَرْسَلْنٰكَ اِلَّا كَآفَّةً لِّلنَّاسِ بَشِيْرًا وَّنَذِيْرًا

wa mā arsalnāka illā kā‘ffa tallinnāsi bashīrañwwa nadhīrā

And We have not sent you but as a bearer of glad tidings and a Warner, for all mankind (34:29*)*

40. He was a plain warner:

قُلْ يٰٓاَيُّهَا النَّاسُ اِنَّمَآ اَنَالَكُمْ نَذِيْرٌمُّبِيْنٌ ۚ 0

qul yā ayyuhannāsu innamā anā lakum naḏīrummubīn

Say, 'O mankind, I am but a plain Warner to you. (22:50)

قُلْ اِنَّمَآ اَنَا مُنْذِرٌ ۖ وَّ مَا مِنْ اِلٰهٍ اِلَّا اللّٰهُ الْوَاحِدُ الْقَهَّارُ 0

qul innamā anā mundhiruñwwa mā min ilāhin illallāhul wāḥidul qahhār

Say, 'I am only a Warner; and there is no God but Allāh, the One, the Most Supreme. (38:66)

41. He was a Messenger of Allāh with guidance and the religion of truth

هُوَ الَّذِيْٓ اَرْسَلَ رَسُوْلَهٗ بِالْهُدٰى وَدِيْنِ الْحَقِّ لِيُظْهِرَهٗ عَلَى
الدِّيْنِ كُلِّهٖ ۙ وَلَوْ كَرِهَ الْمُشْرِكُوْنَ 0

huwalladhī arsala rasūlahū bil hudā wa dīnil ḥaqqi liyuẓhirahū 'aladdīni kulli hī wa lau karihal mushrikūn

He it is Who sent His Messenger with guidance and the religion of truth, that He may make it prevail over every *other* religion, even though the idolaters may dislike it. (9:33)

هُوَ الَّذِيْٓ اَرْسَلَ رَسُوْلَهٗ بِالْهُدٰى وَدِيْنِ الْحَقِّ لِيُظْهِرَهٗ عَلَى
الدِّيْنِ كُلِّهٖ ؕ وَكَفٰى بِاللّٰهِ شَهِيْدًا ۝

huwalladhī arsala rasūlahū bil hudā wa dīnil ḥaqqi liyuẓhirahū 'aladdīni kulli hī wa kafā billāhi shahīdā

He it is Who has sent His Messenger, with guidance and the Religion of truth, that He may make it prevail over *all other* religions. And sufficient is Allāh as a Witness. (48:29)

42. He bore the Trust which the heavens, the earth and the mountains refused to bear

اِنَّا عَرَضْنَا الْاَمَانَةَ عَلَى السَّمٰوٰتِ وَالْاَرْضِ وَالْجِبَالِ فَاَبَيْنَ اَنْ
يَّحْمِلْنَهَا وَاَشْفَقْنَ مِنْهَا وَحَمَلَهَا الْاِنْسَانُ ؕ

innā 'araḍnal amānata 'alassamāwāti wal arḍi wal jibāli fa abaina añyyaḥmilnahā wa ashfaqna minhā wa ḥamalahal insānu

Verily, We offered the Trust to the heavens and the earth and the mountains, but they refused to bear it and were afraid of it. But man bore it. (33:73)

43. He invited humanity to the right path

وَ اِنَّكَ لَتَدْعُوْهُمْ اِلٰى صِرَاطٍ مُّسْتَقِيْمٍ ۝

wa innaka la tad'ū hum ilā ṣirāṭimmustaqīm

And most surely you invite them to a straight path. (23:74)

44. The religion of Islām and the revelation of the Holy Qur'ān was completed through him before his demise

اَلْيَوْمَ اَكْمَلْتُ لَكُمْ دِيْنَكُمْ وَ اَتْمَمْتُ عَلَيْكُمْ نِعْمَتِيْ وَ رَضِيْتُ لَكُمُ الْاِسْلَامَ دِيْنًا ط

al-yauma akmaltu lakum dīnakum wa atmamtu 'alaikum ni'matī wa raḍītu lakumul islāma dīnā

This day have I perfected your religion for you and completed My favor upon you and have chosen for you Islām as religion. (5:4)

45. He was a Messenger who recited the clear Signs of Allāh

قَدْ اَنْزَلَ اللّٰهُ اِلَيْكُمْ ذِكْرًا ۝ رَّسُوْلًا يَّتْلُوْا عَلَيْكُمْ اٰيٰتِ اللّٰهِ مُبَيِّنٰتٍ لِّيُخْرِجَ الَّذِيْنَ اٰمَنُوْا وَ عَمِلُوا الصّٰلِحٰتِ مِنَ الظُّلُمٰتِ اِلَى النُّوْرِ ط

qad anzalallāhu ilaikum dhikrar rasūlañyyatlū 'alaikum āyātillāhi mubayyinātilli yukhrijalladhīna āmanū wa 'amilusṣāliḥāti minaẓẓulumāti ilannūr

Allāh has indeed sent down to you a Reminder -- A Messenger, who recites unto you the clear Signs of Allāh, that he may bring those who believe and do good deeds out of every *kind of* darkness into light. (65:11-12)

46. He was a Messenger who purified and taught the Book of Wisdom

لَقَدْ مَنَّ اللّٰهُ عَلَى الْمُؤْمِنِيْنَ اِذْ بَعَثَ فِيْهِمْ رَسُوْلًا مِّنْ اَنْفُسِهِمْ يَتْلُوْا عَلَيْهِمْ اٰيٰتِهٖ وَيُزَكِّيْهِمْ وَيُعَلِّمُهُمُ الْكِتٰبَ وَالْحِكْمَةَ ج

laqad mannallāhu 'alal mu'minīna idh ba'atha fīhim rasūlammin anfusihim yatlū 'alaihim āyātihī wa yuzakkīhim wa yu'allimuhumul kitāba wal ḥikmata

Verily, Allāh has conferred a favor on the believers by raising among them a Messenger from among themselves, who recites to them His Signs, and purifies them and teaches them the Book and Wisdom. (3:165)

47. He was a moral guide for the followers

وَمَآ اٰتٰكُمُ الرَّسُوْلُ فَخُذُوْهُ ق وَمَا نَهٰكُمْ عَنْهُ فَانْتَهُوْا ج

mā ātākumurrasūlu fa khudhūhu wamā nahākum 'anhu fantahū

And whatsoever the Messenger gives you, take it; and whatsoever he forbids you, abstain from *that.* (59:8)

48. He was commanded to convey Allāh's Message

يٰٓاَيُّهَا الرَّسُوْلُ بَلِّغْ مَآ اُنْزِلَ اِلَيْكَ مِنْ رَّبِّكَ ط وَ اِنْ لَّمْ تَفْعَلْ فَمَا بَلَّغْتَ رِسَالَتَهٗ ط

yā ayyu harrasūlu balligh mā unzila ilaika mirrabik wa illam taf'al famā ballaghta risālatah

O Messenger! convey *to the people* what has been revealed to you from your Lord; and if you do it not, you have not conveyed His Message *at all.* (5:68)

49. He was a human being

قُلْ اِنَّمَآ اَنَا بَشَرٌ مِّثْلُكُمْ يُوْحٰٓى اِلَيَّ اَنَّمَآ اِلٰهُكُمْ اِلٰهٌ وَّاحِدٌ ج

qul innamā anā basharummithlukum yūḥā ilayya annamā ilāhukum ilāhuñwwāḥid

Say, 'I am only a man like yourselves; *but* I have received the revelation that your God is only One God.' (18:111)

50 The name of the Holy Prophet[sa] is mentioned in the Holy Qur'ān

In the Holy Qur'ān the name of the Holy Prophet's[sa] is mentioned in the following four places:

وَمَا مُحَمَّدٌ اِلاَّ رَسُوْلٌ ۚ قَدْ خَلَتْ مِنْ قَبْلِهِ الرُّسُلُ ۗ

wa mā Muḥammadun illā rasūlun qad khalat min qablihirrusul

And Muḥammad is only a Messenger. Verily, *all* Messengers have passed away before him. (3:145)

مَا كَانَ مُحَمَّدٌ اَبَآ اَحَدٍمِّنْ رِّجَالِكُمْ وَلٰكِنْ رَّسُوْلَ اللّٰهِ وَخَاتَمَ النَّبِيّٖنَ ۗ وَكَانَ اللّٰهُ بِكُلِّ شَيْءٍ عَلِيْمًا ۝

mā kāna Muḥammadun abā aḥadimmirrijālikum wa lākirrasūlallāhi wa khātamannabiyyīn wa kānallāhu bi kulli shai'in 'alīmā

Muḥammad is not the father of any of your men, but *he is* the Messenger of Allāh and the Seal of the Prophets; and Allāh has full knowledge of all things. (33:41)

وَ الَّذِيْنَ اٰمَنُوْا وَ عَمِلُوا الصّٰلِحٰتِ وَاٰمَنُوْا بِمَا نُزِّلَ عَلٰى مُحَمَّدٍ وَّ هُوَ الْحَقُّ مِنْ رَّبِّهِمْ ۙ كَفَّرَ عَنْهُمْ سَيِّاٰتِهِمْ وَاَصْلَحَ بَالَهُمْ ۝

walladhīna āmanū wa 'amiluṣṣāliḥāti wa āmanū bimā nuzzila 'alā Muḥammadiñwwa huwal ḥaqqu mirrabbihim kaffara 'anhum sayyi'ātihim wa aṣlaḥa bālahum

But *as for* those who believe and do good works and believe in that which has been revealed to Muḥammad - and it is the truth from their

Lord - He will remove from them their evils and will reform their conduct. (47:3)

مُحَمَّدٌ رَّسُوْلُ اللّٰهِ ؕ وَ الَّذِيْنَ مَعَهٗۤ اَشِدَّآءُ عَلَى الْكُفَّارِ رُحَمَآءُ
بَيْنَهُمْ تَرٰىهُمْ رُكَّعًا سُجَّدًا يَّبْتَغُوْنَ فَضْلًا مِّنَ اللّٰهِ وَ رِضْوَانًا ز

Muḥammadur rasūlullāhi walladhīna ma‘ahū ashiddā’u ‘alal kuffāri ruḥamā’u bainahum tarāhum rukka‘an sujjadañyyab taghūna faḍlamminallāhi wa riḍwānā

Muḥammad is the Messenger of Allāh. And those who are with him are firm against the non-believers, tender among themselves. You see them bowing and prostrating themselves *in Prayer*, seeking grace from Allāh and *His* pleasure. (48:30)

51. God Almighty exalted his name

اَلَمْ نَشْرَحْ لَكَ صَدْرَكَ ۙ وَ وَضَعْنَا عَنْكَ وِزْرَكَ ۙ الَّذِيْۤ
اَنْقَضَ ظَهْرَكَ ۙ وَ رَفَعْنَا لَكَ ذِكْرَكَ ؕ

alam nashraḥ laka ṣadrak, wa waḍa‘nā ‘anka wizrakalladī anqaḍa ẓahrak, wa rafa‘nā laka dhikrak

Have We not opened for you your bosom. And removed from you your burden. Which had *well nigh* broken your back. And We exalted your name? (94:2-5)

52. He was a testifier to the truth of all the Messengers

بَلْ جَآءَ بِالْحَقِّ وَ صَدَّقَ الْمُرْسَلِيْنَ ٥

bal jā'a bil ḥaqqi wa ṣaddqal mursalīn

Nay, he has brought the truth and has testified to the truth of *all* the Messengers. (37:38)

53. Those who annoy Allāh and His Messenger are cursed

اِنَّ الَّذِيْنَ يُؤْذُوْنَ اللّٰهَ وَ رَسُوْلَهٗ لَعَنَهُمُ اللّٰهُ فِى الدُّنْيَا وَالْاٰخِرَةِ
وَاَعَدَّ لَهُمْ عَذَابًا مُّهِيْنًا ٥

innalladhīna yu'dhūnallāha wa rasūlahū la'anahumullāhu fiddunyā wal ākhirati wa a-'adda lahum 'adhāban muhīnā

Verily, those who annoy Allāh and His Messenger - Allāh has cursed them in this world and in the Hereafter, and has prepared for them an abasing punishment. (33:58)

The aforementioned traits of the Holy Prophet[sa] in the Holy Qur'ān are a few of the many excellences he possessed.

The Holy Prophet[sa] States About His High Status

Ḥaḍrat Abū Hurairah[ra] relates that the Holy Prophet[sa] said: "God Almighty has disclosed to me such beautiful words of His glorification and gratitude, which were not disclosed to anyone else before me."

(Ṣaḥīḥ Bukhārī, Kitābut Tafsīr Sūrah Banī Isra'īl, Bāb qaulihi dhurriyyata man ḥamalnā ma'a nūhin)

Ḥaḍrat Anas[ra] relates that the Holy Prophet[sa] said: "Ḥaḍrat Moses[as] was once travelling, when God, the Omnipotent called to him, 'O Moses!' Moses[as] looked around but did not see anyone. Again the voice came, 'O Moses son of 'Imrān!' Again, Moses[as] looked around but did not see anyone. At this, Moses[as] became frightened and his shoulders started to shiver. A third time the voice came: 'O Moses! I am God. There is none worthy of worship except Me.' Hearing this, Moses fell into prostration while proclaiming, '*Labbaik, Labbaik.*' God Almighty said: 'O Moses! Raise up your head.' When Ḥaḍrat Moses[as] raised his head from prostration, God said: 'O Moses! I want you to rest under the shade of My Throne, on the day when there will be no other shade besides the shade of My Throne. Therefore, take care of orphans like a kind father, and of widows, like a loving husband. O Moses! Have Mercy, so that you are treated compassionately. O Moses! What you sow, so will you reap. O Moses! Convey to Banī Isrā'īl that whoever returns to Me while he has refused to accept Ḥaḍrat Aḥmad, I will throw him into Hell, whether he is My Khalīl, Ibrāhīm, or My Kalīm, Mūsā.' Moses[as] asked, 'Who is this Aḥmad?' God Almighty said: 'O Moses! By My Honor and Grandeur! No one is more beloved to Me among my creation than him. I have written his name along with My name in the empyrean. I had written his name with My name two million years before creating the Heaven, the Earth, the Sun, and the Moon. By My Honor and Grandeur! No one will be given permission to enter Heaven before Muḥammad and his followers.' Ḥaḍrat Moses[as] said,

'What kind of people will be the followers of this Prophet?' God Almighty said, 'They will be the ones who praise God Almighty. They will praise God Almighty while ascending to and descending from the heights. They will always be ready to serve the religion. Their flanks will be holy. During the day, they will keep fast while they will pass their nights as monks. I will accept even a few deeds from them.' Ḥaḍrat Moses[as] said, 'Make me the Prophet of this *Ummah* (following).' God Almighty said: 'The Prophet of this *Ummah* will be one of them.' Then Moses[as] said, 'Then make me a member of this *Ummah*.' God Almighty said: 'Your period will be earlier as that Prophet will come later on. Therefore, you can not become a disciple of this Prophet. However, in the next life, I will grant you the company of this Prophet in Heaven.' "

(Al-Khaṣā'iṣal Kubrā lil-Sayūṭī, p 12/1 as quoted in Ḥayatal auliyā' li Abī Na'īmul Mawāhib al-Ladunniyya, p 425 almahdāta ilā man yazīdal 'ilm 'alā aḥādīthal Mishkāt, p 327, Maulvī Sayyed Nūrul Ḥasan Khān ibn Nawāb Ṣiddīq Ḥasan Khān - Nasharaṭṭayyab fī dhikrinnabiyyal ḥabīb[sa]*, p 262, written by Maulvī Ashraf 'Alī Ṣaḥib Thānvī)*

(It is related that the Holy Prophet[sa] said), "Had Moses[as] and Jesus[as] been alive, they would have no alternative other than to accept and obey me."

(Al-yawaqīt wal-Jawāhar compiled by Imām Shi'rānī, p 20/2, Tafsīr Ibni Kathīr Footnote on tafsīr Fataḥul Biyān, p 246/2)

Ḥaḍrat Abū Hurairah[ra] relates that the Holy Prophet[sa] said: "The similitude between me and the previous Prophets can be illustrated as a palace built beautifully. A space for one final stone is left in it. People walk around to see the palace and appreciate its beauty. However, they wonder why space for one stone has been left? It is I who have filled the empty space of the missing stone. Through me, the building has become unique in its construction and beauty. Thus, have I been commissioned as the Seal of the Prophets."

According to another narration the Holy Prophet[sa] said, "I am that stone and I am the Seal of the Prophets."

(Ṣaḥīḥ Bukhārī, Kitābal Manāqib, Bāb khātamannibiyyīn[sa]*; Ṣaḥīḥ Muslim, p. 228/2; Jāmi' Tirmidhī, p. 544/2; Mishkāt, p. 511)*

Ḥaḍrat Jābir[ra] bin 'Abdullāh relates that the Holy Prophet[sa] said: "I have been bestowed five things which have never been given to any Prophet before me. I have been helped with the awe of one month's travel. The whole earth has been purified for me and has been declared a mosque. Wherever any one of my followers notices that it is Prayer time, he can offer Prayer at that place. I have been bestowed the honor of intercession, which has not been given to previous Prophets. I have been sent as a Messenger to all the people, whereas before me, Messengers were sent to particular nations."

(Nasā'ī, Kitābaṭṭahārat, Bāb tayammum biṣṣa'īd)

Ḥaḍrat Abū Hurairah[ra] relates that the Holy Prophet[sa] said: "I have been given superiority over other Prophets in six matters. I have been bestowed a comprehensive message. I have been given veneration. Spoils of war have been made lawful for me. The whole earth has been purified as a mosque or place of worship, for me. I have been sent as a Messenger for the entire creation, and I have been made the Seal of the Prophets."

(Ṣaḥīḥ Muslim, Kitābul Masājid, Bāb al-Masājid wa mawāḍi'aṣṣalāti)

Imām Baihaqī narrates from 'Abdullāh bin Salām[ra] that the most honored (*mu'azzaz*) in the whole of creation is Ḥaḍrat Abul Qāsim.

(Khaṣā'iṣ al-Kubrā, Vol. 2, p.198)

Two Phases of the Life of the Holy Prophet[sa]

The Promised Messiah[as] states:

God Almighty divided the life of the Holy Prophet[sa], into two phases, one phase of hardship and calamities and suffering, and the other of victory; so that during the phase of suffering those high moral qualities might be demonstrated which come into play at such times, and during the phase of victory and authority those high moral qualities might be illustrated which cannot be displayed in the absence of authority. Thus both these types of qualities were perfectly illustrated in the life of the Holy Prophet[sa], by his passing through both these phases and conditions. During the period of trials in Mecca, which extended over thirteen years, the Holy Prophet[sa], demonstrated in practice all the high qualities which a perfectly righteous person should exhibit at such a time, such as trust in God, perfect serenity under suffering, steady and eager carrying out of duties and fearless courage. Observing his steadfastness many of the disbelievers believed in him and thus testified that it is only the one who has complete trust in God who can display such steadfastness and endurance of suffering.

During the second phase, that is to say the phase of victory, authority and prosperity, he demonstrated such high qualities as forbearance, forgiveness, benevolence and courage, so that a large number of the disbelievers believed in him by witnessing his display of those high qualities. He forgave those who had persecuted him, granted security to those who had expelled him from Mecca, bestowed great wealth upon those among them who were in need and having obtained authority over his bitter enemies, forgave them all. Witnessing his high morals many of them testified that such qualities could only be demonstrated by one who comes from God and is truly righteous. That is how all the rancor that his enemies had entertained against him over a long period was washed out of their hearts in an instant. His greatest quality was the one that is set out in the Holy Qur'ān in the following words:

قُلْ إِنَّ صَلَاتِي وَ نُسُكِيْ وَ مَحْيَايَ وَ مَمَاتِيْ لِلّٰهِ رَبِّ الْعٰلَمِيْنَ ۝

qul inna ṣalāti wa nusuki wa maḥyāya wa mamāti lillāhi rabbil 'ālamīn

Say, 'My Prayer and my sacrifice and my life and my death are *all* for Allāh, the Lord of the worlds.' (6:163)

This means that the whole purpose of his life was to demonstrate the glory of God and to provide comfort for His creatures so that through his constant suffering of death they might procure life. No one should be misled by the mention of his death in the cause of God and for the good of His creatures, into thinking that he had at any time (God forbid) contemplated destroying himself, imagining like the ignorant and the insane, that his suicide would be of benefit to others. He was entirely free from any such stupid line of thinking and was wholly opposed to it. The Holy Qur'ān considers anyone who is guilty of self destruction as a great offender, liable to severe chastisement, as it says:

وَلَا تُلْقُوْا بِاَيْدِيْكُمْ اِلَى التَّهْلُكَةِ

wa lā tulqū bi aidīkum ilattahlukah

And cast not yourselves into ruin with your own hands. (2:196)

The true meaning of the verse cited above is, that the Holy Prophet[sa], out of true sympathy, had devoted his life to labor for the welfare of mankind and through supplications and exhortations and enduring their persecution and by every proper and wise means had laid down his life and sacrificed his comfort in this cause; as God the Glorious has said:

لَعَلَّكَ بَاخِعٌ نَّفْسَكَ اَلَّا يَكُوْنُوْا مُؤْمِنِيْنَ ۝

la'allaka bākhi'unnafsaka allā yakūnū mu'minīna

Haply you will grieve yourself to death because they believe not. (26:4)

and

فَلاَ تَذْهَبْ نَفْسُكَ عَلَيْهِمْ حَسَرٰتٍ ط

falā tadh hab nafsuka 'alaihim ḥasarāt

So let not your soul waste away in sighing for them. (35:9)

Thus the wise way of laying down one's life in the service of one's people is to endure hardship in their service in accord with the beneficial law of nature, and to spend one's life working out appropriate projects to that end.

(Philosophy of the Teachings of Islām, pp137-139, Published in 1996)

The Prophet[sa] passed through every imaginable stage of human experience, starting from an impoverished and orphaned childhood and ending as the undisputed ruler of his people. His life has been documented in minute detail and reflects unparalleled faith in God and constant sacrifice in His way. He lived a full and eventful life, packed with action, and has left behind an example of perfect conduct in every sphere of human endeavor. This is only fitting and proper, as he was living interpretation of the Holy Qur'ān, and by personal example lighted the way of mankind for all time to come -- a role not fulfilled adequately by any other Prophet.

(Distinctive Features of Islām, pp. 12-15)

The Exalted Status of the Holy Prophet[sa] in the Sight of the Promised Messiah[as]:

The Promised Messiah[as] writes about the Holy Prophet[sa]:

"The sublime light which was bestowed on man, i.e., the most perfect among them, was not shared by angels nor by stars; nor was in the moon, nor in the sun, or in the oceans and the rivers; it was not to be found in rubies or emeralds, nor in sapphires, nor in pearls: it was not in any earthly or heavenly object. It was possessed only by the perfect man, manifested in the most consummate way in the person of our lord and master, Muḥammad, the chosen one, the chief of all the Prophets, leader of those who live (in the sight of Allāh). So, the light was bestowed on that man and likewise, to a degree, on all who in their several ways were similar to him... Sublime grace was possessed in its most perfect and consummate manifestation by our lord and master, the unlettered Prophet[sa], the truthful one, the one whose truth is testified to, Muḥammad, the chosen one, peace be on him.

(Rūḥānī Khazā'in, Vol. 5, pp. 160-162)

I look always with wonder at this Arab Prophet, whose name is Muḥammad, thousands of blessings and peace be upon him. How exalted his status was! One cannot perceive the ultimate limit of his station, and it is not within the scope of man to fully comprehend the depth and penetration of his ennobling qualities. Alas! due recognition has not been paid to his lofty rank. That unity (i.e., belief in One God) which had disappeared from the world was restored by this same valiant champion. He loved God most intensely, so also his soul was being consumed in deep sympathy for mankind. That is why God, Who was fully aware of the hidden excellences of his heart, exalted him above all the Prophets and all the people of the past and the future, and fulfilled his heart's desires in the span of his lifetime.

(Rūḥānī Khazā'in, Vol. 22: Ḥaqīqatul-Waḥī, pp. 118-119)

Our Holy Prophet[sa] combines in him the names of all the Prophets, for in him are blended the noble qualities we find severally in all the other Prophets. Hence, he is Moses as well as Jesus; he is Adam, he is Abraham, he is Joseph and also he is Jacob. God indicates this in the verse:

فَبِهُدٰىهُمُ اقْتَدِهْ ط

fabi hudāhumuqtadih

So follow you their guidance. (6:91)

Meaning: O Prophet of God, merge in yourself the various teachings of all the Prophets! This shows that the excellence of all the prophets was combined in the Holy Prophet[sa]. In fact, the very name Muḥammad points towards this because it means 'the one who is most highly praised'. The highest praise can only be conceived if it is granted that the very best of virtues and special qualities of all the Prophets are blended in him.

(Rūḥānī Khazā'in, Vol. 5: Ā'īna Kamālāt-e-Islām, p. 343)

I have been made to understand that of all the Messengers, the one who gave the most perfect and purest of teachings full of wisdom, and the one who exhibited in him the noblest of human qualities is the Holy Prophet Muḥammad[sa], our lord and master, may peace and blessings of Allāh be upon him.

(Rūḥānī Khazā'in, Vol. 17: Arba'īn, No. 1 p. 345)

When we examine with fairness and justice all the Prophets of the past, we find that Muḥammad[sa], the Holy Prophet of Islām stands out as the most valiant among them, the one who fully possessed all the qualities of life and was the one most endeared to God.

(Rūḥānī Khazā'in, Vol. 12: Sirāj-e-Munīr, p. 82)

A strange phenomenal event took place in the wilderness of Arabia, when hundreds of thousands of the dead became alive within a few days, and those who had been corrupted through generations took on Divine color. The blind began to see, and the tongues of the dumb began to flow with Divine wisdom. Such a revolution took place in the world as no eye had seen and no ear had heard of before. Do you realize what this was? All this was brought about by prayers during the darkness of nights of one who had been wholly lost in God which created an uproar in the world and manifested such wonders as seemed impossible at the hands of that unlettered helpless person. O Allāh! send down blessings and peace on him and on his followers in proportion to his concern and suffering for the Muslim *Ummah* (the people of Islām), and shower upon him the light of Thy Mercy forever.

(Rūḥānī Khazā'in, Vol. 6: Barakātud Du'ā', pp. 10-11)

For all the children of Adam there is now no Messenger and Intercessor other than the Holy Prophet Muḥammad[sa], the chosen one, may peace and blessings of Allāh be upon him. So you should endeavor to cultivate true love for this magnificent and majestic Prophet and not place anyone else above him in any manner so that you may be counted in Heaven among those who have attained salvation. Remember, salvation is not something which is attainable only after death. Indeed, true salvation is the one which manifests its light in this very world. Who is the one who is delivered? He indeed, who believes that God is Truth and that the Holy Prophet[sa], is the Intercessor between God and mankind. So also he believes that under the firmament of Heaven there is no Prophet equal to him and that there is no book of the status of the Qur'ān. And for none else has God ordained that he should live forever. But with his message and his law, this noble Prophet[sa] lives for ever.

(Rūḥānī Khazā'in, Vol.19: Kashtī Nūḥ, p. 13)

From a study of the life of the Holy Prophet[sa], it will become manifest to every reader that the Holy Prophet of Islām[sa] had no duality in his character and possessed a pure and noble spirit. He was ever ready to lay down his life for God, he pinned no hopes on men and he entertained no fear of them. He reposed his entire trust in Allāh. Having enslaved himself entirely to the will and pleasure of Allāh, he cared not what hazards he would face and what suffering he would be subjected to at the hands of the idolaters as a result of declaring to the world the message of the Unity of God.

(Rūḥānī Khazā'in, Vol. 1: Brāhīn-e-Aḥmadiyya, p. 111)

Is it not a most wonderful thing to have happened that in an age when all the great nations of the world possessed a plentitude of financial, military and intellectual means, a mere penniless orphan, who was powerless, helpless, unlettered and unaided, brought forth such resplendent teachings which, with their conclusive arguments and irrefutable proofs, dumbfounded every opponent? It also exposed the mistakes and faults of such scholars who in their conceit boasted of being great philosophers and men of wisdom. In spite of his being poor and helpless, he rose to great power and dethroned many a mighty king and in their place installed the poor. If this was not from Allāh, what else was it? To conquer and excel the whole world in wisdom, in knowledge and in strength, can all this be accomplished without the help of Allāh?

(Rūḥānī Khazā'in, Vol. 1: Brāhīn-e-Aḥmadiyya p. 191)

Take note how the Holy Prophet of Islām[sa] remained resolute and steadfast in his claim to prophethood from beginning to end in the face of thousands of dangers and a multitude of enemies and threatening opponents. For years on end, he endured such hardship and suffering as increased from day to day; enough to make one despair of success. It is inconceivable for a man, with ulterior worldly motives, to have shown such prolonged and steadfast endurance. Not only that, by putting forth his claim to prophethood, he even lost the support he had previously enjoyed. The price he had to pay for his one claim was to confront a hundred thousand contentions and invite a multitude of calamities to fall upon his head. He was exiled from his homeland and pursued with intent to murder. His home and belongings were destroyed and several attempts on his life were made by poisoning him. Those who were his well-wishers began to harbor ill for him. Friends turned into foes. For an age which seemed like eternity, he braved such hardships as are beyond what a pretender and imposter could suffer through.

(Rūḥānī Khazā'in, Vol. 1: Brāhīn-e-Aḥmadiyya, p. 108)

It would not have been possible for me to have attained this grace if I had not followed the footsteps of my lord and master, the pride of all the Prophets, the best of mankind, Muḥammad, the chosen one, peace and blessings of Allāh be upon him. Whatever I have achieved, I have achieved by following him, and I know from verified reliable experience that no man can reach God and obtain a deeper understanding of His ways without following that Prophet, may peace and blessings of Allāh be upon him. Now, let me also make it known that the very first thing you are rewarded with, after having completely submitted yourself to the instructions and teachings of the Holy Prophet Muḥammad[sa], is that you are granted a new heart which is always rightly inclined, that is to say, a heart which has turned cold upon the love of this material world, and instead it begins to yearn for an everlasting heavenly pleasure. Having achieved this desire this heart is now fit to receive that perfect and purest love - the love of God. Because of your complete obedience to him, all these blessings are bequeathed to you as his spiritual heritage.

(Rūḥānī Khazā'in, Vol.22: Ḥaqīqatul Waḥī, pp. 64-65)

19

Physical Description and Habits of the Holy Prophet[sa]

The Holy Prophet[sa] was a perfect model for all human beings. An observation of the life of the Holy Prophet[sa] clearly shows that his entire life was dedicated to the service of God Almighty and love of humanity. He devoted his whole life to becoming a recipient of Allāh's Guidance, Blessings and Mercy. To achieve these goals he fervently prayed to God Almighty. In fact he prayed so much that his prayers cover every aspect of human life. In short, the Holy Prophet[sa] had the highest moral excellences and was a mercy for mankind.

God Almighty says in the Holy Qur'ān about the Holy Prophet[sa]:

لَقَدْ كَانَ لَكُمْ فِيْ رَسُوْلِ اللّٰهِ اُسْوَةٌ حَسَنَةٌ

laqad kāna lakum fī rasūlillāhi uswatun ḥasanah

Verily you have in the Prophet of Allāh an excellent model. (33:22)

The Holy Prophet[sa] Describes About Himself

Cognizance is my true possession, wisdom is the root of my religion, love is my foundation, zeal is my impetus, remembrance of Allāh is my companion and comforter, steadfastness is my treasure, sorrow is my companion, knowledge is my tool, patience is my covering, contentment is a blessing, poverty is my honor, piety is my profession, my belief is my strength, truthfulness is my associate, obedience is my lineage, struggle in the cause of Allāh is my civility, and Prayer is the comfort of my eyes.

(Ash-Shafā', faṣl fī khaufihī ṣallallāhu 'alihi wasallam min rabbihī wa ṭā'atihī lahū Vol. 1, pp. 85-86; Qāḍī 'Iyāḍ bin Musā)

Ḥaḍrat Abū Sa'īd al-Khudrī[ra] relates that the Holy Prophet[sa] said: "I am the leader of Adam's[as] progeny. However, I am not proud of it. I will be the standard-bearer of the Glory of God. However, I feel no pride of it. On the day of resurrection, Adam and all other Prophets besides him will be gathered under my flag. I will be the first one to be raised on the Day of Judgement, but I do not feel proud about it, as well. The Holy Prophet[sa] continued: 'People will encounter fear on three occasions. They will go to Adam[as] and say to him: 'You are our father, please intercede on our behalf to your Lord.' He will reply to them: 'I had committed a sin (according to you) for which I was expelled from Heaven to the earth. I suggest you go to Noah[as]. Maybe he can help you.' Then they will go to Noah[as] and ask him. Noah[as] will say to them: 'I prayed ill (according to you) for the people of the land unjustly which led to their destruction. I suggest that you go to Abraham[as].' Then they will go to Abraham[as] and ask him. Abraham[as] will say to them: 'I told three lies (according to you).' The Holy Prophet[sa] said: 'In fact none of these were lies, they were just some prudent decisions he made in the interest of faith.' Anyway, Abraham[as] will reply to the people, 'You should go to Moses[as] perchance he can help you.' The people will go to Moses[as] and ask him. Moses[as] will say to them: 'I had killed a person unjustly (according to you), you should go to Jesus[as].' When they go to Jesus[as], he will say to them: 'I had encouraged the people to worship me (according to you) instead of God, you should go to Muḥammad[sa].' Then they will come to me. I will accompany them (to God Almighty). I will be asked, 'Who are you?' I will respond: 'Muḥammad is here.' So the door will be opened. I will be welcome. I will fall in prostration and at this, in an excellent manner praise will be revealed to me from God Almighty, and it will be said to me: 'Raise your head and ask, it will be given. Intercede and your intercession will be accepted; and say, it will be heard. This is the *'Muqām-e-Maḥmūd'* about which God Almighty has said:

عَسٰٓى اَنْ يَّبْعَثَكَ رَبُّكَ مَقَامًا مَّحْمُوْدًا ۝

'asā anyyab'athaka rabbuka maqāmammaḥmūdā

It may be that your Lord will raise you to an exalted station. (17:80)' "

(Jāmi' Tirmidhī, Abwābut Tafsīr Sūrah Banī Israel; Ṣaḥīḥ Bukhārī, Kitābut Tafsīr Sūrah Al-Naḥl; Ṣaḥīḥ Muslim, Kitābul Īmān, Bāb adna ahlil jannah manzilah)

Physical Description and Personality of the Holy Prophet[sa]

Ḥaḍrat Jābir bin Samurah[ra] narrates that once the Holy Prophet[sa] came out during a moon-lit night while he was covering himself with a red sheet: "I looked at him and then at the moon and kept on doing so. By God, he was more beautiful than the moon."

(Jāmi' Tirmidhī, Kitābul Adab, Bāb mā jā'a firrukhsati fillabsil hamrati lirrijāli)

Physically, the hands of the Holy Prophet[sa] were as beautiful and pleasing to gaze upon as everything else about him. They were white and fleshy, with slightly tapering fingers. Ḥaḍrat Anas bin Mālik[ra] said on more than one occasion, "I have never touched any silk or brocade that is softer than the palm of the Messenger[sa] of Allāh nor have I ever smelled musk or scent more fragrant than the fragrance of the Messenger[sa] of Allāh."

(Bukhārī 2:269), Muslim 4:1815)

Ḥaḍrat Wā'il ibn Ḥajar[ra] said, "Whenever I shook hands with the Holy Prophet[sa] or my skin touched his skin, I smelled the scent of musk on my hand for three days."

(Majma' al-Zawā'id 7:33)

Ḥaḍrat Ḥasan bin 'Alī[ra] relates that he asked his maternal uncle, Hind bin Abī Hāla to describe the appearance and features of the Holy Prophet[sa]. Hind bin Abī Hāla was an expert in describing the physical features of the Holy Prophet[sa]. He desired that he describe the physical features of the Holy Prophet[sa] so that he could remember them forever. Hind bin Hāla said:

"The Holy Prophet[sa] had a very commanding personality. His face was bright like the full moon. He was of medium height; that is, he was taller than a short person and slightly shorter than a tall person. He had a large head covered with slightly curly thick hair. The hair reached his ear lobes and there was a prominent partition in his hair. He had a beautiful white complexion, a broad forehead, long and thick eyebrows which were not joined. Rather, there was a white space between the eyebrows, which would become prominent when he was angry. He had an exquisite fine nose which appeared bright and slightly raised to someone glancing at his face. His beard was thick; his cheeks were soft and smooth; his mouth was broad with a shiny full set of teeth with part of gums within the teeth; the corners of his eyes narrowed to a point; his neck was long and lovely, shining like silver with a slight redness. With a balanced well-built body, he had slight plumpness, which looked appropriate and agreeable. His chest and belly were even. His chest was large and broad; joints, strong and full; skin, soft, tender and luminous. His chest and belly were hairless but there was a fine streak of hair from his chest to the navel. There was some hair on both hands which extended to the elbows. There was hair on the shoulders. He had long wrists, wide and fleshy palms, and long and graceful fingers. The soles of his feet were relatively filled with flesh. His feet were soft and smooth to the extent that water would not stay on them. When he walked, he raised his feet fully. He walked in a dignified manner, but a bit quickly, as if he were walking downhill. When he turned his face to any side, he turned it fully. He always kept his eyes lowered to the ground. It seemed as if he looked more towards the ground than his surroundings. He often looked with eyes half-open. He walked behind his Companions[ra] and took care of them. He was always the first to say *'Salām'* to anyone he met."

(Shamā'il Tirmidhī, Bāb fī khalq Rasūlullāh[sa])

Ḥaḍrat Anas bin Mālik[ra] relates that the Holy Prophet[sa] was of medium height, neither too tall nor too short. He had a glowing white complexion, which was neither too white nor too wheatish. His hair was somewhat straight, neither too curly nor absolutely straight. ...

(Al-mu'jamaṣṣaghīr lil-Ṭibrānī, Bābuljīm min ismuhū Ja'far, Vol. 1, p. 118; Dalā'ilunnabuwwatu lil-Baihaqī, Bāb ṣifat laun Rasulullāh[sa], Vol. 1, p. 201)

Ḥaḍrat Ḥasan[ra] bin Alī[ra] relates that he asked his uncle Hind bin Abī Hāla about the Holy Prophet[sa] and his manner of speaking. He stated:

"It always seemed as if the Holy Prophet[sa] was continuously in deep thought and was somewhat perturbed due to some thought. Most of the time he was quiet and did not talk unnecessarily. Whenever he spoke, he spoke very clearly. His conversation was always brief but eloquent and full of wisdom covering various subjects comprehensively but without any extraneous details. Furthermore, there was never any ambiguity in what he said. He never degraded or scorned anyone or made derogatory remarks about anyone. He depicted even the smallest blessing as a great blessing. The quality of giving thanks was very singular in him. He neither spoke evil of a thing nor praised it so much that it reflected his extraordinary liking for the thing. He neither exaggerated in praising a delicious food nor exaggerated in relaying his dislike for an unappetizing food. Moderation was his habit. He never became angry or showed distase concerning a worldly affair. However, when he saw rights being usurped, then no one could face his anger. Until the rights were restored, he remained anxious. He never showed anger or took revenge for any injustice done to him. Whenever he gestured towards something, he always did it with his hand and never by just moving his finger. Whenever he was amazed about something, he showed his amazement by turning his hand upside down. When he emphasized a point, he placed one hand over the other and hit the palm of the right hand with the thumb of the left hand. When he disliked something, he turned his face away, and when he felt happy, he half closed his eyes. His laughter was mostly a broad smile."

(Shamā'il Tirmidhī, Bāb kaifa kāna kalām Rasūlullāh[sa] *)*

Ḥaḍrat 'Abdullāh bin Ḥārith[ra] relates that he did not see anyone smile more than the Holy Prophet[sa].

(Jāmi' Tirmidhī, Abwābul Manāqib, Bāb mā jā' fī bishāshatunnabiyyi[sa] *)*

Ḥaḍrat 'Ā'ishah[ra] relates: "I never saw the Holy Prophet[sa] laugh outright so that his uvula (a small finger-like tissue which hangs from the back of the root of the mouth) could be seen. He just smiled."

(Ṣaḥīḥ Bukhārī, Kitābul Adab, Bāb tabassam waḍḍuḥak)

Ḥaḍrat Qatādah[ra] relates that he heard 'Abdullāh bin Abī 'Utbah[ra] state that he heard Abū Sa'īd Al-Khudrī[ra] say that the Holy Prophet[sa] was more modest than a virgin behind her veil and that when something displeased him they could perceive it in his face.

(Ṣaḥīḥ Muslim, Kitābul Faḍā'il, Bāb kathratah ḥiyā'ih)

Ḥaḍrat Hishām bin 'Urwah relates that his father 'Urwah[ra] narrated: "Someone asked Ḥaḍrat 'Ā'ishah[ra]: 'Did the Holy Prophet[sa] perform any of the household chores?' She replied: 'Yes. He used to mend his shoes, sew his clothes, and did other household chores just like you do in your homes.' "

(Musnad Aḥmad, p. 167/7 - p. 121/6)

Ḥaḍrat Aswad bin Yazīd[ra] relates that he asked Ḥaḍrat 'Ā'ishah[ra]: "What did the Holy Prophet[sa] do in his home? She answered: 'He occupied himself with helping members of his family, and when the time of Prayer came, he would go out for Prayer.'"

(Ṣaḥīḥ Bukhārī, Kitābul Adhān, Bāb man kāna fī ḥajjah ahlihī ... alkh)

Ḥaḍrat Abū Sa'īd Al-Khudrī[ra] relates that the Holy Prophet[sa] fed his camels, undertook various household chores, repaired his shoes, patched torn clothes, and milked his goats. He used to eat food along with his servant and helped him whenever he became tired of grinding wheat. The Holy Prophet[sa] never felt shy of bringing household items from the market. He used to shake hands with everyone, whether rich or poor, and always was the first to say *'Salām'*. He always accepted an invitation, even if it was to eat ordinary dates, and never felt insulted. He was extremely sympathetic, mild-mannered and tender-hearted. His lifestyle was very simple and clean. He always greeted everyone cheerfully and he always had a smile on his face. He never laughed loudly. He was always concerned about the fear of God. However, he did not have an iota of peevishness. He was very humble but not out of weakness or cowardice. He was extremely generous but not extravagant. He was kind-hearted, compassionate, and generous. He used to treat every Muslim compassionately. He never ate so much that he had to burp. He was never covetous of anything. On the contrary, he was always patient, thankful, and content with what he had.

(Usdul Ghābah, Vol. 1, p 29; Qashīriyyah, p. 7; Ash-Shifā', p. 77/1)

Ḥaḍrat 'Abdullāh bin Salām[ra] relates that when the Holy Prophet[sa] came to Medina, he was one of the people who came out to receive him. When he saw the face of the Holy Prophet[sa], he realized that certainly this could not be the face of a false person. At this occasion, the Holy Prophet[sa] said, "O people! Spread the greetings of peace, feed the needy, show tenderness towards kith and kin, offer Prayers while people are sleeping. If you do all of these, you will enter Paradise in peace."

(Sunan Dārmī, Kitābul Isti'dhān, Bāb fī afshā'assalām; Jāmi' Tirmidhī, Abwāb suffatul qayyamah, Vol. 2, p. 72)

The Daily Routine

As far as the daily routine of the Holy Prophet[sa] was concerned, he had divided the day into three parts. One part was reserved to worship and to pray to Allāh, the second part was to take care of the household affairs while the last part was used for his personal needs and activities. However, the major portion of the time reserved for his personal needs was often used to serve humanity.

(Ash-Shifā' Ba-ta'rīf Ḥaqūqul Muṣṭafā, lil-Qāḍī 'Iyāḍ, Vol. 1, p. 174, Dārul Kitāb al-Arabī)

Ḥaḍrat Jābir bin Samurah[ra] relates that after offering the *Fajr* Prayer, the Holy Prophet[sa] remained seated on his Prayer mat till sunrise. During this time, some people talked with each other and laughed over some event of the days of ignorance. At this, The Holy Prophet[sa] also smiled.

(Ṣaḥīḥ Muslim, Kitābul Faḍā'il, Bāb tabassamah ṣallallāhu 'alaihi wasallam[sa] wa ḥusan 'ashratahū wa Kitābuṣ Ṣalāt, Bāb faḍlal jalūs fī miṣlāh ba'daṣṣubha wa faḍlul masājid)

After the congregational Prayer and finishing the *Dhikr-e-Ilāhī* (silent remembrance of Allāh), the Holy Prophet[sa] used to sit among his Companions[ra] for a while. Often he used to ask the Companions[ra] to relate their dreams, if they had seen one. If he liked the dream he used to interpret the dream. Once in a while he used to relate his dream also to his Companions[ra].

(Ṣaḥīḥ Muslim, Kitābur Ru'yā',Bab Ru'yā' an-Nabī[sa]; Ṣaḥīḥ Bukhārī, Kitābur Ru'yā')

After the *Fajr* Prayer, the Holy Prophet[sa] followed the day's program as he had organized in his mind. If anyone of his Companions[ra] was sick he would visit him to inquire about his health and to cheer him up. If someone had passed away, he would attend his or her funeral services and console the deceased person's family. At the end of these routines he would return to his home and would ask for food to eat. If there was nothing to eat at home, he would say, "That is alright, I will fast today."

(Musnad Aḥmad, Vol. 6, p.45)

Patience in Adversity

The Holy Prophet[sa] was always very patient in adversity. He was neither discouraged by adverse circumstances nor did he permit any personal desire to overpower him. His father had died before his birth and his mother died while he was still a young child. Up till the age of eight, he was under the guardianship of his grandfather and after the latter's death he was cared by his uncle, Abū Ṭālib. Both on account of natural affection and also because he had been specially admonished in that behalf by his father, Abū Ṭālib always watched over his nephew with care and indulgence but his wife was not affected by these considerations to the same degree. It often happened that she would distribute something among her own children, leaving out their little cousin. If Abū Ṭālib chanced to come into the house on such an occasion, he would find his little nephew sitting apart, a perfect picture of dignity and without a trace of sulkiness or grievance on his face. The uncle, yielding to the claims of affection and recognizing his responsibility, would run to his nephew, clasp him to his bosom and cry out: "Do pay attention to this child of mine too! Do pay attention to this child of mine too!" Such incidents were not uncommon and those who were witnesses to them were unanimous in their testimony that the young Muḥammad never gave any indication that he was in any way affected by them or that he was in any sense jealous of his cousins. Later in life, when he was in a position to do so, he took upon himself the care and upbringing of two of his uncle's sons, ‘Alī and Ja‘far, and discharged this responsibility in the most excellent manner.

(Life of Muḥammad by Ḥaḍrat Mirzā Bashīruddīn Maḥmūd Aḥmad, Khalīfatul Masīḥ II[ra]*, pp. 327-328, Published in UK, 2005)*

Simple Lifestyle

The Holy Prophet[sa] was extremely simple in the matter of food and drink. He never expressed displeasure with ill-prepared or ill-cooked food. If he could eat such food he would do so to save the person who had prepared it from disappointment. If, however, a dish was unedible, he merely refrained from partaking of it and never expressed his disapproval of it. When any edible food was presented to him he always shared it with those present. On one occasion someone presented him with some dates. He looked around and after making an estimate of the number of people present divided the dates equally among them, each of them receiving seven.

Ḥaḍrat 'Ā'ishah[ra] relates that the Holy Prophet[sa] never ate his fill even of barley bread two successive days till he died.

((Jāmi' Titmidhī, Abwābuz Zuhdi 'an rasūlullah[sa]*, Bāb mā jā'a fī ma'īshatinnabiyyi*[sa] *wa ahlihī)*

Since childhood, the Holy Prophet[sa] showed a high standard of contentment. Umm Aiman[ra], the wet-nurse of the Holy Prophet[sa] relates:

مَا رَاَيْتُ النَّبِيَّ شَكَا صَغِيْرًا وَّ كَبِيْرًا جُوْعًا وَّ لاَ عَطَشًا

mā ra-aitunnabiyya shakā ṣaghīrañwwa kabīran jau'añwwa lā 'aṭashā

I have never seen the Holy Prophet[sa], from his childhood to the old age, complain about hunger or thrist .

(Ibn Sa'd's Al-Ṭabaqāt Al-Kabīr, Vol. 1, p. 168)

Ḥaḍrat Masrūq[ra] relates that he visited Ḥaḍrat 'Ā'ishah[ra] and she ordered food to be served to me. She said, "Never do I eat to a full stomach without crying. I asked her, 'Why?' She said, 'I recall the condition in which Allāh's Messenger[sa] departed from this world. By Allāh, he never had bread and meat to a full belly twice a day.' "

(Jāmi' Titmidhī, Abwābuz Zuhdi 'an rasūlullah[sa], Bāb mā jā'a fī ma'īshatinnabiyyi[sa] wa ahlihī)

Ḥaḍrat Aswad[ra] relates that Ḥaḍrat 'Umar ibn al-Khaṭṭāb[ra] visited the Holy Prophet[sa]. The Holy Prophet[sa] was ill and was lying on a *Qutwānī* bed-sheet and his pillow was filled with *Adhkhar* grass. Seeing this, Ḥaḍrat 'Umar ibn al-Khaṭṭāb[ra] said: "May my father and mother be sacrificed for you! Caesar and Chosroes rest on silky mattresses and you are in such a condition. Hearing this, the Holy Prophet[sa] said: 'O 'Umar! Would you not be happy that you get these comforts in the Hereafter, whereas worldly people have these in this world?' Then Ḥaḍrat 'Umar ibn al-Khaṭṭāb[ra] touched the body of the Holy Prophet[sa] and noticed that he had a very high fever. At this, Ḥaḍrat 'Umar ibn al-Khaṭṭāb[ra] said: 'Messenger[sa] of Allāh, You are a Messenger[sa] of Allāh, yet you have such a high fever.' The Holy Prophet[sa] said: 'In this *Ummah*, it is the Prophet who is tried the most, after that, rank-wise, the virtuous people and the leaders. This has been the case with other Prophets who passed before me.' "

(Msunadul Imāmul A'ẓam, Kitāburriqāq, p. 217)

Ḥaḍrat 'Ā'ishah[ra] relates: "The mattress of the Holy Prophet[sa] was of leather stuffed with the husk of the date-palm tree."

(Ṣaḥīḥ Bukhārī, Kitāburriqāq, Bāb kaifa kāna 'aishannabiyya[sa])

Ḥaḍrat 'Abdullāh bin Mas'ūd[ra] relates the Holy Prophet[sa] slept on a mat and when he got up the impress of the mat was visible on his body. Noticing this, he said: "Messenger[sa] of Allāh, may my father and mother be sacrificed for you! Shall we prepare a mattress for you over this mat which protects you? He said:

مَا اَنَا وَ الدُّنْيَا، اِنَّمَا اَنَا وَ الدُّنْيَا كَرَاكِبٍ اِسْتَظَلَّ تَحْتَ شَجَرَةٍ ثُمَّ رَاحَ وَتَرَكَهَا

mā anā waddunyā, innamā anā waddunyā karākibin istaẓalla taḥta shajaratin thumma rāḥa wa tarakahā

'What have I to do with this world? I am in the world like a traveler who stops in the shade of a tree for a while, then leaves it and moves on.'"

(Ibn-e-Mājah, Abwābuzzuhad ,Bāb mithluddunyā, p. 302)

Ḥaḍrat Abū Mūsā al-Ash'arī[ra] relates: "Ḥaḍrat 'Ā'ishah[ra] showed us a sheet and a thick loin-cloth and told us that the Holy Prophet[sa] was wearing them when he died."

(Ṣaḥīḥ Bukhārī, Kitābul Libās, Bābul aksiyyah; Ṣaḥīḥ Muslim, Kitābul Libās, Bāb a-ttawāḍi' fillibās ... alkh)

Ḥaḍrat Abū Burdah[ra] states that once Ḥaḍrat 'A'ishah[ra] took out and showed me a thick sheet made of coarse cotton cloth and an under garment (*tah band*). She said, "The Holy Prophet[sa] was wearing these clothes at the time of his demise."

(Ṣaḥīḥ Bukhārī, Kiābul Libās, Bāb al-aksiyah)

Humility

The Holy Prophet's[sa] humility knew no bounds. When sitting among his followers, ordinarily clothed, eating the same food as they did, he did not occupy a very special place. Many a time people were mistaken as to who was the Holy Founder of Islām. Ḥaḍrat Abū Bakr[ra], who later became the First Caliph of Islām, was older than he was and perhaps had a longer beard, (I don't know, it is my surmise), but something in him led some strangers to address him as the Prophet of God. With a respectful manner, he would then turn to the Holy Prophet[sa] and lead them to him.

Once, Ḥaḍrat ‘Umar[ra] who later became the Second Caliph of Islām obtained his permission to perform *‘Umrah.* The Holy Prophet of Islām[sa] turned to him and said: "Yes go ahead, perform the *‘Umrah* and please do not forget me in your prayers." Such was the humility of the man, on whose prayers every Muslim depended, that he asked one of his own servants to remember him in his prayers.

(The Seal of Prophets[sa], His Personality and Character, Ḥaḍrat Mirzā Ṭāhir Aḥmad, Khalīfatul Masīh IV[rh], Islām International Publications, 1992)

During the early days of Islām when the Holy Prophet[sa] was living in Mecca, Abū Lahab and ‘Aqbah bin Abī Mu‘īt were his neighbors. Both of them had taken to disturbing the Holy Prophet[sa] to an extreme. They not only opposed the Holy Prophet[sa] outside in the public they also annoyed the Holy Prophet[sa] when he was at his home. They would place all sorts of filth at the door of the house of the Holy Prophet[sa]. Whenever the Holy Prophet[sa] came out of the house and saw the filth he himself removed it from the front of his house and only said, "O the sons of ‘Abd Manāf! What are you doing. Is it the way to treat a neighbor?"

(Ibn Sa‘d's Al-Ṭabqāt Al-Kabīr, Vol. 1, p. 201, Beirut, Lebanon, 1960)

The Holy Prophet[sa] always took good care of the Companions[ra] during travel. He[sa] never gave preference to himself over the others and used to bear the hardships encountered during travel just like the others. When the Holy Prophet[sa] left for the Battle of Badr there were very few rides available to them. One camel was shared by three persons to travel. The Holy Prophet[sa] shared his camel with Ḥaḍrat 'Alī[ra] and Ḥaḍrat Abū Lubābah[ra] and they took turns to ride the camel. When the Holy Prophet[sa] was about to come down from the camel after taking his turn, both of others who were sharing the ride with the Holy Prophet[sa] requested the Holy Prophet[sa] to continue riding the camel as they would walk. The Holy Prophet[sa] said, "Neither you possess more strength to walk than me nor I am less in need of the reward than you."

(Musnad Aḥmad bin Ḥanbal, Vol. 1, p. 411, Al-Maktabul Islāmi lil Ṭaba'h wannashar, Beirut, Lebanon)

Once, Ḥaḍrat 'Aqbah bin 'Āmir Juhanī[ra] visited the Holy Prophet[sa] while he was travelling. The Holy Prophet[sa] made his ride sit down and asked Ḥaḍrat 'Aqbah[ra] to ride the camel. He said, "O Messenger[sa] of Allāh! How can it be that I ride while you are walking? The Holy Prophet[sa] again told 'Aqbah to ride. 'Aqbah again gave the same reply. However, when the Holy Prophet[sa] insisted that he mount the ride, to obey the Holy Prophet[sa], he mounted the ride and the Holy Prophet[sa] started to walk while holding the rein of the ride.

Once, the Holy Prophet[sa] mounted his ride to travel to Qubā'. Ḥaḍrat Abū Hurairah[ra] was with the Holy Prophet[sa]. The Holy Prophet[sa] asked Ḥaḍrat Abū Hurairah[ra] if he would like to ride with him. He said as the Messenger[sa] of Allāh wishes. The Holy Prophet[sa] told him to mount the ride. When Ḥaḍrat Abū Hurairah[ra] tried to mount he could not and fell down. During the fall he held the Holy Prophet[sa] for support. This made the Holy Prophet[sa] also fall down. The Holy Prophet[sa] again mounted the ride and asked Ḥaḍrat Abū Hurairah[ra] to mount the ride. Like before, he could not mount and fell down and pulled down the Holy Prophet[sa] along with him. When the third time the Holy Prophet[sa] asked Ḥaḍrat Abū Hurairah[ra] to mount the ride he said, "I do not want to make you fall down again."

(Zurqānī, Sharḥ Mawāhib al-Ladunniyya, Vol. 4, p. 265, Dārul Ma'rfah, Beirut, Lebanon)

Ḥaḍrat 'Abdullāh bin Abū Bakr[ra] relates that an Arab told him: "In the rush of the Battle of Ḥunain, I severely injured the foot of the Holy Prophet[sa] with a hard sandal I was wearing. The Holy Prophet[sa] tapped me lightly with a whip and said, 'In the name of Allāh! You have hurt me.' I was very much ashamed. I passed the night rebuking myself for hurting the Holy Prophet[sa]. Only God knows how I passed the night. In the morning, someone told me that the Holy Prophet[sa] was asking for me. I became very worried that maybe I was summoned to face the punishment for yesterday's mistake. Anyway, when I went to see the Holy Prophet[sa], he very affectionately said, 'Yesterday, you crushed my foot which caused me severe pain and I hit you lightly with a whip. Take these eighty goats as compensation.' "

(Musnad Dārmī, Bāb fī sakhā'annabiyyu[sa], p. 36/1)

It is related that Ḥaḍrat Usaid bin Ḥuḍair[ra] who was from *Anṣār*, was a very witty person. Once, he was talking wittily while sitting in the company of people, and the Holy Prophet[sa] poked him lightly in his ribs with his stick. At this, he said to the Holy Prophet[sa], "I have to avenge that." The Holy Prophet[sa] said, "Alright, you can take revenge." He replied: "But you are wearing a shirt, while I am not wearing a shirt." At this, the Holy Prophet[sa] raised his shirt. Ḥaḍrat Usaid bin Ḥuḍair[ra] embraced the Holy Prophet[sa] and started to fervently kiss his side, and stated: "Messenger[sa] of Allāh, this was my intention."

(Sunan Abū Dāwūd, Kitābul Adab, Bāb fī qiblatul jasad, Mishkāt, Kitābul Adab, Bābul muṣāfiḥah wal mu'āniqah)

Pleasing Sense of Humor

The Holy Prophet[sa] possessed a very pleasing sense of humor. He used to joke with children to amuse them in simple ways. But his humor would never hurt anyone. There are many reports of his jokes with children and sometimes with old people. His humor was delicate and pleasing - always practiced with an underlying sense of love and never that of derision.

Ḥaḍrat Anas[ra] relates that someone asked the Holy Prophet[sa] for an animal to ride. The Holy Prophet[sa] said that he would give him a baby camel to ride. He said: "What will I do with a baby camel? The Holy Prophet[sa] said, 'Is a camel not the baby of a camel?' "

(Sunan Abū Dāwūd, Kitābul Adab, Bāb mā jā' fil mizāḥ; Jāmi' Tirmidhī, Abwābul bir walṣilah ,Bāb fil mizāḥ)

A woman came to see the Holy Prophet[sa]. The Holy Prophet[sa] asked her about her husband. She told his name. The Holy Prophet[sa] said, "The one with a hole in his eyes." When she returned home she started gazing in her husband's eyes. Her husband said, "What has happened to you." She told him that the Holy Prophet[sa] had told her that their is whitishness in his eyes. Upon hearing this he said, "The white area is not more than the black area in my eyes."

(Sharfunnabī by 'Allāmah Sa'īd Neshāpurī, p. 109)

Ḥaḍrat 'Auf bin Mālik[ra] relates that during the Battle of Tabūk, he appeared before the Holy Prophet[sa]: "The Holy Prophet[sa] was staying in a small leather tent. I greeted the Holy Prophet[sa]. He returned my greetings and told me to come inside the tent. I said: 'Should the whole of me (come inside)?' The Holy Prophet[sa] said, 'Yes, the whole of you come in.' Then, I went inside the tent.' "

(Sunan Abū Dāwūd, Kitābul Adab, Bāb mā jā' fil mizāḥ)

Ḥaḍrat Anas[ra] relates that once the Holy Prophet[sa] said to an old woman: "Old women will not enter Paradise.' The woman, who used to read the Holy Qur'ān, nervously said: "Why will they not enter the Paradise?" The Holy Prophet[sa] said, "Did you not read in the Holy Qur'ān the following?"

إِنَّآ أَنْشَأْنٰهُنَّ إِنْشَآءً ۙ فَجَعَلْنٰهُنَّ أَبْكَارًا ۙ

innā ansha'nā hunna inshā' an fa ja'alnāhunna abkārā

Verily, We have created them a *good* creation. And made them virgins.' "
(56:36-37)

(i.e., Even old women will enter in the Heaven as young and virgin)

(Rawāhushsharaḥ alsinatah with reference to Mishkāt, Bāb almizāḥ, p. 416)

Ḥaḍrat Abū Hurairah[ra] relates that while talking with the Holy Prophet[sa] people said: "O Messenger[sa] of Allāh! You also sometimes joke with us." The Holy Prophet[sa] said, "I do not say anything except the truth."

(Jāmi' Tirmidhī, Abwābul bir walṣilah, Bāb fil mizāḥ)

20

A Synopsis of the High Moral Excellences of the Holy Prophet[sa]

His Character

The character of the Holy Prophet[sa] has so many different facets that it is not possible to deal adequately with it within the space of these pages. Here are just a few examples to illustrate some of the high moral excellences of the Holy Prophet[sa].

Ḥaḍrat Sa'd bin Hishām bin 'Āmir[ra] relates, "I visited Ḥaḍrat 'Ā'ishah[ra] and requested her to tell me about the character of the Holy Prophet[sa]. She stated:

كَانَ خُلُقُهُ الْقُرْاٰنَ

kāna khulquhul Qur'ān

The character of the Holy Prophet[sa] was the Holy Qur'ān.

Then she asked me: 'Did you not read in the Holy Qur'ān where Allāh the Most Honored and Glorious says:

إِنَّكَ لَعَلٰى خُلُقٍ عَظِيْمٍ

innaka la'alā khuluqin 'aẓīm

You do surely possess high moral excellences. (68:5)?' "

(Musnad Aḥmad bin Ḥanbal, p 91/6, dalā'ilunnabuwwatu lil-Baihaqī, p. 309/1)

Ḥaḍrat 'Ā'ishah[ra] relates that the character of the Holy Prophet[sa] was in accordance with the Holy Qur'ān.

(Musnad Aḥmad bin Ḥanbal, Vo. 6, p. 91;Mustadrik lil-Ḥākim tafsīr sūratul Mu'minūn, Vol 2, p. 392, Dalā'ilunnabuwwatu lil-Baihaqī, Bāb dhikr akhbār ruwait fī shamā'ilihī wa ikhlāquhī, p 309/1)

Ḥaḍrat Sa'd bin Hishām[ra] relates that he visited Ḥaḍrat 'Ā'ishah[ra] and said: "O Mother of the Faithful! Tell me about the character and conduct of the Holy Prophet[sa]. She said, don't you read the Holy Qur'ān?' I said, 'Why not! (Certainly, I read the Holy Qur'ān.)' Then Ḥaḍrat 'Ā'ishah[ra] said, 'The character of the Holy Prophet[sa] was the Holy Qur'ān.' "

Another version is: "The character of the Holy Prophet[sa] was in full accordance with the Holy Qur'ān."

(Ṣaḥīḥ Muslim, Kitābus Ṣalāt, Bāb jāmi' ṣalātullail, majma'ul baḥār, Vol.1, p. 372; Dalā'ilunnabuwwatu lil-Baihaqī, p. 308/1)

Ḥaḍrat Ṣafiyyah[ra] states :

مَا رَاَيْتُ اَحَدًا قَطُّ اَحْسَنُ خُلُقًا مِّنَ النَّبِيِّ ﷺ

mā ra-aitu aḥadan qaṭṭu aḥsanu khuluqamminannabiyyi[sa]

I did not see anyone better than the Holy Prophet[sa] in moral excellences.

The Holy Prophet[sa] was a true and honest teacher. He practiced what he preached and preached what he practiced.

Ḥadrat Imām Mālik[ra] relates that the Holy Prophet[sa] said: "I have been commissioned (by Allāh) for the completion of good morals."

There is another narration:

عَنْ اَبِىْ هُرَيْرَةَ رَضِيَ اللّٰهُ عَنْهُ قَالَ قَالَ رَسُوْلُ اللّٰهِ ﷺ اِنَّمَا بُعِثْتُ لِاُتَمِّمَ مَكَارِمَ الْاَخْلَاقِ

'an abī Hurairata[ra] qāla qāla rasūlullāhi[sa] innamā bu'ithtu li utammima makārimal akhlāqi

Ḥadrat Abū Hurairah[ra] relates that the Holy Prophet[sa] said, "I have been commissioned for the completion of noble morals."

(Muwaṭṭā' Imām Mālik, Bāb fī ḥusnul khulq, p. 364; Al-sununul kubrā ma'a jawāhirunnaqī kitābushshahada, Bāb biyān makāramul ikhlāq, p. 192/10)

Ḥadrat 'Ā'ishah[ra] relates that the Holy Prophet[sa] used to pray

اَللّٰهُمَّ اَحْسَنْتَ خَلْقِيْ فَاَحْسِنْ خُلُقِيْ -

allāhumma aḥsanta khalqī fa aḥsin khuluqī

O Allāh! Just as You have made me handsome, make my morals attractive as well.

(Musnad Aḥmad, p. 150/6 - 68/6)

Ḥaḍrat Khadījah[ra] describing the praiseworthy character of the Holy Prophet[sa] said:

كَلاَّ اَبْشِرْ فَوَاللّٰهِ لاَ يُخْزِيْكَ اللّٰهُ اَبَدًا اِنَّكَ لَتَصِلُ الرَّحِمَ وَتَحْمِلُ الْكَلَّ وَتَكْسِبُ الْمَعْدُوْمَ وَتَقْرِى الضَّيْفَ وَتُعِيْنُ عَلٰى نَوَائِبِ الْحَقِّ

kallā abshir fa wallāhi lā yukhzīkallāhu abadan innaka la taṣilurraḥima wa taḥmilul kalla wa taksibul ma'dūma wa taqriḍḍaifa wa tu'īnu 'alā nawā'ibil ḥaqqi

Certainly, it can never happen so. You should be happy. By God! God Almighty will never disgrace you.Surely you take care of your kith and kin, help the oppressed, restore the lost virtues, honor the guest and help the needy.

Ḥaḍrat 'Ā'ishah[ra] relates: "Wherever the Holy Prophet[sa] was given the option to adopt one of two courses, he adopted the easier course, unless it was sinful to do so, in which case he avoided it more than anyone else."

(Ṣaḥīḥ Muslim, Kitābul Faḍā'il, Bāb mubā'idtah salallāhhu alaihi wasallām lil athām wa ikhtiyārah minal mabāḥ)

Trust and Faith in God

When all the plots of Meccan chiefs to stop the Holy Prophet[sa] from spreading the Message of Allāh failed, they offered the Holy Prophet[sa] leadership, wealth and beautiful women to marry to convince him to stop spreading his message. However, the Holy Prophet[sa] refused to accept the offer and told his uncle, Abū Ṭālib, that if the chiefs of Mecca placed the sun in his right hand, and the moon in his left hand, even then he would not stop spreading the message of Allāh.

Ḥaḍrat Jābir[ra] relates that he accompanied the Holy Prophet[sa] on a campaign towards Najd and returned with him. At noon, the party reached a valley of thorny trees where the Holy Prophet[sa] made a stop and his Companions[ra] scattered in search of shade. He hung up his sword on a branch of an acacia tree and lay down in its shade. He recounts: "We also took a siesta and suddenly we heard the Holy Prophet[sa] calling us. We hastened to him and saw that a rustic Arab from amongst the disbelievers was standing near him. The Holy Prophet[sa] said to us: 'This one drew my sword against me while I was asleep. I woke up and saw that he had the sword in his hand. He said to me: 'Who will deliver you from me?' I told him: 'Allāh'; and repeated it three times. The sword fell down from his hand and he could not do anything.' " The Holy Prophet[sa] sat up and imposed no penalty on the man.

Another version is: "We were with the Holy Prophet[sa] in the campaign of *Dhātur Riqā'*. We came to a shady tree and we left him to rest under it. A pagan came and seeing the sword of the Holy Prophet[sa] which was hanging on the tree, drew it, and said to him: 'Do you fear me?' He answered: 'No.' Then the man asked: 'Now who will deliver you from me?' The Holy Prophet[sa] answered: 'Allāh.' Thereupon, the sword fell from the man's hand and the Holy Prophet[sa] having secured it asked him: 'Who will now deliver you from me?' The man said: 'You forgive me.' The Holy Prophet[sa] asked him: 'Will you affirm that there is none worthy of worship save Allāh and that I am His messenger?' The man said: 'No. But I promise you that I will not fight against you, nor will I join those who do so.' The Holy Prophet[sa] let him go free. He went back to his people and told them: 'I have come back to you from one who is the best of mankind.' "

(Ṣaḥīḥ Bukhārī, Kitābal Maghāzī, Bāb Ghazwah Dhātur Riqā'; Fatḥul Bārī 7/416)

Rejected Help from an Infidel

Ḥaḍrat 'Ā'ishah[ra] relates that when the Holy Prophet[sa] left for the Battle of Badr and reached a place called *Ḥarratil Wabarah*, he met a man who was famous for his courage and bravery. The Companions[ra] of the Holy Prophet[sa] were very much delighted to see the man. The man said to the Holy Prophet[sa], "I would like to fight as your subordinate along with you. The Holy Prophet[sa] asked him, 'Do you believe in Allāh and His Messenger?' He said, 'No.' The Holy Prophet[sa] told him to leave as he did not want to get help from an infidel.

Ḥaḍrat 'Ā'ishah[ra] relates that after hearing the response of the Holy Prophet[sa] to his request, the man left. However, when the army reached a place called *Shajarah*, the man came again to the Holy Prophet[sa] and offered his services to fight in the battle. The Holy Prophet[sa] again told him that he did not want help from an infidel. So the man left. However, he came again at the place called *Baida'* and repeated his request. The Holy Prophet[sa] again asked him: 'Do you believe in Allāh and His Messenger?' He replied: 'Yes.' The Holy Prophet[sa] said: 'Now you can come along with us.' "

(Ṣaḥīḥ Muslim, Kitābul Jihād, Bāb karāhtal isti'ānah fil Ghazwah bikāfirīn)

Love of God and Submission to Him

Ḥaḍrat 'Ā'ishah[ra] states that after revelation of the *Sūrah*:

اِذَا جَآءَ نَصۡرُ اللّٰهِ وَالۡفَتۡحُ ۙ

idhā jā'a naṣrullāhi wal fatḥu

When the help of Allāh comes, and the victory (110:2)

The Holy Prophet[sa] used to recite the following prayer in every Prayer:

سُبْحَانَكَ رَبَّنَا وَبِحَمْدِكَ اَللّٰهُمَّ اغْفِرْلِىْ

subhānaka rabbanā wabi ḥamdika allāhummaghfirlī

Holy are You, Our Lord, and all praise is Yours. O Allāh, forgive me,

(Ṣaḥīḥ Bukhārī, Kitābut Tafsīr Sūrah: idha jā'a naṣrullāhi wal fatḥu)

Ḥaḍrat 'Abdullāh bin Ḥuḍair[ra] relates that the Holy Prophet[sa] recited from the pulpit

وَالسَّمٰوٰتُ مَطْوِيّٰتٌۢ بِيَمِيْنِهٖ ؕ سُبْحٰنَهٗ وَ تَعٰلٰى عَمَّا يُشْرِكُوْنَ ٥

wassamāwātu maṭwiyyātum bi yamīnihī subḥānahū wa ta'ālā 'ammā yushrikūn

"So will the Heavens be rolled up by His right Hand. Glory to Him and Exalted is He above that which they associate with Him." (39:68)

Then the Holy Prophet[sa] stated that God Almighty says:

اَنَا الْجَبَّارُ ، اَنَا الْمُتَكَبِّرُ ، اَنَا الْمَلِكُ ، اَنَا الْمُتَعَالُ يُمَجِّدُ نَفْسَهٗ

anal-jabbāru, anal-mutakabbiru, anal-maliku, anal-muta'ālu yumajjidu nafsahū

"I am the One Who has complete power to reform, I am the Exalted, I am the Sovereign, I am the Most High. In this way, God Almighty states His Glory and Grandeur."

The Holy Prophet[sa] kept repeating these words with such force until the pulpit and he himself shook so much that we became apprehensive lest he falls from the pulpit.

(Musnad Aḥmad, p 88/2)

Miraculous Divine Help

During migration from Mecca to Medina when the Holy Prophet[sa], Ḥaḍrat Abū Bakr[ra] and the guide reached the camp of Umm Ma'bad, they asked her for a little milk. She did not have milk at that time to give to them. Her husband had taken the goats out to pasture. Only those goats which were too weak to walk and unable to give milk were left behind. The Holy Prophet[sa] asked Umm Ma'bad for permission to milk one of these goats. She said him to take any one he likes. The Holy Prophet[sa] picked one goat, said, 'In the name of Allāh', and started to milk the goat. Milk started to flow. The Holy Prophet[sa] gave the first bowl full of milk to Umm Ma'bad, the second bowl to Ḥaḍrat Abū Bakr[ra] and the third bowl to the guide. He was the last to drink. Then the Holy Prophet[sa] milked the second goat and gave many bowls full of milk to Umm Ma'bad. When the husband of Umm Ma'bad returned home he was amazed to see so many bowls full of milk while he had left home only those goats which were too weak to walk and unable to give milk.

Ḥaḍrat Anas[ra] relates that Abū Ṭalḥa said to his wife, O Umm Sulaim: "From the weakness in the voice of the Holy Prophet[sa] I have perceived that he has been hungry for a long time. Do you have anything to eat? She said: 'Yes.' She brought out some barley bread. Then she took her headdress and wrapped the bread in a portion of it and concealed it under my cloth. She made me wear (the rest of) it and sent me off to the Holy Prophet[sa]. I found the Holy Prophet[sa] seated in the mosque with other people. I stood near them and the Holy Prophet[sa] asked me: 'Have you been sent by Abū Ṭalḥa?' I said: 'Yes.' He asked: 'Did you bring a meal?' I said: 'Yes.' The Holy Prophet[sa] said: 'Let us go. We will eat at Ṭalḥa's place.' Then the Holy Prophet[sa] along with his Companions[ra] began to walk. I walked ahead of them and told Abū Ṭalḥa what had happened. He told Umm Sulaim: 'The Holy Prophet[sa] is coming with a large company and we do not have enough to feed them all.' She said: 'Allāh and His Messenger[sa] know best.' Abū Ṭalḥa quickly went outside and met the Holy Prophet[sa] on the way and brought him in. The Holy Prophet[sa] said: 'Bring whatever food you have, Umm Sulaim.' So she brought the pieces of bread. He asked them to break the bread into pieces and then Umm Sulaim squeezed the container of butter over them and made into morsels. Then the Holy Prophet[sa] blessed it and said: 'Permit ten to come in.' I called in ten persons; they ate their fill and went out. Then the Holy Prophet[sa] said: 'Permit ten more to come in.' So ten more were called in who ate and went out. Then the Holy Prophet[sa] said: 'Permit ten more to come in.' This went on till everyone had eaten his fill. They were seventy or eighty in all. ' "

According to another narration, then, the Holy Prophet[sa] and all the inhabitants of the house ate and still some food was left.

(Ṣaḥīḥ Bukhārī, Kitābul Manāqib, Bāb alāmātinnabuwwah fil Islām)

Ḥaḍrat Jābir bin ‘Abdullāh[ra] relates that he used to borrow money from a Jew of Medina on the condition that he would repay it when the dates in his palm-tree orchard ripen. This orchard of Ḥaḍrat Jābir bin ‘Abdullāh[ra] was located on the road leading to Rūmah. One year, the date crop was very poor and it seemed that he would not be able to repay the loan. When the time to pick the dates arrived, the Jew came to collect his money. However, Ḥaḍrat Jābir bin ‘Abdullāh[ra] did not have money to repay his loan. Therefore, he asked for an extension of one year towards repayment of his loan. The creditor refused to do so and insisted on immediate repayment of the loan. When the Holy Prophet[sa] came to know about Ḥaḍrat Jābir bin 'Abdullāh's[ra] plight, he told his Companions[ra], "Let us go and ask the Jew for an extension towards repayment of the loan. Accordingly, the Holy Prophet[sa] along with few of his Companions[ra] came to the orchard and talked with the Jew about extending the period of repayment of the loan. However, the Jew said, 'Abul Qāsim! I am not going to give an extension.' Noticing that the Jew would not accept his recommendation, the Holy Prophet[sa] circled the orchard and asked the Jew to give an extension in the repayment of the loan. However, the Jew again refused. Ḥaḍrat Jābir bin 'Abdullāh[ra] relates that in the meantime, he brought fresh dates from the orchard and presented these to the Holy Prophet[sa]. The Holy Prophet[sa] ate the dates and said, 'Jābir! Where is your hut? Make a bed for me in it.' He made a bed for the Holy Prophet[sa] where he rested for a while. When he woke up, he presented him with more fresh dates. He ate a few of the dates and again talked with the Jew. However, the Jew again refused. Then, the Holy Prophet[sa] made another round of the orchard and said, 'Jābir! Start picking dates and repay the loan.' He started to pick dates. During this period, the Holy Prophet[sa] stayed in the hut. Jābir repaid all of the loan to the Jew and many dates were still left over. He told this to the Holy Prophet[sa]. He became very happy and said:

أَشْهَدُ أَنِّيْ رَسُوْلُ اللّٰهِ

ash-hadu annī rasūlullāh

I bear witness that I am a Messenger of Allāh' "

(Ṣaḥīḥ Bukhārī, Kitābal Aṭ'amah, Bāb arraṭab wattamar)

While travelling towards Tabūk for the expedition of Tabūk, the Holy Prophet[sa] and his Companions[ra] encamped at a place on the way. There, the camel of the Holy Prophet[sa] wandered away and was lost. The

Companions[ra] searched the camel all around the encampment area. One person who was sharing the ride with Ḥaḍrat 'Ammārah bin Ḥazam and was probably a newcomer to Islām said, "The Holy Prophet[sa] claims to be a Messenger of Allāh and talks about heavens but he does not know where his camel is." Ḥaḍrat 'Ammārah bin Ḥazam told the Holy Prophet[sa] what the new Muslim had said. The Holy Prophet[sa] said, "By Allāh! I do not know anything except what Allāh tells me and Allāh has told me about my lost camel. My camel is in such and such area of such and such valley. The camel's rein is tangled in the branches of a tree and the camel is stuck there. So go and bring the camel to me." Accordingly, the Companions[ra] went to the place told by the Holy Prophet[sa] and brought back the camel.

(As-Sīratun Nabawiyyah libne Hishām, Ghazwah Tabūk, Vol. 4, pp. 166-167; Sīrah Ibne Hishām, Urdu, Translated by 'Abdul Jalīl Siddiqī, Vol. 2, p. 628, Ghazwah Tabūk, I'tiqād Publishing House, Delhi, India, 1982)

Revelations, Visions and Prophecies

It is apparent from the Holy Qur'ān that some dreams and prophecies came true in the life of the Prophets while others were fulfilled after the passing of them. God Almighty had revealed to the Holy Prophet[sa] glad tidings and admonitions which are mentioned in the Holy Qur'ān. Once, regarding a Divine manifestation scene by the Holy Prophet[sa] during *Kasūf* Prayer he said, "Right here, at this moment, I have been shown by God Almighty the future events which have been promised to you." To the extent that I have been shown hell and heaven. What the Holy Prophet[sa] saw during the manifestation he described was so vivid that seeing the blessings of the heaven he moved forward to fetch them while seeing the ferocity of the hell he moved back.

Some of the dreams, revelations and manifestations of the Holy Prophet[sa] are briefly described here:

1. Marriage with Ḥaḍrat 'Āi'shah[ra]

God Almighty had beforehand revealed to the Holy Prophet[sa] regarding his marriage with Ḥaḍrat 'Āi'shah[ra]. Ḥaḍrat 'Ā'ishah[ra] relates that the Holy Prophet[sa] said to her, "You have been shown to me twice in my dream. I saw you pictured on a piece of silk and someone said to me, 'This is your wife.' When I uncovered the picture, I saw that it was yours. I said, 'If this is from Allāh, it will be accomplished.' "

(Ṣaḥīḥ Bukhārī, Kitāb Faḍā'il Aṣḥābannabī[ra], Bāb tazwījunnabī[sa] 'Āi'shata[ra] wa qudūmihal madīnata wa banā'ihī bihā)

2. False Claimants: Musailimah ibn Ḥabīb (*al-Kadhdhāb*) and Aswad 'Ansī

Ḥaḍrat Ibn 'Abbās[ra] relates that Musailimah ibn Ḥabīb (al-Kadhdhāb) came to Medina while the Holy Prophet[sa] was alive and said: "I will obey Muḥammad[sa] if he entrusts sovereignty to me when he passes away. Many people of his tribe were with him. One day, the Holy Prophet[sa] went to see him. Ḥaḍrat Thābit bin Qais bin Shammās[ra] accompanied the Holy Prophet[sa]. The Holy Prophet[sa] had a thin stick of a date tree in his hand. Musailimah was sitting in the company of his people. The Holy Prophet[sa] told him: 'If you ask for this thin stick, I will not give even this to you. You will not escape God's judgement. If you move backward, God will hamstring you. I have been shown many things concerning your end. Thābit will answer your questions.' Then the Holy Prophet[sa] left. Ḥaḍrat Ibn 'Abbās[ra] relates that he asked Ḥaḍrat Abū Hurairah[ra] what was meant by the comment of the Holy Prophet[sa] that I have been shown a lot of things concerning your end? Ḥaḍrat Abū Hurairah[ra] told him that the Holy Prophet[sa] had told him his dream.' The Holy Prophet[sa] said: 'Once I was asleep and I saw in a dream that I had two gold bracelets in my hand. I became a bit worried about these. In the dream, I was told to blow air on the bracelets. When I blew air on the bracelets, the bracelets disappeared. I interpreted the dream as: After I pass away, there will be two false claimants and liars who will revolt.' " So, the narrator explains that later on, it became clear that one of them was (Aswad) 'Ansī, who revolted in Ṣan'ā' (Yemen) and the second one was Musailimah (*al-Kadhdhāb*), who laid the foundation for the revolt in *Yamāmah.*

(Ṣaḥīḥ Muslim, Kitābar Ru'yā, Bāb ar-Ru'yā annabī[sa]; Ṣaḥīḥ Bukhārī)

3. Death of Aswad 'Ansī

Ḥaḍrat 'Amr bin 'Abdullāh[ra] relates, "God Almighty had informed the Holy Prophet[sa] the night before the assassination of Aswad 'Ansī (the false claimant of the prophethood) about his death. In the morning, the Holy Prophet[sa] told them that Aswad 'Ansī had been killed by a blessed man. Someone asked the Holy Prophet[sa], 'Who is the person who has killed Aswad 'Ansī. The Holy Prophet[sa] said, 'His name is Firozbān Firoz.' "

(Kanzul 'Ummāl)

4. Death of Quraish Leaders of Mecca in the Battle of Badr

God Almighty had shown to the Holy Prophet[sa] in a vision

before the Battle of Badr the death of the *Quraish* leaders. In this regard, Ḥaḍrat Anas[ra] relates, "I was travelling with Ḥaḍrat 'Umar[ra] and we were in the middle of Mecca and Medina when Ḥaḍrat 'Umar[ra] told me, 'One day before the Battle of Badr the Holy Prophet[sa] while pinpointing the place of death of the *Quraish* leaders told him that so and so leader of the *Quraish* will fall at such and such place during the Battle.' Ḥaḍrat 'Umar[ra] then stated, 'The bodies of the leaders of the *Quraish* were found exactly at the places which were pinpointed by the Holy Prophet[sa].' "

Ḥaḍrat 'Umar[ra] said to the Holy Prophet[sa], "O Messeger of Allāh! By God Who has sent you with the Truth, the bodies were found exactly at the places you had pinpointed without the slightest mistake."

(Ṣaḥīḥ Bukhārī, Kitābul Jihād, Bāb mā qīla fī dar' annabī[sa])

5. Prophecy Regarding the Death of Chosroes Pervaiz, the King of Persia

Chosroes Pervaiz, the king of Persia had ordered Bādhān, the Governer of Yemen to imprison the Holy Prophet[sa] and present to him in his court. Bādhān sent his two emissaries to the Holy Prophet[sa] with Chosroes' orders. The Holy Prophet[sa] told them to wait for a short while for his response. After a couple of days the Holy Prophet[sa] told the emissaries of the Governor of Yemen to go back as his Lord has revealed to him that He has killed their lord. When the representatives of the Governor of Yemen returned to him they received the news that Sherawiyyah had assassinated his father Chosroes Pervaiz.

6. Chosroes' Bracelets and Surāqah bin Mālik

Surāqah bin Mālik followed the Holy[sa] Prophet with the intention of arresting or killing him and getting the reward which was fixed by the infidels of Mecca for doing so. When he failed to do so he told to the Holy Prophet[sa] the intentions of his people and wished to offer the Holy Prophet[sa] some provisions for the journey and other things. The Holy Prophet[sa] did not accept his offer. Then he requested the Holy Prophet[sa] to give an undertaking of peace and protection for him in writing. The Holy Prophet[sa] told 'Āmir bin Fuhairah to do so. He wrote a guarantee on a piece of leather. When Surāqah bin Mālik was leaving the Holy Prophet[sa] said, "Surāqah! How would you feel when the bracelets of the king of Persia will be given to you to wear. Surāqah said, 'Chosroes Pervaiz, the King of Persia.' The Holy Prophet[sa] said, 'Yes, the bracelets of Chosroes Pervaiz.' "

After the conquest of Mecca, Surāqah bin Mālik accepted Islām in Ji'rānah. When during the *Khilāfat* of Ḥaḍrat 'Umar[ra] the bracelets of Chosroes were presented to Ḥaḍrat 'Umar[ra] in his court, he called Surāqah bin Mālik and told him to bring forward his hands. Then he gave Surāqah bin Mālik the bracelets to wear which he did.

(As-Siratul Ḥalabiyyah, Vol. 2, p.45, Published in Beirut, Lebanon)

7. The Prophecy Regarding Sea Conquests

Ḥaḍrat Anas[ra] relates that the Holy Prophet[sa] used to visit the house of Ḥaḍrat Umm Ḥarām bint Milḥān[ra]. She was the wife of Ḥaḍrat 'Ubādah bin Ṣāmat[ra]. The Holy Prophet[sa] once visited Ḥaḍrat Umm Ḥarām[ra] who presented food to him. Ḥaḍrat Umm Ḥarām[ra] began massaging the head of the Holy Prophet[sa] gently and he went to sleep. After a little while, he woke up smiling. Ḥaḍrat Umm Ḥarām[ra] asked the Holy Prophet[sa]: "Messenger[sa] of Allāh! Why are you smiling? The Holy Prophet[sa] said: 'In my dream I have seen some of my followers who have left to fight in the way of Allāh. Sitting on the wooden planks after boarding the ships, they looked like kings on thrones.' Ḥaḍrat Umm Ḥarām[ra] said: 'Messenger[sa] of Allāh! Invoke Allāh that He includes me among these people.' So the Holy Prophet[sa] prayed for her and went to sleep again. Again he woke up and was smiling. Ḥaḍrat Umm Ḥarām[ra] asked the Holy Prophet[sa]: 'Messenger[sa] of Allāh! Why are you smiling?' The Holy Prophet[sa] said, 'I have again seen some warriors of mine who were going on a sea expedition, repeating the same dream.' Ḥaḍrat Umm Ḥarām[ra] besought: 'Messenger[sa] of Allāh! Pray that God may include me among these conquerers.' The Holy Prophet[sa] said, 'You will be included in the first group.' " Thus, during the rule of Ḥaḍrat Amīr Mu'āwiyah bin Abū Sufyān[ra], after disembarking from the ship, Ḥaḍrat Umm Ḥarām[ra] entered the island and while riding on a camel she fell and passed away there.

(Ṣaḥīḥ Bukhārī, Kitāb at-Ta'bīr , Bāb Ru'yā' binnahār)

8. Prophecy Regarding the Glory of Islām

During the digging of the trenches in the Battle of Aḥzāb when the Holy Prophet[sa] struck the big solid rock with his pick-axe, there appeared three times a bright flash of light and each time the Holy Prophet said, "*Allāhu Akbar*" in a loud voice. The Companions[ra] asked the Holy Prophet[sa] about the significance of the light and why he said "*Allāhu Akbar*" each time there was the light. The Holy Prophet[sa] smiled and told them, "I struck the rock three times with the pick-axe, and three times I saw the scenes of the future glory of Islām. In the first spark I saw the Syrian palaces of the Roman Empire. I had the keys of those palaces given to me. The second time, I saw the palaces of Persia and Madā'in, and had the keys of Persian Empire given to me. The third time, I saw the gates of Ṣan'ā and I had the keys of the kingdom of Yemen given to me. These are the promises of Allāh.

The conquest of these great empires started during the *Khilāfat* of Ḥaḍrat Abū Bakr[ra] when Ḥaḍrat Khālid bin Walīd and Ḥaḍrat Abū 'Ubaidah[ra] conquered Syria. However, the prophecy was completely fulfilled in the *Khilāfat* of Ḥaḍrat 'Umar[ra] when Ḥaḍrat Sa'd bin abī Waqās[ra] conquered Iran. Thus within a short period of time two great kingdoms, Rome and Persia, surrendered to Muslims.

(Ṣaḥīḥ Bukhārī, Kitab at-Ta'bīr, Bāb Ru'yā allail)

Acceptance of His Prayers

It has always been the case with the Prophets that despite the fact that they are given prophecies and they have very strong faith in the promises given by God, they do not abandon praying to Him (for their success). They do so because they believe that God has power to do whatever He likes - and none can grasp His ways and it is disrespectful for one not to pray to Him.

History tells us that when the Battle of Badr was raging and the

Holy Prophet[sa] was busy praying to God (for victory), Ḥaḍrat Abū Bakr[ra] requested him to stop praying, for he had already been promised victory by God. But the Holy Prophet[sa] continued praying. Some people have opined that it could not be said that the faith of Ḥaḍrat Abū Bakr[ra] was stronger than that of the Holy Prophet[sa]; the *Ma'rifat* (God-realization) of the Holy Prophet[sa] was much greater and the more a man realizes what the situation is, the more he fears. The *Ma'rifat* (God-realization), of the Holy Prophet[sa] made him fear that God has the power to do whatever He likes. One should, therefore, in no case, abandon praying to God.

(Malfūẓāt, Vol. 3, p 267, London Edition, 1984)

The life of the Holy Prophet[sa] was full of incidents where his prayers were accepted. Sometimes, his prayers were accepted by God Almighty as soon as he finished praying or while he was praying. Earlier it is mentioned how God Almighty accepted the prayer of the Holy Prophet[sa] and helped against the enemies in various battles and also God Almighty accepted the prayer of the Holy Prophet[sa] and guided Ḥaḍrat 'Umar[ra] towards Islām. A few more examples of the acceptance of the prayers of the Holy Prophet[sa] are described here:

'Utbah and Mu'attab were the sons of Abū Lahab bin 'Abdul Muṭṭalib and thus cousins of the Holy Prophet[sa]. The Holy Prophet[sa] had an intense desire that both of his cousins accept Islām. Thus, the Holy Prophet[sa] told Ḥaḍrat 'Abbās[ra] to convey the message of Islām to 'Utbah and Mu'attab. Ḥaḍrat 'Abbās[ra] conveyed the message of Islām to them and both of them accepted Islām. Ḥaḍrat 'Abbās[ra] brought both 'Utbah and Mu'attab to the Holy Prophet[sa]. The Holy Prophet[sa] was very happy upon their acceptance of Islām. The Holy Prophet[sa] brought both of them to *Multazim* in the *Ka'bah* and prayed for them. The Holy Prophet[sa] said, "I had asked God Almighty for both of the brothers and God Almighty has given both of them to me."

Ḥaḍrat Shuraḥbīl bin Ṣimṭ[ra] relates that he said to Ka'b bin Murra, "O Ka'b bin Murra, relate to us some *Ḥadīth* of the Holy Prophet[sa]." He said that a man came to the Holy Prophet[sa] and said, "O Messenger[sa] of Allāh! Pray to Allāh for rain." Thereupon the Holy Prophet[sa] raised both his hands and prayed the following:

اَللّٰهُمَّ اسْقِنَا غَيْثًا مَرِيْئًا مَرِيْعًا طَبَقًا عَاجِلاً غَيْرَ رَائِثٍ ' نَافِعًا غَيْرَ ضَارٍّ عَاجِلاً ۔

allāhummasqinā ghaithan marī'an marī'an ṭabaqan 'ājilan ghaira rā'ithin nāfi'an ghaira ḍarrin 'ājilan

O Allāh, give us rain that is wholesome and productive, filling all spaces soon, without delay that is profitable and not harmful.

He said, "Then they came and complained to the Holy Prophet[sa] of (excessive) raining and said, 'O Allāh's Messenger[sa]! The houses have been demolished.' Thereupon the Holy Prophet[sa] prayed the following and the clouds began to disperse:

اَللّٰهُمَّ حَوَالَيْنَا وَلاَ عَلَيْنَا ۔

allāhumma ḥavālainā walā 'alainā

O Allāh, let rain fall on our surroundings and not on us."

(Sunan Ibni Mājah, Kitāb Iqāmatiṣ-Ṣalāti wassunnati fihā, Bāb mājā'a fiddu'ā'i fil istisqā'i)

Once, during a battle, there was an extreme shortage of water and

Muslims were very thirsty. Ḥaḍrat 'Umar[ra] requested the Holy Prophet[sa] to pray for rain. The Holy Prophet[sa] raised his hands and started praying. Suddenly, a cloud appeared and it rained so much that all the water needs of the Muslims were fulfilled and then the cloud disappered.

(Al-Shifā Ba-ta'rīf Ḥaqūqul Muṣṭafā, lil-Qāḍī 'Ayāḍ, Vol. 1, p. 457, As quoted by Baihaqī)

Ḥaḍrat Abū Hurairah[ra] had accepted Islām at the time when the Holy Prophet[sa] was returning to Medina after the fall of Khaibar. He belonged to the *Banī Daus* tribe. His original name was "'Abd Shams" and the Holy Prophet[sa] had changed his name to 'Abdullāh. His family name was Abū Hurairah. The reason for giving him the name of Abū Hurairah was that he had a cat as a pet whom he carried around all the time.

Ḥaḍrat Abū Hurairah's[ra] mother did not accept Islām and was a staunch enemy of Islām. Ḥaḍrat Abū Hurairah[ra] urged her to accept Islām but she refused and abused the Holy Prophet[sa]. Ḥaḍrat Abū Hurairah[ra] was very much saddened because of his mother's attitude. He went to the Holy Prophet[sa] and told him about the attitude of his mother. The Holy Prophet[sa] said:

اَللّٰهُمَّ اهْدِ اُمَّ اَبِیْ هُرَیْرَةَ

allāhummahdi Ummi Abī Hurairah

O Allāh! Guide Abū Hurairah's mother

The Holy Prophet's[sa] prayer was accepted in a strange way. When Ḥaḍrat Abū Hurairah[ra] returned home he found a big change in his mother. Her attitude toward Islām was totally changed and she was openly announcing her acceptance of Islām. Ḥaḍrat Abū Hurairah[ra] immediately went back to the Holy Prophet[sa] and told him the whole incident and requested the Holy Prophet[sa] to pray that God Almighty create love for him and his mother in the hearts of the believers. The Holy Prophet[sa] prayed for that also.

(Al-Aṣābah fī Ma'rafatuṣ Ṣaḥāba, See Undur Abū Hurairah, Vol. 4, p. 243, Published in Egypt)

Once Ḥaḍrat Abū Hurairah[ra] said to the Holy Prophet[sa]: "After listening to what you say, I forget everything quickly. Please pray for me that my memory is sharpened." The Holy Prophet[sa] told Ḥaḍrat Abū Hurairah[ra] to spread his sheet which he was using to cover himself. Ḥaḍrat Abū Hurairah[ra] complied and spread his sheet. The Holy Prophet[sa] prayed over the sheet and told Ḥaḍrat Abū Hurairah[ra] to cover himself with the sheet. Ḥaḍrat Abū Hurairah[ra] relates that since then his memory was so sharp that he did not forget any *Ḥadīth*.

(Jāmi' Tirmidhī, Abwābul Manāqib, Manāqib Abī Hurairah[ra])

This is acceptance of the prayer of the Holy Prophet[sa] that although Ḥaḍrat Abū Hurairah[ra] accepted Islām quite late (in 7 AH) still the traditions related by him are more than those related by some who accepted Islām much earlier than him.

(Jāmi' Tirmidhī, Kitābul Manāqib, Bāb manāqib Abū Hurairah[ra])

According to Ḥaḍrat Ibn Ḥazam[rh] there are 5,374 traditions narrated by Ḥaḍrat Abū Hurairah[ra].

(Abū Hurairah[ra] p. 124, By Maḥmūd Abū Zayya, Published by Mu'ssatul 'ilmi lil Maṭbū'āti Beirut, Lebanon)

Ḥaḍrat Anas[ra] was twelve years old when his parents presented him to the Holy Prophet[sa] as his personal servant. Once, Ḥaḍrat Anas'[ra] mother,

Ḥaḍrat Umm Sulaim[ra] came to the Holy Prophet[sa] and requested him to pray for Anas. The Holy Prophet[sa] prayed that God Almighty may enlarge his provisions and bless his progeny.

(Ṣaḥīḥ Bukhārī, Kitābud Da'wāt, Bāb ad-Du'ā'i bi kathratil māli wal waladi ma'al barakati)

Ḥaḍrat Anas[ra] himself relates that God Almighty accepted the prayer of the Holy Prophet[sa] which he prayed for him and fulfilled it beautifully. "My garden produced fruit twice a year and I had more than eighty sons, daughters and grandchildren." Ḥaḍrat Anas[ra] was around 103-110 years old when he passed away.

(Usud al-Ghābah, Vol. 1, p. 128, Published in Beirut, Lebanon)

The Holy Prophet[sa] prayed for Ḥaḍrat Fāṭimah[ra] that she never suffer from hunger. Ḥaḍrat Fāṭimah[ra] later said that she never suffered from hunger.

(Khaṣā'iṣ Al-Kubrā, Jalāluddīn Al-Suyūṭī, (Urdu) Vol. II, p. 276, Printed in Lahore, Pakistan)

The Holy Prophet[sa] prayed for blessings in Ḥaḍrat 'Abdullāh bin Ja'far's business. As a result of the prayer, whatever Ḥaḍrat 'Abdullāh binJa'far bought he made profit out of it.

(Khaṣā'iṣ Al-Kubrā, Jalāluddīn Al-Suyūṭī, (Urdu) Vol. II, p. 290, Printed in Lahore, Pakistan)

The Holy Prophet[sa] had prayed for the acceptance of the prayers of Ḥaḍrat Sa'd bin Abī Waqqās[ra]. God Almighty accepted the prayer of the Holy Prophet[sa] which is apparent from this tradition. The following tradition shows how beautifully the prayer of Ḥaḍrat Sa'd bin Abī Waqqās[ra] was accepted by God Almighty:

Ḥaḍrat Jābir bin Samurah[ra] relates that the people of Kūfā complained against Ḥaḍrat Sa'd bin Abī Waqqās to Ḥaḍrat 'Umar. Ḥaḍrat 'Umar dismissed Ḥaḍrat Sa'd and appointed Ḥaḍrat 'Ammār as governor of Kūfā. Their complaint was that he could not even lead the Prayer properly. Thus, Ḥaḍrat 'Umar sent for Ḥaḍrat Sa'd to Medina and said to him: "O Abū Isḥāq! They think that you cannot lead the Prayer properly. Ḥaḍrat Sa'd replied: 'O Leader of the Believers! I conducted the Prayer services as did the Holy Prophet[sa], without any change (i.e., no decrease or increase). For instance, in the *'Ishā'* Prayer I made the first two *rak'āt* long and the last two *rak'āt* short.' Ḥaḍrat 'Umar said: 'This is what I thought about you.' Then, he sent some men with Ḥaḍrat Sa'd to Kūfā to inquire about him. They made an inquiry about the complaints in each mosque in Kūfā. All praised Ḥaḍrat Sa'd; but amongst the gathering in the mosque of *Banī 'Abs,* a man whose name was Usāmah bin Qatādah stood up and said: 'Now that we have been placed under the oath, I am compelled to tell that Ḥaḍrat Sa'd did not lead the expeditions, did not distribute the spoils equitably and did not judge justly.' On this Ḥaḍrat Sa'd said: 'I shall make three supplications concerning him: O my Allāh! If this servant of Thine is a liar and has stood up to show off, then do Thou prolong his life and lengthen his adversity and afflict him with trials.,' God Almighty did the same. Thereafter when the man was very old whenever someone asked about his condition he would say: 'I am an old man, afflicted with different trials, and people laugh at me. I am certainly overtaken by the imprecation of Sa'd.' Ḥaḍrat Jābir bin Samurah[ra] who is a narrator of the incident relates: 'I saw this unfortunate man when due to old age his eyebrows fell over his eyes and he roamed the streets teasing the girls and they teased him.' "

(Ṣaḥīḥ Bukhārī, Kitāb aṣ-Ṣalāt, Bāb wajūb qiratal imām)

Once, the Holy Prophet[sa] was offering Prayer in the *Ka'bah* and a few chiefs of the *Quraish* were also sitting there. Abū Jahl asked if there was anyone courageous enough to bring the womb of a camel and place it on top of the Holy Prophet[sa] while he is prostrating. 'Aqba bin Abī Mu'īṭ got up and brought a womb of a camel which was full of blood and filth and placed it on the back of the Holy Prophet[sa] while he was in prostration. Seeing this everyone started to laugh out aloud. When Ḥaḍrat Fāṭimah[ra] came to know about it she ran to the *Ka'bah* and removed that womb from the Holy Prophet[sa]. Then the Holy Prophet[sa] raised his head from the prostration position. It is stated that at this time the Holy Prophet[sa] pronounced the names of those who were bent upon erasing the religion of Islām and prayed for their destruction. It so happened that all of them were killed in the Battle of Badr.

(Ṣaḥīḥ Bukhārī, Kitābul Maghāzī, Bāb du'ānnabī[sa] 'alā kuffāri Quraish)

Love of the Holy Qur'ān

Ḥaḍrat Ibn Mas'ūd[ra] relates: The Holy Prophet[sa] asked me to recite the Qur'ān to him. I said: "Messenger[sa] of Allāh, shall I recite the Qur'ān to you, whereas it is you to whom it has been revealed? He[sa] said: 'I like to hear it recited by another.' So I recited to him a portion from *Sūrah Al-Nisā'* till I came to the verse:

فَكَيْفَ إِذَا جِئْنَا مِنْ كُلِّ أُمَّةٍ بِشَهِيْدٍ وَّ جِئْنَابِكَ عَلٰى هٰٓؤُلَآءِ شَهِيْدًا ۝

fakaifa idhā ji'nā min kulli ummatim bi shahīdiñwwa ji'nā bika 'alā hā 'ulā'ai shahīdā

And how *will it fare with them* when We shall bring a witness from every people, and shall bring you as a witness against these! (4:42)'

Upon this the Holy Prophet[sa] said: 'That is enough for now.' " I looked at him and saw that his eyes were running.

(Ṣaḥīḥ Bukhārī, Kitābut Tafsīr, Bāb qauluhu 'azza wa jalla "fakaifa idhā ji'na min kulli ummatin bi-shahīd")

His Worship and Love for Prayers

According to the traditions, the Holy Prophet[sa] used to begin his day with *Tahajjud* Prayer. Before performing *Wuḍū'* for the *Tahajjud* Prayer he used to clean his teeth with a *Miswāk* (a softened twig of a tree used for cleaning the teeth). He used to offer *Tahajjud* Prayer beautifully and for a long duration, in which he used to recite a large portion of the Holy Qur'ān. He used to stand so long while offering *Tahajjud* Prayers that often his feet used to swell. After offering the *Tahajjud* Prayer he used to lie down to rest for a short period of time. During this time he often used to converse with the family members who were awake. Upon hearing the voice of Ḥaḍrat Bilāl[ra] calling *Adhān*, he would get up and offer two *Sunnah*, which were rather short. Then he would go to *Masjid Nabawī* to lead the *Fajr* Prayer. If due to illness he was unable to offer the *Tahajjud* Prayer he would compensate it by offering *Nawāfil* during the day time.

(Ṣaḥīḥ Bukhārī, Kitābut Tahajjud)

Ḥaḍrat 'Ā'ishah[ra] relates: "The Holy Prophet[sa] stood so long during his voluntary Prayers at a night that the skin of his feet would crack, so I said to him: 'Messenger[sa] of Allāh, why do you stand so long in Prayer when Allāh has suppressed in you all past and future inclination towards sin?' He answered: 'Then should I be a grateful servant of Allāh.'"

(Ṣaḥīḥ Bukhārī, Kitābut Tafsīr Sūrah Al-Fatḥ)

The Holy Prophet[sa] used to wait anxiously for the Prayer time. His mind was always thinking of the mosque and the Prayers. He used to say to Ḥaḍrat Bilāl[ra]:

يَا بِلَالُ أَرِحْنَا بِالصَّلٰوةِ

yā bilālu a-riḥnā biṣṣalāti

O Bilāl! Make me happy by informing me about the Prayer

(Musnad Aḥmad bin Ḥanbal, Vol. 1, Ḥadīth # 364)

Ḥaḍrat 'Ā'ishah[ra] relates: "During the last ten days of *Ramaḍān*, the Holy Prophet[sa] would liven the whole night (i.e., he would keep himself and his family members awake the whole night). He girded up his loins and devoted himself entirely (to offering Prayers and supplication).

(Ṣaḥīḥ Bukhārī, Kitābuṣ Ṣaum, Bābul 'aml fīl 'ashril awākhir min Ramaḍān; Ṣaḥīḥ Muslim, Kitābuṣ Ṣaum, Bābul ijtihād fīl 'ashril awākhir min shaḥri Ramaḍān)

Ḥaḍrat 'Ā'ishah[ra] relates that the Holy Prophet[sa], in the month of *Ramaḍān* and in other months, did not offer more than eleven *rak'āt Nafl* Prayer (in the late hours of the night at *Tahajjud* time). He offered four *rak'āt*. Ask me not how beautiful and for how long he offered these. Then, he offered four *rak'āt* more. Ask me not how beautiful and for how long he offered these. After that, he would offer three *rak'āt*. Ḥaḍrat 'Ā'ishah[ra] relates that she asked the Holy Prophet[sa]: "Do you take a nap before offering the *Vitr* Prayer? He said: 'O 'Ā'ishah! My eyes go to sleep but my mind does not.' "

(Ṣaḥīḥ Bukhārī, Kitābuṣṣaum , Bāb faḍl man qāma Ramaḍān)

Ḥaḍrat Muṭarraf[ra] relates that his father told him that he had seen the Holy Prophet[sa] offer Prayers. Due to pleading and lamenting during Prayers, his chest sounded like a grinding mill.

(Sunan Abū Dāwūd, Kitābuṣṣalāt, Bāb al-bakā' fiṣṣalāt, p. 238/1)

Ḥaḍrat 'Ā'ishah[ra] relates that during the illness that ultimately led to the demise of the Holy Prophet[sa], there was a period when the Holy Prophet[sa] felt better. It was time for Prayer. The Holy Prophet[sa] told her to send a message to Ḥaḍrat Abū Bakr[ra] to lead the Prayer. She sent the message to Ḥaḍrat Abū Bakr[ra] that the Holy Prophet[sa] wanted him to lead the Prayer. Ḥaḍrat Abū Bakr[ra] replied: "I am an old man with a very tender-heart. It will not be possible for me to control my emotions when the Holy Prophet[sa] is unable to lead the Prayer. Therefore, both you and Ḥafṣah[ra] may request the Holy Prophet[sa] to send the message to 'Umar[ra]. The Holy Prophet[sa] replied: ' اَنْتُنَّ صَوَاحِبُ يُوْسُفَ (***antunna ṣawāḥibu Yūsufa***) Both of you are like the women who conspired against Yūsuf. Tell Abū Bakr to lead the Prayer.' When the Holy Prophet[sa] heard the *Mu'edhdhin* say حَيَّ عَلَى الصَّلٰوة (***ḥayya 'alaṣṣalāh***, Come to Prayer), he told some people to help him stand. At this, Ḥaḍrat 'Ā'ishah[ra] said: 'You have already told Abū Bakr to lead the Prayer and you also have an excuse (sickness).' The Holy Prophet[sa] said: 'Help me stand up. My tranquility is in Prayer.' Thus, two men helped the Holy Prophet[sa] stand while his feet stumbled on the ground. When Abū Bakr[ra] realized that the Holy Prophet[sa] was coming for the Prayer he started to move back. The Holy Prophet[sa] indicated to Abū Bakr to stay at his place and he himself sat on his left side. Abū Bakr[ra] repeated the *Takbīr* after it was pronounced by the Holy Prophet[sa]. The other people offering the Prayer followed the *Takbīr* of Abū Bakr[ra] and in this way completed their Prayer. This was the last Prayer offered by the people standing behind the Holy Prophet[sa]. After this, Ḥaḍrat Abū Bakr[ra] led the Prayers during the illness of the Holy Prophet[sa] till he passed away.' "

(Musnad Imāmul A'ẓam, Kitābaṣṣalāt, p. 80)

Thankfulness for Divine Bounties

Ḥaḍrat Abū Hurairah[ra] relates: "One day the Holy Prophet[sa] came out either at day time or at night and saw Ḥaḍrat Abū Bakr[ra] and Ḥaḍrat 'Umar[ra]. He asked them: "What has brought you out of your houses at this time? They said: 'Hunger, O Messenger[sa] of Allāh'. He affirmed: 'By Allāh, in Whose Hands is my life, the same cause has brought me out that has brought both of you out; so come along.' So both of them accompanied him and they went to the house of one of the *Anṣār*. However, he was not at home. When his wife saw the Holy Prophet[sa], she welcomed him. He asked her: 'Where is So and So?' She said: 'He has gone to fetch water.' In the meantime, the *Anṣārī* came back. Seeing the Holy Prophet[sa] and his two Companions[ra], he said: *'Alḥamdulillāh* (Praise be to Allāh). There is no one who has more honored guests today than I have.' He then went out and brought a branch of a date tree bearing ripe and semi-ripe dates and invited them to eat. He then took up a knife and the Holy Prophet[sa] said to him: 'Do not slaughter a goat that is yielding milk.' So he slaughtered another goat for them and they ate and drank. When they had their fill and were refreshed, the Holy Prophet[sa] said to his two Companions[ra]: 'By Him in Whose Hands is my life, you will be called to account for these bounties on the Day of Judgment. Hunger drove you out of your homes and you did not return till you had enjoyed these bounties. ' "

(Ṣaḥīḥ Muslim, Kitābul Ashribah, Bāb jawāz istatbā'ah ghairih ilā dār man yashaqqa bi raḍā bi dhālik)

Truthfulness

The Holy Prophet[sa] had lived among his people for forty years before he was commissioned by God as a Prophet. Even the several critics of his character cannot put a finger on any blemish in his life up to that age. There is no disagreement among historians regarding this fact. As such the Holy Qur'ān challenged those who rejected him by saying:

فَقَدْ لَبِثْتُ فِيْكُمْ عُمُرًا مِّنْ قَبْلِهٖ ط اَفَلَا تَعْقِلُوْنَ ٥

faqad labiththu fīkum 'umurammin qablihī afalā ta'qilūn

I have indeed lived among you a *whole* lifetime before this. Will you not then understand! (10:17)

Do you not see that a man who lived for forty years of blameless life suddenly cannot turn into the most wanton man on earth. He, who never told a lie against his fellow beings, how could he dare speak lies about his Creator, the God he loved so much.

(The Seal of Prophets: His Personality and Character, Islām International Publications Ltd., pp.12-13, Printed in USA, 2007)

Once Abū Jahl said to the Holy Prophet[sa]:

إِنَّا لَا نُكَذِّبُكَ وَلٰكِنْ نُكَذِّبُ بِمَا جِئْتَ بِهٖ

innā lā nukadhdhibuka wa lākin nukadhdhibu bimā ji'ta bihī

We do not belie you but we belie that which you have brought.

(Jāmi' Tirmidhī, Kitābut Tafsīr, Abwābu Tafsīrul Qur'ān, Wa min Sūrah al-An'ām)

The Holy Prophet[sa] was himself so rigid in his standards of truthfulness that he was known among his people as "The Trustworthy" and "The Truthful". Through centuries of Arab history we find that it was only in the case of the Holy Prophet of Islām[sa] that his people conferred the titles of "The Trustworthy" and "The Truthful". This proves that the Holy Prophet[sa] possessed these qualities in so eminent a degree, that within the knowledge and the memory of his people no other individual could be regarded as his equal in these respects.

He was equally anxious that Muslims should adopt the same standards of truth as were observed by himself. He regarded truth as the basis of all virtue, goodness and right conduct. He taught that a truthful person is one who is so confirmed in truth that he is counted as truthful by God.

Excellences in Dealing with Others

Ḥaḍrat Jābir bin 'Abdullāh[ra] relates that the Holy Prophet[sa] said: "When you weigh something to give to someone, give a little extra."

(Ibni Mājah, Abwābuttijārāt, Bāburruijḥān fīlwazn)

Ḥaḍrat Qailah Umm Banī Anmār[ra] relates that at the occasion of one *'Umra*, she met the Holy Prophet[sa] at *Marwah* (a hill, the other is called *Ṣafā*). She told the Holy Prophet[sa] that she was a businesswoman. Her way of doing business was to at first bid a price that was very low. She would slowly raise the price and when it reached the price at which she wanted to purchase, she purchased the goods. Similarly, when she sold an item, at first she would quote a very high price, then slowly lower the price. When it reached the price at which she wanted to sell, she sold the goods. Hearing this, the Holy Prophet[sa] said: "O Qailah! Do not do business like this. Instead, you should fix the price. Tell the price at which you want to purchase the goods. If he wants to sell at that price he can or if he does not then he need not. Similarly, when selling an item, tell them the actual price. If anyone wants to buy at that price, he can do so or leave it."

Devotion Towards Moral Training of the Muslims

Ḥaḍrat Abū Hurairah[ra] relates that once while the Holy Prophet[sa] was sitting in the Mosque, a man came and offered his Prayer. Then he came up to the Holy Prophet[sa] and greeted him. The Holy Prophet[sa] returned his greeting and said: "Go back and repeat your *Ṣalāt* for you have not performed it properly. He went back, performed the *Ṣalāt* and came up to the Holy Prophet[sa] and greeted him. This happened three times. Then the person said: 'By God Who has sent you with the Truth! I cannot perform Prayer better than this. Therefore, tell me the correct way to perform

Prayer.' At this, the Holy Prophet[sa] said: "When you stand for Prayer, first say *Takbīr,* then recite the Holy Qur'ān as much as you can, then with full composure go into *rukū',* then stand up straight, then prostrate with full composure, then get up from prostration and sit completely, then do the second prostration. Perform all of the Prayer like this, slowly and correctly.' "

(Ṣaḥīḥ Bukhārī, Kitābul Adhān, Bāb wajūb Ibrāh lil Imām ajma'ū fī Ṣalāt Kulthūm)

Ḥaḍrat Mālik bin Ḥuwairith[ra] relates: "We were a group of young men of about the same age who came to the Holy Prophet[sa], and we stayed with him for twenty days. He was a most kind and considerate person. He perceived that we were eager to return to our families. He inquired from us about those we had left behind, and we told him. Then he said: 'Now return to your families and stay with them, and teach them and ask them to act upon these, and establish *Ṣalāt* the way you have seen me offer the *Ṣalāt.* At the time of the *Ṣalāt,* one of you should call the *Adhān* and the oldest of you should lead the Prayer.' "

(Ṣaḥīḥ Bukhārī, Kitābul Adhān ,Bābul adhān lil musāfir)

Ḥaḍrat Anas[ra] relates that some Companions[ra] of the Holy Prophet[sa] pledged to forsake the world. One said, "I shall never marry. Another declared, 'I shall always spend the entire night in Prayer and not sleep.' Another announced, 'I shall observe fast every day continuously without breaking the fast.' The Holy Prophet[sa] came to know of this, and said: 'What kind of people are these who say such things? I keep fast and break it, I offer Prayers and sleep too, and I also marry women. He who turns away from my practice is not from me.' "

(Ṣaḥīḥ Bukhārī, Kitābun Nikāḥ, Bāb targhīb finnikāḥ)

Ḥaḍrat 'Alī[ra] relates that owing to the use of a grinding mill, Fāṭimah[ra] had developed calluses on her hands. In those days, few servants were brought to the Holy Prophet[sa]. Fāṭimah[ra] went to see the Holy

Prophet[sa]. However, she was not able to see him. She saw Ḥaḍrat 'Ā'ishah[ra] and told her the reason for her visit. When the Holy Prophet[sa] came out, Ḥaḍrat 'Ā'ishah[ra] told him about Fāṭimah's[ra] visit. Ḥaḍrat 'Alī[ra] relates that after this, the Holy Prophet[sa] visited them. They were lying down on their beds. Seeing the Holy Prophet[sa], they began to get up from the their beds. The Holy Prophet[sa] told them not to arise and sat between them so close that Ḥaḍrat 'Alī[ra] felt the coldness of the feet of the Holy Prophet[sa] on his chest. Then the Holy Prophet[sa] said: "Should I not tell you something which is better than what you seek? At night when you go to bed, repeat: thirty-four times (*Allāhu akbar*), thirty-three times (*Subḥānallāh*), and thirty-three times (*Alḥamdu lillāh*). This is better for you than a servant."

(Ṣaḥīḥ Muslim, Kitābudhdhikr, Bāb at-Tasbīḥ awwalannahar wa 'indannaum)

Ḥaḍrat Anas[ra] relates that the Holy Prophet[sa] passed by a woman who was crying over a grave. He said to her: "Be mindful of thy duty to Allāh and be steadfast. She retorted, 'Leave me alone; you have not been afflicted as I have been.' She had not known who he was. Someone told her, 'That was the Holy Prophet[sa].' She proceeded to the door of the Holy Prophet[sa] and not finding any doorman went in and said to him, 'I had not recognized you.' He said, 'True steadfastness is to be resigned at the beginning of the grief.' "

(Ṣaḥīḥ Bukhārī, Kitābul Janā'iz, Bāb ziyāratul qabūr)

Ḥaḍrat Abū Hurairah[ra] relates that he had seen no one consult his Companions[ra] more than the Holy Prophet[sa].

(Jāmi' Tirmidhī, Abwāb Faḍā'ilul Jihād, Bāb mā jā' fil mashwarah)

Justice and Fair Dealings

The Holy Prophet[sa] was a man of strict and absolute justice.

However, in him we see this complemented with a balanced sense of perfect kindness. In the Battle of Badr, one of the Holy Prophet's[sa] uncles, while fighting on the side of the idolators, was arrested by the Muslims. Along with the other prisoners, his hands and feet were bound against posts in the mosque. In those days there were no prisons. Someone had tied these men rather harshly. The Holy Prophet[sa], whose home was adjacent to the mosque, could not sleep that night. It is reported that he was restless and kept turning in the bed. His Companions[ra] noticed and asked him what was causing him distress. He told them that he could hear the groaning of his uncle 'Abbās from the mosque. Someone then went and loosened the ties of 'Abbās. After a while the Holy Prophet[sa] no longer heard any moaning, but he became worried and inquired as to why the sounds had stopped. Somebody said that the ties of 'Abbās had been loosened. He said: "If you have done this to 'Abbās, then do it to every prisoner." This was how his justice supplemented his kindness.

The Arabs were greatly given to favoritism and applied different standards to different persons. Even among the so-called civilized nations of today, one observes a reluctance to bring prominent persons or those occupying high positions or offices to account for their doings, though the law is enforced rigorously against the common citizen. The Holy Prophet[sa] was, however, unique in enforcing uniform standards of justice and fair dealing.

On one occasion a case came before the Holy Prophet[sa] in which a young woman belonging to a highly respectable family was found to have committed theft. This caused great consternation as, if the normal penalty were imposed upon the young woman, a leading family would be humiliated and disgraced. Many were anxious to intercede with the Prophet[sa] on behalf of the offender but were afraid to do so. Eventually Usāmah bin Zaid[ra] who was much loved by the Holy Prophet[sa] was prevailed upon to undertake the mission. So Usāma spoke to the Holy Prophet[sa] and the Holy Prophet[sa] said to him: "Do you seek to intercede in the matter of the penalties prescribed by Allāh the Exalted?' Then he stood up and made an address in which he said: 'Those who were before you were ruined because they would excuse a high-placed one if he committed theft and would exact the prescribed penalty from a poor one who stole. I call Allāh to witness that were Fāṭimah, daughter of Muḥammad[sa], to steal, I would cut off her hand."

(Ṣaḥīḥ Muslim, Kitābul Ḥadūd, Bāb qata'assariq ashsharīf wa ghairih; Ṣaḥīḥ Bukhārī, Kitāb Faḍā'il Aṣḥābunnabī[ra]*, Bāb Dhikri Usāma bin Zaid*[ra]*)*

The Holy Prophet[sa] once owed money to a Jew. The Jew thought it was overdue, whereas it was not so. He confronted him and demanded his money using very harsh words, and charged that all the *Quraish* were one lot of bad debtors who never honored their promises. He had not only insulted the Holy Prophet[sa] but also his tribe. Ḥaḍrat 'Umar[ra], who was also present, became extremely incensed and his hand went for his sword. The Holy Prophet[sa] stopped 'Umar, who had now used some abusive words against the Jew and was perhaps about to strike him, and said: "'Umar, you should have behaved differently. First, you should have told me to be mindful of the contract and pay on time; then you should have told him to be kind in his demands and merciful to his debtors." Then he turned to another of his Companions[ra] and said: 'Still there are three days. I know the limit is not yet crossed, but pay him whatever I owe and add some more because of the harsh attitude of 'Umar.' "

This was his behavior when openly insulted in the company of his Companions[ra]. His sense of justice was supreme. It was absolute, not in any way connected to his personal, tribal or religious loyalties.

(The Seal of Prophets[sa]*, His Personality and Character, Ḥaḍrat Mirzā Ṭāhir Aḥmad, Khalīfatul Masīh IV*[rh]*, Islām International Publications, 1992)*

On one occasion a prisoner was brought to the Holy Prophet[sa] who had been guilty of the murder of many Muslims. Ḥaḍrat 'Umar[ra], who was also present, believed that the man duly deserved the imposition of the death penalty and he looked repeatedly at the Prophet[sa] expecting that the

Prophet[sa] would at any moment indicate that the man should be put to death. After the Holy Prophet[sa] had dismissed the man, Ḥaḍrat 'Umar[ra] suggested that he should have been put to death as that was the only appropriate penalty. The Prophet[sa] replied: "If that is so, why did you not kill him ?" Ḥaḍrat 'Umar replied: "O Messenger[sa] of Allāh! If you had given me an indication by winking your eye, I would have done so." To this the Prophet[sa] rejoined: "A Prophet does not act equivocally. How could I have winked my eye to indicate the imposition of a death penalty upon the man while I was talking amicably with him ?"

(As-Sīratun Nabawiyyah libne Hishām, Vol. 2, p. 217)

Fulfillment of the Covenants

The Holy Prophet[sa] was very particular with regard to the fulfillment of covenants. On one occasion an envoy came to him on a special mission and, after he had remained in his company for some days, was convinced of the truth of Islām and suggested that he might declare his loyalty to it. The Prophet[sa] told him that this would be improper as he was there in a representative capacity and it was incumbent upon him to return to the headquarters of his government without making a new allegiance. If after he had returned home he still felt convinced of the truth of Islām, he could return as a free individual and declare his acceptance of it.

(Sunan Abū Dāwūd, Kitābul Jihād, Bāb Wafa bi'l 'Aḥd)

Trustworthiness

People used to leave their precious things and property in trust with the Holy Prophet[sa] and this continued till he migrated from Mecca to Medina. The Holy Prophet[sa] performed this duty for both friends and enemies in a very honorable way. Even at the time when he was migrating from Mecca to Medina and was in great distress, he was conscious of and worried about returning the property and other precious things to their owners. He entrusted these things to Ḥaḍrat 'Alī and instructed him to give these things to their owners before coming to Medina.

The Holy Prophet[sa] used to say that often it happens that he finds a date on the bed or any other place in the house and starts to eat while he is hungry but he does not eat it thinking that it may not be from charity.

(Ṣaḥīḥ Bukhārī, Kitābul Luqṭah, Bāb idhā wajada tamrata fiṭṭarīqi)

Generosity

Ḥaḍrat Anas[ra] relates that whenever someone asked the Holy Prophet[sa] for something in the name of Islām, he always gave it to them. He further relates that once a man came to the Holy Prophet[sa] and he[sa] gave him a flock of goats scattered over a valley. When the man returned to his people he said to them: "O my people! Accept Islām, for Muḥammad[sa] bestows as if he has no fear of poverty." Even when a person out of a worldly motive became a Muslim, in due course, Islām became dearer to him than the world and all it contains.

(Ṣaḥīḥ Muslim, Kitābul Faḍai'l, Bāb mā su'ila Rasūlullāh ṣalallāhu 'alaihi wasallam[sa] shai'an qaṭ faqāla lā; Musnad Aḥmad, p 108-175/3)

Ḥaḍrat Ibn 'Abbās[ra] relates that the Holy Prophet[sa] was the most generous person, and he was at his best in generosity and benevolence during the month of *Ramaḍān* when Gabriel visited him every night, and recited the Qur'ān to him, and when the generosity of the Holy Prophet[sa] used to increase, faster than the rain-bearing breeze.

(Ṣaḥīḥ Bukhārī, Kitāb Bad'u al-Khalq, Bāb dhikrul Malāikatu; Riyāḍuṣ Ṣāliḥīn, Kitābul Faḍā'il, Bāb al-Jūd wa fi'l al-ma'rūf minal khair fī shahri ramaḍān)

Whenever anyone asked him for something, he (always gave and) never said "no".

(Ṣaḥīḥ Muslim, Kitābul Faḍā'il, Bāb mā su'ila Rasūlullāh[sa] *....)*

Ḥaḍrat Jubair bin Muṭ'im[ra] relates that while he was walking with the Holy Prophet[sa] during the return from Ḥunain, some rustics caught hold of him and started begging from him. They pushed him under a tree and someone snatched away his cloak. The Holy Prophet[sa] came to a halt and said: "Restore my cloak to me; had I at my disposal camels equal to the number of the leaves of this thorny tree I would have distributed all of these among you and you would not have found me a miser or a liar or a coward."

(Ṣaḥīḥ Bukhārī, Kitābul Jihād mā kānannabiyyu[sa] *yu'ṭil muwillafata qulūbihim; Mishkāt, Bāb fī akhlāqhu wa shamā'ilahū ... alkh)*

Ḥaḍrat 'Ā'ishah[ra] relates that she slaughtered a goat. The Holy Prophet[sa] asked: "How much meat is left? She answered: 'A shank.' He said: 'All of it is saved except the shank (i.e., all that you have distributed is saved owing to the reward we get for it).' "

(Jāmi' Tirmidhī, Abwāb Ṣifatul qiyāmah; At-Targhīb wa't-Tarhīb, p. 129/2)

Bravery

The Holy Prophet[sa] was a dauntless, courageous person who never refrained from approaching danger head on. In his lifetime he fought many defensive battles, however he never initiated a single offensive war. He[sa] was usually found in the most dangerous areas of the battle, where fighting would rage like a wild fire. It is reported by a narrator that when the Holy Prophet[sa] was sought during a battle, they would look for him in that part where combat was at its fiercest and he would always be in the midst of it.

Ḥaḍrat Anas bin Mālik[ra] relates that the Holy Prophet[sa] was the most beautiful, generous, and brave man among all the men.

Once, Medina was full of rumors that the Romans were preparing a large army for its invasion. During that time the Muslims were always on the *qui vive* at night. One night sounds of an uproar came from the desert. The Muslims hurried out of their homes and some of them assembled in the mosque, and waited for the Holy Prophet[sa] to appear and to give them directions to meet the contingent. Soon, they saw the Holy Prophet[sa] on a horse coming back from the direction of the noise. They then discovered that, at the very first sound of alarm, the Prophet[sa] had mounted a horse and gone in the direction from which the sound had come to determine whether there was any reason for alarm and had not waited for people to collect together so that he could proceed in a company. When he returned he assured his Companions[ra] that there was no cause for alarm and that they could return to their homes and go to sleep.

(Ṣaḥīḥ Muslim, Kitābul Faḍā'il, Bāb fī shujā'atun Nabī[sa], Ṣaḥīḥ Bukhārī, Kitābul Jihād)

The Holy Prophet[sa] was badly injured in the Battle of Uḥud. His face was covered with blood. A disbeliever belonging to the Meccan opposition, Ubayy bin Khalf was making preparations for a long time and had raised a horse specifically for this purpose so that he could ride on it and kill the Holy Prophet[sa]. He used to feed barley to the horse daily. When he saw the Holy Prophet[sa] spurring his horse he went towards the Holy Prophet[sa]. He was shouting, "If I fail to kill the Holy Prophet[sa] my life will be useless!" When the Companions[ra] saw him coming they wanted to stand in his way to protect the Holy Prophet[sa]. The Holy Prophet[sa] told the Companions[ra] to get away and let him come. The Holy Prophet[sa] who was profusely bleeding faced the attacker and hit at his neck with his spear so forcefully that he ran away while he was screaming. Someone asked him why he was screaming since it is a superficial wound. He said it is not a superficial wound. It is a wound inflicted by Muḥammad. Ubayy died with that wound.

(As-Sīratun Nabawiyyah libne Hishām, Vol. 3, p. 89)

Kindheartedness

Hinda bint 'Utbah, the wife of Abū Sufyān[ra] was a staunch enemy of the Holy Prophet[sa] and the Muslims. In the battles against the Muslims she would incite the enemy soldiers against the Muslims by reciting the verses usually recited at the battlefield to arouse the martial spirit of soldiers. In the Battle of Uḥud she treated the body of Ḥaḍrat Ḥamzah[ra] in a most demeaning way. She cut out the liver of the Holy Prophet's[sa] uncle, Ḥaḍrat Ḥamzah[ra] who was killed in the battle and had chewed it up. Mūsā ibn 'Uqbah narrated that Waḥshī gouged the liver of Ḥamzah ibn 'Abdul Muṭṭalib and took it to Hinda bint 'Utbah and she ate it.

(Ibni Kathīr, Al-Bid'ayah wan-Nihāyah, Vol. 4, p. 43).

Even on the day Mecca had fallen to the Muslims Hinda bint 'Utbah was so outraged that when her husband told her about the surrender she violently shook his beard in disgust. She called upon the Meccans to come and to kill him for his treachery in having agreed to surrender instead of fighting the Muslims. However, when she realized what had happened she joined a group of women and went to see the Holy Prophet[sa]. When she went to see the Holy Prophet[sa] she was sure that the death penalty was the only punishment she deserved and that is what she would get because of her misbehavior. She was frightened. When the women took the oath of allegiance she disguised herself and joined the other women. During the ceremony when she spoke, the Holy Prophet[sa] recognized her voice. She immediately said:

فَاعْفُ عَمَّا سَلَفَ , عَفَا اللّٰهُ عَنْكَ

fa'fu 'ammā salafa, 'afallāhu 'anka

(O Messenger of Allāh) Forgive what has passed. God will forgive you.

Despite the fact that she had dishonored the body of his beloved uncle in a most barbaric way, the Holy Prophet[sa] accepted her request for forgiveness and pardoned her.

Another person who deserved severe punishment was Habbār who had cut the girth of the camel which carried Ḥaḍrat Zainab[ra], the daughter of the Holy Prophet[sa] when she was leaving for Medina. Habbār's action had caused Ḥaḍrat Zainab[ra] to fall from the camel and thus suffer a miscarriage. The miscarriage resulted in her death. When Habbār appeared in front of the Holy Prophet[sa], he professed his misconduct and begged for his forgiveness. He also told the Holy Prophet[sa] that he had accepted Islām. The Holy Prophet[sa] forgave him.

'Ikrimah who was the son of Abū Jahl, the bitterest enemy of the Holy Prophet[sa], was one of the Meccan commanders in the Battle of Uḥud. He is the one who had spotted the inadequately guarded rear pass and had led the attack which ended in near disaster for the Muslims.

When Mecca fell, 'Ikrimah left the town and proceeded to the coast, intending to cross over to Ethiopia, being convinced that he could have no security in Mecca or anywhere near it. His wife approached the Holy Prophet[sa] and asked whether 'Ikrimah could return to Mecca while professing his idolatrous beliefs. The Holy Prophet[sa] replied that faith was a matter of conscience and conscience was free. If 'Ikrimah returned to Mecca he would not be mistreated, and could live there in security professing whatever he chose to believe in. On this assurance she followed 'Ikrimah and persuaded him to return to Mecca. On arrival there, he went to the Holy Prophet[sa] and received in person the assurance which the Holy Prophet[sa] had already given to his wife. Thereupon he announced his acceptance of Islām, and the Holy Prophet[sa] asked him if there were anything he wished for. 'Ikrimah replied that he could wish for no greater bounty than God had already bestowed upon him in opening his heart to the acceptance of Islām, but he did desire that the Holy Prophet[sa] should pray to God to forgive him for all the enmity that he had borne toward the

Holy Prophet[sa] and the Muslims.

The Holy Prophet[sa] prayed accordingly and then bestowed his own cloak on 'Ikrimah, saying: "He who comes to me believing in God can claim my house as his." 'Ikrimah proved himself a sincere and zealous believer and set the seal on his faith by laying down his life in defense of it on one of the Syrian battlefields some years later.

(The Excellent Examplar - Muḥammad, Chaudhari Muḥammad Ẓafrullā Khān, p. 237, Routledge & Kegal Paul, London, UK)

Self-Control and Tolerance

Ḥaḍrat 'Abdullāh bin Salām[ra] relates that when Allāh the Exalted desired to guide Zaid bin Sa'nah, he said: "When I beheld the countenance of the Holy Prophet[sa], I saw all the signs of prophethood in his face except two characteristics I knew not whether he possessed. One was that his tolerance would overpower his anger and the second was that no matter how much he was provoked and treated rudely, he would exhibit great tolerance. So, I was looking for a chance to determine whether or not these signs were present in him." Zaid bin Sa'nah further relates that one day, the Holy Prophet[sa] came out of his house with 'Alī bin Abī Ṭālib. In the meantime, a rider who appeared to be a Bedouin came and said to the Holy Prophet[sa]: 'The people of a tribe in the town of 'Baṣra' have accepted Islām and I had told them that were they to accept Islām, their provisions would be enlarged. However, due to lack of rain, they are facing a drought. I am worried that greed may cause them to leave Islām, as greed of enlarging their provisions had made them accept Islām. It is requested that, if it is proper then you please send them some provisions to help them.' Hearing this, the Holy Prophet[sa] looked towards Ḥaḍrat 'Alī[ra]. Ḥaḍrat 'Alī[ra] told the Holy Prophet[sa] that at present there was nothing available which could be sent to help them. Zaid bin Sa'nah relates that he came to the Holy Prophet[sa] and said: 'O Muḥammad! You can sell dates to me from a particular plantation on a fixed value, and on a fixed time.' The Holy

Prophet[sa] said: 'O Jewish one! I can sell the dates for a fixed value and for a fixed time but without the condition that the dates must be from the specified orchard.' He agreed to it. So, the Holy Prophet[sa] made a deal with me. I gave the Holy Prophet[sa] eighty *Mithqāl* in advance on condition that he would give me a certain amount of dates on such a date.' The Holy Prophet[sa] gave the gold to the man and told him to distribute it equally to the distressed people and help them. Zaid bin Sa'nah relates, 'A couple of days were still left in the period for repayment of the debt when I came to the Holy Prophet[sa]. I seized him by the collar, pulled his sheet and said angrily, O Muḥammad! Won't you give me what is my right? By God! You know very well that you people are very bad in repayment of loans and I also know very well your habit of putting off repayment.' At that time, I was looking at Ḥaḍrat 'Umar[ra]. His eyes were whirling like a boat in a storm. He angrily looked towards me and said, 'O enemy of Allāh! How dare you say to the Messenger[sa] of Allāh what I am hearing, and treat him so rudely. By God, Who has sent him with Truth! Were I not afraid of him, I would have cut your head with the sword.' The Holy Prophet[sa], who was calmly looking towards Ḥaḍrat 'Umar[ra] and smiling, said, 'O 'Umar! Instead of showing anger, what both of us deserve is that you tell me about a good way of repayment and to him about a good manner of demanding it. Although a couple of days remain in the due date for repayment, he probably needs money sooner. Therefore, give him what is due to him and give him twenty *Ṣā'* (a unit of weight) dates extra.' When I was paid, I asked, ''Umar[ra] why am I being paid extra?' 'Umar[ra] said, 'The Holy Prophet[sa] had told me to pay you twenty *Ṣā'* extra for my acting harshly with you..' I asked Ḥaḍrat 'Umar[ra], 'Do you know who I am?' Ḥaḍrat 'Umar[ra] said: 'No. Who are you?' I told him that I am Zaid bin Sa'nah. Ḥaḍrat 'Umar[ra] asked: '*Ḥibar* (i.e., the Jewish learned man)?' I said: 'Yes. The Jewish learned man.' 'Umar[ra] said: Then, why did you behave so?' I replied: 'I saw all the signs of prophethood in the Holy Prophet[sa] when I beheld his face, except the two. One of these was that his tolerance would overpower his anger and the second was that no matter how much he was provoked and treated rudely he would exhibit great tolerance. I have tested him for the presence of both these signs. O ‘Umar! I make you my witness that I am very happy in accepting Allāh as my Lord, Islām as my religion, and Muḥammad[sa] as my Prophet. Furthermore, I make you witness that I am a wealthy man and I give half of my wealth as charity for the followers of the Holy Prophet[sa].' Ḥaḍrat ‘Umar[ra] said: 'You should say: I give it as charity for some followers of the Holy Prophet[sa]. How can it be enough for all of them?' I said, 'Alright, it should be spent for the needs of some of the followers of the Holy Prophet[sa].' After this, Zaid bin Sa‘nah came to the Holy Prophet[sa] and said, 'I bear witness there is none worthy of worship besides Allāh and Muḥammad[sa] is His Messenger. That is, I believe in this credo.' " Thus, Zaid bin Sa‘nah took initiation at the hands of the Holy Prophet[sa], and took part in many battles with the Holy Prophet[sa]. He died on the way returning from the Battle of Tabūk. May God Almighty have Mercy upon him.

(Mustadrik Ma‘attalkhīṣ Kitāb Marifataṣṣaḥābah, Vol. 3, p. 605)

The Holy Prophet[sa] always exercised complete self-control. Even when he became a Sovereign, he always listened to everybody with patience, and if a person treated him with impertinence, he bore it and never attempted any retaliation. In the East, one way of showing respect for a person to whom one is addressing, is to address him not by his personal name. The Muslims used to address the Holy Prophet[sa] as: "O Messenger[sa] of Allāh", and non-Muslims used to address him as "Abul Qāsim" *(i.e.,* Qāsim's father: Qāsim being the name of one of his sons). On one occasion, a Jewish person came to him in Medina and started a discussion with him. In the course of the discussion, he repeatedly addressed him as "O Muḥammad, O Muḥammad" The Holy Prophet[sa] paid no attention to his form of address and went on patiently expounding the matter under discussion to him. His Companions[ra], however, were getting irritated at the discourteous form of address adopted by his interlocutor till one of them, not being able to restrain himself any longer, admonished the Jewish person not to address the Holy Prophet[sa] by his personal name but to address him as Abul Qāsim. The Jewish person said that he would address him only by the name which his parents had given him. The Holy Prophet[sa] smiled and said to his Companions[ra]: "He is right. I was named Muḥammad at the time of my birth and there is no reason to be upset at his addressing me by that name." Sometimes people stopped him in the way and engaged him in conversation, explaining their needs and conveying their requests to him. He always stood patiently, and let them go on and proceeded only after they had finished. On occasion, people kept hold of his hand for some time when shaking hands with him, and though he found this inconvenient and time-consuming he was never the first to withdraw his hand. People went freely to him and laid their troubles and difficulties before him and asked him for help. If he was able to help he never declined a request. Sometimes he was pestered with requests and they were unreasonably pressed, but he went on complying with them as far as he was able. On occasion, after complying with a request, he would admonish the person concerned to have greater trust in God and to avoid asking others for relief. On one occasion, a devout Muslim asked him several times for money and each time he complied with his request, but in the end said: "It is best for a man to put his trust in God and to avoid making requests." The person concerned was a sincere man. Out of regard for the feelings of the Holy Prophet[sa], he did not offer to return what he had already received but he declared that in future he would never make a request to anybody under any circumstances. Years later, he was taking part in a battle, mounted on a charger, and in the thick of it, when the din and confusion and the clash of arms were at their highest, and he was surrounded by his enemies, his whip fell from his hand. A Muslim soldier who was on foot, perceiving his predicament, bent down to pick up the whip for him but the mounted man begged him to desist and jumped from his horse and picked up the whip himself, explaining to the soldier that he had long since promised the Holy Prophet[sa] that he would never make any request to anybody and that if he had permitted the soldier to pick up the whip for him it would have amounted to his having made an indirect request and would thus have rendered him guilty of breaking his promise to the Holy Prophet[sa].

Love for Humanity

Ḥaḍrat Jābir[ra] relates that the Holy Prophet[sa] said: "You and I are as if a person kindles a fire, and moths and such rush to fall into it, and he strives to protect them from the fire. Likewise, I hold you from the back to save you from the fire of Hell while you struggle to slip out of my hands."

(Ṣaḥīḥ Muslim, Kitābul Faḍā'il, Bāb shafqata Sallallāhu 'alaihi wassalam 'alā ummatihī)

On the day of 'Aqabah, the Holy Prophet[sa] presented himself to Ibn 'Abd Yālīl bin 'Abd Kulāl and got no response to the message he delivered to them. So he left grieved and depressed, and felt no relief unil he arrived at Qarn Tha'lib. Then he raised his head and saw a cloud that was shielding him from the sun in which he beheld Gabriel who called to him and said: 'Allāh, the Most Honored and Glorious, has heard what your people have said to you and the response they have made to you and has sent the Angel of the Mountains to you so that you may direct him to do what you might wish to be done to them.' Then the Angel of the Mountains called to him, and offered him the greeting of peace and said: 'Muḥammad, indeed Allāh has heard what thy people have said to you. I am the Angel of the Mountains, and my Lord has sent me to you, so that you might give me your direction concerning that which you would wish done to them. If you would so wish, I would press down upon them the two great mountains.' The Holy Prophet[sa] answered him: 'Indeed not, I am hoping that Allāh will make out of their progeny such people as would worship Allāh, the One, not associating aught with Him.'"

(Ṣaḥīḥ Muslim, Kitābul Jihād, Bāb mā laqannabiyya[sa] min idhil mushrikīna wal munāfiqīn)

The Holy Prophet[sa], not only rejected the destruction of his people but prayed fervently for their guidance in these words:

اَللّٰهُمَّ اهْدِ قَوْمِىْ فَاِنَّهُمْ لَا يَعْلَمُوْنَ

allāhummahdi qaumī fa innahum lā y'lamūn

O Allāh! Guide my people to the right path as they do not know.

(Tafsīr al-Alwasī, Vol. 5, p. 75; Barīqata Maḥmūdiyya fī Sharḥ Ṭarīqata Muḥammadiyyah wa Shrī'ata Nabawiyyah, Vol. 3, p. 371)

Ḥaḍrat Usāmah bin Zaid[ra] relates that the Holy Prophet[sa] passed by a company of people which was comprised of Muslims, idol worshippers and Jewish people, he greeted them with the salutation of peace 'Salām'.

(Ṣaḥīḥ Bukhārī, Kitābul Isti'dhān, Bāb fittaslīm fī majlis fīhi ikhlāṭ minal muslimīn walmushrikīn, p. 924/2)

Love for the Companions[ra]

Once at the request of certain tribes, the Holy Prophet[sa] sent seventy *Ḥuffāẓ* (Those who had committed the whole Qur'ān to memory) to convey the message of Islām. *Banū Sulaim* and some other tribes treacherously killed the *Ḥuffāẓ* at a place called, Bi'r Ma'ūnah. When the enemy after killing Ḥaḍrat Ḥarām bin Milḥān, the leader of the group, surrounded the rest of the party, they prayed, "O Allāh! At present, we do not have any other means to convey a message to the Holy Prophet[sa], we beg You to convey our *Salām* and the news of our martyrdom to the Holy Prophet[sa] and that we are pleased with our Lord and our Lord is pleased with us." God Almighty through Gabriel informed the Holy Prophet[sa]. At that time, the Holy Prophet[sa] was sitting in the company of his Companions[ra] and suddenly he said, "*Wa 'Alaikussalām*". Then, the Holy Prophet[sa] addressed the Companions[ra] and told them that your brothers were attacked by the enemies and all of them have been martyred. At the time of their martyrdom they prayed to God Almighty to convey their *Salām* and the message that they are pleased with their Lord and their Lord is pleased with them.

The Holy Prophet[sa] was very saddened to hear of the martyrdom of these seventy Companions[ra]. Ḥaḍrat Anas[ra] relates that the Holy Prophet[sa] was never saddened at the demise of anyone as much as he was at the martyrdom of these seventy Companions[ra]. The Holy Prophet[sa] kept on praying by raising his hands for help from Allāh in the last *rak'at* of the Prayer.

(Sīrah Ḥalabiyyah, Vol. 3, pp. 243-244)

Treatment of the Non-Muslims

Respect for the Non-Muslim Delegates

The Holy Prophet[sa] not only emphasized the desirability of tolerance in religious matters but set a very high standard in this respect. A delegation from a Christian tribe of *Najrān* visited him in Medina to exchange views on religious matters. It included several Church dignitaries. The conversation was held in the mosque and extended over several hours. At one stage, the leader of the delegation asked for permission to depart from the mosque, and to hold their religious service at some convenient spot. The Holy Prophet[sa] said that there was no need for them to go out of the mosque, which was itself a place consecrated to the worship of God, and they could hold their service in it.

(Zurqānī, Sharḥ Mawāhib al-Ladunniyya, Vol. 5, pp. 186-187; Zād al-Ma'ād, Vol. 2, pp. 35-36)

Once, a delegation from the monastery of St. Catherine wrote a pronouncement to the effect that their monastery should be protected when Islām became victorious in that part of the world.

The Holy Prophet[sa] immediately accepted the request and wrote orders to that effect. The order reads: "No one should ever interfere with the property of the Monastery, nor with the figure of the cross or any other article which represents their faith. They should not be molested in any manner whatsoever. Anyone ignoring this will not be one of us."

Charter of Privileges

In 628 C.E. the Holy Prophet[sa] of Islām granted a Charter of Privileges to the monks of St. Catherine Monastery in Mt. Sinai. It consisted of several clauses covering all aspects of human rights including such topics as the protection of Christians, freedom of worship and movement, freedom to appoint their own judges and to own and maintain their property, exemption from military service, and the right to protection in war. This document is excellent guidance for all the Muslim states for dealing with the non-Muslim minorities. The following is the text of the Charter:

This is the document which Muḥammad, son of 'Abdullāh, God's Prophet, Warner and Bearer of glad-tidings, has caused to be written so that there should remain no excuse for those coming after. I have caused this document to be written for Christians of the East and the West, for those who live near, and for those of the distant lands, for the Christians living at present and for those who will come after, for those Christians who are known to us and for those as well whom we do not know.

1. Any Muslim violating and abusing what is therein ordered would be regarded as violator of God's testament and would be the breaker of His promise and would make himself deserving of God's curse, be he a king or a subject.

2. I promise that any monk or wayfarer, etc., who will seek my help on the mountains, in forests, deserts or habitations,

or in places of worship, I will repel his enemies with all my friends and helpers, with all my relatives and with all those who profess to follow me and will defend him, because they are my covenanted. And I will defend the covenanted against the persecution, injury and embarrassment by their enemies in lieu of the poll-tax they have promised to pay.

3. If they will prefer themselves to defend their properties and persons, they will be allowed to do so and will not be put to any inconvenience on that account.

4. No bishop will be expelled from his bishopric, no monk from his monastery, no priest from his place of worship, and no pilgrim will be detained in his pilgrimage.

5. None of their churches and other places of worship will be desolated or destroyed or demolished. No material of their churches will be used for building mosques or houses for the Muslims, any Muslim so doing will be regarded as recalcitrant to God and His Prophet.

6. Monks and bishops will be subject to no tax or indemnity whether they live in forests or on the rivers, or in the East or West, North or South. I give them my word of honor. They are on my promise and covenant and will enjoy perfect immunity from all sorts of inconveniences.

7. Every help shall be given them in the repair of their churches. They shall be absolved from wearing arms. They shall be protected by the Muslims. Let this document be not disobeyed till the Judgment Day.

(Al-Wathā'iqul Siyāsiyya lil 'Ahdi Nabawī wal Khilāfatur Rāshida, By Dr. Muḥammad Hamīdullāh, pp. 187-190, Beirut, Lebanon)

In a tradition, Ḥaḍrat Abū Hurairah[ra] narrates that two men were quarreling. One was a Muslim and the other a Jew. The Muslim said, "I swear by that Being Who chose Muḥammad[sa] over all the worlds and granted him excellence over others." The Jew replied, "I swear by that Being Who granted excellence to Moses[as] over all the worlds and chose him."

On this the Muslim slapped the Jew. The Jew took the complaint to the Holy Prophet[sa], who asked the Muslims for details and then said:

لَا تُخَيِّرُوْنِيْ عَلٰى مُوْسٰى

lā tukhayyirūnī 'alā Mūsā

Do not give me preference over Moses.

(Ṣaḥīḥ Bukhārī, Kitābul Khuṣūmāti, Bāb mā yudhkaru fil-Askhāsi wal-khuṣūmati bainal Muslim wal-Yahudī)

Respect for the Dead

Ḥaḍrat Jābir[ra] relates that they were in the company of the Holy Prophet[sa] when a funeral procession passed by. Seeing it, the Holy Prophet[sa] stood up. When they walked towards the coffin to help carry it, they discovered that it was a funeral of a Jewish person. They said: "Messenger[sa] of Allāh! This is the funeral procession of a Jewish person." He observed, "Death is a matter of grief and awe; therefore, when you see a funeral passing by you should stand up."

(Sunan Abū Dāwūd, Kitābuljanā'iz, Bāb al-qiyām liljanāzah)

Ḥaḍrat 'Abdur Raḥmān bin Abī Lailā[ra] relates that Ḥaḍrat Sahl bin Ḥanīf[ra] and Ḥaḍrat Qaist bin Sa'd bin 'Ubādah[ra] were in Qādisiyyah, when a funeral procession passed by them. Seeing the funeral procession, both stood up. People told them that it was the funeral procession of someone (a non-Muslim) from this area. Hearing this, both of them said: "A funeral procession passed by the Holy Prophet[sa]; seeing that, he stood up. Someone said to the Holy Prophet[sa] that it was a funeral cortege of a Jew. The Holy Prophet[sa] replied:

أَلَيْسَتْ نَفْسًا؟

a-laisat nafsā

'Was he not a human being?' "

(Nasā'ī, Kitābul Janā'iz, Bāb al-qiyām li-janāzah ahlishshirk)

Appreciation of the Service to Mankind

The Holy Prophet[sa] paid special deference to those who devoted their time and substance to the service of mankind. The Arab tribe, the *Banū Ṭā'ī*, started hostilities against the Prophet[sa] and in the ensuing battle, their forces were defeated and some were taken prisoner. One of these was the daughter of Ḥāṭim Ṭā'ī, whose generosity had become a proverb amongst the Arabs. When Ḥāṭim's daughter informed the Holy Prophet[sa] of her parentage he treated her with great consideration and as the result of her intercession, he remitted all the penalties imposed upon her people on account of their aggression.

(Sīrah Ḥalabiyyah, Vol. 3, p. 227)

Treatment of the Uncultured

The Holy Prophet[sa] was particularly considerate towards those who, from lack of cultural training, did not know how to behave. On one occasion a dweller of the desert who had only recently accepted Islām, was sitting in the company of the Holy Prophet[sa] in the mosque, got up and walked away a few paces and sat down in a corner of the mosque to pass water. Some of the Companions[ra] of the Prophet[sa] arose to stop him from doing so. The Prophet[sa] restrained them, pointing out that any interference with the man was bound to cause inconvenience to him and might possibly cause him injury. He told his Companions[ra] to leave the man alone and to clean the spot later.

Serving a Disbeliever

Ḥaḍrat Abū Hurairah[ra] relates that a disbeliever stayed with the Holy Prophet[sa] as his guest. The Holy Prophet[sa] had the goats milked for him. The man drank the milk from seven goats, one by one. On the next day, the disbeliever became a Muslim. The Holy Prophet[sa] had one goat milked for him. He drank all of it. When the second goat was milked for him, he could no longer drink all the milk. At this, the Holy Prophet[sa] said: "A believer drinks just enough to fill a single intestine and a disbeliever drinks enough to fill seven intestines."

(Jāmi' Tirmidhī, Abwāb al-Aṭa'mah, Bāb innal mu'min yakulu fī ma'ī wāḥid)

Helping the Oppressed and Orphans

The Holy Prophet[sa] would stand up to even a most tyranical enemy to help an oppressed person. A stranger by the name of Al-Arashī bought a camel from Abū Jahl. Abū Jahl started making various kinds of lame excuses with respect to payment of the price of the camel. Al-Arashī came to a gathering of the *Quraish* and asked for help in collecting money from Abū Jahl. He told them that he was a traveler and asked them, "Is there anyone who could make Abū Jahl pay the price of the camel which he had sold? He is keeping my camel without payment." The Chiefs of the *Quraish* jokingly directed him towards the Holy Prophet[sa] and said, "He can get you the money for your camel from Abū Jahl." Al-Arashī went to the Holy Prophet[sa] and requested his help to get his money from Abū Jahl. The Holy Prophet[sa] walked along with the stranger. The Chiefs of the *Quraish* sent a man to follow them to find out how Abū Jahl responded to the Holy Prophet[sa]. The Holy Prophet[sa] knocked on the door of the house of Abū Jahl. Abū Jahl asked, "Who is there?" The Holy Prophet[sa] responded, 'It is Muḥammad. Come out.' Seeing the Holy Prophet[sa] at his door Abū Jahl's face turned pale. The Holy Prophet[sa] said, 'Give this man what is due to him.' Abū Jahl said, 'Alright.' The Holy Prophet[sa] told him that he would not leave the place till he paid what was due to the man.' Abū Jahl went inside the house, brought the money and gave it to the man. Then, the Holy Prophet[sa] returned. Al-Arashī was so pleased that he went to the Chiefs of the *Quraish* and said, 'May Allāh reward Muḥammad. He has made Abū Jahl pay the money that was due to me from him.' In the meantime the messenger of the *Quraish* whom they had sent to follow the Holy Prophet[sa] also returned. He told the Chiefs that today, he had seen a very strange scene. The Holy Prophet[sa] told Abū Jahl to pay the money to the stranger and Abū Jahl immediately paid him the money. After a short time Abū Jahl also joined the Chiefs of the *Quraish.* The Chiefs asked him, what happened to you? He told them, 'As soon as I heard the voice of Muḥammad I felt shock and awe. When I came out I saw a furious camel next to Muḥammad. I felt that if I refused to pay the money the camel would tear me into pieces.' "

(As-Sīratun Nabawiyyah libne Hishām, Vol. 2, pp. 29-30)

Ḥaḍrat Sahl bin Sa'd[ra] relates that the Holy Prophet[sa] said: "I and the one who takes care of an orphan will be together like this in the Heaven. He indicated his first finger and the middle finger touching on top with a little gap between the two in the middle and said, 'like this.' "

(Ṣaḥīḥ Bukhārī, Bạb faḍl min ya'ūl yatīman)

Ḥaḍrat Abū Hurairah[ra] relates that the Holy Prophet[sa] said: "The best house among the houses of Muslims is the one in which an orphan is treated well and the worst house is the one in which an orphan is treated badly."

(Ibni Mājah, Abwābul Adab, Bāb ḥaqqul yatīm)

Ḥaḍrat Anas bin Mālik[ra] relates that Umm Sulaim (the mother of Ḥaḍrat Anas[ra]) was the guardian of an orphan girl. The Holy Prophet[sa] once saw the girl and said to her smilingly, "Oh! You have grown so big. May your age not be prolonged. Weeping, the orphan girl went to see Umm Sulaim. Umm Sulaim said, 'Dear daughter! Why are you crying?' She said, 'The Holy Prophet[sa] has cursed me that my age may not prolong anymore. Now I will not have a long life and will die soon.' Umm Sulaim hurriedly took her covering and went to see the Holy Prophet[sa]. The Holy Prophet[sa] asked her, 'What is the matter? What brings you?' She said, 'Messenger[sa] of Allāh! Did you imprecate this orphan girl that her age may not prolong?' The Holy Prophet[sa] said, 'Why do you say so?' Umm Sulaim said, 'You have said to this orphan girl that her age may not prolong.' The Holy Prophet[sa] smiled and said, 'I said this to the girl just for amusement. Umm Sulaim! Don't you know that God Almighty had granted acceptance to my request that I am a human being, I feel happiness like other people, and also become angry like other people, if I turn angry and curse someone who does not deserve the curse in the sight of Allāh, may God make my curse a source of virtue, and nearness to God. O My God! Grant her Your nearness on the Day of Judgement. That is, change it to a prayer for goodness.' "

(Ṣaḥīḥ Muslim, Kitābul bir walṣilah, Bāb man la'natannabī[sa])

Love for the Poor

Ḥaḍrat Anas[ra] relates that Ẓāhir bin Ḥarām[ra], a Companion of the Holy Prophet[sa] who lived in a village and was somewhat ugly, used to bring the produce of the village to the Holy Prophet[sa] as a gift. In return, the Holy Prophet[sa] used to give him something as a gift when he departed. The Holy Prophet[sa] used to say: "Ẓāhir is my rustic friend, and I am his urban friend. The Holy Prophet[sa] deeply loved him. The Holy Prophet[sa] once saw Ẓāhir selling produce in a market. The Holy Prophet[sa] went behind him and covered his eyes with his hands in such a way that he was unable to see him. At this, he said: 'Leave me.' When he turned and saw that it was the Holy Prophet[sa], he touched his back with the chest of the Holy Prophet[sa] and rubbed a lot. The Holy Prophet[sa] jokingly said, 'Who will buy this slave from me?' Hearing this, he said: 'O Messenger[sa] of Allāh! By God! You will be at a loss.' At this, the Holy Prophet[sa] said: 'In the sight of Allāh, you are not a petty person. Rather, you are a very precious and unique person.' "

(Shamā'il At-Tirmidhī bāb mā jā'a fī ṣiftih mazāh Rasūlullāh[sa])

Ḥaḍrat 'Abdullāh bin Abī Aufā[ra] relates that the Holy Prophet[sa] never frowned upon or avoided walking along with and helping the impoverished and the widows.

(Musnad Dārmī bāb fittawāḍi' Rasūlullāh[sa])

Ḥaḍrat Abū Hurairah[ra] relates that a dark-skinned woman (The narrator is unsure whether it was a woman or perhaps a young man) used to take care of the mosque. The Holy Prophet[sa] missed her and inquired about her, and was told that she had died. He said, "Why did you not let me know?" The Companions[ra] considered it a death of an ordinary person, and thought that there was no need to inform and trouble the Holy

Prophet[sa]. He then said, "Show me the grave." On being shown it he prayed over it and said, "These graves are filled with darkness but Allāh illuminates them as a result of my prayers."

(Ṣaḥīḥ Muslim, Kitābul Janā'iz, Bābaṣṣalātu 'alal qabr)

Love for Children

The Holy Prophet[sa] loved children very much and used to treat them nicely. Whenever he passed by them or met them he always said *Salām* to them. He[sa] was very frank with the children and used to give them a lot of attention and love. He[sa] joked with them, teased, amused and entertained them. Whenever the Holy Prophet[sa] returned from a trip, children used to run to see and receive him. The Holy Prophet[sa] used to make them sit with him in the back and in the front on his ride.

A Bedouin once saw that the Holy Prophet[sa] was hugging the children and he said, "I have several children but I have never kissed them." The Holy Prophet[sa] said, "What can I do if God Almighty took away love from your heart." Then the Holy Prophet[sa] said, "The one who does not have mercy on people, God also does not have mercy on him."

(Sunan Abū Dāwūd, Kitābul Adab, Bāb qiblatiṣṣibyān)

Ḥaḍrat 'Ā'ishah[ra] relates that a Bedouin came to the Holy Prophet[sa] and said, "You kiss the children. We don't kiss them." The Holy Prophet[sa] said, "I cannot put mercy in your heart after Allāh has taken it away from it."

(Ṣaḥīḥ Bukhārī, Kitābul Adab, Bāb raḥmatal wald wa taqbīlih, wa mu'ānaqah)

Ḥaḍrat Jābir bin Samrah[ra] relates: "Once I offered Prayer behind the Holy Prophet[sa]. After the Prayer the Holy Prophet[sa] went to his family and I also went along with him. When he reached the house, many children were standing there to welcome him. The Holy Prophet[sa] stopped there and he tickled the cheeks of each child with his hand. Although I had accompanied the Holy Prophet[sa], he tickled my cheek also. When he touched my cheek I felt such a pleasant smell in his hand as if he had just taken it out of a perfume bottle."

(Ṣaḥīḥ Muslim, Kitābul Faḍā'il, Bāb ṭayyab rā'iḥatannabbi[sa])

Ḥaḍrat Abū Qatādah[ra] relates: "Once I came to the mosque to offer *Ẓuhr* or *'Asr* Prayer. We were waiting for the Holy Prophet[sa]. Ḥaḍrat Bilāl[ra] after calling the *Adhān* had informed the Holy Prophet[sa] that it was time to lead the Prayer. However, it was delayed and we were waiting for him to come. The Holy Prophet[sa] came and he was carrying on his shoulders Umāmah the daughter of Ḥaḍrat Zainab and Abul 'Āṣ. The Holy Prophet[sa] entered the mosque while he was carrying Umāmah on his shoulders and stood at his Prayer mat to lead the Prayer. We stood behind him. The Holy Prophet[sa] said *Takbīr* in this condition and we also said *Takbīr*. The Holy Prophet[sa] did *Qiyām* while he was carrying Umāmah and when he bowed down for *Rukū'* he[sa] removed Umāmah from his shoulders and made her sit on the floor. After performing *Rukū'* and *Sajdah* (prostration) when he was going to stand for the *Qiyām*, he again picked Umāmah and made her sit on his shoulders. The Holy Prophet[sa] completed the Prayer in this way. He used to remove Umāmah from his shoulders before doing *Rukū'* and *Sajdah* and then before standing for the *Qiyām* he would pick up Umāmah and make her sit on his shoulders."

(Sunan Abū Dāwūd, Kitābaṣṣalah, Bāb al-'Aml fiṣṣalāh)

Ḥaḍrat Anas[ra] relates that the Holy Prophet[sa] was very frank with them: "Sometimes he called my younger brother lovingly: Abū 'Umair! What happened to your *Mamolah* (wagtail: a small bird with long wing feathers and a long tail that wags up and down)? "'Umair had a pet wagtail with whom he used to play till it died."

(Ṣaḥīḥ Bukhārī, Kitābul Adab, Bāb al-inbisāṭ)

Treatment of Women

Ḥaḍrat Abū Qatādah Ḥārith[ra] relates that the Holy Prophet[sa] said: "I stand up to lead the Prayer having it in mind to lengthen it. Then I hear the cry of an infant and I shorten the Prayer fearing lest I should make it burdensome for its mother."

(Ṣaḥīḥ Bukhārī, Kitābuṣ Ṣalāt, Bāb akhfiṣṣalāt 'inda bakā' ṣabiyyi)

Ḥaḍrat Anas[ra] relates that the Holy Prophet[sa] was on a journey and Anjasha, a black slave, was singing *'Uḥdiya'* (songs of the camel handlers) while driving the camels, which spurred the camels to walk fast. At this, the Holy Prophet[sa] said: "O Anjasha! Sing a little slowly. Mind the crystal on the camels (i.e., Ladies)."

(Ṣaḥīḥ Muslim, Kitābul Faḍā'il fī raḥmatun-Nabī[sa] linnisā')

Ḥaḍrat Abū Ṭufail[ra] relates that he saw the Holy Prophet[sa] at a place called, Ji'rānah. The Holy Prophet[sa] was distributing meat, when a woman arrived. The Holy Prophet[sa] spread a sheet of cloth for her to sit and she sat on it. He asked the people: "Who is this woman to whom the Holy Prophet[sa] is giving so much respect? People told him that she is the foster-mother of the Holy Prophet[sa]."

(Sunan Abū Dāwūd, Kitābul Adab, Bāb fil bir wālidain)

Ḥaḍrat Usāma[ra] relates that the foster-mother of the Holy Prophet[sa], Ḥaḍrat Ḥalīma, came to Mecca and mentioned to the Holy Prophet[sa] about the shortage of food and death of the animals. The Holy Prophet[sa] discussed with Ḥaḍrat Khadījah[ra] and gave his foster-mother forty goats and a camel laden with things.

(Ibn Sa'd's Al-Ṭabqāt Al-Kabīr, Vol. 1, p. 113, Beirut, Lebanon, 1960)

In the Battle of Ḥunain, the Muslims captured 6,000 prisoners of war belonging to *Banū Hawāzin.* These prisoners included people belonging to the tribe of Ḥaḍrat Ḥalīma and some of them were her relatives. Their deputation came to the Holy Prophet[sa] talked about their link with his foster-mother and requested freedom. The Holy Prophet[sa] after discussing the request with *Anṣār* and *Muhājirīn* freed the prisoners.

(Ibn Sa'd's Al-Ṭabqāt Al-Kabīr, Vol. 1, p. 114, Beirut, Lebanon 1960)

Abū Hurairah[ra] relates that a man came to the Holy Prophet[sa] and inquired: "Messenger[sa] of Allāh! Which of all the people is best entitled to kind treatment and the good companionship from me?"

He replied: "Your mother."
"And after her, O the Holy Prophet[sa]?" He[sa] replied: "Your mother."
"And after her, O the Holy Prophet[sa]?" He[sa] replied: "Your mother."
"And after her?" He[sa] replied: "Your father."

Another version is: The man asked: "Prophet of Allāh[sa]! Who is best entitled to my kind treatment?" He replied: "Your mother, then your mother, then your mother, then your father, and then your relatives, your near relatives in order of nearness."

(Ṣaḥīḥ Bukhārī, Kitābul Adab, Bāb min a-ḥaqqunnāsi biḥusnaṣṣuḥbati wa Muslim)

Ḥaḍrat Abī Sa'īd Al-Khudrī[ra] relates that they were sitting in the company of the Holy Prophet[sa] when a woman came to the Holy Prophet[sa] and said: "My husband Ṣafwān bin Mu'aṭṭal hits me when I offer Prayer, makes me break my fast when I keep fast, and offers *Fajr* Prayer after the sunrise." Ṣafwān was present in the gathering. The Holy Prophet[sa] asked him about the complaints. He said: "O Prophet[sa] of Allāh! She says that I hit her when she offers Prayer. It is because she recites two *Sūrahs* in the Prayer, and I forbade her." At this, the Holy Prophet[sa] said: "If you recite just one *Sūrah*, it is enough for people." Then Ṣafwān said: "With regards to her complaint about my telling her to break the fast, the truth is that she keeps on fasting continuously. You know I am a young man. I do not have that much patience." At this the Holy Prophet[sa] said: "A woman should not keep voluntary fast without her husband's permission." Said Ṣafwān: "Now, regarding her last complaint that I offer *Fajr* Prayer after the sunrise: Everyone knows that my tribesmen have the habit of getting up late." At this, the Holy Prophet[sa] said, "Alright, offer your Prayer when you get up."

(Sunan Abū Dāwūd, Kitābuṣ Ṣaum, Bāb al-Imrata tasūmu bighair idhan zaujihā; Mishkat, p. 282)

Treatment of Neighbors

Ḥaḍrat Abū Dharr[ra] relates that the Holy Prophet[sa] said: "Let not any of you neglect the least chance of doing good; if you can do no more at least meet your brother with a smile on your face. "

(Ṣaḥīḥ Muslim , Kitābul Bir Walṣilah, Bāb istijāb ṭalāqatal wajhi 'indalliqā'')

Ḥaḍrat Abū Dharr[ra] relates that the Holy Prophet[sa] said: "Abū Dharr! When you buy meat and put the cooking pot on the fire, add a little more water and send a portion of the broth to your neighbor."

(Ṣaḥīḥ Muslim, Kitābul Bir Walṣilah ,Bāb alwaṣiyyah biljār wal iḥsān ilaih)

Ḥaḍrat 'Ā''ishah[ra] relates that she asked the Holy Prophet[sa] who has stronger claim as a neighbor? The Holy Prophet[sa] said: "If you are invited by two persons at the same time, accept the invitation of the one the door of whose house is nearer to yours than that of the other, for he has a stronger claim upon you as a neighbor. But if one invites you before the other, accept the invitation of the one who invites you first."

(Ṣaḥīḥ Bukhārī, Kitābul Adab, Bāb Ḥaqqul Jiwāri fī qurbil abwābi)

The Holy Prophet[sa] said about the rights of a neighbor:

"Do you know what are the rights of a neighbor? It is his right that if he asks you for help, you should help; if he begs for a loan, you should lend; and if he becomes destitute you should render him aid. If he is ailing you should tend him; if he dies you should join in the funeral rites; if good befalls him you should felicitate him, and if he is afflicted by a calamity you should comfort and console him. You should not raise your structure higher than his obstructing the passage of the breeze towards it, without his consent. If you bring home some fruit, send your neighbor a portion of it as a present. If you are unable to do so take it inside secretly and do not let your children come out with it causing distress to your neighbor's children. Let not the smell of food from your cooking pot disturb your neighbor unless you are ready to share it with him."

(Majma'uz Zawā'id, Haithamī, Vol. 8, Kitābul Birre Waṣṣilah, Bāb Ḥaqquljar; Wisdom of the Holy Prophet[sa], pp. 19-20, Chaudharī Muḥammad Ẓafrullā Khān, Islam International Publications Limited, Islamabad, UK, 1995)

Treatment of Slaves

Ḥaḍrat Imām Abū Ḥanīfah[ra] relates that Ḥaḍrat 'Aṭā told him that he heard the following incident from several Companions[ra] of the Holy Prophet[sa]: "Ḥaḍrat 'Abdullāh bin Rawāḥah[ra] owned a slave-girl who used to graze a flock of his goats. Ḥaḍrat 'Abdullāh bin Rawāḥah[ra] had instructed her to take special care of one particular goat. She did and it grew into a stout goat. One day, the shepherdess was busy taking care of some other animals when a wolf attacked the stout goat and devoured it. Ḥaḍrat 'Abdullāh bin Rawāḥah[ra], not seeing the goat in the flock of goats, asked the slave-girl about the goat. The shepherdess told him the whole incident. Hearing it, he forcefully slapped the shepherdess. Later on, Ḥaḍrat 'Abdullāh bin Rawāḥah[ra] felt remorse about slapping the shepherdess and related the incident to the Holy Prophet[sa]. The Holy Prophet[sa] took the matter very seriously and told ‘Abdullāh bin Rawāḥah[ra] that he had slapped the face of a believer. He replied: 'O Messenger[sa] of Allāh! She is an ignorant woman from Abyssinia who does not know anything about religion.' The Holy Prophet[sa] called the shepherdess and asked her, 'Where is God?' She replied, 'In Heaven.' Then the Holy Prophet[sa] asked her, 'Who am I?' She replied, 'Messenger[sa] of Allāh.' Hearing her responses, the Holy Prophet[sa] told ‘Abdullāh bin Rawāḥah[ra]: 'She is a believer. Free her.' Ḥaḍrat ‘Abdullāh bin Rawāḥah[ra] freed her.' "

(Musnad Al-Imāmul A‘ẓam, al-Īmān wal-Islām)

Another tradition recounts that once a Companion was beating up his slave which the Holy Prophet[sa] happened to see. He expressed great anger. On this the Companion freed his slave. The Holy Prophet[sa] remarked that if he had not freed the slave he would have come under the chastisement of God.

(Ṣaḥīḥ Muslim, Kitābul Īmān, Bāb Suḥbatil mamāliki ... Ḥadīth No. 4308)

Treatment of Servants and Laborers

Ḥaḍrat ‘Ā’ishah[ra] relates: "The Holy Prophet[sa] never hit any servant whether a male or a female with his hand. However, he fought well in the cause of Allāh. Even if someone tormented him, he did not take revenge on that person. However, when Allāh's Laws were violated, he reacted for the sake of Allāh, the Most Honored and Glorious."

(Ṣaḥīḥ Muslim, Kitābul Faḍā’il, Bāb mubā‘idtah lil athām wa ikhtiyārah minal mabāḥ)

Ḥaḍrat Ibn ‘Umar[ra] relates that the Holy Prophet[sa] said: "Pay the laborer his wages before his sweat dries."

(Sunan Ibni Mājah, Kitāb Arrahūn, Bāb ajrul ajrā’)

Treatment of Animals

The Holy Prophet[sa] was sent by God Almighty as a blessing for everything in the world. Animals are also creatures of God Almighty. Therefore, the Holy Prophet[sa] established the best examples of affectionate love for and good treatment of the animals so that others also could follow his ways of treating and loving the animals.

The Holy Prophet[sa] warned people against cruelty to animals and enjoined kind treatment on them. He often used to relate the instance of a Jewish woman who was punished by God for having starved her cat to death. He also used to relate the story of a woman who found a dog suffering from thirst near a deep well. She took off her shoe and lowered it into the well and thus drew up some water. She gave the water to the thirsty dog to drink. This good deed earned her God's forgiveness for all her previous sins.

Ḥaḍrat ʻAbdullāh bin Masʻūd[ra] relates: "While we were in the course of a journey along with the Holy Prophet[sa] we saw two young doves in a nest and we caught them. They were still very small. When their mother returned to the nest, not finding her little ones in it, she began to fly wildly around close to us. When the Holy Prophet[sa] arrived at the spot he observed the dove he said, "Who has tortured the sparrow by taking her children away from her? Immediately set free the children."

(Sunan Abū Dāwūd, Kitābul Adab, Bāb Qataludhdhar)

Ḥaḍrat Suhail[ra] relates that the Holy Prophet[sa] passed by a camel whose belly due to hunger had shrunk to his back after contraction. The Holy Prophet[sa] said, "Fear Allāh regarding these helpless animals. Ride these animals and eat their meat only when they are healthy."

(Sunan Abū Dāwūd, Kitābul Jihād bāb mā yu'mar bih minal qiyām ʻaladdawwab wal bahā'im)

Ḥaḍrat ʻĀ'ishah relates that one day she mounted such a camel which was headstrong and was bothering her a lot. She started to run the camel right and left. When the Holy Prophet[sa] saw this he said, "Be gentle."

(Ṣaḥīḥ Muslim, Kitābul Bir waṣṣilah, Bāb fī faḍlurrifq)

The Holy Prophet[sa] was travelling along with some of his Companions[ra]. On the way a bird had laid an egg. A person picked up the egg. The bird came and started to fly in pain and restlessness around the Holy Prophet[sa]. The Holy Prophet[sa] said, "Who has hurt the bird by snatching her egg?" The person said, "O Messenger[sa] of Allāh! I have picked up the egg." The Holy Prophet[sa] said, "Have pity on the bird and leave the egg at the place where you picked it."

'Abdullāh bin Mas'ūd relates, that on one occasion, they observed an ant-hill and, placing some straw on top of it, they set fire to it; whereupon they were rebuked by the Holy Prophet[sa].

On one occasion, the Prophet[sa] observed a donkey being branded on the face. He inquired the reason for this and was told that the Romans had recourse to this practice for the purpose of identifying high-bred animals. The Prophet[sa] said that as the face was a very sensitive part of the body, an animal should not be branded on the face and that if it had to be done the branding should be done on its haunches.

(Jāmi' Tirmidhī, Abwāb Faḍā'il Jihād 'an Rasūlallāh[sa], Bāb mā jā'a fittaḥrīshi bainal bahā'imi wal wasmi fil wajhi)

Ḥaḍrat 'Abdullāh bin Ja'far[ra] relates that, one day, the Holy Prophet[sa] made him sit on the back of his ride and told him some confidential matters which he would never tell anyone. The Holy Prophet[sa] cared very much about privacy regarding the call of nature and liked the barrier of a wall or a bush. Accordingly, once the Holy Prophet[sa] went to the garden of an *Anṣār* to relieve himself. A camel, seeing the Holy Prophet[sa], started to cry bitterly and tears started to drip from its eyes. The Holy

Prophet[sa] walked to the camel and patted its head and seat. The camel became calm. Then the Holy Prophet[sa] asked, "Who is the owner of the camel?" An *Anṣārī* youth told the Holy Prophet[sa] that the camel belonged to him. The Holy Prophet[sa] said to him, "Do you not fear God? God has made you owner of the camel and the camel is complaining that you keep him hungry and make him work hard."

(Sunan Abū Dāwūd, Kitābul Jihād, Bāb mā yu'mar bih minal qiyām 'aladdawab walhā'im)

Ḥaḍrat Anas[ra] relates that the name of one of the camels of the Holy Prophet[sa] was *'Aḍbā'*. She would not let any other camel excel her and always won a race. A Bedouin once came and his camel ran faster than all other camels. It hurt the feelings of the Muslims. The Holy Prophet[sa], realized this and said: "It is a tradition of God Almighty that the one who rises to heights in the world, God causes him to fall also."

(Ṣaḥīḥ Bukhārī, Kitāb al-Jihād, Bāb nāqatannabī[sa])

Visiting the Sick

Ḥaḍrat Umm 'Alā'[ra] relates that she was sick when the Holy Prophet[sa] visited her and said: "Umm 'Alā! Be happy. God Almighty removes the sins of a Muslim due to sickness just like fire removes grime from silver and gold."

(Sunan Abū Dāwūd, Kitābul Janā'iz, Bāb 'iyādatunnisā)

Ḥaḍrat 'Ā'ishah[ra] relates that when the Holy Prophet[sa] visited any member of his family who was sick he would touch the unwell person with his right hand and would supplicate:

اَللّٰهُمَّ ، رَبَّ النَّاسِ! اَذْهِبِ الْبَاْسَ ، اِشْفِ ، اَنْتَ الشَّافِيْ ، لَا شِفَآءَ اِلَّا

شِفَآؤُكَ ‘ شِفَآءً لَّا يُغَادِرُ سَقَمًا -

allāhumma rabbannāsi, adh-hibil ba'sa, ishfi, antashshāfi lā shifā'a illā shifā'uka, shifā'allā yughādiru saqamā

O Allāh, Lord of mankind, remove the affliction and bestow healing, You are the Great Healer. There is no healing save Your healing, a healing that leaves no ill behind.

(Ṣaḥīḥ Muslim, Kitābussalām, Bāb istiḥbāb raqiyyatal marīḍ)

Ḥaḍrat Anas[ra] relates that a Jewish boy who served the Holy Prophet[sa] fell ill. The Holy Prophet[sa] visited him, sat down near his head and said: "Accept Islām. The boy looked at his father who was sitting next to him. The father said: 'Obey, Abul Qāsim; whereupon the boy accepted Islām.' When the Holy Prophet[sa] left him he affirmed: 'All praise is due to Allāh Who has delivered him from the Hell-Fire.' "

(Ṣaḥīḥ Bukhārī, Kitābul Janā'iz, Bāb 'idha aslamaṣṣabi famāta hal yuṣallī 'alaih)

Extraordinary Patience

The Holy Prophet[sa], throughout his life, had to encounter a succession of bitter experiences. He was born an orphan as his mother died while he was still a small child and he lost his grandfather at the age of eight. After marriage he had to bear the loss of several children, one after another, and then his beloved and devoted wife Ḥaḍrat Khadījah[ra] died. Some of the wives he married after Ḥaḍrat Khadījah's[ra] death died during his lifetime and towards the close of his life he had to bear the loss of his son Ibrāhīm. He bore all these losses and calamities cheerfully, and none of them affected in the least degree either his high resolve or the serenity of his disposition. His private sorrows never were revealed in public and he always met everybody with a benign countenance and treated all with uniform benevolence. On one occasion he observed a woman who had lost a child occupied in loud lamenting over her child's grave. He admonished her to be patient and to accept God's will as supreme. The woman did not know that she was being addressed by the Holy Prophet[sa] and replied: "If you had ever suffered the loss of a child as I have, you would have realized how difficult it is to be patient under such an affliction." The Prophet[sa] observed: "I have suffered the loss not of one but of seven children," and passed on. Except when he referred to his own losses or misfortunes in this indirect manner, he never cared to dwell upon them nor did he permit them in any manner to interfere with his unceasing service to mankind and his cheerful sharing of their burdens.

Ḥaḍrat Anas[ra] relates that the Holy Prophet[sa] came to his son Ibrāhīm, when he was nearing his end and his eyes began to run, whereupon Ḥaḍrat 'Abdur Raḥmān bin 'Auf[ra] exclaimed: "Messenger[sa] of Allāh, even you? The Holy Prophet[sa] said: 'Ibn 'Auf, this is but the tenderness of the heart.' He wept again and said:

إِنَّ الْعَيْنَ تَدْمَعُ ، وَالْقَلْبَ يَحْزَنُ ، وَلاَ نَقُوْلُ اِلاَّ مَا يَرْضٰى رَبُّنَا ، وَاِنَّا بِفِرَاقِكَ يَا اِبْرَاهِيْمُ! لَمَحْزُوْنُوْنَ

innal 'aina tadma'u wal qalba yaḥzanu walā naqūlu illā mā yarḍā rabbunā wa innā bi firāqika yā ibrāhīmu la maḥzūnūna

'The eye sheds tears and the heart is sorrowful, but we utter only that which should please our Lord. We are indeed grieved, Ibrāhīm, by your parting.' "

(Ṣaḥīḥ Bukhārī, Kitābul Janā'iz, Bāb qaulunnabī[sa] anā bikal maḥzūnūn)

Ḥaḍrat Usāmah bin Zaid[ra], loved by the Holy Prophet[sa] and the son of one loved by him[sa], relates that a daughter of the Holy Prophet[sa], Ḥaḍrat Zainab[ra], sent word to him that her son was at his last breath and begged him to go to her. He sent his salutation to her with the message: "To Allāh belongs that which He bestowed and to Him belongs that which He takes. Everything has its term fixed by Him. Let her be steadfast, therefore, and hope for His Grace and Mercy. She sent back word to him begging him for the sake of Allāh to go to her. He stood up and proceeded to her accompanied by Ḥaḍrat Sa'd bin 'Ubādah[ra], Ḥaḍrat Mu'ādh bin Jabal[ra], Ḥaḍrat Ubayy bin Ka'b[ra], Ḥaḍrat Zaid bin Thābit[ra] and others. When he arrived the child was presented to him and he took it in his lap. Observing its distress his tears began to run, whereupon Sa'd said: 'Messenger[sa] of Allāh, what is this?' He answered: 'This is compassion which Allāh has placed in the hearts of His servants and Allāh has compassion for such of His servants who are compassionate to others.' "

(Nasā'ī, Kitābul Janā'iz, Bāb al-amr biliḥtisāb waṣṣabr)

As a Judge

Ḥaḍrat 'Ā'ishah[ra] relates that the *Quraish* were worried about the case of a *Makhzūmī* woman who had committed theft and wondered who should intercede on her behalf with the Holy Prophet[sa]. Some said: "Who can venture to do so except Usāmah bin Zaid[ra] who is much loved by the Holy Prophet[sa]? So Usāmah spoke to him and the Holy Prophet[sa] said to him: 'Do you seek to intercede in the matter of the penalties prescribed by Allāh the Exalted?' Then he stood up and made an address in which he said: 'Those who were before you were ruined because they would let off a high-placed one if he committed theft and would exact the prescribed penalty from a poor one who stole. I call Allāh to witness that were Fāṭimah, daughter of Muḥammad[sa], to steal, I would cut off her hand.' "

(Ṣaḥīḥ Muslim, Kitābul Ḥadūd, Bāb qata'assariq ashsharīf wa ghairih)

Ḥaḍrat Ummi Salamah[ra] relates that two men who had a dispute between themselves about ownership of an inheritance were brought to the Holy Prophet[sa]. Since it was an old property dispute, neither of the parties had proof to support his claim. After hearing the claims of both men, the

Holy Prophet[sa] said: "I am but a human being. You bring your disputes to me for a judgement. It might happen that someone is more articulate in presenting the case than the other and I might decide in his favor based on what I hear. But if I decide in favor of the one who is more articulate and the decision is against the rightful person, in such a situation, one should not take advantage of the decision and should not usurp the right of his brother. It will be merely a piece of fire I allot to him. If he takes it, it will turn into a snake wrapped around his neck on the Day of Judgement. Hearing this, both parties cried, and each said: 'O Messenger[sa] of Allāh! I do not want anything, give it to my brother.' The Holy Prophet[sa] said: 'If both of you agree, then divide the property into two parts and select a part by drawing lots. When the lot of either of the disputants falls upon a part of the property, he will take that part of the property and bestow the other part to the other person.' "

(Sunan Abū Dāwūd, Kitābal Qaḍā', Bāb fī qaḍā' al-qāḍī idha akhṭā)

Loving Father and Grandfather

Ḥaḍrat 'Ā'ishah[ra] relates that no one resembled the Holy Prophet[sa] more in appearance, talk and gait than Ḥaḍrat Fāṭimah[ra].

According to another narration, whenever Ḥaḍrat Fāṭimah[ra] visited the Holy Prophet[sa], he stood up to receive her, kissed her hand, and seated her on his own seat. Similarly, whenever the Holy Prophet[sa] visited Ḥaḍrat Fāṭimah[ra], she stood up, kissed the blessed hands of the Holy Prophet[sa], and seated him on her place.

(Sunan Abū Dāwūd, Abwābul adab, Bāb fil qiyām)

Ḥaḍrat 'Ā'ishah[ra] and Ḥaḍrat Ummi Salamah[ra] relate that the Holy Prophet[sa] told them to prepare Ḥaḍrat Fāṭimah[ra] as a bride so that they marry her to Ḥaḍrat 'Alī[ra]: "We fixed her room beautifully. We made soft pillows and mattresses from date-palm skin. Then we arranged dates and raisins to eat and sweet water to drink. We drove a stick in the ground to hang clothes and water-skin. Thus, no marriage ceremony was as beautiful as that of Ḥaḍrat Fāṭimah[ra]."

(Ibni Mājah kitābunnikāḥ, Bābul walīmah)

Ḥaḍrat Abū Hurairah[ra] relates that the Holy Prophet[sa] kissed his grandson Ḥasan bin 'Alī. 'Aqra' bin Ḥābis, who was with the Holy Prophet[sa] at the time and said: "I have ten sons and have never kissed any of them. The Holy Prophet[sa] looked at him and said, 'He who has no compassion will receive none.' "

(Ṣaḥīḥ Bukhārī, Kitābul Adab, Bāb raḥmatal wald wa taqbīlah, p 887/2)

Ḥaḍrat 'Abdullāh bin Ja'far[ra] relates that whenever the Holy Prophet[sa] returned from a journey, the children in the family of the Holy Prophet[sa] used to go out to welcome him. He relates: "Once, when the Holy Prophet[sa] returned from a journey, I was the first who was brought to him. The Holy Prophet[sa] held me in his lap. Then, one of the sons of Ḥaḍrat Fāṭimah[ra], either Imām Ḥasan[ra] or Imām Ḥusain[ra], was brought to the Holy Prophet[sa]. He seated his grandson behind himself. Thus, we entered Medina while three of us were sitting on the same camel in such glory."

(Musnad Aḥmad, p 203/1)

Ḥaḍrat Ibn A'bud[ra] relates that Ḥaḍrat 'Alī[ra] asked him: "Should I not tell you a story about Fāṭimah[ra], the daughter of the Holy Prophet[sa] and I? Among all the relatives, Fāṭimah[ra] was the most beloved of the Holy Prophet[sa]. Ḥaḍrat 'Alī[ra] narrated, 'Due to the use of a grinding mill and fetching water with the water-skin, Fāṭimah[ra] had developed corns on her hands and the marks of the water-skin on her chest. Her clothes used to become dirty due to sweeping dust in the house. In the meantime, a few servants were brought to the Holy Prophet[sa]. I said to Fāṭimah[ra] that a few servants have been brought to the Holy Prophet[sa], and if you ask him for a servant, you will get one. So, go to the Holy Prophet[sa] and ask him for a servant. She went to see the Holy Prophet[sa]. However, there were many people sitting in the company of the Holy Prophet[sa] so she came back without asking him about the servant. The next day, she went again. The Holy Prophet[sa] asked her the purpose of her visit. She remained silent." Ḥaḍrat 'Alī[ra] says that he said, 'Messenger[sa] of Allāh! I tell you about the purpose of her visit. Due to the use of a grinding mill and fetching water with the water-skin, she[ra] has developed corns on her hands and water-skin marks are visible on her chest. You had said that when servants are brought to you, you would give her one. Therefore, give her a servant so that she does not have to do such heart-rending work.' Hearing this, the Holy Prophet[sa] said, 'Fāṭimah! Fear Allāh. Fulfill your duties to Allāh. Do your household chores with your own hands. At night when you go to bed, repeat: thirty-three times *Subḥānallāh*, thirty-three times *Alḥamdulillāh* and thirty-four times *Allāhu Akbar*. This makes the total one hundred. This act is better than desiring a servant.' Ḥaḍrat Fāṭimah[ra] said, 'I submit to the Will of Allāh and His Messenger[sa].'"

(Sunan Abū Dāwūd, Kitābu Kharaj walfī wal imārah, Bāb fī biyān mawāḍi' qasamal khams)

Ḥaḍrat 'Umar bin Abī Salama[ra], a step-son of the Holy Prophet[sa], relates: "The Holy Prophet[sa] was at the house of Ḥaḍrat Ummi Salamah[ra] when the following verse was revealed to him:

اِنَّمَا يُرِيدُ اللّٰهُ لِيُذْهِبَ عَنْكُمُ الرِّجْسَ اَهْلَ الْبَيْتِ وَيُطَهِّرَكُمْ تَطْهِيْرًا ۞

innamā yurīdullāhu li ydhhiba 'ankumurrijsa ahlal baiti wa yuṭahhirakum taṭhīrā

Surely Allāh desires to remove from you *all* uncleanliness, O Members of the Household, and purify you completely. (33:34)

The Holy Prophet[sa] sent for Ḥaḍrat Fāṭimah[ra], Ḥaḍrat Ḥasan, and Ḥaḍrat Ḥusain and covered them with a sheet. Ḥaḍrat 'Alī[ra] was standing behind them. The Holy Prophet[sa] covered him also with the sheet. Then he supplicated to God Almighty:

اَللّٰهُمَّ هٰؤُلَآءِ اَهْلُ بَيْتِىْ فَاذْهَبْ عَنْهُمُ الرِّجْسَ

allāhumma hā'ulā'i ahlu baitī fadh-hab 'anhumurrijsa

O my Lord! They are also members of my Household. Remove from them *all* uncleanliness (and make them righteous).

Ḥaḍrat Ummi Salamah[ra] said, 'Can I be included with them?' The Holy Prophet[sa] said: 'Ummi Salamah! You have your own status and your status is better.' "

(Jāmi' Tirmidhī, Abwāb Tafsīr ul Qur'ān, wa min Sūrah al-Aḥzāb, p. 152/2)

21

Wives of the Holy Prophet[sa] (Mothers of the Faithful)

The Holy Prophet[sa] married twelve times. Non-Muslims often make an issue that it was against the commandment of the Holy Qur'ān that a Muslim should not have more than four wives at a time. However, if we look at the circumstances under which those marriages took place it reveals that it was an absolute necessity to do so. First of all he did not marry a woman while Ḥaḍrat Khadījah[ra] was alive. It was after her demise that he married other women. Polygamy was common at that time and the commandment of Allāh limiting the number of wives one can have with certain conditions had not yet come. All the women he married were widows or divorcees except Ḥaḍrat 'Ā'ishah[ra]. None of the women who married the Holy Prophet[sa] was forced into marriage. They married him of their own free will. Furthermore, whenever he married a woman it was for the abolishing of certain old traditions such as not marrying the wife of an adopted son or a widow with children. Furthermore some of the women he married were quite old. So the reason for marrying more than four wives was based on piety and for the religous needs of the time. The Holy Prophet[sa] married the following pious ladies:

1. Ḥaḍrat Khadījah[ra]

Ḥaḍrat Khadījah[ra], the daughter of Khuwailid bin Asad bin 'Abdul

'Uzzā bin Quṣayy, was an intelligent and rich businesswoman. She was twice married before her marriage to the Holy Prophet[sa]. Her first marriage was with Abū Hālah ibn Zurārah al-Tamīmī. She bore two children from this marriage, named, Hind and Ḥārith. After the demise of her first husband she married 'Ātīq ibn 'Ā'yidah al-Makhzūmī. From this marriage she had a daughter who was also named Hind. After the demise of 'Atīq ibn 'Ā'yidah al-Makhzūmī, Ḥaḍrat Khadījah[ra] married the Holy Prophet[sa]. She was a well respected pious rich lady and due to her piety was known as '*Ṭāhira*" (i.e., the pure one).

Ḥaḍrat Khadījah[ra] was a shrewd businesswoman. She preferred to manage the business herself. She was a widow and there were several men who sought to marry her. However, she refused to marry any one of them. She was well aware of the truthfulness and excellent character of the Holy Prophet[sa] who from his early youth was known as the truthful and the trustworthy. Thus, both the Holy Prophet[sa] and Ḥaḍrat Khadījah[ra] possessed unique qualities. At first, Ḥaḍrat Khadījah[ra] acquired his services for taking care of her business. She was very much impressed with the character and other qualities of the Holy Prophet[sa]. Her servant, Maisrah who had accompanied the Holy Prophet[sa] during the business trip was also full of praise for the Holy Prophet[sa]. Soon she proposed to the Holy Prophet[sa] to marry her. The Holy Prophet[sa] took advice from his relatives and then agreed to marry Ḥaḍrat Khadījah[ra]. Abū Ṭālib performed the *Nikah* of the Holy Prophet[sa] with Ḥaḍrat Khadījah[ra] with a dowry of 500 *Dirhams*. The marriage took place in 595 AD. She was 40 years old at the time of her marriage with the Holy Prophet[sa] while the Holy Prophet[sa] was 25 years old.

Ḥaḍrat Khadījah[ra] was the first one among men and women to accept Islām. All of the children of the Holy Prophet[sa] except Ibrāhīm were born to Ḥaḍrat Khadījah[ra]. Ḥaḍrat Khadījah[ra] gave birth to seven children, the sons were named Qāsim, Ṭāhir and Ṭayyab, and the four daughters named, Ḥaḍrat Zainab[ra], Ḥaḍrat Ruqayyah[ra], Ḥaḍrat Ummi Kulthūm[ra] and Ḥaḍrat Fāṭimah[ra]. All the children of Ḥaḍrat Khadījah[ra] from marriages before she married the Holy Prophet[sa] accepted Islām.

Ḥaḍrat Khadījah[ra] died at the age of 65 years and the Holy Prophet[sa] at that time was 50 years old. Thus, till the age of 50 years the Holy Prophet[sa] had one wife, Ḥaḍrat Khadījah[ra]. She passed away in the month of *Ramaḍān* in 10 AH and was buried in the "*Jannat-e-Mu'allā*" graveyard. Ḥaḍrat Khadījah[ra] was with the Holy Prophet[sa] during of the siege of *Shi'b-e-Abī Ṭālib* and at an old age she endured the hardships of the siege for two to three years.

The Holy Prophet[sa] loved Ḥaḍrat Khadījah[ra] so much that even after she had passed away and he had several other wives when anything reminded him of Ḥaḍrat Khadījah[ra] he used to become full of emotions and kept her memory alive in various ways. Once, Ḥaḍrat Hālah[ra], a sister of Ḥaḍrat Khadījah[ra], whose voice was very close to Ḥaḍrat Khadījah's[ra] voice came and asked the Holy Prophet[sa] permission to come inside the house. When, the Holy Prophet[sa] heard her voice he immediately said it must be Hālah and old memories of Ḥaḍrat Khadījah[ra] overwhelmed him.

2. Ḥaḍrat Saudah[ra]

After the sad demise of Ḥaḍrat Khadījah[ra], the Holy Prophet[sa] married Ḥaḍrat Saudah[ra] bint Zam'ah ibn Qais ibn 'Abd Shams who was the widow of Sakrān bin 'Amr, who was one of the servants of the Holy Prophet[sa]. Ḥaḍrat Saudah was one of the early Muslims. She had accepted Islām before her husband. According to the traditions, Ḥaḍrat Saudah[ra] migrated to Abyssinia with her husband, after being persecuted by the

Polytheists of Mecca. Ḥaḍrat Saudah[ra] was the first woman to emigrate to Abyssinia for the sake of her religion. Her husband died when the couple returned to Mecca. She had a son from her first husband named Sakrān ibn ‘Amr ibn ‘Abd Shams. After her husband's death she was living with her father. At the same time the Holy Prophet[sa] after the demise of Ḥaḍrat Khadījah[ra] himself was taking care of his children. A relative of the Holy Prophet[sa], Khaula bint Ḥākim who was married to ‘Uthmān bin Maẓ‘ūn, pointed out to the Holy Prophet[sa] that his children need a mother. She proposed that he marry Ḥaḍrat ‘Ā’ishah[ra] who was the daughter of his dear friend, Ḥaḍrat Abū Bakr[ra], or Ḥaḍrat Saudah[ra] who was a widow of his servant Sakrān bin ‘Amr. The Holy Prophet[sa] told Khaula to talk with both families. Accordingly, Khaula delivered the proposal first to Ḥaḍrat Abū Bakr[ra] and his wife, Umm Rumān[ra]. Then, she went to Ḥaḍrat Saudah bint Zam‘ah and conveyed the message to her. Ḥaḍrat Saudah and her family agreed to the proposal. Thus, in the month of *Shawwāl*, 3 BH (February/March, 619 AD) the *Nikāh* of the Holy Prophet[sa] was performed with both Ḥaḍrat ‘Ā’ishah and Ḥaḍrat Saudah[ra]. Four hundred *Dirhams* were fixed as the *Ḥaq Mehr* for each of them. Ḥaḍrat Saudah's[ra] marriage ceremony took place right away while the marriage ceremony of Ḥaḍrat ‘Ā’ishah[ra] was delayed due to her being of a relatively young age. Ḥaḍrat Saudah[ra] was a middle-aged woman at the time of her marriage with the Holy Prophet[sa]. According to one tradition she was fifty years old at the time of her marriage to the Holy Prophet[sa]. Thus she was very suited to taking care of the children, and immediately after the marriage she took over the care of the children and the household work. When Ḥaḍrat Saudah[ra] grew old she gave up her share of the Holy Prophet's[sa] time in favor of Ḥaḍrat ‘Ā’ishah[ra]. She had the honor of performing *Ḥajj* in the company of the Holy Prophet[sa]. She passed away in 27 AH at the age of 75 years.

3. Ḥaḍrat 'A'ishah[ra]

Ḥaḍrat 'Ā'ishah[ra] was born to Ḥaḍrat Abū Bakr[ra] and Ḥaḍrat Zainab[ra] four years after the beginning of the prophethood of the Holy Prophet[sa]. Thus, Ḥaḍrat 'Ā'ishah[ra] was the only wife of the Holy Prophet[sa] who was a Muslim by birth. The rest of the wives of the Holy Prophet[sa] had accepted Islām either by themselves or along with their parents. Her *Nikāh* with the Holy Prophet[sa] was performed in 619 AD. When the Holy Prophet[sa] and Ḥaḍrat Abū Bakr[ra] got settled in Medina after the migration from Mecca, Ḥaḍrat Abū Bakr[ra] sent his slave to Mecca to bring his wife and Ḥaḍrat 'Ā'ishah[ra] to Medina. Her marriage ceremony with the Holy Prophet[sa] was performed when she was close to 12 years old.

Ḥaḍrat 'Ā'ishah[ra] relates that the Holy Prophet[sa] said to her, "You have been shown to me twice in my dream. I saw you pictured on a piece of silk and someone said to me, 'This is your wife.' When I uncovered the picture, I saw that it was yours. I said, 'If this is from Allāh, it will be accomplished.' "

(Ṣaḥīḥ Bukhārī, Kitāb Faḍā'il Aṣḥābannabī[sa], Bāb tazwījinnabī[sa] Khadījata wa faḍlihā[ra])

The Holy Prophet[sa] loved Ḥaḍrat 'Ā'ishah[ra] very much and he, with the permission of the other wives, spent the last days of his life with Ḥaḍrat 'Ā'ishah[ra] in her apartment and passed away there in her lap.

The high status of Ḥaḍrat 'Ā'ishah[ra] as a commentator, narrator of *Ḥadīth* and the one having the knowledge of Islāmic Law is well established. Whenever, the Companions[ra] of the Holy Prophet[sa] faced a tough question to tackle they usually consulted Ḥaḍrat 'Ā'ishah[ra] and were always satisfied with her answer to the question. She is quoted as source for many *Aḥādīth*. She has narrated 2210 *Aḥādīth* out of which 316 *Aḥādīth* are mentioned in both *Ṣaḥīḥ Al-Bukhārī* and *Ṣaḥīḥ Muslim*. The Holy Prophet's[sa] personal life is the topic of many traditions quoted by her.

Ḥaḍrat 'Urwah bin Zubair[ra] relates that he has seen no one more knowledgable than Ḥaḍrat 'Ā'ishah[ra] in the knowledge of the Holy Qur'ān, patrimony, *Ḥalāl* and *Ḥarām*, *Fiqh*, poetry, medicine, *Ḥadīth*, Arabs and genealogies.

Ḥaḍrat Umm Hānī'[ra] relates that the Holy Prophet[sa] said: "O 'Ā'ishah! Your mark should be knowledge and the Holy Qur'ān."

(Musnad Imāmul A'ẓam , Kitābal 'Ilm, p. 20)

Ḥaḍrat 'Amr bin al-'Āṣ[ra] relates that once he asked the Holy Prophet[sa], "Whom do you love the most amongst the people? He said, ' 'Ā'ishah.' "

(Ṣaḥīḥ Muslim, Kitāb Faḍā'il Aṣḥābah[ra], Bāb faḍā'il 'Ā'ishah[ra])

Ḥaḍrat 'Ā'ishah[ra] narrated that the Holy Prophet[sa] said to her, "I know when you are pleased or angry with me. I said, 'How do yo know that?' He said, When you are pleased with me, you swear like this:

لاَ وَ رَبِّ مُحَمَّدٍ

lā wa rabbi Muḥammad

No, by the Lord of Muḥammad

However, when you are angry with me, then you swear like this:

لاَ وَ رَبِّ اِبْرَاهِيْمَ

lā wa rabbi Ibrāhīm

No, by the Lord of Ibrāhīm

Then, I said, 'Yes, but by Allāh, O Messenger[sa] of Allāh, I leave out only your name. There is not a slightest change in my love for you.' "

(Ṣaḥīḥ Muslim, Kitāb Faḍā'il Aṣḥābah[ra], Bāb faḍā'il 'Ā'ishah[ra])

Ḥaḍrat 'Ā'ishah[ra] relates that she was travelling with the Holy Prophet[sa] when she competed in a race with the Holy Prophet[sa]. Ḥaḍrat 'Ā'ishah[ra] passed ahead of the Holy Prophet[sa]. However, when she had gained some weight they had another race in which the Holy Prophet[sa] passed ahead of her in the race and he said: "O 'Ā'ishah! I have avenged my defeat in the previous competition."

(Sunan Abū Dāwūd, Kitābul Jihād, Bāb fissabaq 'alarrajul)

Ḥaḍrat 'Ā'ishah[ra] spent nine years with the Holy Prophet[sa]. She lived for 48 years after the sad demise of the Holy Prophet[sa]. She passed away in 57 AH when she was 66 years old. She is buried in "*Jannatul Baqī*'" in Medina. She accompanied the Holy Prophet[sa] in the Battles of Uḥud and . During the Battle of Uḥud she used to carry water and give it the wounded. She had the honor of performing *Ḥajj* in the company of the Holy Prophet[sa].

There were two incidents in the life of Ḥaḍrat 'Ā'ishah[ra] which are well discussed and recorded, one is the accusation of the enemies of Islām that Ḥaḍrat 'Ā'ishah[ra] was underage at the time the Holy Prophet[sa] married her and the other is the incident when the hypocrites falsely accused Ḥaḍrat 'Ā'ishah[ra] of an immoral behavior and spread a lot of propaganda about it. The second incident was very painful for both the Holy Prophet[sa] and Ḥaḍrat 'Ā'ishah[ra]. However, God Almighty revealed the facts to the Holy Prophet[sa] and exonerated Ḥaḍrat 'Ā'ishah[ra].

Ḥaḍrat 'Ā'ishah's[ra] Age at the Time of Her Marriage With the Holy Prophet[sa]

Some of the Orientalists criticize that the Holy Prophet[sa] married women of very young age and particularly they mention that Ḥaḍrat 'Ā'ishah[ra] was of an unusually young age when the Holy Prophet[sa] married her. This criticism is unwaranted. The fact is that at the time of the Holy Prophet[sa] it was customary to marry a girl who had reached puberty irrespective of how old she was. Due to the climate of the area and diet of the people the girls usually achieved puberty at a very young age. Ḥaḍrat 'Ā'ishah[ra] was about nine years old when her parents requested to perform her *Nikāh* with the Holy Prophet[sa], and that was according to the Arab customs. She was married to the Holy Prophet[sa] when she was twelve years old. If it was objectionable to marry a girl at a young age, certainly the Holy Prophet[sa] would not have married his daughters at a young age. The first marriages of Ḥaḍrat Zainab[ra], Ḥaḍrat Ruqayyah[ra], and Ḥaḍrat Ummi Kulthūm[ra], the daughters of the Holy Prophet[sa], took place at a very young age. When Ḥaḍrat Ruqayyah[ra] married a second time with Ḥaḍrat 'Uthmān[ra], she was less than 12 years old. When she migrated with her husband, Ḥaḍrat 'Uthmān[ra], to Abyssinia she was 12 years old.

Ḥaḍrat Mirzā Bashīr Aḥmad[ra] has presented the following view about the age of Ḥaḍrat 'Ā'ishah[ra] at the time of her marriage with the Holy Prophet[sa] which is based on a tradition narrated by

Ibn Sa'd in his '*Ṭabaqāt*: "Ḥaḍrat 'Ā'ishah[ra] was born in the beginning of the 4th year of prophethood. As the Holy Prophet[sa] migrated from Mecca in the month of *Rabī'ul Awwal* of 14th *Nabuwwah* (prophethood), the age of Ḥaḍrat 'Ā'ishah[ra] at the time of migration comes to a few months more than 10 years. She got married in the month of *Shawwāl* of 2 AH. Thus the difference between migration and her marriage is a few months less than two years. By adding up this period with her age at the time of the marriage, which is a few months more than 10 years, gives us her age of 12 years at the time of her marriage."

Slander Against Ḥaḍrat 'Ā'ishah[ra] by the Hypocrites

While returning from the Battle of *Banū Muṣṭaliq* Ḥaḍrat 'Ā'ishah[ra] was with the Holy Prophet[sa]. When the army reached near Medina the Holy Prophet[sa] ordered the army to move during the night time. When Ḥaḍrat 'Ā'ishah[ra] heard the order she went away for human needs. When she returned she noticed that her necklace was missing. To search for the necklace Ḥaḍrat 'Ā'ishah[ra] went back to the place where she had gone earlier. In the meantime, the members of the caravan picked up the *Haudah* (a seat used on a camel, in which the ladies travel) and placed it on the camel without realizing that Ḥaḍrat 'Ā'ishah[ra] was not inside the *Haudah.* Since Ḥaḍrat 'Ā'ishah[ra] was of a young age and also slender, she did not weigh much, so the caravan people did not notice her absence. When Ḥaḍrat 'Ā'ishah[ra] returned after searching for her necklace, the caravan had already left. Ḥaḍrat 'Ā'ishah[ra] stayed at the same place and since it was late at night she fell sleep. Ḥaḍrat Ṣafwān bin Mu'aṭṭal[ra], one of the Companions[ra] of the Holy Prophet[sa], who was assigned the duty to come back after the caravan has left to check that nothing was left behind, found Ḥaḍrat 'Ā'ishah[ra] sleeping there. He made Ḥaḍrat 'Ā'ishah[ra] sit on his camel and brought her to the Muslim army. Ḥaḍrat 'Ā'ishah[ra] returned to Medina with the army. The hypocrites used this incidence to slander Ḥaḍrat 'Ā'ishah[ra] and spread wrong information about her. The leader of this conspiracy was 'Abdullāh bin Ubayy bin Salūl. When Ḥaḍrat 'Ā'ishah[ra] came to know of the slander against her she went to her parents' house and stayed there till she was cleared of the slander by God Almighty through revelation to the Holy Prophet[sa].

This incident is mentioned in the Holy Qur'ān as follows:

إِنَّ الَّذِيْنَ جَآءُوْ بِالْإِفْكِ عُصْبَةٌ مِّنْكُمْ ۚ لَا تَحْسَبُوْهُ شَرًّا لَّكُمْ ۚ
بَلْ هُوَ خَيْرٌ لَّكُمْ ۚ لِكُلِّ امْرِىءٍ مِّنْهُمْ مَّا اكْتَسَبَ مِنَ الْإِثْمِ ۚ وَ
الَّذِيْ تَوَلّٰى كِبْرَهٗ مِنْهُمْ لَهٗ عَذَابٌ عَظِيْمٌ ٥ لَوْلَآ إِذْ سَمِعْتُمُوْهُ
ظَنَّ الْمُؤْمِنُوْنَ وَ الْمُؤْمِنٰتُ بِأَنْفُسِهِمْ خَيْرًا ۙ وَّ قَالُوْا هٰذَآ إِفْكٌ
مُّبِيْنٌ ٥

innalladhīna jā'ū bil ifki 'uṣbatumminkum lā taḥsabūhu sharrallakum bal huwa khairullakum likullimri'immin hummaktasaba minal ithmi walladhī tawallā kibrahū minhum lahū 'adhābun 'aẓīm lau lā idh sami'tumūhu ẓannal mu'minūna wal mu'minātu bi anfusihim khairañwwa qālū hādhā ifkummubīn

Verily, those who brought forth the lie are a party from among you. Think it not to be an evil for you; nay, it is good for you. Every one of them shall have *his share of* what he has earned of the sin; and he among them who took the chief part therein shall have a grievous punishment. Why did not the believing men and believing women, when you heard of it, think well of their own people, and say, 'This is a manifest lie?' (24:12-13)

Then the punishment for false accusation of adultery was promulgated through the revelation of the following:

وَالَّذِيْنَ يَرْمُوْنَ الْمُحْصَنٰتِ ثُمَّ لَمْ يَأْتُوْا بِاَرْبَعَةِ شُهَدَآءَ فَاجْلِدُوْهُمْ ثَمٰنِيْنَ جَلْدَةً وَّلَا تَقْبَلُوْا لَهُمْ شَهَادَةً اَبَدًا ۚ وَاُولٰٓئِكَ هُمُ الْفٰسِقُوْنَ ۙ

walladhīna yarmūnal muḥṣanāti thumma lam ya'tū bi arba'atin shuhadā'a fajlidūhum thamānīna jaldatañwwa lā taqbalū lahum shahādatan abadan wa ulā'ika humul fāsiqūn

And those who calumniate chaste women but bring not four witnesses -- flog them with eighty stripes, and never admit their evidence *thereafter*, and it is they that are the transgressors. (24:5)

In pursuit of the above Qur'ānic injunction, those who had spread the false accusation of Ḥaḍrat 'Ā'ishah[ra] were flogged eighty stripes each. Ḥaḍrat 'Ā'ishah's[ra] health improved and she returned to her quarter. Soon she reclaimed her previous high status in the heart and mind of the Holy Prophet[sa] and with all the Muslims.

An Interesting Episode

Ḥaḍrat Muḥammad bin Qais[ra] bin Makhramah bin Muṭṭalib once said: "Should I relate to you an incident from myself and my mother? We speculated that he was going to relate from his mother. However, he said: 'Ḥaḍrat 'Ā'ishah[ra] once said that she was going to tell us about an incident: 'One night, when it was the turn of the Holy Prophet[sa] to stay with me, the Holy Prophet[sa] changed his clothes, took off his shoes and went to bed. After a short while, the Holy Prophet[sa], thought that I had fallen asleep, silently got out of the bed, changed his clothes, put on his shoes, and went outside. However, I was awake. So, I covered myself well with a sheet and followed the Holy Prophet[sa]. I saw him enter the *Jannatul Baqī'* where he prayed for a long time. Then he raised his hands thrice and turned back. I also turned back. When the Holy Prophet[sa] walked fast, I also walked fast. When he walked faster, I walked faster than him. I reached the house before him and lay on the bed. The Holy Prophet[sa] came inside and asked: 'O 'Ā'ishah! What is the matter? Why are you out of breath?' I said, 'Nothing.' The Holy Prophet[sa] said: 'There is something. Tell me or my All-Knowing God will tell me.' I said: 'O Messenger[sa] of Allāh! May my father and mother be sacrificed for you! And I told him everything.' The Holy Prophet[sa] said, 'So, the shadow I saw in front of me at some distance was you?' I said: 'O Messenger[sa] of Allāh! Yes, It was me.' He nudged me and said: 'Do you think that the Messenger[sa] of Allāh will transgress, be unjust to you and usurp your rights?' I thought (to myself) that people keep matters secret from others, but Allāh Knows all. Then the Holy Prophet[sa] said: 'The fact is that Gabriel had come to me silently so that you would not find out about it. That is why I kept it secret from you. Gabriel did not want to face you while you were sleeping in your night dress and I also thought that since you were asleep it was not proper to wake you up. Gabriel called me outside and said: 'Your Lord commands you to visit the *Jannatul Baqī'* and pray for the forgiveness (of the martyrs).' 'Ā'ishah asked: 'What should we pray at the graves of our elders?' The Holy Prophet[sa] said to supplicate:

اَلسَّلَامُ عَلٰى اَهْلِ الدِّيَارِ مِنَ الْمُؤْمِنِيْنَ وَالْمُسْلِمِيْنَ وَيَرْحَمُ اللّٰهُ الْمُسْتَقْدِمِيْنَ مِنَّا وَ الْمُسْتَاْخِرِيْنَ وَ اِنَّا اِنْ شَاءَ اللّٰهُ بِكُمْ لَلَاحِقُوْنَ ۔

assalāmu 'alā ahliddiyāri minal mu'minīna wal muslimīna wa yarḥamullāhul mustaqdimīna minnā wal musta'khirīna wa innā inshā 'allāhu bikum la lāḥiqūn

O Muslims! Peace and blessings of Allāh be upon the dwellers of the graveyard. The Mercy of Allāh be upon all those who have preceded us and those who will join later on. God willing, surely, soon we will join you .' "

(Ṣaḥīḥ Muslim, Kitābul Janā'iz, Bāb mā yuqāl 'idhā dakhūlul qabūr waddu'ā li ahlihā)

The Battle of the Jamal (Camel)

After the death of the Holy Prophet[sa], in the early days of the *Khilafat* of Ḥaḍrat 'Alī[ra], an insurrection was led against Ḥaḍrat 'Alī[ra] by the supporters of Ṭalḥa and Az-Zubair. Ḥaḍrat 'Ā'ishah[ra] joined them in the battle and fought against the forces of Ḥaḍrat 'Alī[ra]. During the battle Ḥaḍrat 'Ā'ishah[ra] was mounted on a camel. That is why this battle is called, the "Battle of Jamal". After a pitch battle amongst the forces of Ḥaḍrat 'Alī[ra] and the rebels, the rebels were defeated. Both Ṭalḥa and Az-Zubair were killed and Ḥaḍrat 'Ā'ishah[ra] was taken in protective custody. Ḥaḍrat 'Ā'ishah[ra] was allowed to return to Medina under the supervision of her brother, Ḥaḍrat Muḥammad bin Abū Bakr[ra], who was fighting with the forces of Ḥaḍrat 'Alī[ra].

4. Ḥaḍrat Ḥafṣah[ra]

Ḥaḍrat Ḥafṣah[ra] was the daughter of Hadrat Umar[ra]. She was first married to Ḥaḍrat Khunais bin Ḥudhāfah As-Sahmī[ra] who participated in the Battle of Badr. Upon returning from Badr to Medina, Ḥaḍrat Khunais[ra] became ill and died due to the illness. Thus, Ḥaḍrat Ḥafṣah[ra] became a widow at a very young age. She was just 20 years old. Ḥaḍrat 'Umar[ra] started to look for a suitable match for her. Ḥaḍrat 'Umar[ra] first asked Ḥaḍrat Abū Bakr[ra] to marry Ḥaḍrat Ḥafṣah[ra]. However, Abū Bakr[ra] refused. Then, Ḥaḍrat 'Umar[ra] asked Ḥaḍrat 'Uthmān[ra] to marry his daughter, Ḥafṣah[ra]. Ḥaḍrat 'Uthmān[ra] also excused himself. Ḥaḍrat 'Umar[ra] felt sadness due to these refusals. He went to the Holy Prophet[sa] and complained about the refusal by Ḥaḍrat Abū Bakr[ra] and Ḥaḍrat 'Uthmān[ra] to marry his daughter. The Holy Prophet[sa] had earlier mentioned to Ḥaḍrat Abū Bakr[ra] about his intention to marry Ḥaḍrat Ḥafṣah[ra]. This was the reason that Ḥaḍrat Abū Bakr[ra] had refused to marry Ḥaḍrat Ḥafṣah[ra]. The Holy Prophet[sa] himself sent the message to Ḥaḍrat 'Umar[ra] to marry Ḥaḍrat Ḥafṣah[ra]. Ḥaḍrat 'Umar[ra] happily agreed to the proposal and the marriage of Ḥaḍrat Ḥafṣah[ra] to the Holy Prophet[sa] took place in the month of *Sha'bān*, 3 AH (i.e., February 625). Ḥaḍrat Ḥafṣah[ra] being the daughter of Ḥaḍrat 'Umar[ra] had high status amongst the wives of the Holy Prophet[sa]. Ḥaḍrat Ḥafṣah[ra] could read and write which she had learned from Ḥaḍrat Shifā' bint 'Abdullāh. She possessed a copy of the Holy Qur'ān. She had the opportunity to perform *Ḥajj* in the company of the Holy Prophet[sa]. She passed away in 45 AH at the age of 63 years. There are 60 *Aḥādīth* in the book of the *Aḥādīth* which were related by Ḥaḍrat Ḥafṣah[ra].

5. Ḥaḍrat Zainab bint Khuzaimah[ra]

Ḥaḍrat Zainab[ra] was first married to Ḥaḍrat Ṭufail[ra]. When Ḥaḍrat Ṭufail[ra] divorced her, she was married to Ḥaḍrat 'Ubaidah[ra] who was the brother of Ḥaḍrat Ṭufail[ra]. Ḥaḍrat 'Ubaidah[ra] was martyred in the Battle of *Badr.* She married a third time with Ḥaḍrat 'Abdullāh bin Jaḥsh[ra] who was martyred in the Battle of Uḥud. Thus, Ḥaḍrat Zainab[ra] had lost her husbands one after the other in two battles. This gave her a unique status due to which the Holy Prophet[sa] sent the message to marry her which she accepted. She was married to the Holy Prophet[sa] in *Ṣafr*, 4 AH (i.e., July 625) at the age of 30 years. However, she passed away just a couple of months after the marriage in *Rabī 'ul Ākhir*, 4 AH. She was buried in the *Jannatul Baqī'* graveyard. Due to her passion for serving the poor she was often called as the "*Ummul Masākīn*".

6. Ḥaḍrat Ummi Salamah[ra]

In the early days of Islām when the *Quraish* were persecuting Muslims in Mecca, Ḥaḍrat Ummi Salamah[ra] bint Abī Umayyah[ra] with her husband, 'Abdullāh ibn 'Abdul Asad, and their son migrated to Medina. However, on the way to Medina Ummi Salamah's[ra] tribe stopped them and refused to let Ḥaḍrat Ummi Salamah[ra] go with her husband. Thus, her husband left for Medina with his son without her. She was really saddened and for a year she would sit in front of her house and cry remembering her husband and son whom she missed so much. Ultimately, someone from her tribe took pity upon her and convinced the tribe's people to let her go to her husband. So she was united with her family in Medina and there she gave birth to three more children and then her husband was martyred in the Battle of Uḥud. After a few months of her becoming a widow, Ḥaḍrat Abū Bakr[ra] sent a message to marry her. However, she politely refused. Then,

Ḥaḍrat 'Umar[ra] asked her to marry him. Again she refused to marry. She had four children (Salamah, 'Umar, Zainab and Durra) and no assets or income to support them. Under these circumstances, the Holy Prophet[sa] sent her a message to marry her. Initially, she was reluctant. However, later on she agreed to marry the Holy Prophet[sa]. This marriage became an excellent example for the Muslims of marrying widows with children.

With respect to age, Ḥaḍrat Ummi Salamah[ra] was the oldest of the wives of the Holy Prophet[sa]. Probably, this was the reason that the Holy Prophet[sa] in his daily routine of visiting his wives after the *'Aṣr* Prayer used to visit first Ḥaḍrat Ummi Salamah[ra] and at the last Ḥaḍrat 'Ā'ishah[ra], and then he would go to the quarter of the wife whose turn was on that day.

Ḥaḍrat Ummi Salamah[ra] was always seeking blessings from the Holy Prophet[sa]. One such an incident is mentioned in one of the traditions which is as follows:

Ḥaḍrat Abū Mūsā narrates, "I and Ḥaḍrat Bilāl were with the Holy Prophet[sa] when he was encamping at Ji'rānah (a place between Mecca and Medina) during the Battle of *Ṭā'if.* A Bedouin came to the Holy Prophet[sa] and said, 'Won't you fulfill what you have promised me?' The Holy Prophet[sa] said, 'Rejoice.' The Bedouin said, 'You have said to me 'rejoice' too many times.' Then the Holy Prophet[sa] turned to me and Bilāl and said, "The Bedouin has refused the good tidings, so you both accept them.' Bilāl and I said, 'We accept them.' Then the Holy Prophet[sa] asked for a bowl of water and washed his hands and face in it. Then he took a mouthful of water and spit it back into the bowl and said, 'Drink of it and pour on your faces and chests and be happy at the good tidings.' So they both did as instructed by the Holy Prophet[sa]. Ḥaḍrat Ummi Salamah[ra] who was seeing all this from behind a curtain called and said, 'Keep some blessed water for your mother.' So they left some water for her."

(Ṣaḥīḥ Bukhārī, Kitābul Maghāzī, Ghazwah Ṭā'if)

Ḥaḍrat Ummi Salamah[ra] died at the age of eighty-four. She was the last one to die amongst the wives of the Holy Prophet[sa]. She had migrated to Abyssinia and also to Medina. She could read and thus played a major role in the education and moral training of the Muslim women. There are 349 *Aḥādīth* in the books of the *Aḥādīth* which are related by Ḥaḍrat Ummi Salamah[ra]. She had the opportunity to travel with the Holy Prophet[sa] during the battles of *Aḥzāb*, *Ḥudaibiyyah*, *Khaibar*, *Wādī al-Qurā*, *Fadak*, the Conquest of Mecca, *Ḥunain*, *Auṭās* and *Ṭā'if*. In this regard she had superiority over all other wives of the Holy Prophet[sa]. Furthermore, she also had the opportunity to perform *Ḥajj* in the company of the Holy Prophet[sa].

7. Ḥaḍrat Zainab bint Jaḥsh[ra]

Ḥaḍrat Zainab bint Jaḥsh[ra] was a cousin of the Holy Prophet[sa]. Ḥaḍrat Zaid[ra] was a slave of Ḥaḍrat Khadījah[ra] who had given Ḥaḍrat Zaid[ra] to the Holy Prophet[sa]. The Holy Prophet[sa] had freed him and had raised him as a son. The Holy Prophet[sa] thought that Ḥaḍrat Zainab[ra] would be a good match for Ḥaḍrat Zaid[ra]. Furthermore, the marriage of an ex-slave with a woman belonging to a noble family would set a good example of marriage based on qualities other than the nobility or wealth of a person. The family of Ḥaḍrat Zainab[ra] was shocked at the proposal and refused to marry Ḥaḍrat Zainab[ra] with Ḥaḍrat Zaid[ra]. At that time, this verse of the Holy Qur'ān was revealed:

وَمَا كَانَ لِمُؤْمِنٍ وَّ لَا مُؤْمِنَةٍ اِذَا قَضَى اللّٰهُ وَرَسُوْلُهٗۤ اَمْرًا اَنْ يَّكُوْنَ
لَهُمُ الْخِيَرَةُ مِنْ اَمْرِهِمْ ؕ وَمَنْ يَّعْصِ اللّٰهَ وَرَسُوْلَهٗ فَقَدْ ضَلَّ ضَلٰلًا
مُّبِيْنًا ۟

wa mā kāna li mu'miniñwwa lā mu'minatin idhā qaḍallāhu wa rasūluhū amran añyyakūna lahumul khiyaratu min amrihim wa mañyya'ṣillāha wa rasūlahū faqad ḍalla ḍalālammubīnā

And it behooves not a believing man or a believing woman, when Allāh and His Messenger have decided a matter, that there should be a choice for them in the matter concerning them. And whoso disobeys Allāh and His Messenger, surely strays away in manifest error. (33:37)

Thus, the family of Ḥaḍrat Zainab[ra] agreed to marry their daughter with Ḥaḍrat Zaid[ra]. However, the marriage had problems and was not a happy marriage. Ḥaḍrat Zaid[ra] was patient for a long time but the situation did not change. Ultimately, Ḥaḍrat Zaid[ra] divorced Ḥaḍrat Zainab[ra]. In those days it was a custom to free a slave and adopt him as a son. The adopted son was given the family name and he was eligible for inheritance as their own sons. Similarly, they considered marriage to an adopted son's wife forbidden as it was to the wife of their blood-related son. However, an adopted son was not like a blood-related son in the sight of Allāh.

When Ḥaḍrat Zaid[ra] divorced Hadrat Zainab[ra], the Holy Prophet[sa] was commanded by Allāh to marry Ḥaḍrat Zainab[ra]. The underlying reason for this marriage was to establish that an adopted son is not like a blood-related son. Because of the long-established tradition of accepting an adopted son as a blood-related son among the Arabs, it was difficult for them to understand this new order that the adopted son is not the same as a blood-related son. Their reservation changed with the revelation of the following verse of the Holy Qur'ān:

وَ اِذْ تَقُوْلُ لِلَّذِيْٓ اَنْعَمَ اللّٰهُ عَلَيْهِ وَ اَنْعَمْتَ عَلَيْهِ اَمْسِكْ عَلَيْكَ زَوْجَكَ
وَ اتَّقِ اللّٰهَ وَ تُخْفِيْ فِيْ نَفْسِكَ مَا اللّٰهُ مُبْدِيْهِ وَتَخْشَى النَّاسَ ۚ وَ اللّٰهُ
اَحَقُّ اَنْ تَخْشٰىهُ ؕ فَلَمَّا قَضٰى زَيْدٌ مِّنْهَا وَطَرًا زَوَّجْنٰكَهَا لِكَيْ لَا يَكُوْنَ

عَلَى الْمُؤْمِنِيْنَ حَرَجٌ فِيٓ اَزْوَاجِ اَدْعِيَآئِهِمْ اِذَا قَضَوْا مِنْهُنَّ وَطَرًا ط
وَكَانَ اَمْرُ اللّٰهِ مَفْعُوْلًا ۝

wa idh taqūlu lilladhī an'amallāhu 'alaihi wa an'amta 'alaihi amsik 'alaika zaujaka wattaqillāha wa tukhfī fī nafsika mallāhu mubdīhi wa takhshannāsa wallāhu aḥaqqu an takhshāhu fa lammā qaḍā zaidumminhā waṭaran zawwajnākahā likai lā yakūna 'alal mu'minīna ḥarajun fī azwāji ad'iyā'ihim idhā qaḍau minhunna waṭaran wa kāna amrullāhi maf'ūlā

And *remember* when you did say to him on whom Allāh had bestowed favors and on whom you *also* had bestowed favors: 'Keep your wife to yourself, and fear Allāh.' And you did conceal in your heart what Allāh was going to bring to light, and you were afraid of the people, whereas Allāh has better right that you should fear Him. Then, when Zaid had accomplished his want of her s*o as to have no further need of her,* We joined her in marriage to you, so that there may be no hindrance for the believers with regard to the wives of their adopted sons, when they have accomplished their want of them. And Allāh's decree must be fulfilled. (33:38)

Accordingly, the Holy Prophet[sa] obeyed the commandment of Allāh and married Ḥaḍrat Zainab[ra]. The marriage took place sometime before the Battle of Muṣṭaliq either in *Jamādī aththānī* or in *Rajab,* 5 AH (i.e., 626 AD). Ḥaḍrat Zainab[ra] was a cousin of the Holy Prophet[sa]. Her brother, Ḥaḍrat Abū Aḥmad bin Jaḥsh acted as her guardian at the *Nikāh* Ceremony. The *Ḥaq Mahr* was fixed as 400 *Dirhams.* On the second or the third day of the wedding the *Walīma* was held. Due to the special significance of this marriage the *Walīma* function was rather elaborate. At the time of the marriage Ḥaḍrat Zainab[ra] was 37 years old. She was a very charitable woman. She was expert in sewing clothes. She used to sew the clothes and distribute these among the poor. The Holy Prophet[sa] once said about her that she was the mother of the charitable. Once the Holy Prophet[sa] said to his wives:

اَسْرَعُكُنَّ لَحَاقًا بِی اَطْوَلُکُنَّ یَدًا

asra'u kunna laḥāqan bi aṭwalukunna yadan

(In the hereafter) the one (amongst you) who will meet me the first is the one who has longest hands

(Ṣaḥīḥ Muslim, Kitāb Al-Faḍā'il Aṣ-Ṣaḥābah, Bāb faḍā'il Zainab Ummil Mu'minīn[ra])

Ḥaḍrat 'Ā'ishah[ra] states that upon hearing this saying of the Holy Prophet[sa] all the wives of the Holy Prophet[sa] started measuring the length of their hands by placing a hand on a wall. Ḥaḍrat Saudah[ra] had the longest hands. However, Ḥaḍrat Zainab[ra] was the one who passed away before the other wives of the Holy Prophet[sa]. Then we realized that what was meant by having the longest hands in the saying of the Holy Prophet[sa] was that the one who is the most charitable.

(Ṣaḥīḥ Bukhārī, Kitābuz Zakāt, Bāb ayyu ṣadqatu afḍal)

During his *Khilāfat*, Ḥaḍrat 'Umar[ra] sent a pile of gold to Ḥaḍrat Zainab[ra] which was her share of the gold which fell into their hands as war booty when the Persians were defeated by the Muslims. Ḥaḍrat Zainab[ra] told her maid to call the poor of Medina and distribute the gold among them. When all of the gold was distributed, Ḥaḍrat Zainab[ra] asked her maid to remove the cover from another pile. When she removed the cover there were eighty *Dinārs*. Ḥaḍrat Zainab[ra] accepted the *Dinars* as her share and thanked God Almighty.

Ḥaḍrat Zainab[ra] was a very broadminded, pious and honest woman.

Although she had some personal differences with Ḥaḍrat 'Ā'ishah, when the Holy Prophet[sa] asked Ḥaḍrat Zainab[ra] for her observation about the incident of slander against Ḥaḍrat 'Ā'ishah by the hypocrites, she said it is nothing but clearly a slander against Ḥaḍrat 'Ā'ishah[ra].

Ḥaḍrat Zainab[ra] passed away in 20 AH at the age of 52 years in Medina. She travelled along with the Holy Prophet[sa] during the Conquest of Mecca and Battles of *Ḥunain*, *Auṭās* and *Ṭā'if.* She also had the honor of performing *Ḥajj* with the Holy Prophet[sa].

8. Ḥaḍrat Juwairiyyah[ra]

The tribe of *Banū Muṣṭaliq* was preparing to attack the Muslims. When the Muslims came to know of their preparations to attack them, they attacked first and defeated the enemy. Ḥaḍrat Juwairiyyah bint al-Ḥārith[ra] belonged to the tribe of *Banū Muṣṭaliq* and was one of the prisoners captured in the Battle of Muṣṭaliq. The prisoners were brought to Medina and were distributed among the Muslims. During the division of the prisoners, an *Anṣār*, Ḥaḍrat Thābit bin Qais[ra] was given custody of her. Her name was Barrah. Barrah made an agreement with Ḥaḍrat Thābit bin Qais[ra] about her freedom based on the principle of '*Mukātbat*'. That is, if she paid him such an amount as ransom she would become a free woman. She was worried that she will be used to collect a large amount of ransom from her father. She went to see the Holy Prophet[sa] and talked with him about her dilemma. She told the Holy Prophet[sa] that she is the daughter of a chief of *Banū Muṣṭaliq* and she needs assistance with the payment of her freedom money. The Holy Prophet[sa] understood the problem and wanted to save her and her tribe from further difficulties. The Holy Prophet[sa] thought that the marriage with her would open the ways for spreading the message of Islām to her tribe's people. Therefore, he decided to pay the ransom for her freedom and to marry her. The Holy Prophet[sa] sent her the proposal for marriage which she wholeheartedly accepted. The Holy Prophet[sa] changed her name from Barrah to Juwairiyyah. The marriage took place in *Sha'bān*, 5 AH. (i.e., December, 626). At the time of her marriage Ḥaḍrat Juwairiyyah[ra] was 25 years old. After marrying Ḥaḍrat Juwairiyyah[ra], the Holy Prophet[sa] felt it against the status of a Prophet[sa] that his in-laws were his prisoners. Accordingly, the Holy Prophet[sa] freed hundreds of prisoners without collecting any ransom and all the war booty collected from *Banū Muṣṭaliq* was returned.

(As-Sīratun Nabawiyyah libne Hishām, Vol. 3, p.295)

This had a positive effect upon the *Banū Muṣṭaliq* tribe. Ḥaḍrat 'Ā'ishah[ra] used to say that Ḥaḍrat Juwairiyyah[ra] turned out to be a very blessed person for her tribe. This openheartedness of the Holy Prophet[sa] won the hearts and minds of the people of the *Banū Muṣṭaliq* tribe and they soon accepted Islām. Ḥaḍrat Juwairiyyah[ra] had the honor of performing *Ḥajj* in the company of the Holy Prophet[sa]. Ḥaḍrat Juwairiyyah[ra] was 70 years old when she passed away in *Rabī'ul Awwal*, 50 AH. According to one tradition she passed away at the age of 75 years in 56 AH. There are seven *Aḥādīth* attributed to Ḥaḍrat Juwairiyyah[ra] in the various books of the *Aḥādīth.*

According to one tradition, the father of Ḥaḍrat Juwairiyyah[ra] came to the Holy Prophet[sa] to request the freedom of his daughter. Staying in the company of the Holy Prophet[sa] he accepted Islām and then he married his daughter willingly to the Holy Prophet[sa]. According to another tradition when Ḥārith, the father of Ḥaḍrat Juwairiyyah[ra], came to see the Holy Prophet[sa] he said to the Holy Prophet[sa] that he is a leader of a tribe as such his daughter could not be kept as a prisoner. The Holy Prophet[sa] told him that Ḥaḍrat Juwairiyyah[ra] should be asked for her opinion. If she would like to get freedom and go home we would let her go. However, if she decides to stay with us then she can stay with us. When Ḥaḍrat Juwairiyyah[sa] was asked for her opinion, she preferred to become a Muslim and stay in the company of the Holy Prophet[sa]. Accordingly, the Holy Prophet[sa] freed her and then married her.

9. Ḥaḍrat Ṣafiyyah[ra]

Ḥaḍrat Ṣafiyyah[ra] was the daughter of Ḥuyyay ibn Akhṭab, the chief of the *Banū Naḍīr* tribe. She was brought to the Holy Prophet[sa] as a captive after the Battle of Khaibar in which the Muslims had defeated the Jews. At the time of the distribution of the prisoners of war she was allotted to Ḥaḍrat Diḥyah Kalbī[ra]. One of the Companions[ra] of the Holy Prophet[sa] mentioned to the Holy Prophet[sa] that Ḥaḍrat Ṣafiyyah[ra] who had been given to Ḥaḍrat Diḥyah Kalbī[ra] is a princess of *Banū Naḍīr* and *Banū Quraiẓa.* She deserves none other than you. Accordingly, the Holy Prophet[sa] sent the message to Ḥaḍrat Diḥyah Kalbī[ra] regarding his decision to marry Ḥaḍrat Ṣafiyyah[ra]. Hadrat Diḥyah Kalbī[ra] sent Ḥaḍrat Ṣafiyyah[ra] to the Holy Prophet[sa]. The Holy Prophet[sa] treated her with respect and told her that if she would like to stick to her religion there would not be any pressure put on her to change her decision. However, if she accepts Islām it will be a blessing for her. Ḥaḍrat Ṣafiyyah[ra] accepted Islām as her religion. At this, the Holy Prophet[sa] freed her and gave her the option that either she can become his wife or go back to her family. Ḥaḍrat Ṣafiyyah[ra] preferred to marry the Holy Prophet[sa]. Accordingly, the Holy Prophet[sa] married her and her freedom was considered as her *Ḥaq Mehr.* The marriage took place in *Ṣafr*, 7 AH (i.e., June, 628). At the time of her marriage, Ḥaḍrat Ṣafiyyah[ra] was 17 years old. When Ḥaḍrat Ṣafiyyah[ra] agreed to marry the Holy Prophet[sa], the Companions[ra] of the Holy Prophet[sa] were keen to see whether she observed *Purdah* or not. If she observed *Purdah* that meant she is the

Mother of the Faithful. The Holy Prophet[sa] made her observe *Purdah* from which everyone came to know that she had become the Mother of the Faithful. On the third day after returning from Khaibar when the Holy Prophet[sa] along with his Companions[ra] reached a place called *Sahbā*, proper arrangements were made for the wedding ceremony. Ḥaḍrat Umm Sulaim[ra], the mother of Ḥaḍrat Anas bin Mālik[ra] prepared Ḥaḍrat Ṣafiyyah[ra] as a bride and the wedding took place. The next day, the Holy Prophet[sa] told Ḥaḍrat Bilāl[ra] to spread the tablecloth. Dates, cheese and butter were placed on the tablecloth which everyone ate together. This was the *Walīma* ceremony. There was no bread or meat served in this function.

Being the daughter of a great chief, the only way she could avoid being a slave was to marry the Holy Prophet[sa]. Her father Ḥuyyay Ibn Akhṭab was a staunch enemy of the Holy Prophet[sa] and was determined to destroy Islām. However, Ḥaḍrat Ṣafiyyah[ra] accepted Islām and became the wife of the Holy Prophet[sa]. Ḥaḍrat Ṣafiyyah[ra] had difficulty adjusting as wife of the Holy Prophet[sa] because the other wives of the Holy Prophet[sa] belonged to the *Quraish* and other Arab tribes and they considered themselves better than Ḥaḍrat Ṣafiyyah[ra] who came from a Jewish family. She was so annoyed with the attitude of the other wives of the Holy Prophet[sa] that she could not bear it any more. So she complained to the Holy Prophet[sa] while her eyes were overflowing with tears. The Holy Prophet[sa] told her to tell his other wives who annoy her that she is better than them as the Holy Prophet[sa] is her husband, Moses[as] is her great granduncle and Aaron[as] is her great grandfather. This made her happy and after this talk with the Holy Prophet[sa] she never felt inferior to anyone of the wives of the Holy Prophet[sa].

(Jāmi' Tirmidhī, Abwābul Manāqib Fī Faḍli Azwājin Nabiyyi[sa])

Ḥaḍrat Ṣafiyyah[ra] was a widow of Kinānah ibn al-Rabī', a Chief of Khaibar who was killed in the siege of Khaibar, when she was married to the Holy Prophet[sa]. The Holy Prophet[sa] saw that Ḥaḍrat Ṣafiyyah[ra] had a mark on her face which appeared to be an impression of a hand. The Holy Prophet[sa] asked Ḥaḍrat Ṣafiyyah[ra] about the mark on her face. Ḥaḍrat Ṣafiyyah[ra] stated the following:

"I saw the moon fall in my lap in a dream. I related the dream to my husband. No sooner had I related the dream than my husband gave a heavy slap on my face and said, 'You desire to marry the king of Arabia'"

The moon was the national emblem of Arabia. The moon in the lap denoted some intimate connection with the king of Arabia.

(Life of Muḥammad[sa], Ḥaḍrat Mirzā Bashīruddīn Maḥmūd Aḥmad, p. 125)

Ḥaḍrat Ṣafiyyah[ra] passed away in the month of *Ramaḍān*, 50 AH. At the time of her demise she was 60 years old. During the travel from Khaibar to Medina she accompanied the Holy Prophet[sa]. She also had the opportunity to perform *Ḥajj* along with the Holy Prophet[sa]. There are ten *Aḥādīth* in the books of the *Aḥādīth* which have been related by Ḥaḍrat Ṣafiyyah[ra].

When the Holy Prophet[sa] became seriously ill, Ḥaḍrat Ṣafiyyah[ra] along with the other wives of the Holy Prophet[sa] was with the Holy Prophet[sa]. Seeing the Holy Prophet[sa] in such a condition, Ḥaḍrat Ṣafiyyah[ra] said, "I wish that the Holy Prophet[sa] becomes completely healthy and I get his disease." Hearing this, the other wives looked at each other. At this, the Holy Prophet[sa] said:

وَاللّٰهِ اِنَّهَا لَصَادِقَةٌ

wallāhi innahā laṣādiqatun

By Allāh! She is truthful.

An Interesting Episode

Ḥaḍrat Ṣafiyyah bint Ḥuyyay[ra], the Mother of the Faithful relates: "The Holy Prophet[sa] was in retreat in the mosque, and I went there to see him one evening. After finishing talking with me he stood up to accompany me a part of the way. Two men passed by us and when they saw the Holy Prophet[sa] they quickened their pace. The Holy Prophet[sa] called out to them: 'Stop a moment. This is my wife, Ṣafiyyah bint Ḥuyyay.' They expostulated: 'Holy is Allāh, Messenger[sa] of Allāh.' The Holy Prophet[sa] observed: 'Satan courses through a man's mind like the circulation of the blood, and I apprehended lest Satan might create suspicion in your minds.' Or he said something similar to it.' "

(Ṣaḥīḥ Bukhārī, Kitābul I'tikāf, Bāb hal yakhrujul mu'takif li ḥawā'ijih, p 272/1, Ṣaḥīḥ Muslim, p 202/9)

10. Ḥaḍrat Ummi Ḥabībah[ra]

Ḥaḍrat Ummi Ḥabībah[ra] was the daughter of Hadrat Abū Sufyān[ra] who at one time was a staunch enemy of the Holy Prophet[sa] and had fought against the Muslims in many battles. Her actual name was Ramla bint Abū Sufyān. She had accepted Islām along with her husband, 'Ubaidullāh ibn Jaḥsh[ra]. 'Ubaidullāh ibn Jaḥsh[ra] was the brother of Ḥaḍrat Zainab[ra], the wife of the Holy Prophet[sa]. Both had migrated to Abyssinia where their daughter Ḥabībah was born. After the birth of Ḥabībah she became known as Ummi Ḥabībah. In Abyssinia her husband embraced Christianity. He tried to persuade her to do the same. However, she held on to Islām. She found herself in a terrible situation. She did not want to stay with her husband and could not go to her father who was an arch enemy of the Holy Prophet[sa]. She separated from her husband and lived with her daughter under miserable conditions. However, she remained a staunch Muslim. Allāh rewarded her for her steadfastness in Islām.

When the Holy Prophet[sa] sent a message to king Negus through 'Amr bin Umayyah al-Zumar asking him to let the immigrants return. He also asked the king to perform his *Nikāh* with Ḥaḍrat Ummi Ḥabībah[ra]. Upon receiving this message the king started to make preparations for the marriage. One day a maid of Negus, the king of Abyssinia, brought to her a message from the king. The message was that the Holy Prophet[sa] would like to marry her. Ḥaḍrat Ummi Ḥabībah[ra] was overjoyed to receive the marriage proposal. She accepted the proposal and in happiness gave her silver bangles and rings as a gift to the maid. The king prepared the dowry for Ḥaḍrat Ummi Ḥabībah[ra] and asked her to appoint someone as her guardian. She appointed Ḥaḍrat Khālid ibn Sa'īd ibn al-'Ās[ra] as her guardian. It was the Will of God that she was chosen to be the wife of the Holy Prophet[sa]. The marriage ceremony took place in Abyssinia even though the Holy Prophet[sa] was not present there. The king invited Ḥaḍrat Ja'far[ra] and other Muslims present in Abyssinia for the *Nikāh* ceremony and he himself delivered the *Khuṭbah Nikāh*. Ḥaḍrat Khālid ibn Sa'īd[ra] made a speech in reply to the king's sermon. On behalf of the Holy Prophet[sa], Negus offered a dowry of four hundred *Dinars* to Ḥaḍrat Ummi Ḥabībah[ra]. It was a large sum of money which she badly needed at that time. A huge wedding feast was prepared on behalf of the Holy Prophet[sa] after the ceremony. The *Nikāh* ceremony was held in the month of *Muḥarram*, 7 AH (i.e., May 628).

In those days, it was difficult for the Muslims to travel from Abyssinia to Medina. Therefore, Ḥaḍrat Ummi Ḥabībah[ra] lived in Abyssinia for six years and when the situation changed and the Muslims were able to return from Abyssinia to Medina she went back to Medina and lived with the Holy Prophet[sa]. It was Negus who made the arrangements to send her to Medina by boat under the supervision of Shurāḥbīl bin Ḥasana. When Ḥaḍrat Ummi Ḥabībah[ra] arrived in Medina from Abyssinia she was thirty years old.

Ḥaḍrat Ummi Ḥabībah[ra] had such a high degree of honor for the Holy Prophet[sa] that she would not mind sacrificing her love for her father for the sake of the Holy Prophet[sa]. Once, Abū Sufyān came to Medina to see the Holy Prophet[sa] to get the time period of the *Ḥudaibiyyah* Pact extended. At first, he went to the house of his daughter, Ḥaḍrat Ummi Ḥabībah[ra]. There, when he was about to sit at the bed of the Holy Prophet[sa], Ḥaḍrat Ummi Ḥabībah[ra] immediately folded the bed. Abū Sufyān realized that something is wrong. So he asked Ḥaḍrat Ummi Ḥabībah[ra], "Does the bed not deserve me or do I not deserve the bed?" Ḥaḍrat Ummi Ḥabībah[ra] told him that the bed belongs to the Holy Prophet[sa] and he being a disbeliever and impure person does not deserve to sit on this bed.

Ḥaḍrat Zainab bint Abī Salmah[ra] relates: "I visited Ḥaḍrat Ummi Ḥabībah[ra], wife of the Holy Prophet[sa] when her father Abū Sufyān had died. She sent for a yellow perfume and rubbed it on one of her maids and then rubbed it on both her own cheeks and said: "I had no desire for perfume except that I heard the Holy Prophet[sa] say from the pulpit: 'It is not permissible for a woman who believes in Allāh and the Last Day that she should mourn a dead person for more than three days except in the case of her husband when the period of mourning is four months and ten days.' Zainab then continued, 'I then visited Zainab bint Jaḥsh when her brother died and she sent for perfume and rubbed some of it on herself and said, 'I have no need for perfume except that I heard the Holy Prophet[sa] say from the pulpit: 'It is not permissible for a woman who believes in Allāh and the Last Day that she should mourn a dead person for more than three days except in the case of her husband when the period is four months and ten days.' "

(Ṣaḥīḥ Bukhārī, Kitābul Janā'iz, Bāb aḥadādal mirāta 'ala ghairi zaujihā)

Ḥaḍrat 'Ā'ishah[ra] relates that when Ḥaḍrat Ummi Ḥabībah[ra] was close to her last days, she called me and said, "During our lives once in a while it happened that I did or said things which were unpleasant to you, I apologize for that. Please forgive me." I prayed for her that may God Almighty ignore her shortcomings and forgive her. Then, Ḥaḍrat Ummi Ḥabībah[ra] said, 'You have made me happy, may God Almighty keep you also happy.' Then Ḥaḍrat 'Ā'ishah[ra] called Ḥaḍrat Ummi Salmah[ra] and said the same which she had said to me.' "

Ḥaḍrat Ummi Ḥabībah[ra] passed away in 44 AH in Medina. At the time of her death she was 67 years old. She had the honor of performing *Ḥajj* in the company of the Holy Prophet[sa]. She had related 65 *Aḥādīth.*

11. Ḥaḍrat Mariah al-Qibṭiyyah[ra]

Ḥaḍrat Mariah al-Qibṭiyyah[ra] belonged to Egypt and had started serving in the palace of Muqawqis, the ruler of Egypt, at a very young age. When the Holy Prophet[sa] wrote a letter to Muqawqis and sent it to him through his messenger, Ḥāṭib bin Abī Balta'ah, inviting him to accept Islām, Mauqawqis treated the letter with great respect. He put it in an ivory box and kept it in a safe place. He asked the messenger of the Holy Prophet[sa] to tell him in detail about the Holy Prophet[sa]. After the conversation he said to the carrier of the message of the Holy Prophet[sa], "I was expecting the appearance of a Prophet[sa]. However, I was expecting the Prophet[sa] to come from Syria. My people are Coptic Christians who, I think, will not accept the new Messenger. I also hate to give up my kingdom for the sake of the Messenger[sa]." As a symbol of his great respect for the Holy Prophet[sa], Muqawqis sent back a letter, many precious presents such as a special kind of honey, one thousand *Mithqāl* gold, 20 pieces of a special kind of soft cloth and two sisters, Mariah and Sīrīn to the Holy Prophet[sa]. He also sent a sturdy donkey of gray color which was named as "*Duldul*" and a donkey, named " *'Afīr*". He wrote a letter to the Holy Prophet[sa] in which he had stated that the girls who are being sent to the Holy Prophet are sisters and have high status among the Coptic Christians. The sisters arrived in Medina in 7 AH (628 AD). On the way from Egypt to Medina Ḥaḍrat Ḥāṭib bin Abī Balta'ah[ra] preached to the girls about Islām. Both of the girls accepted Islām before reaching Medina. An old man by the name of Maboar who was accompanying the two girls did not accept Islām during the travel to Medina. However, on arrival in Medina, after some time, he also accepted Islām. On arrival in Medina both sisters along with the king's letter and the gifts were presented to the Holy Prophet[sa]. The Holy Prophet[sa] married Ḥaḍrat Mariah al-Qibṭiyyah[ra] and Ḥaḍrat Ḥassān bin Thābit[ra] married Sīrīn. Ḥaḍrat 'Ā'ishah[ra] relates that in the beginning the Holy Prophet[sa] kept Ḥaḍrat Mariah[ra] in the house of Ḥartha bin al-'Amān and then later on he moved her to another place in Medina which was known as *Al-'Aliya.* Till her last days Ḥaḍrat Mariah[ra] lived there. In *Dhul Hijja*, 8 AH (i.e., March 630) a son was born to Ḥaḍrat Mariah[ra] whom the Holy Prophet[sa] had named, 'Ibrāhīm'. The Holy Prophet[sa] was very happy at the birth of a son as all his earlier sons had died in infancy. Ḥaḍrat Ibrāhīm lived for 15 to 16 months and passed away in *Rabīul Awwal*, 10 AH. The Holy Prophet[sa] upon his demise stated,

لَوْ عَاشَ لَكَانَ صِدِّيْقًا نَّبِيًّا

lau 'āsha lakāna siddīqannabiyyan

If he had lived, he would have been a Truthful Prophet.

The tradition relating to it is as follows:

Ḥaḍrat Ibn 'Abbās[ra] relates that when Ḥaḍrat Ibrāhīm[ra], the son of the Holy Prophet[sa] died, the Holy Prophet[sa] led his funeral Prayer and said: "If my son, Ibrāhīm had lived, he would have been a *Siddīq* (Truthful) Prophet, and his maternal grand-parents' family, who are Coptic Egyptians, would have been liberated from bondage."

(Sunan Ibni Mājah, Kitābul Janā'iz, Bāb mā jā' fiṣṣalāta 'alā ibn rasūlullāh wa dhikr wafātih, p 237/1 Maṭba' 'Ilmiyyah 1313 H)

Ḥaḍrat Mariah[ra] passed away in 16 AH during the *Khilāfat* of Ḥaḍrat 'Umar[ra].

12. Ḥaḍrat Maimūnah[ra]

Ḥaḍrat Maimūnah[ra] who was daughter of Ḥārith and Hind was first married to Mas'ūd bin 'Umair Thaqfī. When Mas'ūd bin 'Umair divorced her, she married Abū Ruham bin 'Abdul 'Uzza. After the death of Abū Ruham she lived for some time as a widow. Ḥaḍrat 'Abbās[ra] who was the brother-in-law of Ḥaḍrat Maimūnah[ra] was concerned about her marriage. He conveyed his concerns to the Holy Prophet[sa]. Thus, the Holy Prophet[sa] married Ḥaḍrat Maimūnah[ra] at the suggestion of Ḥaḍrat 'Abbās[ra]. Ḥaḍrat 'Abbās[ra] made the announcement of Ḥaḍrat Maimūnah's[ra] *Nikāh* with the Holy Prophet[sa] with a *Ḥaq Mahr* of 400 *Dirhams.* The marriage took place in *Dhul Qa'da*, 7 AH (i.e., March 629). At that time she was 36 years old. Before her marriage with the Holy Prophet[sa] her name was Barrah. The Holy Prophet[sa] changed her name to Maimūnah just like he had changed the name of Ḥaḍrat Juwairiyyah[ra]. Ḥaḍrat Maimūnah[ra] was the real sister of Ḥaḍrat Ummul Faḍl[ra], the wife of Hadrat 'Abbas[ra] who was the uncle of the Holy Prophet[sa]. Ḥaḍrat Maimūnah[ra] who was the last one to become the Mother of the Faithful passed away in 51 AH. At the time of her demise she was 80 years old. Although, her *Nikāh* ceremony took place in Medina, her wedding took place at a place called, *'Sarif*. Ḥaḍrat Maimūnah[ra] before her demise had picked '*Sarif* for her burial. Accordingly, in 51 AH, she was buried at '*Sarif* which is 7 miles from Mecca and close to *Tan'īm.* She had the honor of performing *Ḥajj* in the company of the Holy Prophet[sa]. There are 67 *Aḥādīth* which were narrated by her.

22

Life of the Wives of the Holy Prophet[sa]

The Holy Prophet[sa] states about the good treatment of the family:

خَيْرُكُمْ خَيْرُكُمْ لِأَهْلِهِ وَأَنَا خَيْرُكُمْ لِأَهْلِي

khairukum khairukum li ahlihī wa anā khairukum li ahlī

The best amongst you is the one who is best in treatment of his family and I am better than all of you in treatment of the family.

(Jāmi' Tirmidhī, Abwābul Manāqib, Bāb faḍl az azwājunnabī[sa])

It was the routine of the Holy Prophet[sa] that he would visit his wives daily in their quarters and then he would go to the quarter of the wife where he was to stay for the night. In the evening all the wives would get together in the quarter of the wife of the Holy Prophet[sa] where he was staying and after socializing for some time they would go back to their own houses.

The Holy Prophet[sa] used to take good care of his wives and their sensibilities. However, their lives were very simple as was the life of the Holy Prophet[sa]. Most of them belonged to well-to-do familes.

Separation of the Holy Prophet[sa] from his Wives for One Month

In 9 AH, the Holy Prophet[sa] isolated himself from all his wives and started to live in a cabin which was located above the quarter of Ḥaḍrat 'Ā'ishah[ra]. He stayed there for one month. It is stated that the cause of this separation was that the Holy Prophet[sa] was annoyed when he learned about the desires of his wives to raise their standard of living. The wives of the Holy Prophet[sa] were living a simple life like the Holy Prophet[sa]. However, when the Muslims became prosperous after receiving war booty and their living standard improved, the wives of the Holy Prophet[sa] desired an improvement in their living standard. So they consulted among themselves and then mentioned to the Holy Prophet[sa] about their desire to live a prosperous life. The Holy Prophet[sa] felt that in their request there was a desire for worldly things over spiritual things. He had married them so that they could live as desired by Allah. He wanted to see his wives have higher moral standards as compared to other women and live an exemplary life. So the Holy Prophet[sa] did not like his wive's attitude and was a bit annoyed. Thus, the Holy Prophet[sa] separated for one month from his wives. After one month's separation the following verses of the Holy Qur'ān were revealed to the Holy Prophet[sa]:

يٰۤاَيُّهَا النَّبِيُّ قُلْ لِّاَزْوَاجِكَ اِنْ كُنْتُنَّ تُرِدْنَ الْحَيٰوةَ الدُّنْيَا وَ زِيْنَتَهَا
فَتَعَالَيْنَ اُمَتِّعْكُنَّ وَ اُسَرِّحْكُنَّ سَرَاحًا جَمِيْلًا 0 وَاِنْ كُنْتُنَّ تُرِدْنَ اللّٰهَ وَ
رَسُوْلَهٗ وَ الدَّارَ الْاٰخِرَةَ فَاِنَّ اللّٰهَ اَعَدَّ لِلْمُحْسِنٰتِ مِنْكُنَّ اَجْرًا عَظِيْمًا 0

yā ayyuhannabiyyu qulli azwājika in kuntunna turidnal ḥayātaddunyā wa zīnatahā fata'ālaina umatti'kunna wa

usarriḥkunna sarāḥan jamīlā. wa in kuntunna turidnallāha wa rasūlahū waddāral ākhirata fa innallāha a'adda lil muḥsināti minkunna ajran 'aẓīmā

O Prophet! say to your wives, 'If you desire the life of this world and its adornment, come then, I will provide for you and send you away in a handsome manner. But if you desire Allāh and His Messenger and the Home of the Hereafter, then truly Allāh has prepared for those of you who do good a great reward.' (33:29-30)

Thus, God Almighty gave the wives of the Holy Prophet[sa] the choice that they can either live the life of austerity or of luxury.

Although the wives of the Holy Prophet[sa] belonged to rich families they chose the second option and lived simple and exemplary lives. Ḥaḍrat 'Ā'ishah[ra] relates that when one month of separation of the Holy Prophet[sa] from his wives had passed, and the verses of the Holy Qur'ān had been revealed, the Holy Prophet[sa] gave the following option:

خَيَّرْنَا رَسُوْلَ اللّٰهِ ﷺ فَاخْتَرْنَا اللّٰهَ وَرَسُوْلَهٗ

khayyarnā rasūlallāhi fakhtarnallāha wa rasūlahū

The Holy Prophet[sa] gave us the option (to be divorced) and we picked Allāh and His Messenger.

(Ṣaḥīḥ Bukhārī, Bāb man khairunnisā' wa Qaulillāh ta'ālā)

We picked Allāh and His Messenger.

Ḥaḍrat 'Ā'ishah[ra] further relates that the wives of the Holy Prophet[sa] lived a simple life just like the Holy Prophet[sa]:

مَا كَانَ لِاِحْدَانَا اِلاَّ ثَوْبٌ وَاحِدٌ

mā kāna liḥdānā illā thaubun wāḥidun

Each one amongst us (the wives of the Holy Prophet[sa]) did not have more than one (pair of) clothes.

(Ṣaḥīḥ Bukhārī, Kitābul Ḥaiḍ, Bāb hal taṣallil m ar'atu fi thaub ḥāḍat fīh)

Some Other Events in the Life of the Wives of the Holy Prophet[sa]

Some of the events in the life of the wives of the Holy Prophet[sa] which shed light on the household atmosphere of the Holy Prophet[sa] are briefly mentioned here:

Ḥaḍrat 'Ā'ishah[ra] relates that when the Holy Prophet[sa] returned home from one of the battles the cupboard in her room was covered with a curtain. The wind blew and it displaced the curtain. In the cupboard were some dolls of Ḥaḍrat 'Ā'ishah[ra]. The Holy Prophet[sa] asked: "O 'Ā'ishah! What is this? Ḥaḍrat 'Ā'ishah[ra] said: 'These are my dolls. 'Among the dolls, he also saw a horse with two wings of paper. The Holy Prophet[sa] asked, 'What is this?' Ḥaḍrat 'Ā'ishah[ra] said, 'It is a horse.' The Holy Prophet[sa] pointing to the wings of the horse asked, 'What is this?' Ḥaḍrat 'Ā'ishah[ra] said, 'These are its wings.' The Holy Prophet[sa] said, 'A horse with wings?' At this, Ḥaḍrat 'Ā'ishah[ra] said, 'Did you not hear that the horses of Ḥaḍrat Sulaimān had wings?' Hearing this, the Holy Prophet[sa] laughed out so loud that I could see his back teeth (i.e., he burst into laughter).' "

(Bukhārī, Kitābul Adab, Bāb al-La'bu bil bināt; Sunan Abū Dāwūd, Kitābul Adab, Bāb filla'b bil bināt)

Ḥaḍrat 'Ā'ishah[ra] stated that once at the occasion of *'Īd* some Ethiopians were showing war tactics, the Holy Prophet[sa] asked her if she would like to see the jugglery? Then, he made her stand behind him. For a long time I watched the fun standing behind him while my chin was resting on his shoulders and my cheeks were touching his cheeks. He stood while bearing her weight on his shoulders till the time that I got tired. Then he said, "It is enough, you should go home now."

(Ṣaḥīḥ Bukhārī, Kitābul 'Īdain, Bāb al-Ḥarab walid raq yuamal 'Id)

The Holy Prophet[sa] was once returning from the Battle of 'Usfān. Ḥaḍrat Ṣafiyyah[ra] daughter of Ḥuyyay was riding the camel with the Holy Prophet[sa]. When the camel stumbled both of them fell off the camel. Ḥaḍrat Abū Ṭalḥa[ra] rushed to support the Holy Prophet[sa], the Holy Prophet[sa] said: 'Take care of the woman.'

(Ṣaḥīḥ Bukhārī, Kitābul Jihād walsair, Bāb mā yaqūl idhā raja'a minal Ghazwah)

Despite the excellent treatment by the Holy Prophet[sa] of his wives once in a while human nature used to come into play. The following traditions explains some such incidents in the life of the wives of the Holy Prophet[sa]:

Ḥaḍrat 'Ā'ishah[ra] relates, "I did not feel jealous of any of the wives of the Holy Prophet[sa] as much as I did of Khadījah though I did not see her, but the Holy Prophet[sa] used to mention her very often, and whenever he slaughtered a sheep, he would cut its parts and send them to the friends of Khadījah. When I sometimes said to him, 'You treat Khadījah as if there is no other woman on earth except Khadījah.' He would say, Khadījah was such and such, and from her I had children.' "

(Ṣaḥīḥ Bukhārī, Kitābul Faḍā'il Aṣḥābannabī[ra]*, Bāb tazwījinnabī*[sa] *Khadījata wa faḍlihā*[ra]*)*

Ḥaḍrat ‘Ā’ishah[ra] relates that the wives of the Holy Prophet[sa] were in two groups. One group consisted of Ḥaḍrat Ḥafṣah[ra], Ḥaḍrat Ṣafiyyah[ra], and Ḥaḍrat Saudah[ra], and the second group included, Ḥaḍrat Ummi Salamah[ra], Ḥaḍrat Zainab[ra], and the other wives. All the Muslims knew that the Holy Prophet[sa] loved Ḥaḍrat ‘Ā’ishah[ra] most. Therefore, anyone who wanted to give a gift to the Holy Prophet[sa] would wait for the Holy Prophet's[sa] turn to stay with Ḥaḍrat ‘Ā’ishah[ra]. Thus, when the Holy Prophet[sa] stayed with her, people sent gifts for him and this annoyed the wives in the other group. After consulting each other, the wives in the other group decided to say to the Holy Prophet[sa] that he should suggest to the people that they could give gifts to him even when he was with any one of the other wives. Ḥaḍrat Ummi Salamah[ra] was nominated to convey this message to the Holy Prophet[sa]. When Ḥaḍrat Ummi Salamah[ra] mentioned it to the Holy Prophet[sa], he kept quiet and did not respond. The next day, the other wives asked her about the Holy Prophet's[sa] response. She told them that the Holy Prophet[sa] did not give a response. They told her to talk again with the Holy Prophet[sa]. The next time the Holy Prophet[sa] came to her house she again mentioned the message the wives wanted to convey to him. Again, the Holy Prophet[sa] did not respond. Then, the wives told Ḥaḍrat Ummi Salamah[ra] to keep talking about it with the Holy Prophet[sa] until he gave a response. When the third time Ḥaḍrat Ummi Salamah[ra] mentioned the matter to the Holy Prophet[sa], he said: "Ummi Salamah! Why do you annoy me concerning ‘Ā’ishah[ra]? ‘Ā’ishah's[ra] status is exalted as it is only in her bed that I receive revelation. Hearing this response, Ḥaḍrat Ummi Salamah[ra] regretted her words and apologized to the Holy Prophet[sa] for the mistake. Then, this group of wives sent Ḥaḍrat Fāṭimah[ra] as their representative to say to the Holy Prophet[sa] that he should do justice with all wives. When Ḥaḍrat Fāṭimah[ra] gave the message to the Holy Prophet[sa], he said: 'Dear Daughter! Do you not love whom I love?' Ḥaḍrat Fāṭimah[ra] said: 'Why not? Certainly, I love the person whom you love.' When Ḥaḍrat

Fāṭimah[ra] told the wives about her conversation with the Holy Prophet[sa], they asked her to talk again with the Holy Prophet[sa]. However, she did not agree to do so. Then, the wives sent Ḥaḍrat Zainab[ra] as their representative to the Holy Prophet[sa]. Ḥaḍrat Zainab[ra] forcefully presented the case to the Holy Prophet[sa]. She said: 'Your wives demand that for God's sake you do justice and do not give preference to bint Abū Quḥāfah[ra] only. Love other wives also the way you love her.' Ḥaḍrat Zainab[ra] talked so enthusiastically that her voice became a bit loud and she reviled Ḥaḍrat 'Ā'ishah[ra]. The Holy Prophet[sa] kept listening quietly. However, Ḥaḍrat 'Ā'ishah[ra] gave her such a stern reply that she was silenced and she could not say anything else. At this, the Holy Prophet[sa] smiled and said: 'She is really the daughter of Abū Bakr[ra].'"

(Ṣaḥīḥ Bukhārī, Kitāb al-Hibah, Bāb man ihdā ila ṣāḥibah wa taḥarrā ba'ḍ nisā'ih)

Ḥaḍrat Anas[ra] relates that the Holy Prophet[sa] was at the house of one of the Mothers of the Faithful, when one of the other wives sent food in a bowl. At this, the lady of the house hit the hand of the man who brought the bowl. This caused the bowl to fall to the ground. The bowl broke and the food fell to the ground. The Holy Prophet[sa] picked up both pieces of the bowl and put them together. Then, he collected the food and put it back in the bowl. While doing so, he was saying (with displeasure): "You are ruined. Take and eat it." He repeated it many times which made the wife in the house realize her mistake and she felt ashamed. She brought a new bowl. The Holy Prophet[sa] gave this new bowl in place of the broken one to the man who had brought the bowl and kept the broken bowl in the house of his wife who had broken it.

(Sunan Ibni Mājah, Abwābal aḥkām bāb al-ḥakam fīman kasr shai'an)

The Incident of Honey

The Holy Prophet[sa] once visited one of his wives and she served honey to him. The Holy Prophet[sa] was very much fond of honey and liked the honey served to him. So the Holy Prophet[sa] stayed there some time extra than his normal stay in the house of the wife he was visiting. His other wives did not like his extra stay in the house of his wife who had served him honey. When the Holy Prophet[sa] went to the quarter of another wife, he told her the reason for his coming late to visit her. One of the wives of the Holy Prophet[sa] told another wife that sometime the honey bees make honey from smelly plants. Therefore, let us tell the Holy Prophet[sa] that sometime a bad smell comes from his mouth after eating honey. This way, the Holy Prophet[sa] will stop visiting the wife who serves him honey. Accordingly, one of the wives of the Holy Prophet[sa] followed the plan and said to the Holy Prophet[sa] that a bad smell of honey which is probably prepared from smelly plants was coming from his mouth. The Holy Prophet[sa] was very sensitive and disliked bad smells. He did not like that a bad smell of honey came from his mouth. Therefore, he swore not to eat honey again. At this, God Almighty revealed the following to him:

يٰٓاَيُّهَا النَّبِيُّ لِمَ تُحَرِّمُ مَآ اَحَلَّ اللّٰهُ لَكَ ۚ تَبْتَغِيْ مَرْضَاتَ اَزْوَاجِكَ ؕ
وَاللّٰهُ غَفُوْرٌ رَّحِيْمٌ 0 قَدْ فَرَضَ اللّٰهُ لَكُمْ تَحِلَّةَ اَيْمَانِكُمْ ۚ وَاللّٰهُ مَوْلٰىكُمْ ۚ
وَهُوَ الْعَلِيْمُ الْحَكِيْمُ 0

yā ayyuhannabiyyu lima tuḥarrimu mā aḥallallāhu laka tabtaghī marḍāta azwājika wallāhu ghafūrurraḥīm qad faraḍallāhu lakum taḥillata aimānikum wallāhu maulākum wa huwal 'alīmul ḥakīm

O Prophet! why do you forbid *yourself* that which Allāh has made lawful to you, seeking the pleasure of your wives? And Allāh is Most Forgiving, Merciful. Allāh has indeed made incumbent upon you the dissolution of your vows, *concerning the aforementioned*, and Allāh is your Guardian; and He is All-Knowing, Wise. (66:2-3)

23

Children of the Holy Prophet[sa]

Except for one son, Ibrāhīm, all the other children of the Holy Prophet[sa] were born to Ḥaḍrat Khadījah[ra]. The children born to Ḥaḍrat Khadījah[ra] included three boys, Qāsim, Ṭāhir and Ṭayyab, and four girls, Zainab, Ruqayyah, Ummi Kulthūm and Fāṭimah. According to some traditions a fourth boy was born to Ḥaḍrat Khadījah[ra] whose name was 'Abdullāh. However, general concensus is that 'Abdullāh was another name of Ṭayyab. All of these children were born before the beginning of the prophethood of the Holy Prophet[sa].

Sons of the Holy Prophet[sa]

All the male children of the Holy Prophet[sa] died in their childhood. All sons except Ibrāhīm were born before the beginning of the prophethood of the Holy Prophet[sa]. Abul Qāsim, the family name of the Holy Prophet[sa], was based on the name of his son Qāsim. Ibrāhīm was born in April 630 AD to Ḥaḍrat Mariyah al-Qibṭiyyah. The Holy Prophet[sa] performed Ibrāhīm's *'Aqīqa* on seventh day of his birth. Two rams were sacrificed. The hair from his head was shaved by Abū Hind. The Holy Prophet[sa] distributed silver equivalent in weight to the weight of the hair removed from Ibrāhīm's head to the poor. The Holy Prophet[sa] appointed Ḥaḍrat Umm Burdah wife of Ḥaḍrat Brā' bin Aus as wet-nurse for his son, Ibrāhīm.

Daughters of the Holy Prophet[sa]

All of the boys had died at an early age. However, all of the girls lived a long life and accepted Islām. Except Ḥaḍrat Fāṭimah[ra], none of the daughters of the Holy Prophet[sa] produced an ongoing lineage.

Ḥaḍrat Zainab[ra]

Ḥaḍrat Zainab[ra] who was married to Abū al-'Āṣ bin Rabī' had lost a child due to miscarriage during her migration to Medina. Later on a boy, 'Alī and a daughter, Umāmah were born to her. The boy died at an early age. The girl, Umāmah survived and after the demise of Ḥaḍrat Fāṭimah, she became the wife of Ḥaḍrat 'Alī[ra]. Ḥaḍrat Zainab[ra] passed away in 8 AH.

Ḥaḍrat Ruqayyah[ra] and Ḥaḍrat Ummi Kulthūm[ra]

Ḥaḍrat Ruqayyah[ra] and Ḥaḍrat Ummi Kulthūm[ra] were engaged to 'Utbah and 'Utaybah respectively who were the children of Abū Lahab, an uncle of the Holy Prophet[sa]. Abū Lahab severely opposed the Holy Prophet[sa]. Accordingly, the engagements of Ḥaḍrat Ruqayyah[ra] and Ḥaḍrat Ummi Kulthūm[ra] were broken before their marriage. After that Ḥaḍrat Ruqayyah[ra] and Ḥaḍrat Ummi Kulthūm[ra], one after the other, became wives of Ḥaḍrat 'Uthmān[ra]. This is the reason that Ḥaḍrat 'Uthmān[ra] is called, *Ḍunnūrain* (i.e, the one with two lights). Both of them did not have any progeny. Ḥaḍrat Ruqayyah[ra] had a boy who was born dead. Her second child, 'Abdullāh, passed away when he was two years old. Ḥaḍrat Ummi

Kulthūm[ra] did not bear any children. Ḥaḍrat Ruqayyah[ra] passed away during the time of the Battle of Badr while Ḥaḍrat Ummi Kulthūm[ra] passed away after the Conquest of Mecca.

Ḥaḍrat Fāṭimah[ra]

Ḥaḍrat Fāṭimah[ra] who was loved by the Holy Prophet[sa] the most was married to Ḥaḍrat 'Alī[ra] after the migration to Medina. She bore two children, Ḥaḍrat Ḥasan[ra] and Ḥaḍrat Ḥussain[ra]. The progeny of Ḥaḍrat Ḥasan[ra] and Ḥaḍrat Ḥussain[ra] are called, "*Sayyed*". Ḥaḍrat Fāṭimah[ra] passed away 6 months after the sad demise of the Holy Prophet[sa].

Ḥaḍrat Fāṭimah[ra] loved the Holy Prophet[sa] very much. Once, the Holy Prophet[sa] was walking through a street when an evil person threw dirt on the head of the Holy Prophet[sa] in the presence of other people. When the Holy Prophet[sa] returned home with dirt on his head Ḥaḍrat Fāṭimah quickly brought water, washed his head and started to cry profusely. The Holy Prophet[sa] consoled her and said, "Daughter, do not cry. God Almighty Himself will protect your father and all these agonies will be dispelled."

(Tarīkh Ṭabrī, Vol. 2, p. 80, Press Istiqāmah, Cairo)

24

The Farewell Address of the Holy Prophet[sa] at the Occasion of the Last Pilgrimage (Ḥajjatul Widā') and His Illness

In the ninth year of the *Hijrah*, the Holy Prophet[sa] went on a pilgrimage to Mecca. This was the first *Ḥajj* performed by the Holy Prophet[sa] during his prophethood. Thus this event was of great significance as the Holy Prophet[sa] himself was practically showing the proper way of performing various rites of the *Ḥajj*. God Almighty states in the Holy Qur'ān about the *Ḥajj*:

وَاَذِّنْ فِى النَّاسِ بِالْحَجِّ يَاْتُوْكَ رِجَالاً وَّ عَلٰى كُلِّ ضَامِرٍ يَّاْتِيْنَ مِنْ كُلِّ
فَجٍّ عَمِيْقٍ 0 لِّيَشْهَدُوْا مَنَافِعَ لَهُمْ وَيَذْكُرُوا اسْمَ اللّٰهِ فِىْٓ اَيَّامٍ
مَّعْلُوْمٰتٍ عَلٰى مَا رَزَقَهُمْ مِّنْۢ بَهِيْمَةِ الْاَنْعَامِ ۚ فَكُلُوْا مِنْهَا وَ اَطْعِمُوا
الْبَآئِسَ الْفَقِيْرَ 0 ثُمَّ لْيَقْضُوْا تَفَثَهُمْ وَلْيُوْفُوْا نُذُوْرَهُمْ وَلْيَطَّوَّفُوْا
بِالْبَيْتِ الْعَتِيْقِ 0

wa adhdhin finnāsi bil ḥajji ya'tūka rijālañwwa 'alā kulli ḍāmiriñyya'tīna min kulli fajjin 'amīqilli yash hadū manāfi'a lahum

wa yadhkurusmallāhi fī ayyāmimma'lūmātin 'alā mā razaqa hummim bahīmatil an'āmi fa kulū minhā wa aṭ'imul bā'isal faqīr thummal yaqḍū tafathahum wal yūfū nudhūrahum wal yaṭṭawwafū bil baitil 'atīq

And proclaim unto mankind the Pilgrimage. They will come to you on foot, and on every lean camel, coming by every distant track. That they may witness its benefits for them and may mention the name of Allāh, during the appointed days, over the quadrupeds *of the class of* cattle that He has provided for them. Then eat you thereof and feed the distressed, the needy. Then let them accomplish the task of cleansing themselves, and fulfill their vows and go around the Ancient House. (22:28-30)

On the day of the pilgrimage, the Holy Prophet[sa] received the revelation containing the famed verse of the Holy Qur'ān:

اَلْيَوْمَ اَكْمَلْتُ لَكُمْ دِيْنَكُمْ وَ اَتْمَمْتُ عَلَيْكُمْ نِعْمَتِىْ وَ رَضِيْتُ لَكُمُ الْاِسْلَامَ دِيْنًا ط

al yauma akmaltu lakum dīnakum wa atmamtu 'alaikum ni'matī wa raḍītu lakumul islāma dīnā

This day have I perfected your religion for you and completed My favor upon you and have chosen for you Islām as religion. (5:4)

This verse said in effect that the message which the Holy Prophet[sa] had brought from God and which by word and deed he had been expounding all these years, had been completed. Every part of this message was a blessing. The Message now completed, embodied the highest blessings which man could receive from God. The Message is epitomized in the name *'Al-Islām'*, which means submission. Submission was to be the religion of Muslims, the religion of mankind.

The Holy Prophet[sa] recited this verse in the valley of *Muzdalifah*, where the pilgrims had assembled. Returning from *Muzdalifah*, the Holy Prophet[sa] stopped at *Minā*. It was the eleventh day of the month of *Dhul Ḥijjah*. The Holy Prophet[sa] while sitting on his camel, facing a large gathering of Muslims and delivered an address in loud voice, famed in history as the farewell address of the Holy Prophet[sa]. Rabī'ah ibn Umayyah ibn Khalaf repeated the sermon after him sentence by sentence.

The Farewell Address

In the course of the address the Holy Prophet[sa] said:

"O men, lend me an attentive ear. For I know not whether I will stand before you again in this valley and address you as I address you now. Your lives and your possessions have been made immune by God to attacks by one another until the Day of Judgement. God has appointed for every one a share in the inheritance. No 'Will' shall now be admitted which is prejudicial to the interests of a rightful heir. A child born in any house will be regarded as the child of the father in that house. Whoever contests the parentage of this child will be liable to punishment under the Law of Islām. Anyone who attributes his birth to some one else's father, or falsely claims someone to be his master, God, His angels and the whole of mankind will curse him.

O men, you have some rights against your wives, but your wives also have some rights against you. Your right against them is that they should live chaste lives, and not adopt ways which may bring disgrace to the husband in the sight of his people. If your wives do not live up to this, then you have the right to punish them. You can punish them after due inquiry has been made by a competent authority, and your right to punish has been established. Even so, punishment in such a case must not be severe. But if your wives do not do such things, and their behavior is not such as would bring disgrace to their husbands, then your duty is to provide for them food and garments and shelter, according to your own standard of living.

Remember you must always treat your wives well. God has charged you with the duty of looking after them. Woman is weak and cannot protect her own rights. When you married, God appointed you the trustees of those rights. You brought your wives to your homes under the Law of God. You must not, therefore, insult the trust which God has placed in your hands.

O men, you still have in your possession some prisoners of war. I advise you, therefore, to feed them and to clothe them in the same way and style as you feed and clothe yourselves. If they do anything wrong which you are unable to forgive, then pass them on to someone else. They are part of God's creation. To give them pain or trouble can never be right.

O men, what I say to you, you must hear and remember. All Muslims are as brethren to one another. All of you are equal. All men, whatever nation or tribe they may belong to, and whatever station in life they may hold, are equal.

While he was saying this the Prophet[sa] raised his hands and joined the fingers of the one hand with the fingers of other and then said:

Even as fingers of the two hands are equal, so are human beings equal to one another. No one has any right, any superiority to claim over another. You are as brothers.

Proceeding, the Holy Prophet[sa] said:

Do you know what month this is? What territory we are in? What day of the year it is today?

The Muslims said in reply, they knew it was the sacred month, the sacred land and the day of the *Ḥajj*.

Then the Holy Prophet[sa] said:

Even as this month is sacred, this land inviolate, and this day holy, so has God made the lives, property and the honor of every man sacred. To take any man's life or his property, or attack his honor, is as unjust and wrong as to violate the sacredness of this day, this month, and this territory. What I command you today is not meant only for today. It is meant for all times. You are expected to remember it and to act upon it until you leave this world and go to the next to meet your Maker.

In conclusion he said:

What I have said to you, you should communicate to the ends of the earth. Perhaps those who have not heard me may benefit by it more than those who have heard.

(Ṣiḥaḥ Sitta, Ṭabarī, Hishām and Khamīs)

The Holy Prophet's[sa] address is an epitome of the entire teaching and spirit of Islām. It shows how deep was the Holy Prophet's[sa] concern for the welfare of man and the peace of the world; also how deep was his regard for the rights of women and other weak creatures. The Holy Prophet[sa] knew his end was near. He had hints from God about his death.

(Life of Moḥammad[sa], Ḥaḍrat Mirzā Bashīruddīn Maḥmūd Aḥmad, p. 160-162)

Ḥaḍrat Ibn 'Abbās[ra] relates that at the Farewell Pilgrimage, the Holy Prophet[sa] said: "O People! What day of the year is today? They replied: 'It is the venerable day of *'Arfah.*' Then he asked, 'Do you know what city it is?' They replied, 'It is the sacred city of Mecca.' Then he asked, 'What month is this?' They replied, 'It is the sacred month of *Dhulḥijjah.*' Then the Holy Prophet[sa] said, 'Listen! Your bounties, your lives and your honors are as sacred, and their disrespect is as unlawful for you, as this day, this city and this month are revered and sacred for you and as their disrespect is unlawful for you.' He[sa] repeated this several times. Then he raised his head up towards the sky and said: 'O Allāh! Did I convey

Your Message?' He[sa] repeated the words هَلْ بَلَّغْتُ *(hal ballaghtu)* many times. Ḥaḍrat Ibn 'Abbās[ra] says, in fact it was a clear testimony given by the Holy Prophet[sa] to Allāh the Exalted that he has conveyed and made the people understand (the message) in the best possible way. Then the Holy Prophet[sa] (while addressing the audience) said: 'Those who are here, listening to me, should convey my message to those who are not here.' He continued, 'Do not become infidels after I depart lest you start slaying each other.' "

(Musnad Aḥmad, Vol. 1, p 230)

The Holy Prophet's[sa] Illness

Two months after returning from the farewell pilgrimage, the Holy Prophet[sa] fell ill. The illness that ultimately led to his demise had started while he was in the house of Ḥaḍrat Maimūnah[ra]. Despite his illness the Holy Prophet[sa] continued to move from one wife's house to the other wife's house depending upon whose turn it was. When the Holy Prophet[sa] became severely ill he desired to stay in Ḥaḍrat 'Ā'ishah's house which was close to the mosque. However, the Holy Prophet[sa] felt shyness about asking for permission to do so from the other wives. The Holy Prophet[sa] told Ḥaḍrat Fāṭimah[ra] to ask about this from his wives which she did. All the wives agreed that the Holy Prophet[sa] could stay at Ḥaḍrat 'Ā'ishah's[ra] house. Thus, the Holy Prophet[sa] moved to Ḥaḍrat 'Ā'ishah's[ra] house.

The Holy Prophet's[sa] Mosque (*Masjid Nabawī*) was adjacent to his residence. One day the Holy Prophet[sa] stood by the window and looked outside at the Muslims getting ready to say *Fajr* Prayer behind Ḥaḍrat Abū Bakr[ra]. The people looked at the Holy Prophet's[sa] face and waited for him to join them. He smiled at them and indicated with his hand for Ḥaḍrat Abū

Bakr[ra] to go ahead with leading the Prayer. That was the last time the Muslims saw their Prophet's[sa] face; that day at noon, the Holy Prophet[sa] passed away. At the time of his demise on May 26, 632 AD* in Medina, Islām had spread throughout Arabia.

Ḥaḍrat 'Ā'ishah[ra] relates that she heard the Holy Prophet[sa] saying in his last illness till his last breath:

اَللّٰهُمَّ اغْفِرْ لِيْ وَارْحَمْنِيْ وَاَلْحِقْنِيْ بِالرَّفِيْقِ الْاَعْلٰى

allāhummaghfirlī warḥamnī wa al-ḥiqnī birrafīqil a'lā

Allāh, forgive me and have mercy on me and grant me nearness to the Companion, the Most High."

(Ṣaḥīḥ Bukhārī, Kitābul Marḍī, Bāb nahī tumanniyal marīḍil maut)

Ḥaḍrat 'Ā'ishah[ra] relates that the Holy Prophet[sa] passed away when he was sixty-three years old.

(Ṣaḥīḥ Bukharī, Kitabul Maghāzī, Bābwafātinnabī[sa])

* *History of Aḥmadiyyat Vol. 3, p. 555 (printed as footnote): The Daily Jang Karachi September 28, 1958: According to the modern investigation of Dr. Muḥammad Shahīdullāh, Professor, Rajshahi University, Bangladesh the Holy Prophet[sa] passed away on 1st Rabī'ul Awwal, 11th Hijrī which corresponds to 26th May, 632. According to the book 'Attaufīqātil Ilhāmiyyah' 1st Rabī'ul Awwal, 11th Hijrī corresponds to 27th May, 632 AD instead of 26th May, 632 AD. The Promised Messiah and Mahdī[as] passed away on 26th May, 1908 and was buried on 27th May, 1908. This concurrence of the two dates apparently becomes an interpretation of the tradition of the Holy Prophet[sa]*

Funeral Prayer and Burial

The Holy Prophet[sa] passed away on Sunday night. His body was kept for two nights and then on Tuesday afternoon he was buried. Ḥaḍrat 'Alī[ra] and Ḥaḍrat Faḍl bin 'Abbās[ra] bathed the Holy Prophet[sa], while Ḥaḍrat Usāmah bin Zaid[ra] and Ḥaḍrat Aus bin Khaulah[ra] poured the water.' "

(Musnad Abī Ḥanīfah[sa], Kitābul Faḍāi'l, p. 180)

At the time of his demise, the Holy Prophet[sa] was wearing a sheet and a *tah band* (a cloth worn round the waist) made of a thick coarse cotton cloth. It was customary in those days to remove clothes before giving a bath to a deceased person. However, no one felt comfortable enough to remove the clothes of the Holy Prophet[sa] to give him a bath. Thus, the people had two different opinions. Some people were in favor of removing the clothes while others were against doing so.

Ḥaḍrat 'Ā'ishah[ra] relates that at the critical moment of making a decision, God Almighty guided them. Suddenly, everyone felt drowsiness and their heads bowed down while they were standing. Then, they heard a Divine Voice saying, "Give a bath to the Messenger of Allāh in his clothes."

(As-Sīratun Nabawiyyah libne Hishām, Jahaz Rasūlullāh[sa] wa Dafinah, Vol. 4, p. 313)

So, the Companions[ra] were guided through revelation and the Holy Prophet[sa] was given a bath without removing the clothes he was wearing at the time of his demise.

The Holy Prophet[sa] had given directions about his funeral Prayer before his demise which were followed. First, Ḥaḍrat 'Alī[ra], then Ḥaḍrat 'Abbās[ra], then *Ahl-e-Bait*, and then the other relatives of the Holy Prophet[sa] offered the funeral prayer of the Holy Prophet[sa]. Everyone offered the funeral prayer individually. After that people in groups of ten to twelve entered the room to offer the funeral prayer. However, everyone offered the funeral prayer individually. The first group of people to offer the funeral prayer consisted of Ḥaḍrat Abū Bakr[ra], Ḥaḍrat 'Umar[ra] and some *Anṣār* and *Muhājirīn.*

After all the men had offered the funeral prayer of the Holy Prophet[sa], first the women and then the children offered the funeral prayer. There was no *Imām* for the funeral prayers. Everyone offered the funeral prayer individually. The funeral prayers continued for a whole day and the Holy Prophet[sa] was buried thirty-two hours after his demise.

(As-Sīratun Nabawiyyah libne Hishām, Vol.2, p. 663).

The day this came to pass was Tuesday.

(Ibn Kathīr, Vol. 4, p. 517).

Ḥaḍrat Abū Bakr[ra] consulted the Companions[ra] of the Holy Prophet[sa] regarding the place where the Holy Prophet[sa] should be buried. Some Companions[ra] suggested that he should be buried in *Jannatul Baqī'* while the others suggested that he should be buried in the mosque. Ḥaḍrat 'Ā'ishah[ra] mentioned that she had seen in a dream that three moons have fallen into her room. Based on Ḥaḍrat 'Ā'ishah's[ra] dream it was decided that the Holy Prophet[sa] should be buried in Ḥaḍrat 'Ā'ishah's[ra] room. Accordingly, the body of the Holy Prophet[sa] was moved to one side in the room and a grave was dug at the place where his bed was when he passed away. Ḥaḍrat Abū 'Ubaidah al-Jarrāh[ra] was an expert in digging a grave in the Meccan's style and Ḥaḍrat Abū Ṭalḥa[ra] was expert in digging a grave as the people of Medina did. Ḥaḍrat 'Umar[ra] sent his messenger to both of them with the intention that whosoever comes first will dig the grave. The messenger did not find Ḥaḍrat Abū 'Ubaidah[ra]. Thus, Ḥaḍrat Ṭalḥa[ra] came and dug the grave for the burial of the Holy Prophet[sa].

The Holy Prophet[sa] had passed away in the room of Ḥaḍrat 'Ā'ishah[ra]. This room had two doors. One of the doors opened in the courtyard while the other door opened in the *Masjad-e-Nabawī*. After being bathed, the Holy Prophet's[sa] body was placed on a cot in Ḥaḍrat 'Ā'ishah's[ra] room. After digging the grave the cot on which the body of the Holy Prophet[sa] was placed after giving him a bath was kept next to the grave.

Ḥaḍrat Imām Mālik[ra] relates that he was informed that the Holy Prophet[sa] passed away on Monday and he was buried on Tuesday. People in many separate groups offered the funeral Prayer of the Holy Prophet[sa]. No one led the funeral Prayer. Some people thought to bury the Holy Prophet[sa] near the pulpit, while others thought to bury him in the *Jannatul Baqī'*. Ḥaḍrat Abū Bakr[ra] said that he heard the Holy Prophet[sa] say, "A Prophet is buried where he dies." Therefore, a grave for the Holy Prophet[sa] was prepared in the same room. The removal of his clothes to give him a bath was being considered when a Heavenly voice told them not to do so. Thus, the Holy Prophet[sa] was bathed with his clothes on.

(Muwaṭṭā' Imām Mālik, jami'aṣṣalāt 'alal janā'iz bāb fī dafanalmayyat)

Ḥaḍrat 'Ā'ishah[ra] relates, "It was one of the favors of Allāh bestowed upon me that Allāh's Messenger[sa] passed away in my house on the day of my turn while he was leaning against my chest and Allāh made my saliva mix with his saliva at the time of his demise. Ḥaḍrat 'Abdur Raḥmān[ra] came to my house with a *Miswāk* (bark of a tree usually softened before using for cleaning the teeth) in his hand and I noticed that the Holy Prophet[sa] was looking towards the *Miswāk*. I said to the Holy Prophet[sa], 'Should I get the *Miswak* for you.' He nodded in the affirmative. So I took the *Miswāk* and asked the Holy Prophet[sa] whether I should soften the

Miswāk for him. Again he nodded in affirmative. So I softened the *Miswāk* and gave it to him. He cleaned his teeth with the *Miswāk*. There was a water container close to the Holy Prophet[sa]. The Holy Prophet[sa] dipped his hand in the water, rubbed it on his face and said:

لَاإِلٰهَ اِلاَّ اللّٰهُ , اِنَّ لِلْمَوْتِ سَكَرَاتٍ

lā ilāha illallāhu, inna lil mauti sakarātin

None is worthy of worship except Allāh. Death has its agonies

Then the Holy Prophet[sa] raised his hand up and kept saying this till he passed away and his hand dropped down:

فِي الرَّفِيْقِ الْأَعْلٰى

firrafiqil a'lā

With the Companion, the Most High.

(Ṣaḥīḥ Bukhārī, Kitābul Maghāzī, Bāb maraḍinnabiyyi wa wafātihī)

The Last Will of the Holy Prophet[sa]

Ḥaḍrat 'Alī[ra] and Ḥaḍrat Anas[ra] relate, "The last will that the Holy Prophet[sa] made at the time when he was breathing his last breath was:

اَلصَّلٰوةَ وَمَا مَلَكَتْ اَيْمَانُكُمْ

aṣṣalāta wa mā malakat aimānukum

(Take care of) Prayer and those who are under your submission

(Sunan Ibn-e-Mājah, Kitābul Waṣāya, Bāb hal auṣā Rasūlullāh[sa] *)*

Some have stated that the last words the Holy Prophet[sa] spoke were:

لَا تَجْعَلْ قَبْرِىْ وَثَناً

lā taj'al qabrī wathanan

O my Allāh! Do not let my grave become a place of infidelity

(Musnad Aḥmad)

Ḥaḍrat 'Ā'ishah[ra] relates:

مَا تَرَكَ رَسُوْلُ اللّٰهِ ﷺ دِيْنَارًا وَ لَا دِرْهَمًا وَ لَا شَاةً وَ لَا بَعِيْرًا وَ لَا اَوْصٰى بِشَىْءٍ

mā taraka rasūlullāhi dīnāran wa lā dirhaman, wa lā shātan, wa lā ba'īran wa lā auṣā shai'in

The Holy Prophet[sa] nor left any Dinar, any Dirham, any goat or any camel as his inheritance neither he made a will for anything.

(Sunan Ibni Mājah, Kitābul Waṣāyā, Bāb hal auṣā Rasūlullāh[sa] *)*

25

SOME IMPORTANT DATES AND EVENTS IN THE LIFE OF THE HOLY PROPHET MUḤAMMAD

Ṣallallāhu 'alaihi wasallam

A.D. DATES	AGE (Lunar Calendar)	HIJRAH DATES
April 20, 571		**9 or12 Rabī-I 52 BH**

Birth of the Holy Prophet of Islām[sa] at Mecca, 50 days after Abraha's retreat. His father had died in *Yathrib* (later Medina) a few months before his birth.

April 27, 571	**8 days**	**16 or 19 Rabī-l 52 BH**

Ḥaḍrat Ḥalīma Sa'diyya was appointed wet nurse.

During 573	**2 years**	**50 BH**

Visit with his Mother, Ḥaḍrat Āmina at Mecca.

During 577	**6 years**	**46 BH**

Return to Mecca under the care of his mother just before her sad demise.

During 579	**8 years**	**44 BH**

His guardian and grandfather Ḥaḍrat 'Abdul Muṭṭalib died and guardianship passed on to his uncle, Abū Ṭālib.

During 583 **12 years and 2 months** **40 BH**

First visit to Syria with a trading caravan.

June 586 **15 years and 7months** **37 BH**

Tribal Battle of *Fijār* between *Quraish* and *Qaiṣ*.

July 586 **15 years and 8 months** **37 BH**

Pledge of Fuḍūl at the house of 'Abdullāh bin Jud'ān to help the needy and the oppressed.

July 595 **25 years** **28 BH**

Second journey to Syria.

September 595 **25 years and 2 months** **28 BH**

Marriage with Ḥaḍrat Khadījah[ra].

June 598 **28 years** **25 BH**

Birth of his son, Qāsim.

June 600 **3o years** **23 BH**

Birth of his daughter, Ḥaḍrat Zainab[ra].

During 603 **33 years** **20 BH**

Birth of his daughter, Ḥaḍrat Ruqayyah[ra].

During 604 **34 years** **19 BH**

Birth of his daughter, Ḥaḍrrat Ummi Kulthūm[ra].

During 605 **35 years** **18 BH**

Renovation of *Ka'bah* and placement of *Ḥajr-e-Aswad* (Black Stone).
Birth of his daughter Ḥaḍrat Fāṭimah[ra].

February 9, 610 — 40 years and 1 day — 9 Rabi-l, 12 BH

First Revelation in the Cave of *Ḥirā'*.

August 14, 610 — 40 years and 6 months — 18 Ramaḍān, 12 BH

Continuation of Revelation of the Holy Qur'ān.
Ministry of the Holy Prophet Muḥammad[sa].
Acceptance of Islām by Ḥaḍrat Khadījah[ra], Ḥaḍrat Abū Bakr[ra], Ḥaḍrat 'Alī[ra], Ḥaḍrat Zaid[ra].

During 614 — 43 years and 6 months — 9 BH

Open invitation to join Islām under Allāh's Command.

April 615 — 45 years and 4 months — 7 BH

A group of Muslims emigrates to Abyssinia.

September 30, 615 — 46 years — 7 BH

Blockade of Shi'b-e-Abī Ṭālib.

During 616 — 46 years — 6 BH

Ḥaḍrat Ḥamzah[ra] and Ḥaḍrat 'Umar[ra] accept Islām.

January 619 — 49 years and 5 months — Ramaḍān, 3 BH

Abū Ṭālib, uncle of the Holy Prophet[sa] and a few days later, Ḥaḍrat Khadījah[ra] wife of the Holy Prophet[sa] die.

February 619 — 49 years and 6 months — 3 BH

Marriage with Ḥaḍrat Saudah[ra].

March 619 **49 years and 7 months** **3 BH**

Nikāh ceremony with Ḥaḍrat 'Āi'shah[ra]. Journey to *Ṭā'if,* about 40 miles from Mecca, for call to Islām.

March 8, 620 **50 years and 4 months** **27 Rajab, 2 BH**

Spiritual Journey of *Mi'rāj.* Five formal Prayers made obligatory for Muslims.

July 620 **50 years and 9 months** **2 BH**

Deputation from Medina accepts Islām.

During 621 **51 years and 9 months** **Dhulḥaj, 1 BH**

First Pledge of *'Aqaba.*

June 622 **52 years and 9 months** **3 Months BH**

Second Pledge of *'Aqaba.*

September 10, 622 **52 years and 11 months** **27 Ṣafar,**

Hijrat (migration) from Mecca to the cave of *Thaur.*

September 13, 622 (Monday) **1 Rabī-l**

Emigration to Medina begins

September 20, 622 **8 Rabī-I, 1 AH**

Arrival at *Qubā'.*

September 23, 622 **53 years** **11 Rabī-I, 1 AH**

First mosque of Islām constructed at *Qubā'.*

September 24, 622 — 53 years — 12 Rabī-I, 1 AH

Arrival at Medina after the first Friday Prayer at *Qubā's* Mosque.

October 622 — 53 years and 1 month — 1 AH

Construction of the Holy Prophet's[sa] Mosque at Medina.
Ḥaḍrat Bilāl's[ra] call for Prayer (*Adhān*).

November 622 — 53 years and 2 months — Rabī-II, 1 AH

Brotherhood compacts between *Anṣār* (Muslims from Medina) and *Muhājirīn* (immigrants from Mecca).

December 622 — 53 years and 4 months — Jamadī-ul-Ākhar

Treaty with Jews of Medina.

August 14, 623 — 53 years and 11 months — 12 Ṣafar, 2 AH

Permission to fight in self-defense (*Jihād-e-Aṣghar*) revealed by Allāh.

August 31, 623 — 53 years and 11 months — 29 Ṣafar, 2 AH

Ghazwah of *Waddān* (*Ghazwah:* Military expedition or battle under the direct command of the Holy Prophet[sa])

September 623 — 54 years — Rabī-I, 2 AH

Ghazwah of *Bu'at* and of *Ṣafwān.*

December 623 — 54 years and 3 months — Jamādī-ul-Ākhar

Ghazwah *Dhul-'Ashir.*

January 624 — 54 years and 4 months — Rajab, 2 AH

Ḥaḍrat Salmān Fārisī[ra] joins Islām.

February 624 **54 years and 5 months** **Sha'bān**

Revelation and change of *Qiblah* (direction to face for Prayer, *Ṣalāt*) towards *Ka'bah*. Fasting in the month of *Ramaḍān* becomes obligatory.

March 8-13, 624 **54 years and 6 months** **12-17 Ramaḍān**

Ghazwah of *Badr*.

March 21, 624 **54 years and 6 months** **25 Ramaḍān**

Ghazwah of *Banī Sulaim*.

March 24/25, 624 **54 years & 6 months** **28 Ramadan/1 Shawwāl**

Initiation of *'Īdui Fiṭr* and *Zakātul Fiṭr* (Alms at the *'Īdul Fiṭr*).

April 624 **54 years and 7 months** **Shawwāl**

Zakāt became obligatory for Muslims. *Nikāh* and Marriage ceremony of Ḥaḍrat Fāṭimah[ra], his daughter.

April 10, 624 **54 years and 7 months** **15 Shawwāl**

Ghazwah of *Banū Qainuqā'*.

May 29, 624 **54 years and 8 months** **5 Dhul-Ḥajj**

Ghazwah of *Ṣawīq*.

July 624 **54 years and 10 months** **Muḥarram, 3 AH**

Ghazwah of *Ghaṭafān*.

October 624 **55 years and 1 months** **Rabī-II**

Ghazwah of *Baḥrān*.

January 625 **55 years and 6 months** **Sha'bān**

Marriage with Ḥaḍrat Ḥafṣah[ra].

March 22, 625 **55 years and 6 months** **6 Shawwal**

Ghazwah of *Uḥud*.

March 24, 625 **55 years and 7 months** **8 Shawwal**

Ghazwah of *Humra-ul-Asad*.

May 625 **55 years and 9 months** **Dhul-Ḥajj**

Marriage with Ḥaḍrat Zainab Bint Khuzaimah[ra].

August 625 **56 years** **Rabi-l, 4 AH**

Ghazwah of *Banū Naḍāir*. Prohibition of drinking in Islām.

October 625 **56 years and 3 months** **Jamadī-l**

Ghazwah *Dhātur-Riqā'*.

March 626 **56 years and 7 months** **Shawwal**

Marriage with Ḥaḍrat Ummi Salma[ra].

April 626 **56 years and 8 months** **I dhī Qa'd**

Ghazwah of *Rasūluh*.

August 24, 626 **57 years** **25 Rabi-l, 5 AH**

Ghazwah of *Sūratul*.

December 28, 626	**57 years and 4 months**	**3 Sha'ban**

Ghazwah of *Banū Muṣṭa1iq*. Nikāḥ with Ḥaḍrat Jawairiyyah bint Ḥārith[ra].

February 627	**57 years and 7 months**	**Shawwal**

Marriage with Ḥaḍrat Zainab bint Jaḥsh[ra].

March 24, 627	**57 years and 8 months**	**1 Dhi Qa'd**

Revelation for *Ḥijāb* (*Purdah*), rules of modesty.

March 31, 627	**57 years and 8 months**	**8 Dhi Qa'd**

Ghazwah of *Aḥzāb* or *Khandaq* (Ditch).

April 627	**57 years and 9 months**	**DhuI-Ḥajj**

Ghazwah of *Banī Quraiẓah*.

July21, 627	**57 years and 11 months**	**1 Rabī-l, 6 AH**

Ghazwah of *Banū Liḥyān*.

August 627	**58 years and 1 month**	**Rabī'-ul-Ākhar**

Ghazwah of *Dhī Qarad* (or *Ghā'iba*).

March 13, 628	**58 years and 7 months**	**1 Dhī Qa'd**

Ghazwah of *Ḥudaibiyyah*.

March 628	**58 years and 7 months**	**Dhī Qa'd**

Prohibition of marriage with non-believers.

April 628	**58 years and 9 months**	**DhuI-Ḥajj**

Nikāḥ with Ḥaḍrat Ummi Ḥabībah.

May 628 58 years and 9 months 1 Muḥarram, 7 AH

Invitations sent to various rulers to join Islām.

During June 628 58 years and 10 months Muḥarram

Ghazwah *Khaibar*. Return of Muslims from Abyssinia. Deputation from Ashri' īn accepts Islām. *Nikāḥ* with Ḥaḍrat Ṣafiyyah[ra]. Ghazwah of *Wādī'ul Qurā'* and *Taim*.

March 629 59 years and 8 months Dhi Qa'd

Performance of *'Umra* (*'Umratul Qaḍā*). *Nikāḥ* with Ḥaḍrat Maimūnah[ra].

During June 629 60 years Safar 8 AH

Ḥaḍrat Khālid bin Walīd[ra] and Ḥaḍrat 'Amar bin Al-'Āṣ[ra] accept Islām.

August 629 60 years and 2 months Jmādī-I

Ghazwah of *Mauṭa*.

January 1, 630 60 years and 6 months 10 Ramaḍān

Ghazwah of *Fatḥ* Mecca (*Ghazwah Fatḥul A'ẓam*) Fall of Mecca.

During January 630 60 years and 7 months Shawwal

Ghazwah of *Ḥunain* (or *Auṭās* or *Hawāzin*). Ghazwah of *Ṭā'if.*

February 24, 630 60 years and 7 months 5 Dhī Qa'd

Arrival in *Ji'rānah*. Deputation from *Hawāzin* accepts Islām.

April 630 60 years and 10 monthS Mubarram 9 AH

Regular establishment of Department of *Zakāt* and *Ṣadaqa*, and appointment of officers.

May 630 — 60 years and 11 months — Safar

Deputation from *Ghadra* accepts Islām.

June 630 — 61 years — Rabī-I

Deputation from *Ballī* accepts Islām.

August 630 — 61 years and 2 months — Jamādī-ul-Ākhar

Ummul Mu'minīn Ḥaḍrat Mariah[ra] gave birth to a son, Ibrāhīm.

October 630 — 61 years ana 4 monins

Ghazwah *Tabūk*, the last great battle lead by the Holy Propnet[sa]. Ordinance of *Jizya*, tax on non-believers seeking protection from Muslims and exemption from military service in defense of the country they were living in as its citizens.

February 631 — 61 years and 8 months — Dhi Qa'd

Pilgrimage journey of Ḥaḍrat Abū Bakr Siddique[ra].

March 631 — 61 years and 9 months — Dhul-Ḥajj

Ḥajj (pilgrimage of *the Ka'bah* in Mecca) made Obligatory by Allāh.
Prohibition of interest in Islām. Visit by a deputation from *Banū Ḥanīfa*.
Deputations from *Ṭai, Hamdan, Banī Asad and Banī 'Abbās*, all accept Islām.

During 631 — 62 years and 6 months — Ramaḍān, 10 AH

Deputation from *Ghuttan* accepts Islām.

February 23, 632 — 62 years and 8 months — 25 Dhi Qa'd

Departure from Medina for Mecca for *Ḥajjatul Widā'* (Last Pilgrimage).

March 1, 632 | 62 years and 9 months | 4 Dhul-Ḥajj

Entry into Mecca for *Ḥajjatul Widā'*.

March 6, 632 (Friday) | 62 years and 9 months | 9 Dhul Ḥajj

Ḥajjatul-Widā', departure for *'Arafāt.*

March 10, 632 (Tuesday) | 62 years and 9 months | 13 Dhul-Ḥajj

Return from *Minā, Ḥajjatul-Widā'*.

April 11, 632 | 62 years and 10 months | 15 Muḥarram, 11 AH

Arrival of deputation from *Nakha'*, last deputation received by the Holy Prophet[sa].

May 24, 632 | 62 years and 11 months | 28 Ṣafar, 11 AH

Sariyya Usāma bin Zaid[ra], last successful military mission during the Holy Prophet's[sa] life. (*Sariyya*: Military expedition under a commander appointed by the Holy Prophet[sa])

May 13, 632 Wednesday | 62 years and 11 months | 18 Ṣafar, 11 AH

The Holy Prophet[sa] falls ill while he was at Ḥaḍrat Maimūnah's[ra] house

May 19, 632 | 62 years and 11 months | 22 Ṣafar, 11 AH

The Holy Prophet[sa] moved to Ḥaḍrat 'Ā'ishah's[ra] house.

May 21, 632 | 62 years and 11 months | 25 Ṣafar, 11 AH

The Holy Prophet[sa] lead the last *Ṣalāt* before his departure from this world. The Holy Prophet[sa] appointed Ḥaḍrat Abū Bakr[ra] as *Imāmuṣ Ṣalāt* in his place.

The Holy Prophet[sa] offered his last Prayer in congregation in the Mosque lead by Ḥaḍrat Abū Bakr[ra].

May 26, 632 (Tuesday) 63 years and 4 days 1 Rabi-I, 11 AH

The Holy Prophet[sa] passed away. *Innā lillāhi wa innā ilaihi rāji'ūn.*

May 27, 632 (Wednesday) 2 Rabi-I, 11 AH

The Holy Prophet[sa] was buried in Ḥaḍrat 'Ā'ishah's[ra] house.

According to the lunar calendar, the Holy Prophet of Islām[sa] lived and accomplished his mission in 63 years and 4 days, equivalent to 61 years and 48 days of the solar calendar (April 20, 571 to May 26, 632). *Janāzah* (funeral) Prayer and burial was completed on Wednesday, 2 Rabī'ul Awwal, 11 A.H. (i.e., May 27, 632), nearly 32 hours after his demise.

Glossary of Terms and Abbreviations

Abī:	Father of
Abū:	Father of
AD:	Anno Domini, the Year of the Lord, denoting Christian era.
Adhān:	The call for Prayers.
AH:	After *Hijra* of the Holy Prophet of Islām[sa].
Ahl-e-Bait	Members of the family of the Holy Prophet[sa].
Banī:	A tribe or clan.
Banū:	A tribe or clan.
B.H.:	Before *Hijra*
Bin:	Son of.
Bint:	Daughter of.
Dirham:	An Islāmic silver currency weighing approximately 3.12 grams
Ghazwah:	Military expedition or battle under the direct command of the Holy Prophet[sa].
Ḥadīth:	A saying of the Holy Prophet[sa].
Ḥadīth-e-Qudsī:	Revelation of the Holy Prophet[sa] other than the revelation of the Holy Qur'ān.
Ḥaḍrat:	Revered

Ḥāfiẓ	One who knows the entire text of the Holy Qur'ān by heart; plural *"Ḥuffāẓ."*
Hājirah:	Hāgar
Ḥajj	Islāmic pilgrimage to Mecca during the month of *Dhul-Ḥijjah.*
Hijra:	The migration of the Holy Prophet[sa] from Mecca to Medina.
Ibn:	Son of
Ibrāhīm[as]:	Prophet Abraham[as]
Ismā'īl[as]:	Prophet Ishmael[as]
Iḥrām	Pilgrimage garb, two white unsewn cotton robes worn by pilgrims
Jihād:	Strife, Concerted effort.
Jizyah	A poll-tax
Khandaq	Moat, ditch
Qiblah	Direction to face for Prayer
Sajdah	Prostration
Ṣalāt:	Formal worship; Daily Prayers.
Sariyyah:	Military expedition under a commander appointed by the Holy Prophet[sa].
Shari'ah	Islāmic legislative system
Tahajjud:	Voluntary Prayer offered during the last part of the night.

Ṭawāf	Circling around the *Ka'bah*
Umm/Ummi:	Mother of
Ummul Mu'minīn:	Mother of the believers (Wife of the Prophet).
Umrah	The lesser pilgrimage done outside the month of *Ḥajj*
Zakāt:	Prescribed alms on property and wealth.

Raḍiallāhu 'anhā:	May Allāh (God Almighty) be pleased with her. A prayer for the believing ladies who had the opportunity of accepting the Holy Prophet[sa].
Raḍiallāhu 'anhu:	May Allāh (God Almighty) be pleased with him. A prayer for the Companions of the Holy Prophet[sa].
Ṣallallāhu 'alaihi wasallam:	May peace and blessings of Allāh be upon him. A prayer for the Holy Prophet[sa].

Lunar months in Islāmic Calendar

1. **Muḥarram** (The sacred month)
2. **Safar** (The month which is void)
3. **Rabī'ul Awwal** (Rabī-I) (The first spring)
4. **Rabi'uth-Thānī (Rabī-Il)**, (The second spring)
5. **Jamādil-Ūlā (Jamādī-ul Awwal or Jamādī-I)** (The first month of dryness)
6. **Jamādī ul Ukhrā (Jamādī-ul-Ākhar)** (The second month of dryness)
7. **Rajab** (The revered month)
8. **Sha'bān** (The month of division)
9. **Ramaḍān** (the month of great heat)
10. **Shawwāl** (The month of hunting)
11. **Dhil Qa'da (Dhī Qa'd)** (The month of rest)
12. **Dhil Ḥajj (Dhul Ḥajj or Dhul Ḥajja)** (The month of pilgrimage)

BIBLIOGRAPHY

1. Life of Muḥammad[sa], Ḥaḍrat Mirzā Bashīrud Dīn Maḥmūd Aḥmad, Khalīfatul Masīḥ II[ra], Qadian, India, Published in 2003.
2. The Seal of Prophets: His Personality and Character, Ḥaḍrat Mirzā Ṭāhir Aḥmad, Khalīfatul Masīḥ IV[rh], Islām International Publications, Islām International Publications, Ltd., Islamabad, UK, Published in 1992.
3. The Blessed Model of the Holy Prophet Muhammad and the Caricatures, Ḥaḍrat Mirzā Masroor Aḥmad, Khalīfatul Masīḥ V[aba], Islām International Publications, Islām International Publications, Ltd., Islamabad, UK, Published in 2006.
4. Sīrat Khātamun Nabiyyīn, (Urdu) Ḥaḍrat Mirzā Bashīr Ahmad[ra], Vol. I, II and III, Qadian, India, 1947
5. Ḥadīqatuṣ Ṣāliḥīn (Urdu), Ḥaḍrat Malik Saifur Raḥmān, Naẓārat-e-Ishā'at, Rabwah, Pakistan
6. The Excellent Exemplar - Muḥammad, Chaudharī Muḥammad Ẓafrullā Khān, alislam.org
7. Wisdom of the Holy Prophet[sa], Chaudharī Muḥammad Zafrullā Khān, alislam.org
8. Uswah Insān-e-Kāmil (Examplary Life of the Perfact Man[sa]) (Urdu), Ḥāfiz Muẓaffar Aḥmad, Rabwah, Pakistan.
9. Sīrat Khātamun Nabiyyīn[sa] (Urdu, Unpublished), Hadī 'Alī Chaudhary, Toronto, Canada.
10. The Life of the Holy Prophet of Islām[sa], Mukhtār A. Cheema, alislam.org.
11. Sawāneh and Sīrar Ḥaḍrat Khātamun Nabiyyīn Muḥammad[sa], Malik Muḥammad Fahīm, Advocate (Urdu), 254-G Block, Model Town, Lahore, Pakistan. Published in 2006.
12. Shamā'il Muḥammad[sa], 'Abdus Samī Khān (Urdu), Majlis Khuddāmul Aḥmadiyya Pakistan, Rabwah, Pakistan.
13. Ḥaḍrat Muḥammad Muṣṭafā[sa] Kā Bachpan (Urdu), Amatul Bārī

Nāsir, Lajna Imā'illāh Distt. Karachi, Karachi, Pakistan
14. Sīrat-e-Ṭayyabah Maḥbūb-e-Kibriyyā Ḥaḍrat Muḥammad Muṣṭafā Aḥmad Mujtabā, Khātamun Nabiyyīn[sa] (Urdu), Mas'ūd Aḥmad Khurshīd Sanorī, USA
15. Invocations of the Holy Prophet[sa], Ḥaḍrat Muḥammad Muṣṭafā[sa], Dr. Karīmullāh Zīrvī, Aḥmadiyya Movement in Islām, 1500 Good Hope Road, Silver Spring, MD 20905, USA, Published in June 2005.
16. Welcome to Aḥmadiyyat, the True Islām, Dr. Karīmullāh Zīrvī, Aḥmadiyya Movement in Islām, 1500 Good Hope Road, Silver Spring, MD 20905, USA, Published in June 2003.
17. Glossary of Islāmic Terms, 'Ā'isha Bewley, Ṭā-Hā Publishers, Ltd., London, UK, Published in 1998.
18. A History of Arab Peoples, Albert Hourānī, The Belknap Press of Harvard University Press, Cambridge, MA, 1991
19. Durūd Sharīf (Urdu), Ḥaḍrat Maulavī Muḥammad Ismā'īl Ḥalālpūrī, Ist Published in 1939, Second Edition.
20. The Holy Prophet[sa] of Islām, Dr. Rashīd S. A'ẓam, Al-Ḥaqqa Publishers International, Apex, NC, USA, 2004
21. The Concise Encyclopedia of Islām, Cyril Glasse, Stacey International London, 1989.
22. The Life of Muḥammad, Muḥammad Ḥusein Haykal, Translated by Ismā'īl Rājī al-Fārūqī, American Trust Publications, Kuala Lumpur, 1976.
23. The Life of Muḥammad The Prophet[sa], Syed Sa'īd Akhtar Rizvī, Dār-es-Salām, Tanzania, 1999
24. Ibn Sa'd's Al-Ṭabaqāt Al-Kabīr, Vols. I & II, S. Mo'īnul Ḥaq, Kitāb Bhavan, New Delhi, India.
25. The Life of Muḥammad (A translation of Ibn Isḥāq's Sīrat Rasūlullāh), A. Guillaume, Oxford University Press, Oxford, UK.
26. Atlas on the Prophet's[sa] Biography, Dr. Shawqī Abū Khalīl, Dārussalām, Riyadh, 2004.

INDEX

'Abbād bin Bishar, 190
'Abbās, 60, 95, 137, 205, 206, 230, 319, 334, 404,407,424, 428
Abān bin Sa'īd bin al-'Ās, 243
'Abd Manāf bin Zuhra, 43, 297
'Abd Shams, 321, 376
'Abd Yalail bin 'Abd Kulāl, 75
'Abdullāh, 42, 45, 49
'Abdullāh bin Abī Aufā, 152, 356
'Abdullāh bin Abī 'Utbah. 290
'Abdullāh bin Abū Bakr, 97, 299
'Abdullāh bin Arqam al-Zuhrī, 243
'Abdullāh bin Ḥārith, 290
'Abdullāh bin Ḥudhāfa, 174
'Abdullāh bin Huḍair, 308
'Abdullāh bin Ja'far , 73, 365, 323, 371
'Abdullāh bin Jaḥsh, 388
'Abdullāh bin Jubair, 137
'Abdullāh bin Ka'b, 215
'Abdullāh bin Mas'ūd, 296, 364
'Abdullāh bin Muḥammad, 51
'Abdullāh bin Rawāḥah, 194, 243, 362
'Abdullāh bin Sa'd bin Abī Sarḥ, 243
'Abdullāh ibn Salām, 161, 276, 291, 342
'Abdullāh bin Ubayy bin Salūl, 113,131, 148, 229, 383
'Abdullāh ibn 'Abdul Asad, 388
'Abdullāh ibn Abū Rabī'ah, 66
'Abdullāh ibn Jud'ān, 50
'Abdul Muṭṭalib, 36, 42, 46, 47, 48, 71,175,176, 204, 206
Abdur Raḥmān bin Abī Laila, 352
'Abdur Raḥmān bin 'Auf, 58, 368
'Abdur Raḥmān bin Mālik Mudlijī, 99
'Abdur Raḥmān bin 'Uyainah, 169
Abraha, 42, 175
Abul Ḥakam (see under Abū Jahl)
Abul Qāsim, 194, 276, 311, 344, 367, 414
Abū Aḥmad bin Jaḥsh, 392
Abū al-'Āṣ, 71
Abū al-'Āṣ bin Rabī', 415
Abū 'Āmir Ash'arī, 208
Abū 'Āmir Madanī, 212
Abū Ayyūb Anṣārī, 107
Abū Barā' 'Āmir bin Mālik, 145
Abū Bakr, 58, 64, 78, 91, 97, 100, 101, 103, 104, 126, 138, 186, 198, 243, 297, 299, 309, 318, 328, 329, 378, 386, 387, 411, 425, 426,
Abū Burdah, 296
Abū Dharr Ghaffārī, 168
Abū Dujānah, 190
Abū Hālah bin Zrah Tamīmī, 375
Abū Ḥamzah, 81
Abū Ḥanīfah, 362
Abū Hind, 414
Abū Hurairah, 142, 274, 275, 276, 298, 301, 304, 314, 321, 322, 329, 331, 333, 351, 353, 355, 356, 360, 371
Abū Isḥāq, 137, 324
Abū Jahl, 62, 68, 70, 71, 96, 324, 330, 341, 354
Abū Jandal, 165
Abū Khaisamah, 217
Abū Lahab, 59, 60, 65, 71, 96, 297, 319, 415
Abū Lubābah, 158
Abū Mūsā, 202, 213, 389
Abū Mūsā Ash'arī , 192, 208, 296
Abū Qatādah, 169, 219, 358
Abū Qatādah Ḥārith, 359
Abū Qubais, 176, 198
Abū Ruham bin 'Abdul 'Uzza, 404
Abū Sa'īd Al-Khudrī, 210, 286, 290, 291 360,
Abū Sufyān, 96, 123, 124, 136, 138, 139, 170, 205, 206, 317, 340, 399, 401
Abū Ṭalḥa, 319, 427, 409, 425

Abū Ṭālib, 48, 49, 57, 60, 63, 71, 72, 293, 306, 375
Abū 'Ubaidah, 318
Abū 'Ubaidah al-Jarrāh, 425
Abū 'Umair, 358
Abū 'Umayyah, 52, 71
Abwa', 48
Abyssinia, 30, 64, 66, 80, 91, 170, 178, 362, 377, 381, 389, 399
Adam, 81, 85, 255, 281, 282, 286
'Aḍbā', 366
Addas, 74
'Afir, 402
'Ā'ishah, 53, 75, 88, 90, 91, 97, 119, 290, 291, 294,295,296, 302, 303, 304, 305, 307, 313, 326, 327, 333, 338, 357, 366, 369, 374 , 377, 378, 380, 381, 382. 384, 386, 389, 393,395. 401, 406, 407, 408, 409, 410, 422, 423, 424, 425, 426, 428
Al-Abā', 224
Al-Akhḍar, 224
Al-'Aliya, 403
Al-'Amrī, 218
Al-Arashī, 353
Al-'Āṣ bin Wā'il as-Sahmī, 99
Al-Faifā', 224
Al-Ḥajar , 224
Al-Ḥārth, 193
Al-Ḥārth bin 'Umair al-Azdī, 193
Al-Ḥātim, 81
Al-Ḥijr, 81
Al-Jārūd, 81
Al-Miqdād bin 'Amr, 123
Al-Muṭ'am, 72
Al-Rajjī', 146
Al-Ṣa'īd, 224
Al-Shaqq, 224
Al-'Urayd, 136
Al-Wādīul Qurā, 224
'Ala ibn Ḥaḍramī, 181
'Alī, 57, 60, 61, 96, 186, 187, 188, 190, 243, 298, 333, 337, 343, 370, 371, 372, 386, 415, 416, 424, 425, 428
'Amr bin al-'Āṣ, 66, 167, 183, 379
'Amr bin 'Abdullāh, 314
'Amr bin Hishām (see under Abū Jahl)
'Amr bin Umayyah al-Ḍarmī, 178
'Amr ibn Lu'āba, 175
'Amr ibn Umayyah, 146
Āminah bint Wahb, 42, 43, 46, 48
'Āmir bin Fuhairah, 98, 316
'Āmir bin al-Sakn, 227
'Āmir bin al-Ṭufail, 146
'Āmir bin Umayyah al-Zumar, 400
'Ammār, 324
'Ammārah bin Ḥazam, 312
'Ammār bin Yāsir, 192, 228
Anas bin Mālik, 81, 109, 274, 287, 289, 300, 301, 310, 315, 317, 323, 332, 333, 337, 339, 348, 355, 356, 357, 358, 364, 365, 366, 367, 368, 411, 427
'Aqabah, 75, 94 , 95, 216, 346
'Aqbah' bin 'Āmir Juhanī, 298
'Aqra' bin Ḥābis, 371
Arqam, 69
Arwa, 49
Asad bin Zurārah, 106
Ashama ibn Abjar, 178
'Āsim bin Adī, 227
'Āsim bin Thābit al-Anṣārī, 142
Asmā', 97
'Āsma bint 'Amr, 94
Aswad, 295
Aswad Ansī, 313, 314
Aswad bin Yazīd, 291
'Atīq bin 'Āyid Makhzūmī, 375
'Auf bin Mālik, 300
Aus bin Khaulah, 424
'Ayād bin Bishr, 192
Az-Zubair, 50, 386
Bādhān, 177, 315
Baḥīrah, 49
Baḥrain, 181
Baida', 307
Bait-e-Riḍwān, 163

Baitul Māl, 209
Baitul Ma'mūr, 83
Banī 'Abd bin 'Adī, 99
Banī 'Abd Manāf, 59, 95
Banī/Banū 'Abdul Muṭṭalib, 55, 56, 59, 66, 70
Banī ad-Dail, 99
Banī 'Alīm, 182
Banī Daus, 321
Banī Ḥārith bin Khazraj, 206
Banī Nabit, 110
Banī Nahd, 182
Banī Salimah, 217, 218
Banī Tāim, 59
Banī Zuhra, 59
Banū 'Abs, 324
Banū 'Āmir, 145, 184
Banū 'Amr bin 'Auf, 105, 110, 225
Banū Asad, 59
Banū 'Auf, 94, 111, 113, 117, 154, 158
Banū Aus, 111, 117
Banū Bakr, 203
Banū Fazārah, 168
Banū Ghanam bin 'Auf, 225
Banū al-Ḥārith, 110, 111, 117
Banū Ḥāritha, 161
Banū Hāshim, 41, 70, 95, 96
Banū Hawazin, 203, 208, 209, 360
Banū Hudhail, 142, 145
Banū Jatham, 203
Banū Jusham, 110, 117
Banū Ka'b, 203
Banū Kalab, 203
Banū Khazraj, 94, 109, 113, 154, 212
Banū Lihyān, 142
Banū Makhzūm, 59
Banū Muṣṭaliq, 147, 382, 392, 394, 395
Banū al-Nabit, 110
Banū Naḍīr, 108, 135, 149, 160, 161, 184, 396
Banū Najjār, 106, 110, 111, 117
Banū Qainuqā', 108, 113, 161, 184
Banū Quraiẓah, 108, 113, 153,161, 184, 396
Banū Sa'd, 45, 188,203
Banū Sāi'dah, 110, 117
Banū al-Shutaibah, 111, 117
Banū Sulaim, 136,145, 347
Banū Tāim, 59
Banū Tā'ī, 352
Banū Tha'labah, 117
Banū Thaqīf, 203
Banū Zuhrah, 59
Barā' bin Aus, 414
Barah bint 'Abdul 'Uzza, 43
Bark al-Ghimād, 92
Barrah (Juwairiyyah), 394, 404
Barrah (Maimūnah), 404
Battle of Aḥzāb, 147, 149, 318, 390
Battle of Auṭās, 203, 208, 209, 390, 394
Battle of Badr, 123, 127, 135, 137, 142, 144, 202, 216, 230, 298, 307, 314, 319, 325, 334, 387, 416
Battle of Dhātur Riqā', 191, 306
Battle of Fadak, 389
Battle of Fijār, 50
Battle of Hudaibiyyah, 390
Battle of Ḥunain, 203, 205, 206, 207, 208, 209, 299, 338, 360, 390, 394
Battle of Jamal, 386
Battle of Khaibar, 120, 186, 188, 189, 191, 321, 390, 396
Battle of Muṣṭaliq, 147, 382, 392, 394
Battle of Mu'tah, 193
Battle of Tabūk, 121, 212, 215, 223, 224, 226, 229, 300, 311, 344
Battle of Uḥud, 75, 122, 123, 137, 147, 202, 339, 340, 380, 388
Battle of Wādī al-Qurā, 188, 189, 191, 390
Bilāl bin Rabāh, 58, 64, 169, 326, 358, 389, 397
Bi'r Ma'ūnah, 145, 347
Bishr, 120
Brā' bin Aus, 414
Brā' bin 'Āzib, 137
Budail bin Warqā', 163
Burāq, 81
Buṣrā, 44, 49, 193
Chosroes Pervaiz, 122, 163, 170, 174, 177, 295, 315, 316

Copts, 179, 180
David, 51
Dhanb Kawākib, 224
Dhātazzarāb, 224
Dhātil Khaṭmā, 224
Dhātun Nitāqain, 98
Dhī Khushab, 224
Dhī Qarad, 168
Dhil Jaifah, 224
Dhil-Marwah, 224
Dhū Awān, 227
Dhul Ḥulaifah, 167
Dhumarwah, 167
Dihyah al-Kalbī, 170, 396
Ḍirār Mosque, 225, 227
Duldul, 402
Durra bin Ummi Salamah, 388
Durayd ibn al-Ṣimmah, 208
Egypt, 25, 30, 34, 170, 179, 180, 402
Ethopia (see under Ḥabshah)
Faḍl bin 'Abbās, 424
Fāṭimah, 51, 323, 324, 333, 369, 369, 370,371, 372, 376, 410, 414, 415, 416, 422
Fāṭimah bint 'Amr, 49
Fāṭimah bint al-Khaṭṭāb, 68
Fadak, 187, 188
Firozbān Firoz, 314
Ghassān, 182, 219
Ghaṭafān, 135, 168, 191
Habbār, 341
Ḥabīb bin 'Uyainah, 169
Ḥabshah, 66
Ḥaḍrāmī Tribe, 182
Ḥafṣah, 328, 386
Ḥajar, 202, 224
Hājirah, 31, 34, 39
Ḥajj, 36, 39, 50, 94, 234, 240, 377, 380, 387, 390, 394, 398, 402, 404, 417
Ḥajjatul Widā', 417
Ḥajr, 83
Ḥajr-e-Aswad, 52
Hālah, 376
Ḥalīma, 45, 47
Hamdān, 182
Ḥamzah, 60, 65, 68, 81,340
Hanẓalā bin al-Rabī' al-Asadī, 243
Ḥarām ibn Milḥān, 145
Ḥārith (a Meccan leader), 142
Ḥārith (husband of Ḥalīma), 46, 47
Ḥārith (son of Khadījah), 375
Ḥārith (father of Maimūnah) , 404
Ḥārith (father of Juwairiyyah, 395
Ḥārith bin 'Abdul Muṭṭalib, 206
Ḥārith bin Abī Hālah, 64
Ḥarrah, 105
Ḥartha bin al-'Amān, 403
Harratil Wabarah, 307
Ḥasan bin 'Alī, 240, 288,, 289, 372, 416
Ḥassan bin Thābit, 181,403
Ḥāṭib binAbī Balta'ah, 179, 402
Ḥāṭim Ṭā'ī, 352
Hawāzin (Tribe of) , 45, 50, 203
Heraclius, 28, 163, 170
Ḥijāz, 29, 188
Hilāl bin Umayyah al-Wāqifī, 218
Ḥilful Fuḍūl, 50
Hind (son of Khadījah), 375
Hind bin Abī Hāla, 288, 289,
Hind bint Abī Ṭālib, 77
Hinda bint 'Utbah, 340
Hira (town), 29
Ḥirā' (cave), 53, 55, 57
Hishām ibn 'Amr, 71
Hishām ibn 'Urwah, 290
Ḥubāb bin Mundhir, 190
Hubal, 33, 139, 201
Hudā, 142
Ḥudaibiyyah Pact, 162, 168, 182, 186, 188, 205, 390, 401
Ḥudhaifa bin Yamān, 121
Hudhail, 145
Ḥusain bin 'Alī, 371, 372
Ḥuyyay bin Akhṭab, 153, 185, 396, 397,
Ibn 'Abbās, 59, 87, 126, 127, 170, 313, 337, 403, 421
Ibn Ab'ud, 371

Ibn Abī Kabsha, 173
Ibn Abī Saraḥ, 198
Ibn Dāghinah, 92
Ibn Ḥazam, 322
Ibn Shahāb, 99, 104
Ibn Ummi Mahtūm, 168
Ibni 'Umar, 160
Ibrāhīm (the Prophet) , 31, 34, 38, 41, 118, 200, 274, 367, 368, 380
Ibrāhīm (son of Muḥammad[sa]), 367, 368, 375, 402, 403, 414
'Ikrimah, 162, 341
Imām Abū Ḥanīfa, 362
Imām Jalaluddīn Suyūṭī, 48
Imām Mālik, 304, 426
Imām Zuhrī, 174
Iran, 26, 29, 174, 177, 318
Iraq, 26
Isḥāq, 34
Ismāīl, 31, 34, 37, 38, 41, 118
Isrā ', 77, 84
Jābir, 150, 151, 235, 306, 346, 351
Jābir bin 'Abdullāh, 276, 310, 331
Jābir bin Samrah, 357
Jābir bin Samurah, 287, 292, 323
Ja'far bin Abū Ṭālib, 67, 194, 195
Jafnah, 111, 117
Jannatul Baqī', 380, 385, 388, 425, 426
Jannat-e-Mu'allā, 376
Jatham, 203
Jesus ('Īsā) 82, 85, 178, 275, 281, 286
Ji'rānah, 207, 209, 316, 359, 388
Jubair bin Muṭ'im, 256, 330
Juwairiyyah, 386, 338
Ka'bah, 32, 39, 40, 42, 47, 52, 62, 64, 70, 89, 118,131, 152, 175, 183, 193, 200, 233, 240, 319, 324
Ka'b bin Ashraf, 135
Ka'b bin Mālik, 215, 219
Ka'b bin Murra, 320
Ka'b ibn Sa'īd ibn al-'Āṣ, 399
Ka'b ibn Zaid, 146
Khadījah, 21, 51, 53, 55, 72, 80. 305, 359, 367, 374, 376, 390, 409, 414
Khaibar, 149, 185, 186,187, 188, 191, 221, 390, 396, 397
Kharāsh bin Umayyah, 163
Khaula bint Ḥākim, 377
Khālid bin Sa'īd bin al-'Ās, 243, 400
Khālid bin Walīd, 162, 166, 183,196, 318
Khazraj, 94, 108, 113, 154, 158, 206, 212
Khubaib, 142
Khunais bin Ḥudhaifah As-sahmī, 397
Khuwailid bin Asd bin 'Abdul 'Uzzā bin Quṣayy, 51, 374
Khuzā', 163
Kūfā, 323
Madā'in, 152
Madrān, 224
Maḥārib, 191
Maḥrāz bin Naḍlah, 169
Maimūnah, 404,422
Maisrah, 375
Makhramah bin Muṭṭalib, 384
Mālik bin 'Auf Naṣry, 203
Mālik bin al-Dukhshum, 227
Mālik bin Huwairith, 332
Mālik bin Ju'sham, 99
Mālik bin Sa'sa'a, 81
Ma'n bin 'Adī, 227
Manṣūr bin 'Ikrimah, 70
Marr al-Zahrān, 182
Mariah al-Qibṭiyyah, 181, 402
Marwah, 36, 183, 331
Masjid Nabawī, 106, 326, 422
Masjid al-Qiblatain, 119
Masrūq, 295
Mas'ūd bin 'Umair Thaqfī, 404
Mecca, Conquest of, 197
Mid'am, 189
Mi'rāj, 77, 81
Mirzā Bashīr Aḥmad, 381
Mirzā Bashīruddīn Maḥmūd Aḥmad, 79
Moses, 51, 55, 67, 83, 124, 274, 281, 351, 397
Mu'adh bin Jabal, 217, 368
Mu'aiqīb bin Abī Fāṭimah, 243
Mu'attab bin Abū Lahab, 319
Mu'āwiyyah bin Abū Sufyān, 317

Muḍād ibn 'Amr, 31
Muḥammad bin Qais, 384
Muḥayyiṣah bin Mas'ūd, 189
Multazim, 319
Mundhir bin 'Amr, 145
Mundhir bin Sāwā al-'Abdī, 181
Muqām-e-Ibrāhīm, 201
Muqawqis, 179, 402
Murarah bin Ar-Rabī' al-Amrī, 218
Musailimah ibn Ḥabīb (al-Kadhahāb), 313
Mūsā (see under Moses)
Muṣ'ab ibn 'Umair, 94
Muṭarraf, 327
Muṭ'im bin Adī, 76
Najd, 145, 191,306
Najrān, 348
Nakhal, 191
Nakhla, 76
Naṣr (a branch of Hawāzin), 203
Negus, 66, 170, 178, 399
Nineveh, 75
Nūn bin Yūsha', 189
Nuṣaybah, 94
Oman, 30
Qādisiyyah, 352
Qailah Umm Banī Anmār, 331
Qais bin Sa'd, 352
Qarn Tha'lib, 75, 346
Qāsim, 51, 376, 414
Qubā', 97, 103, 105, 212, 225, 298
Quṣayy, 43, 62
Rabāḥ 168
Rabī'ah bin Rafi', 208
Rabī'ah bin Umayyah, 419
Ramla bint Abū Sufyān, 399
Rome, 25, 173, 193, 318
Rukānah, 61
Rūmah, 310
Ruqayyah, 51, 376, 381, 414, 415
Sa'd bin Abī Waqqās, 119, 323
Sa'd bin 'Āmir, 136
Sa'd bin Hishām bin 'Āmir, 302, 303
Sa'd bin Mu'ādh, 158
Sa'd bin 'Ubādah, 168, 190, 210, 368
Sa'd bin Zaid, 168
Ṣadr Ḥauḍī, 224
Ṣafā, 36, 59, 183, 331
Ṣafiyyah bint Ḥuyayyī, 154, 303, 396, 397, 398, 409
Ṣafwān bin Mu'aṭṭal, 360, 382
Ṣafwān bin Umayyah, 64
Sahbā, 189, 396
Sahl, 106
Sahl bin Ḥunaif, 190
Sahl bin Ḥanīf, 352
Sahl bin Sa'd, 186, 356
Sa'īd ibn Zaid, 68
Sakrān bin 'Amr, 375
Sal', 220
Salām bin Mushkam, 120
Salamah (son of Durayd), 208
Salamah bin al-Akwa', 168, 208
Salamah bin Ummi Salamah, 388
Ṣalātul Khauf, 192
Salmān Fārisī, 149
Samurah, 206
Ṣan'ā, 152
Sārah, 34
Sarif, 404
Saudah bint Zam'ah, 376, 393, 410
Shajarah, 307
Shaqq-e-Ṣadr, 47
Shaqta Banī 'Uzrah, 224
Sherawiyyah, 177, 315
Shi'bi Abī Ṭālib, 70, 72
Shifā' bint 'Abdullāh, 387
Shīmā, 206
Shuraḥbīl, 193
Shuraḥbīl bin Ḥasana, 243, 400
Shuraḥbīl bin Ṣimṭ, 320
Sidratul Muntahā, 83
Sīrīn, 181, 402
St. Catherine, 348
Suhail, 106, 145, 364
Suhail bin 'Amr, 164
Sulaimān, 408
Surāqah bin Mālik, 99, 316
Sūqul Lail, 43
Suwailum, 229

Syria, 25, 27, 30, 31, 43, 44, 51, 104, 123, 124, 152, 161, 165, 168, 170, 181, 188, 191, 193, 212, 318, 342, 402
Syriac, 161
Tabūk, 217
Ṭāhir, 375, 414
Ṭā'if, 72
Ṭalḥa bin 'Abdullāh, 50, 58
Ṭalḥa bin 'Ubaidullāh, 141, 220, 229
Taymā', 187, 191
Ṭayyab, 376, 414
Thābit bin Qais, 313, 394
Thanītah, 224
Thaur, 97, 98, 100
Ṭufail, 207, 387
'Ubadah, 387
'Ubadah bin Ṣāmat, 317
'Ubaidullah ibn Jaḥsh, 399
Ubayy bin Ka'b, 243, 368
Ubayy bin Khalf, 339
'Ukaz Fair, 50
Umāmah, 358, 415
Umayyah bin Khalaf, 64
Umm Aiman, 47, 48, 294
Umm 'Alā, 366
Umm Burdah bin Khaulah, 414
Umm Ḥakīm, 49
Umm Hānī, 77, 80, 84, 379
Umm Ḥarām bint Milḥān, 317
Umm Jamīl, 65
Umm Ma'bad, 103, 309
Umm al-Qurā, 201
Umm Rumān, 377
Ummi Ḥabībah, 399
Ummi Kulthūm, 51, 376, 381, 414, 415
Ummi Salamah, 166, 369, 370, 372, 388, 389, 410
Umm Sulaim, 310, 323, 355, 397
Ummul Faḍl, 404
Ummul Masākīn, 388
'Umair, 358
'Umar bin Abī Salama, 372
'Umar bin al-Khaṭṭāb, 68, 70, 86, 123, 127, 138, 241, 295, 324, 336
'Umar bin Umayya al-Ḍamrī, 178
'Umar bin Ummi Salamah, 388
'Umru bin 'Auf, 105
'Urayd, 91
'Urwah, 163
'Urwah bin Zubair, 75, 104, 379
Usaid bin Ḥuḍair, 299
Usāmah bin Qatādah, 324
Usāmah bin Zaid, 144, 335, 347, 368, 369, 424
'Usfān, 142, 409
'Utbah bin Abū Lahab, 319, 415
'Utbah bin Rābī'ah, 65, 96
'Utbah bin Usaid, 167
'Utbah bin Abū Lahab, 319
'Utaybah bin Abū Lahab, 415
'Uthmān bin 'Affān, 58, 163, 191, 198, 243, 381, 387, 415
'Uthmān bin Maz'ūn, 66, 377
'Uthmān bin Ṭalḥa, 201
'Uyainah bin Ḥiṣn, 168
Wahb bin 'Abd Manāf, 43
Waḥshī, 227, 340
Waraqah bin Nauful, 47, 54
Wāthila ibn al-Asqa, 41
Yaḥya (John), 82
Yamāmah, 182, 202, 314
Yathrib, 43, 47, 94, 97, 107, 110, 112, 117, 202,
Yazīd bin Sufyān, 191
Yemen, 27, 32, 175, 177, 182, 213, 314, 315
Ẓāhir bin Ḥarām, 356
Zaid bin Dathinah, 142
Zaid bin Ḥāritha, 73, 193
Zaid bin Sa'nah, 342
Zaid bin Thābit, 161, 209, 243, 368
Zainab bint Muḥammad[sa], 51, 71, 341, 358, 368, 376, 381, 414, 415
Zainab (wife of Abū Bakr), 378
Zainab (wife of Salām), 120
Zainab bint Abī Salmah, 401
Zainab bint Jaḥsh, 390, 392, 393, 399, 410,
Zainab bint Khuzaimah, 387

About the Author

Dr. Karimullah Zirvi was born on May 20, 1940 in Lahore, Pakistan. He completed his undergraduate education in 1959 at Ta'līmul Islām College in Rabwah, Pakistan. He obtained his B.Ed. in 1961 at Central Training College in Lahore. He taught at Ta'līmul Islām High School in Ghatialian, Pakistan for one year. In 1963, he completed his M.Sc. degree in Chemistry from Karachi University and secured the second position in the University.

In 1964, Dr. Zirvi was awarded a Fulbright-Hays Award and a Research Grant from the University of Louisville, Louisville, Kentucky for Post-Graduate studies. In 1968, he completed his Ph.D. in Pharmacology in the laboratory of Dr. Charles H. Jarboe. His thesis was entitled, "Synthesis and Pharmacology of Centrally Active Imides and Amides of Certain Cyclobutanecarboxylic Acids."

After completing his post-doctoral work at the University of Louisville, he became a Senior Research Officer at Pakistan Council of Scientific & Industrial Research (PCSIR) Labs in Peshawar, Pakistan. In 1972, he joined Pahlavi University in Shiraz, Iran as an Associate Professor in the Department of Pharmacology. During this time, he was awarded an International Cancer Research Technology Transfer (ICRETT) Award from Deutsches Krebsforschungszentrum, Heidelberg, Germany. In 1978, Dr. Zirvi and his family emigrated to the United States of America where he took up a position as a visiting scientist at the University of Louisville.

He was a research scientist at the University of California San Diego in La Jolla, California from 1979 to 1980. Then he moved to Vanderbilt University in Nashville, Tennessee where he worked as a research scientist in the Department of Chemistry. In 1982, Dr. Zirvi joined the faculty at the University of Medicine and Dentistry of New Jersey (UMDNJ). There he taught and did research in oncology until he retired in 1993 as an Associate Professor. During his research career he was awarded an NIH Research Grant, VA Research Grant and a New Jersey State Cancer Research Grant. He is the author of over 65 peer-reviewed publications and holds a patent. Dr. Zirvi's biographical sketch is also published in Asia/Pacific Who's Who (Vol. VII, p. 656) and Asian/American Who's Who (Vol. V).

Dr. Zirvi is an active member of U.S.A. *Jamā'at.* He has held many positions over the years which include *Ṣadr Anṣārullāh* USA from 1993 to 1999. As *Ṣadr Anṣārullāh,* he published several special issues of *Al-Nahl* magazine which included a special tribute to the life of Professor Dr. Abdus Salam, Nobel Laureate of Physics. He was the National Ta'lim (Education) Secretary USA from 1998 to 2007. He has been General Secretary (1983 to 2000) and Vice President (2000-present) of the North New Jersey *Jamā'at.* In addition, he has been a past President of the Aḥmadiyya Muslim Scientists Association as well as the General Secretary of the Aḥmadiyya Muslim Medical Association (AMMA) from 1982 to 1996. In 1993, he, along with Dr. Imtiaz Chaudhary (then President of the AMMA), visited Aḥmadiyya Hospitals in Sierra Leone, Liberia and the Gambia and delivered surgical instruments and medicines which were collected from Ahmadi doctors in the USA. He is also the Editor of the Aḥmadiyya Gazette USA and *An-Noor* since May 2004.

Dr. Karimullah Zirvi currently lives in Fair Lawn, New Jersey with his wife, Amatul Latif Zirvi. She is the daughter of the late Malik Saifur Rahman Sahib, former *Muftī Silsilah 'Āliyyah Aḥmadiyya* and the late Amatul Rashid Shaukat Sahibah, former Editor of the *Miṣbāḥ*, Rabwah, Pakistan. Dr. Zirvi has three sons (Nasir Zirvi, Dr. Monib Zirvi, Dr. Khalid Zirvi) and one daughter (Sumra Zirvi) and seven grandchildren.

Other publications by Dr. Zirvi include:

- Words of Wisdom
- Welcome to Aḥmadiyyat, the True Islām
- Invocations of the Holy Prophet Muḥammad Muṣṭafā[sa]
- Ta'līmul Qur'ān

£. 7.00